Additional Praise for

PRIMETIME PROPAGANDA

"Ben Shapiro's *Primetime Propaganda* will knock the Hollywood left on its heels. It turns out they're spiking the popcorn with left-wing politics, a fact that Shapiro establishes with interviews, anecdotes, and quotes from those in a position to know. Get deprogrammed: read Shapiro's book—and wake up to what you're watching."

—Ann Coulter, author of *Guilty: Liberal "Victims" and Their Assault on America*

"Ben Shapiro's *Primetime Propaganda* is vitally important, devastatingly thorough, and shockingly revealing. By going into the belly of the Tinseltown beast, Shapiro has done Americans a true service, exposing the Hollywood machine for what it is: a pawn of the Democratic Party, a corrupt bureaucracy dedicated to preserving its monopoly, and an out-of-touch group of leftists willing to use their entertainment as vehicles for their radial liberalism. After reading *Primetime Propaganda*, you'll never watch TV the same way again. It's a must-buy and a must-read."

—Mark Levin, author of *Liberty and Tyranny*

"*Primetime Propaganda* is brilliant, entertaining, and impeccably researched, proving beyond a reasonable doubt that Hollywood is indeed propagandizing on behalf of leftism and doing so with full intent. Ben Shapiro is a fabulous writer, and *Primetime Propaganda* is his most important book yet—perhaps the most incisive book ever written about the Tinseltown establishment."

—David Limbaugh, author of *Crimes Against Liberty*

"For forty years, Hollywood has pretended that left-wing McCarthyism does not exist in the television industry. In *Primetime Propaganda*, Ben Shapiro blows that lie apart, proving over and over again that Hollywood stole the American narrative and fights relentlessly to keep it its exclusive domain. Shapiro shows beyond a shadow of a doubt, using insiders' own words, that Hollywood liberalism is a motivated ideological force bent on shoving its politics down America's throat."

—Andrew Breitbart, publisher of *Big Hollywood* and author of *Hollywood, Interrupted* and *Righteous Indignation*

Also by Ben Shapiro

Project President: Bad Hair and Botox on the Road to the White House

Porn Generation: How Social Liberalism Is Corrupting Our Future

Brainwashed: How Universities Indoctrinate America's Youth

PRIMETIME PROPAGANDA

THE TRUE HOLLYWOOD STORY OF HOW THE LEFT TOOK OVER YOUR TV

Ben Shapiro

BROADSIDE BOOKS
An Imprint of HarperCollins*Publishers*
www.broadsidebooks.net

HarperCollins books may be purchased for educational, business, or sales promotional use. For information, please e-mail the Special Markets Department at SPsales@harpercollins.com.

Broadside Books™ and the Broadside logo are trademarks of HarperCollins Publishers.

A hardcover edition of this book was published in 2011 by Broadside Books, an imprint of HarperCollins Publishers.

FIRST BROADSIDE BOOKS PAPERBACK EDITION PUBLISHED 2012

The Library of Congress has cataloged the hardcover edition as follows:

Shapiro, Ben.

Primetime propaganda : the true Hollywood story of how the left took over your TV / by Ben Shapiro.

p. cm.

Includes index.

Summary: "The story of how the most powerful medium of mass communication in human history became a propaganda tool for one side of the political spectrum: the left side"—Provided by publisher.

ISBN 978-0-06-193477-3 (hardback)

1. Television programs—United States—History—20th century. 2. Mass media and propaganda—United States—History—20th century. 3. Popular culture—United States—History—20th century. 4. Liberalism—United States—History—20th century. I. Title.

PN1992.3.U5S534 2011

791.450973—dc22

2011006275

ISBN 978-0-06-193478-0 (paperback)

18 19 20 OV/LSC 20

To my wife, Mor,

whose love, comfort, and understanding make our life journey

such a magnificent adventure

Contents

Prologue: How Conservatives Lost the Television War

"Television! Teacher, mother, secret lover."
—Homer Simpson

I was born in the shadow of the Hollywood sign. When the doctors pulled me out of my mom in 1984 at Saint Joseph's Hospital in Burbank, California, I was two blocks down from the beige buildings housing the sound studios of NBC, where they were busily filming *Night Court*, starring Harry Anderson. Across the street was the headquarters for Disney, which looked a bit decrepit; a few years later, Disney would refurbish the Team Disney building by adding a façade of the Seven Dwarfs holding up the roof—and a few years after that, Disney would add the ABC buildings to its Burbank estate. Drive down Alameda Boulevard for about a mile, and there stood the massive Warner Bros. studios, complete with enormous posters advertising upcoming TV shows and movies. Keep going, make a right on Lankershim, and you'd be staring at Universal Studios, where Mr. T and the cast of *The A-Team* were filming on the back lots.

I've loved Hollywood ever since.

Both of my parents work in Hollywood. My cousins, who lived around the corner from our small two bedroom house in Burbank, were Hollywood dreamers too. My aunt got two of my cousins into the movies. One cousin had a bit part in the Tom Hanks vehicle *Turner & Hooch*. His younger sister became a true Hollywood star, playing the little girl in *Mrs. Doubtfire*, Richard Attenborough's *Miracle on 34th Street*, *Matilda*, *A Simple Wish*, and *Thomas and the Magic Railroad*.

My family isn't unusual in Los Angeles; everybody in Hollywood wants to be "in the biz." Every waiter writes scripts, goes on auditions, or attends acting class—generally, all three. Everyone has "a project." Nathanael West labeled California the place where people "come to die." More accurately, it's the place where people come to wait tables.

I narrowly escaped an acting career in Hollywood myself. When I was fifteen months old, my mom's friend, Jean, was making a documentary about child care. She asked if my dad could bring me to the filming. Dad agreed, and he talked with me in front of the cameras. Because I was an early talker, Jean was favorably impressed, and suggested that Dad get me into commercials.

"He's cute, he's bright, he'll be a natural," she told him.

"You must be nuts," said Dad.

That was the end of my Hollywood acting career. If it hadn't been for Dad, maybe I'd be giving an inane Oscar speech right now. More likely, I'd be waiting tables.

Dad kept me out of TV and movies because he wanted me and my three younger sisters to have a "Norman Rockwell childhood": two-parent home, no drugs, no alcohol, no premarital sex. That also meant that Dad monitored the sort of TV we watched. When I was growing up, Dad used to go to the video store and pick up old copies of *The Dick Van Dyke Show*, one of the cleanest shows of all time—Rob (Van Dyke) and Laura (Mary Tyler Moore) have a son, Richie, apparently without copulating, since they sleep in separate beds.

As we grew up, Dad tried to ban us from watching most of the contemporary TV shows. *The Simpsons* was off-limits, as was *Friends*. Forget about *Murphy Brown*. These were shows, Dad said, that promoted particular social agendas: the stupidity of fathers, the substitution of friends for family, the normalization of out-of-wedlock pregnancy.

Good luck, Dad. My sisters and I ended up watching all the shows our friends watched. So I've seen virtually every episode of *The Simpsons*. I currently own all ten seasons of *Friends*—my wife is a huge fan, and I gave them to her as a Hanukkah present. I know the ins and outs of *Dawson's Creek*, the trials and tribulations of *The Practice*, even the ups and downs of *Becker* (there's not much showing at 3:00 P.M. on TBS). During finals week of my first year at Harvard Law School, I watched the first two seasons of *Lost*. When I was in college, I staked out a shoot of *24* near my parents' house for five hours to get a picture with Kiefer Sutherland.

Then one day, as I was watching *Friends*, it struck me: Dad was right. It was "The One with the Birth." Ross's lesbian ex-wife, Carol, is having his baby. And Ross is understandably perturbed that Carol and her lesbian lover will be bringing up his child. While Ross is going quietly cuckoo, Phoebe approaches him. "When I was growing up," she tells him, "you know my dad left, and my mother died, and my stepfather went to jail, so I barely had enough pieces of parents to make one whole one. And here's this little baby who has like three whole parents who care about it so much that they're fighting over who gets to love it the most. And it's not even born yet. It's just, it's just the luckiest baby in the whole world."

Pregnant lesbians and three-parent households portrayed as not only normal, but admirable. This wasn't exactly *Dick Van Dyke*.

And it wasn't one random episode of *Friends*. The propagation of liberal values was endemic to the industry. While Ross was busy walking his lesbian ex-wife down the aisle for her wedding to her new lover, Samantha was chatting graphically about oral sex with Charlotte on *Sex and the City*; Shavonda and Sarah were going topless and French kissing each other on *The Real World: Philadelphia*; a gay man and a single woman were considering whether to have a baby together on *Will & Grace*; Kate was deciding in favor of abortion on *Everwood*; and the city of Springfield was legalizing gay marriage on *The Simpsons*.

It hit me that I was watching the culture being changed before my eyes. These weren't just television episodes—they were pieces of small-scale, insidiously brilliant leftist propaganda.

And they weren't merely anecdotal incidents. They were endemic to the industry—no matter where I turned, I began to see that liberal politics pervaded entertainment. The shows that pushed the cultural envelope received the greatest media attention and often the greatest number of viewers. The shows that embraced traditional values—well, there weren't any shows that openly embraced traditional values.

The overwhelming leftism of American television was too universal to be merely coincidence. It had to be the product of a concerted effort, a system designed to function as an ideological strainer through which conservatism simply could not pass. And the more I investigated, the more I saw that Hollywood was just that: a carefully constructed mechanism designed by television's honchos to blow a hole in the dike of American culture. Television's best and brightest wanted to set America sliding down the slippery slope away from its Judeo-Christian heritage and toward a more cultivated, refined, Europeanized sensibility.

And they succeeded. This book tells the story of that success, a success planned by some, coordinated by others, and implemented by a vast group of like-minded politically motivated people infusing their values both consciously and unconsciously into their work.

It is no great shocking revelation that television is liberal. Conservatives like Robert Bork and Donald Wildmon, among others, have criticized television for years.

Typically, such critics have tackled television from a purely moral perspective, in a tone of opprobrium, responding in a largely sporadic fashion to a series of daily outrages; they pick up on the most egregious abuses of broadcasting liberty, attacking the content that comes across their screens.

Everything these critics say is accurate—television has been the most impressive weapon in the left's political arsenal. But to the evident frustration of conservative cultural critics, this moralistic argument has been utterly ineffective. I know, because I made precisely the same arguments in *Porn Generation: How Social Liberalism Is Corrupting Our Future*. In that book, I looked at the television industry and analyzed many of the shows on the small screen. Like Bork and Wildmon, I was highly critical of television's liberal content, and called for a boycott of particular advertisers, as well as tighter FCC regulation of television content.

The argument failed for one main reason: television is *awesome*.

Nobody wants to turn off the television because *television is great*! Television is just too much fun for people to turn it off. We come home from a long day at work and we want to space out, so we flip on the tube. We've been doing it for generations. My dad tried the cultural conservative argument—turn off the television and preserve your values!—and we all watched television anyway. Hell, each night after I finished working on that day's portion of *Porn Generation*, I flipped on the TV to wind down, and watched some of the very shows I was criticizing. Arguing that television is liberal and that therefore every true conservative should read a book during dinner is unreasonable.

No matter how much critics like Bork and Wildmon exhort the public to hit the OFF button, nobody's responding; indeed, if nothing else is clear by now, it is that conservative critics totally underestimate the staying power and popular appeal of television. Even conservatives who complain about television still watch it—in fact, according to the *Hollywood Reporter*, conservatives actually boost television's most successful shows to the top of the ratings.[1] Conservative viewers aren't boycotting advertisers. They aren't voting with their remotes. They're watching because they enjoy it.

Moreover, even if everything they say is technically correct, cultural conservatives undermine their own credibility on the issue of television by attacking its content. Everybody who watches television has a favorite show. Nobody wants to believe that *that* show is instrumental in destroying America's moral fabric. Even more important, most conservatives believe that they are impervious to the seductive siren call of television liberalism. When cultural conservatives attack television political content, therefore, they alienate just about everyone: liberal Americans who like the content, conservative Americans who think the content doesn't have any effect on them and object only when some shrill comment about Reagan or Bush or Palin emanates from their TV set, and moderates who are indifferent and annoyed by shrieking political debate about their favorite evening entertainment. The traditional conservative critique, therefore, ticks Americans off rather than awakening them—the vast majority respond with a simple, effective phrase: "Lighten up!"

In fact, the typical conservative critique plays right into the hands of the liberals who program television, in two important ways. First, it allows liberals to point their fingers at conservative censorship, arguing that they want to set up a slippery slope toward fascism. This is a fallacious argument from a Constitutional perspective—the First Amendment was created to protect political speech, not curse words or fart jokes—but it works, playing on Americans' well-founded distrust of government interference in private choices. Of course, by pointing at the conservative slippery slope, liberals obscure the fact that they are pushing just as hard in the opposite direction, down a slippery slope toward moral relativism and, ultimately, nihilism. But the conservative emphasis on censorship and boycotts allows liberals to create a false dichotomy between crackdowns on free speech on the one hand and unmitigated liberalism on the other. Given such a choice, Americans will choose unmitigated liberalism every time, since they see it as the lesser of two evils.

Second, the moralistic conservative argument allows liberals to suggest that conservatives are curmudgeons and cranks who still think *Father Knows Best* ought to top the ratings. Liberals point to the fact that the shows conservatives love to critique are overwhelmingly successful. The market has therefore justified the existence of liberal-oriented shows, and if conservatives don't like those shows, that's because they are extremists out of touch with mainstream values. (They are also hypocrites who cite the free market selectively.) Television liberals also point to the age of their consumers as evidence that conservatives are past their prime—television has targeted young people since the late 1960s, and if conservatives reject today's programming, that's because they're crotchety old bores who want to turn back the clock to the monochrome culture of the 1950s.

Every point the liberals make is correct. The traditional conservative critique is worse than useless in the long run—it forces conservatives to turn their backs on modern television or embrace it without reservation. When conservatives treat television as the Golden Calf, they leave no choice but to lay low the unbelievers—and most of us prefer to continue occasionally glancing at the offending cow. Cultural conservatives who believe that television must be cast out like a leper leave us no in-between. Forced to choose, even most conservatives will side with liberals, in practice, by watching what liberals watch in the privacy of their homes.

I understand why cultural conservatives have lost the argument about television, because I'm not one of the old-style, fire-and-brimstone types who insist that television must be discarded in order to save America. Perhaps that's because I'm a member of that younger generation that grew up on television. I'm right in the sweet spot for most television producers—I'm twenty-seven years old, male, and middle-upper-class.

I'm married and shop for my family. I'm the gold standard for advertisers and programmers.

I understand why cultural conservatives find television so damn frustrating. But I also understand why Americans have rejected the conservative arguments on television outright, even if they sympathize with the underlying rationale. Americans love TV, and they're not all that interested in hearing it criticized.

In short, the traditional conservative argument has failed. What then can conservatives do?

We can make a new argument. That argument is made in *Primetime Propaganda*.

This book isn't the typical moralizing conservative critique of industry content, haphazard or hit-and-run. It doesn't focus on shows from the outside, a strategy that fails because it ignores the inherent subjectivity of content analysis. Instead, it focuses on the industry *behind* the scenes, and tells the inside story of liberal television from the mouths of those who have shaped it. *Primetime Propaganda* examines the political orientation and history of television since its inception, not through secondary sources but by looking at the actual words and deeds of the most important figures in TV over the last sixty years. The book makes a case that Hollywood content isn't merely or accidentally leftist, but is consciously designed by liberal creators and executives to convert Americans to their political cause. This case was built over the course of thousands of hours and dozens of interviews, from the palatial estates off Sunset Boulevard to the entertainment skyscrapers of New York City, from the lots of Warner Bros. and ABC and Sony Pictures Studios to the delis and trendy coffee houses of Hollywood.

Primetime Propaganda is also a *constructive* exposé of the television industry, rather than a frontal assault on its existence. The goal here is to understand the sway of television, to gauge and measure it, and to insist that television's power be used to entertain rather than indoctrinate. It just so happens that focusing on entertainment rather than political propaganda is also how television can save itself.

First, though, the television industry is going to have to admit that it has a problem: it's ideologically xenophobic. Most conservatives in Hollywood don't work today, at least not openly. That's not because conservatives are untalented or unqualified or incapable of empathy, as many on the left ridiculously contend. It's because liberals employ a mirror form of McCarthyism on a large scale.

That's a controversial contention, and one I used to doubt. When I began writing this book, I thought the claim of anti-conservative discrimination was overblown, self-serving nonsense put out by unsuccessful conservatives who just couldn't hack it in Hollywood. After all, many of those who complain that they can't get work *can't* make the grade.

I wasn't sure there *was* discrimination against conservatives—until it happened to me.

If you spend too much time in Hollywood, you find yourself gradually and inexorably drawn toward the bright lights. The U.S. television and movie industry overall employs almost 2.5 million people across the country and pays them over $140 billion in total wages annually. If the biz were a country, it would produce a higher GDP than Hungary, New Zealand, and Peru. And that's not even looking at the cultural influence of the industry, which is its main cachet.

Working in television is paradise. The cash is stunning, and you get it by writing *fiction*. If you're a member of the Writers Guild of America, one hour-long episode of scripted television will earn you $30,000, plus residuals if your episode is rerun. That's a lot of green for a very small amount of work. And that's just for lower-level writers. If you're a showrunner, the cash is even better. If you're a show creator and writer, you can start looking for prime real estate on the south coast of France.

When I started interviewing the creators and executives in the industry, I thought I was immune. Not even close. It started when I interviewed Leonard Goldberg, a former head of programming at ABC and the man responsible, along with Aaron Spelling, for *Charlie's Angels*, *Family*, *Starsky & Hutch*, *Fantasy Island*, and other massive hits. He was also on the board at CBS.

At the interviews, I habitually wore my Harvard Law School baseball cap. That served two purposes. First, it informed the interview subject that this was going to be a well-informed, serious book. Second, it put interview subjects at ease; many liberals in Hollywood fear conservatives in an almost pathological way, believing that they're all nuts, and the Harvard Law cap assured them that I would be reasonable.

Goldberg spotted the cap, of course, and asked me about it. I told him a few Harvard Law stories. Then he leaned forward and said, "You know, you're a great talker. And I know you're a great writer. Why don't you write a pilot for a series about Harvard Law?"

I sat there for a minute. Then the butterflies started fluttering in my stomach. There's nothing more exciting than having a major producer ask *you* to write a television series.

So I wrote the pilot. Goldberg liked the basic material, and we started developing it. Everything was going great. I was learning at the feet of a true master. Then Goldberg got caught up producing a new movie, *Unknown*, with Liam Neeson, Diane Kruger, Frank Langella, and January Jones, and then after that, a new TV show for CBS called *Blue Bloods*.

I had to wait—a not uncommon phenomenon in Hollywood, where everyone is waiting for the big break. In the meantime, I decided to write another pilot and pass it around town to see if it drew any interest. To my delight, it drew interest from a major agent in town, who called me in for a meeting.

Now, meetings in Hollywood are a big deal. If you've ever seen *Tootsie*, you know that it's almost impossible to get in to see your *own* agent, let alone to get a meeting with an agent who isn't representing you. This agent didn't just set a meeting—he told me he was bringing along two of his agent colleagues.

The meeting went well. It went so well, in fact, that when the meeting ended, the top agent suggested I write a spec script for CBS's *The Good Wife*—that's how most writers break into the business, by becoming staff on an already-existing show. He also told me as I left that this had been one of the best meetings he'd had in decades.

I drove home singing to myself.

I watched every episode of *The Good Wife* (I hadn't seen any at the time), then wrote the one-hour spec script. The agent made some pertinent comments, which were well-taken. I made the edits and turned it back in. This whole process took about three weeks.

After several weeks, I hadn't heard anything back, so I called to check in—I'd heard from other writers that staying on top of your agent was par for the course. I left a message.

A few minutes later, the agent called back. "One of our agents Googled you and found your website," he told me. My stomach dropped. "I'm not sure we can represent you, because he thinks your political views will make it impossible for you to get a job in this town."

Just like that. Straight out.

I called up a high-ranking lawyer at Fox Broadcasting, a wonderful person I trusted—and a liberal. The first two words out of the lawyer's mouth were: "Holy shit." The lawyer couldn't believe that this was even an issue—or rather, that it was hitting me square between the eyes. "This is crazy," said the lawyer. "Sure, there's a blacklist in this town, but you're not discussing politics with these people. You're not an extremist." The lawyer recommended that I write the agent an e-mail.

In the e-mail, I respectfully told the agent that my politics didn't matter and that I would never bring politics up on the set—a requirement for conservatives, since liberal talk on the set is the only kind of talk that falls into the "approved speech" category. I told him I wasn't abrasive, and that I'd spent years at UCLA and Harvard Law talking to liberals—that, after all, the agent had spoken with me several times and politics had never come up. That I had plenty of close friends who were liberals. That I should be judged on my talent alone, not on my politics.

He called me back and agreed. "Listen," he said, "I have no problem with your politics. It's just that my agent started sending your sample around, and it got to a producer on one of the shows. He said that he knew who you were, and that he'd never work with you. The whole reason I'm even dealing with you is because your writing has what I'm always looking for—that sparkle. But let me get back to you."

The agent wasn't trying to be a bad guy. He was just warning me that I'd have trouble getting work because of the McCarthyesque nature of the business. And he was right to do so—he only makes money if I get a job. Finally we decided to give it a go anyway.

I'm not the only conservative in Hollywood. There are thousands of us, but we remain in the shadows. Outspoken conservatives are less likely to get jobs, as many of the liberal television folks I interviewed openly admitted. Conservatives are less likely to get meetings or pitches. They are more likely to be excluded from social circles—and Hollywood is a social business. Can conservatives succeed? Only by exercising incredible discretion. Do conservative storylines make it onto television? Only occasionally, and in general, only when they're innocuous. Is it possible that conservative writers don't make it in Hollywood because they stink? Yes. But if 50 percent of the country is conservative, you'd expect at least 30 percent of the Hollywood crowd to be. It isn't.

It's a leftist oligarchy. Television is written by liberals, produced by liberals, and greenlit by liberals. Americans watch it because it's clever and fascinating. And they're taken in by the pernicious political messages inserted by the creators, whether consciously or unconsciously.

In *Primetime Propaganda*, you'll learn how the industry truly operates. You'll learn who the decision makers, the power brokers, the influential artists who create our programming truly are. You'll find out what you've really been watching all these years, and how those behind the scenes have shaped hearts and minds across the globe.

Some readers, no doubt, will shy away from this exposé of their favorite shows, networks, producers, and writers. Americans feel about television the way we feel about sausage and magic tricks—we love to consume them, but we don't want to know their secrets. We feel that knowing how sausage is made, magic tricks are performed, or television is created will somehow detract from our enjoyment.

Understanding the television industry, however, doesn't tarnish the magic of the final product—it actually enhances it. When we realize how many elements it takes to bring a vision to the screen, we're awed. When we understand what was going through the creators' heads from inception to filming, we love television even *more*.

At the same time, though, we must understand that television is the exclusive domain of a select few who use the mystique of the industry to mask their own political propagandizing. We must correct that state of affairs if we want to improve television.

After reading *Primetime Propaganda*, you'll be awakened to what's really going on behind the small screen, and you'll be stunned to learn that you've been targeted by generations of television creators and programmers for political conversion. You'll find out that the box in your living room has been invading your mind, subtly shaping your opinions, pushing you to certain sociopolitical conclusions for years.

The next step is fixing the problem. After looking at television from every angle, thoroughly scrutinizing it, we'll learn how to stop this liberal living-room invasion by *engaging* with the industry rather than running away from it.

There is no more subversive social force than culture—and there has been no more powerful voice in our culture than television. Television has been weaponized by those who would use it to cajole, convince, and convert. Until now, we have been ignorant of what goes on behind the curtain of that Great and Powerful Oz.

Now we raise that curtain.

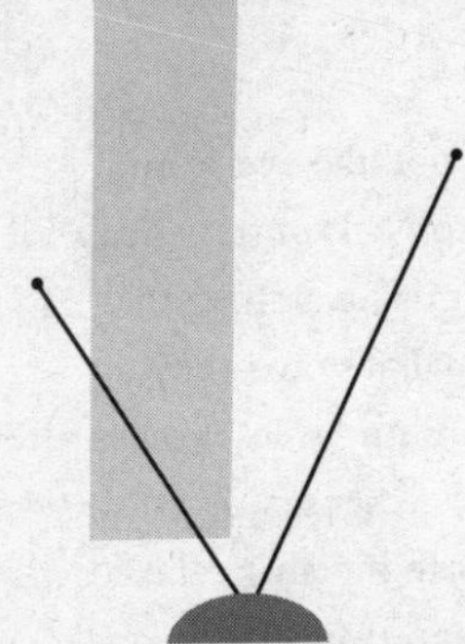

INTRODUCTION: THE POLITICAL PERVERSION OF TELEVISION

For millennia, the power to convey thoughts and images to millions of people simultaneously was restricted to God. According to the Bible, when God appeared at Mount Sinai, he provided evidence of his omnipotence by demonstrating his omnipresence. "You have been shown in order to know that God, He is the Supreme Being," Moses told the Jews. "From Heaven he let you hear His voice in order to teach you, and on earth He showed you His great fire, and you heard His words amid the fire."

Today, such pyrotechnics could appear on any episode of *Lost*, and they could reach a hundred times the number of people God spoke to directly at Sinai. Jesus, restricted as he was by human form, didn't engage in global telepathy. If Jesus had appeared today, he would have had it much better—as Andrew Lloyd Webber put it in *Jesus Christ, Superstar*, "If you'd come today you would have reached a whole nation—Israel in 4 B.C. had no mass communication." That is, as long as Jesus didn't have to go up against *American Idol* in primetime. In that case, Jesus would have been canceled by ex-NBC president Jeff Zucker within three weeks.

The power of an instrument that spoon-feeds tens of millions at a time on a twenty-four-hour basis is almost unimaginable. We are addicted to television as a constant source of information, entertainment, a break from our dreary workdays, an escape. We may not like everything that's on the TV, but we can't turn it off. According to Nielsen statistics, U.S. viewers spend four hours, thirty-five minutes per day watching television. And they don't always do it because they love what's on—they do it because it acts as a sort of narcotic. TV isn't crystal meth (unless you're watching *Twin Peaks*), but it's certainly alcohol for the senses. According to *Scientific American*, people watching TV "reported feeling relaxed and passive. The EEG studies similarly show less mental stimulation, as measured by alpha brain-wave production, during viewing than during reading. . . . Habit-forming drugs work in similar ways." In short, scientists conclude that "TV does seem to meet the criteria for substance dependence."[1] The power of television ought not to be taken lightly.

Yet it is. Despite the unthinkable reach and draw of television, intellectual snobs have derided it as "the boob tube" for decades. Television watching, in this view, is the escapist pastime of morons, who consume ever-increasing amounts of homogeneous tripe day in and day out. And because television is so manifestly awful, it has barely any impact on the tides of history. Steve Jobs of Apple sums it up: "You go to TV to turn your brain off."

This sort of snobbery—the idea that television is garbage, that people are irresistibly drawn to garbage, and that garbage has no impact on people's worldviews—is as wrong as it is snooty. Television is largely *not* garbage: It's generally well written, well produced, well acted, and well shot. Yes, much of it exploits sex and violence. And yes, much of it relies on clichés and jokes dating back to the Cretaceous period and tortuous plot devices that strain credulity. But by and large, television has provided a medium for an artistic explosion that rivals any in human history.

That is not the whole story, though. Television isn't just a tool for artistic expression. Here's the untold secret: For almost its entire existence, television has been gradually perverted by a select group of leftist individuals who have used its power to foster social change through cultural "messaging." The "television is garbage" meme is a criticism designed as a call to action for those in the television industry: a call to make TV an artistic vanguard for liberal social change, rather than a conduit for basic entertainment.

Vanguardism is the buzzword in Hollywood. Those who inhabit the golden shores of Malibu and the sweeping lawns of Sunset Boulevard are of an almost uniform political bent—virtually all vote Democrat, fervently support gay marriage, see abortion as a sacrosanct human right, approve of higher taxes, despise religion, think guns are to blame for crime, maintain that businesspeople are corrupt and union organizers are saints, feel that conservatives are racists, sexists, and homophobes, and sneer at rural right-wingers in "flyover country." Almost all voted for Barack Obama. Almost all hated George W. Bush.

And yet almost all of them are also quite wealthy, the ironic beneficiaries of a capitalist system many of them openly criticize as biased and unfair. How can they justify benefiting from that system even as they hold their liberal beliefs with such fervent conviction?

By attacking the status quo. Many if not most successful television creators lived in relative poverty before hitting it big, a fact that shapes their perspective for the rest of their lives. Since creative success is as rapid as it is unpredictable, many writers feel that they've made it to the top almost purely on luck, and they extrapolate from their own experience to the capitalist system at large. The difference between those who succeed and those who fail is simply a matter of luck, in this view, which is why Hollywood types (and liberals in general) like to speak about the "fortunate" and "less fortunate" rather than the rich and the poor. These creators, who feel that capitalism has somehow worked out to their benefit, but who also remember a time when capitalism worked against them, have to reconcile their newfound lifestyles with their socialist sensibilities.

At the same time, many of these artists were cultural outsiders in their original small-town communities and therefore rejected the values of mainstream society as a defense. This is to some extent the nature of the artistic beast: Artists of all sorts consistently engage in the self-aggrandizing "outsider" delusion that their job is to "speak truth to power." The result is a liberalism that continually attacks the prevailing power structure.

The history of such cultural liberalism is long and celebrated. It stretches back all the way to the 1863 Salon des Refusés, when artists rejected from the Paris Salon formed their own salon celebrating avant-garde art. For today's artists, however, it's not just about rejecting the status quo—it's about shock value in toto. It's not enough to reject society—they must forcibly enlighten the society that rejected them. They do this by shocking middle-class sensibilities. In *Bobos in Paradise*, David Brooks points out that the "hallmark of the bourgeois-bohemian feud" was *"Epater les bourgeois!"*—literally, to shock the middle class.[2] But shocking the public is no longer merely an incidental hallmark of liberalism—it is the dominant goal for the television left. During the 1960s, artists and creators went out of their way to shock the American middle class in order to forward their liberal agenda: feminism, gay rights, racial preferences, bigger government. When the smoke cleared, however, the artists had largely gotten what they wanted—with their help, the civil rights movement had achieved its major goals. This presented a problem for television liberals—how could they continue to rebel against the status quo if there was nothing left to rebel *against*? And so Hollywood has become largely oriented toward shock for shock's sake; its continuing rebellion against bourgeois morality and taste is the sign of a vestigial avant-garde impulse that has become detached from any serious moral purpose.

Why does Hollywood continue to push this empty vanguardism? Because it has no other choice. They're stuck in their ways; their heroes were rebels, and in order to justify their own success, they too must rebel. Just as every journalist still wants to be Bob Woodward, every television writer still wants to be Norman Lear. The problem is obvious—Lear had Nixon, Watergate, Vietnam, and racism. Today's writers have . . . transfats. But the quest to push the envelope persists. Brooks's description of bobos—the class of bohemian bourgeois that now dominates the political and cultural heights of our society—perfectly characterizes the Hollywood elite: "The people who thrive in this period are the ones who can turn ideas and emotions into products. These are highly educated folk who have one foot in the bohemian world of creativity and another foot in the bourgeois realm of ambition and worldly success."[3]

Vanguardism has been a significant and growing strain within television since the beginning. The story is a generational one. Although the original television executives were generally successful conservative businessmen, the intellectuals who commented upon television were influential Marxist thinkers like Theodor Adorno, who ripped television as a medium that reinforced capitalist conformity.[4] Adorno's former boss, television researcher Paul Lazarsfeld, suggested in Congressional hearings that the government mandate "quality" programming at the expense of ratings and endorse collusion among broadcasters rather than competition; the audiences, Lazarsfeld said, would be adjusted to the programming, rather than the other way around.[5]

These sorts of criticisms were taken seriously by government regulators—so much so that by 1961, JFK-appointed FCC Commissioner Newton Minow famously told the National Association of Broadcasters that television was "a vast wasteland." We're not talking about the era of *Married . . . with Children* and *Roseanne*—we're talking about the era of *Gunsmoke* and *Howdy Doody*. In that speech, Minow actually threatened government action against broadcasters: "Clean up your own house or the government will do it for you." Quoting JFK, he explained, "I urge you, I urge you to put the people's airwaves to the service of the people and the cause of freedom."[6] (Minow, not coincidentally, was a supporter of Barack Obama throughout his law school days—Obama met his wife at Minow's Chicago law firm—and supports his agenda through and through.)

Minow's speech was an early form of vanguardism—an elitist attempt to stump for "higher quality" programming that would "educate" the American public. At the time, the conservative executives largely ignored Minow—they were too busy catering to the wants of the American public and making big money by doing it. But the next generation of Hollywood executives, many of whom were also creative types from the advertising centers on Madison Avenue, began to take Minow's criticisms seriously and made real attempts to balance entertainment and social messaging—for every *Gilligan's Island*, there would be a socially oriented program like *That Was the Week That Was*. Hollywood thought that Americans would watch both shows, be entertained, and come away enlightened, too.

Unfortunately for the left, Americans wanted to watch entertaining shows, not shows geared toward political reeducation. As the 1960s progressed, and members of the television industry became more and more disillusioned with the American people's lowbrow tastes, a solution presented itself to the television executives and creators: If they could merge lowbrow entertainment with liberal political messaging, they could have the best of both worlds—ratings *and* propaganda power.

It worked. Hollywood, with its godlike power, has succeeded far beyond its wildest dreams, shaping America's styles, tastes, politics, and even family structures. That success left the next generation of Hollywood creators and executives bereft of causes; today's television writers refuse to rebel against a political and cultural system they built. But they haven't stopped propagandizing in primetime. Instead, they've shifted toward empty vanguardism and the promotion of sophisticated irony—at least until a new conservative bogeyman can be found.

Based on the testimony of hundreds of writers, producers, actors, and television executives—the most important figures in television over the last sixty years—it is abundantly clear that television has evolved from a medium for entertainment and advertising into a funnel for socially liberal messages. It is controlled by a small coterie of largely like-minded executives who are geared toward pleasing a like-minded cadre of advertisers who seek to cater to a like-minded corps of consumers. Content is provided by a like-minded clique of creative artists, who have generally studied under like-minded mentors and interact with like-minded colleagues. Everyone in Hollywood goes to the same restaurants, belongs to the same clubs, and sits in the same seats at Lakers games. Almost all of them think alike, too. Hollywood is still the land where dreams are made—but those dreams are increasingly the dreams of European-style progressives, who support and reinforce one another within their wealthy, cloistered bubble. The political and ideological purity in the television industry is almost awe-inspiring. Hollywood, in the cultural and democratic sense, is no longer American.

This isn't to say that everything on television is liberal. That would be a ridiculous claim, unjustified by the evidence. Sports and history channels are apolitical, aside from the occasional Donovan McNabb controversy. And I'm not tackling the news media here—that subject has been exhaustively covered by the likes of Ann Coulter and Bernie Goldberg.

Even within the pure entertainment arena, there are shows that can be seen as neutral or conservative-leaning, shows that by their very nature seem to endorse the current social order. Many of these are crime procedurals that start with the premise that the criminal justice system works, that crime exists, and that basic social values have to be affirmed from time to time by violent means (think *Hawaii 5-0, Blue Bloods, Cops, CSI,* or *Law & Order*). Others are sitcoms that seem to promote family values, though those seem rarer and rarer these days. Reality television shows avoid politics more than scripted. Within those semi-conservative subsets of television, however, liberalism tends to paper over the conservative underpinnings, as we'll discuss. The most conservative shows are those that provide a modicum of balance. By contrast, the most liberal shows ignore conservatism outright, or openly decry it as brutal, sadistic, racist, and homophobic.

What do the percentages look like in terms of political breakdown? Political content varies channel by channel, of course. Shows themselves vary episode to episode. In rough terms, however, primetime drama and comedy skew liberal the vast majority of the time on network television and nearly always on cable. Children's and daytime television also typically skew liberal. Because there are so many shows, however, and because there is such high churn—shows premiere and are dumped within weeks in some cases—the better approach is to examine them one by one.

To that end, in the chapters that follow we will tackle the most influential and popular shows in television history, and examine them politically. I have, of course, been forced to pick and choose to a certain extent, though where I omit a major show I attempt to explain that omission. In no way should this listing be construed as complete—a full catalog of shows broadcast over the last sixty years can be found in the *Encyclopedia of Television* distributed by the Museum of Broadcast Communication, which runs some 3,000 pages.

Meanwhile, I would encourage liberal readers to focus on the broader point of my critique: the television industry is completely dominated by liberals, as even most liberals agree, including the television figures I interviewed. Many will admit that their liberal values seep into their work—and some openly boast of it. Most, however, refuse to acknowledge the clear evidence of discrimination against conservatives and conservatism within television. Instead, liberals within the industry typically offer three explanations for the leviathan bias of entertainment programming.

First, liberal creators, executives, and producers argue that their shows are not liberal, but rather realistic. *Realism* is a favorite buzzword in Hollywood—every great show must be "realistic." Sandy Grushow, former head of the entertainment division at Fox television network, told me that shows like *Married . . . with Children*; *The Simpsons*; *In Living Color*; *Beverly Hills, 90210*; *Melrose Place*; *Party of Five*; and *The O.C.* "all spoke with a more realistic voice . . . as a culture, we seem to have a desire to express, to embrace, as we grow older as a country, that which feels more authentic. More honest. More real."[7] If *The O.C.* is "authentic," then so are Pamela Anderson's boobs.

In one sense, of course, all shows are realistic. That is because all comedies and dramas must be *specific*—they must revolve around a few characters involved in one plot and perhaps a subplot. Television is not a statistical study—it is by nature anecdotal. And it is not difficult to find anecdotes. Television creators can open the newspaper each morning, read a particular story, and base a plotline on that story. That plotline would clearly be realistic. What television's executives and creators generally fail to recognize is that television acts as a magnifying glass—by focusing on one particular case among thousands, television inflates that case to gargantuan proportions. People assume when they watch television that if an event is shown on television, it must be representative of similar events—part of a larger social trend. Television creators *know* that. The question, therefore, is not whether their portrayals are realistic but whether that "realism" is broadly representative of the world at large.

This is where Hollywood creators and executives fall short. They pick realistic stories that often spring from their own daily lives. But their shows do *not* reflect the daily lives of those who watch them. Hollywood executives and creators disproportionately come from major urban areas that skew liberal, and so they mainly concern themselves with urban liberal themes. What they consider realistic will almost certainly vary from what a family of five in Birmingham, Alabama, would find plausible and familiar. There are many Wills and Graces and Ellens in Los Angeles, San Francisco, Chicago, and New York. There are comparatively few in

Jackson, Mississippi, or Butte, Montana. But these liberal creators and executives suffer from chronic Pauline Kael syndrome—Kael, a film and television critic for the *New Yorker*, hilariously stated in the aftermath of Nixon's trouncing of McGovern in 1972, "I live in a rather special world. I only know one person who voted for Nixon. Where they are I don't know. They're outside my ken. But sometimes when I'm in a theater I can feel them." Those in Hollywood think they can "feel" those in Jackson or Butte or Birmingham. But for the most part they've never met them, and they certainly don't agree with them.

The second, stronger argument leveled by Hollywood leftists is that their programming is not designed to be leftist—it simply responds to market conditions. This is the argument that people watch what they want to, and what they want to watch is liberal programming. This, of course, absolves television's creative minds of any responsibility for what they put on the air. As Marta Kaufman, cocreator of *Friends*, one of the most successful and liberal shows of all time, told me, "Our feeling was always, if you don't like what you're watching . . . just turn it off."[8] Michele Ganeless, president of Comedy Central, told me the same thing: "The great equalizers are . . . the television ratings. People watch what they want to watch; nobody's forcing them to watch television. So if it doesn't appeal to someone's sensibilities, they're not going to watch it."[9]

There is certainly support for this argument. The art of television is inherently intertwined with business. And that business is astonishingly profitable—the writers, producers, and executives I interviewed populate mansions and high-rise condominiums that would make Michael Jackson's plastic surgeon blush. There's a reason everyone wants to get into "the biz."

But the market argument makes one critical assumption: It presumes that producers, executives, and creators are all working in synchronicity to produce the products best suited for the market. There is no evidence that this is the case. In fact, the evidence points to precisely the opposite conclusion. As my study will reveal, Hollywood has jiggered the market to meet its own ends and has made America more liberal in the process.

The market to which Hollywood caters does not accurately reflect the market for television as a whole. People tend to forget that those in the television industry are not interested in ratings per se but in advertiser dollars. Every network must convince advertisers that *its* viewers are the most valuable. It does so by focusing on certain segments of the viewing public. Hollywood has, in fact, *defined* the market to which it caters—young, urban audiences—and then convinced advertisers on Madison Avenue that these audiences are worth more than other audiences. Television executives have made the case for decades that older people, rural people—people, in short, who trend conservative—are not worth as much in advertising terms as younger, hipper, wealthier urban consumers. The programming the industry produces therefore targets those audiences.

For example, suppose your show, starring Angela Lansbury, gets an 11 Nielsen rating and a 20 share (this means that 11 percent of all households with TVs were tuned in to your show, and that 20 percent of households watching TV at the time were tuned in to your show), and pulls in 12.6 million viewers, but only 4.5 million of them are age 18 to 49. A show starring Hilary Duff that gets 4.6 million 18-to-49 viewers may earn more than your show, even if it gets a 4 rating and an 8 share and only pulls in 4.6 million viewers total. The viewers have to be the *right* viewers—as defined by the liberals in the television industry, and their consumers in the ad industry. This is actually nonsensical—the evidence suggests that the focus on the 18-to-49 crowd has been entirely misplaced, and for both business and political reasons.

This strategy of *narrowcasting*—directing programming at a narrow segment of viewers rather than "broadcasting" at Americans as a whole—inherently leads to liberalism as well. The new television industry ideal is total fragmentation of the audience, with specially directed shows aimed at Dad, Mom, Billy, and Jane. This market-driven strategy has had wide-ranging social and political effects.

Once upon a time, Dad, Mom, Billy, and Jane used to sit together and watch *Sing Along with Mitch*. Family cohesion seemed to grow. Then television began targeting Dad, Mom, Billy, and Jane separately. Families stopped watching TV together. Family time turned into individual time. Family interests became individual interests. Dad, Mom, Billy, and Jane were compartmentalized. The splintering of viewership meant the separation of family members from one another in terms of viewing habits. In Robert Putnam's *Bowling Alone*, the political scientist makes the case that our "social capital" is disintegrating—that as a society, we are becoming less communal, more atomistic. In large part, he blames television, which we are increasingly watching alone rather than with family. "[D]ependence on television for entertainment is not merely *a* significant predictor of civic disengagement," Putnam writes. "It is *the single most consistent* predictor that I have discovered."[10] It is also likely to be the single most significant predictor of family disengagement, now that we have discarded family viewing for targeted viewing patterns.

Breaking apart family viewing meant more than simply fracturing family time; it meant treating each individual member of the family as an adolescent, free of care and responsibility. Targeting Dad qua Dad meant producing a very different show than targeting Dad as a member of a family audience. Dad qua Dad probably watches Spike TV and enjoys sports, violence, and boobs, whereas Dad as family member probably likes Bill Cosby. Mom qua Mom watches *Sex and the City* rather than identifying with Debra Barone. Without Mom and Dad there, Billy's probably watching MTV. And Jane is in the other room, checking out what's on CW. Everyone is turned into an adolescent, their particular needs and desires catered to. Family roles are thus undermined by the compartmentalized consumption of television.

The role of the father on television provides a particularly illuminating example. When television shows were *broad*cast, fathers were portrayed as responsible heads of households who cared for their wives and children and put bread on the table. Think *Father Knows Best.* That's because fathers wanted to be seen this way, mothers wanted to see their husbands this way, and children wanted to see their dads this way.

Soon, however, the television industry began targeting younger audiences. Unsurprisingly, the result was Archie Bunker and *All in the Family*, where the father figure still had some residual authority but no real authority; he was a benighted bigot constantly bested by his more tolerant and cleverer son-in-law. This image of fatherhood fell into line perfectly with young adults' perceptions of fathers—old fashioned and close-minded—flattering young people's sensibilities. Archie was given just enough humanity—and made midfifties—to avoid alienating young dads and moms, who could identify more with Meathead and Gloria than Archie and Edith.

Later, marginalized forces within the television industry began targeting even younger audiences, whom they felt they could then pipeline into more mature programming. That led to Fox's *The Simpsons*, where Homer Simpson became the adolescent's picture of the father: moronic, abusive, drunk, foolish. By narrowing the audience further and further, TV's iconic fathers were tailored to those increasingly small targets—and the chain from responsible adult to grown-up teenager was made complete, both on television and in the American mind.

Even if the market is properly calculated, and we leave aside the normative argument that fragmentation of programming destroys family viewing and undermines the family structure, there is no evidence that a variety of programming is being provided. The majority of it emanates from one side of the political aisle. In fact, when quasi-conservative programming hits the airwaves, it often blows out liberal programming. Yet in their monomaniacal quest to push the envelope for status and reward, everyone looks for the next *Friends*, not the next *Cosby Show*; everyone seeks out the next *Will and Grace*, not the next *Everybody Loves Raymond*. Everybody wants to do an updated *All in the Family*; nobody wants to do an updated *Waltons*. As for the tough-on-terrorists action show *24*—let's just say that it died the moment Janeane Garofalo entered the set.

But liberal market-manipulation goes well beyond programming choices. Liberals in television actually corrupt the market by working with nonmarket entities to gain special advantages. They regularly cater to government, which can guarantee them special favors, and liberal interest groups, which can push government to do so. As we will show in a subsequent chapter, television executives work hand-in-glove with both government officials and interest groups in a relationship that can only be described as a Celluloid Triangle. Executives and creators are careful not to offend groups that can organize boycotts, unless those groups are conservative; executives and creators are careful to cultivate liberals in Washington, who provide them with massive tax benefits and kickbacks. FCC regulation has almost always cut in a liberal direction, since the FCC is only active when it violates the First Amendment by cracking down in the name of "diversity" and the "public interest."

Television is a complex industry. It should accordingly respond to business forces just like any other. But just like the music, publishing, and news industries, it has become old, archaic, set in its ways. It therefore refuses to contemplate unorthodox notions about the value of conservative viewers, older viewers, rural viewers, and the distorting role of government. And so its programming leans left as a business matter, too, not a purely creative one.

Television creators' third argument justifying liberal domination of television is that liberals are simply more empathetic, creative, and talented than their right-wing counterparts. This argument is obviously disgustingly discriminatory. Few Hollywoodites admit this sort of xenophobia openly—that could be grounds for a lawsuit—but it exists in precisely the same way that racism dominated American companies during the Jim Crow era. The reason companies weren't hiring blacks, argued the racists, was that blacks were unqualified, incapable of performing well at their jobs. Today, the xenophobes argue that conservatives aren't getting jobs in Hollywood because they are plodding rubes who crib their scripts from old episodes of *Leave It to Beaver.*

This is false and insulting. As we'll see, even successful conservatives who come out of the closet in Hollywood often experience worse discrimination than gays who come out of the closet in society more broadly. They lose friends. They lose contacts. Most important, they lose jobs.

Most liberals in Hollywood aren't insane anticonservative jackasses. Far from it: Most are forthright, kind, and generous people who want to use their talents to benefit humanity. Hollywood liberals are not all Elizabeth Taylors, getting married time and again, or Lindsey Lohans, boozing and smoking and sexing their way up the ladder. Most are good family people with loving spouses and happy, well-adjusted children. Many of them don't even try to infuse their politics into their shows, and some even bend over backward to present a conservative viewpoint.

But there are plenty who are more than willing to shut conservatives and the conservative viewpoint out of the business. And when conservatives shut *themselves* out because they object to liberalism on television, they do liberals a favor. In Hollywood, we're still looking for our Jackie Robinsons to go silently about their business, proving with each script that talent doesn't only come with Democratic Party charter membership.

It will take time. Liberals dominate this business, and many discriminate. Not only do they discriminate—they use their power to promote their choice political causes in an obvious, hamhanded, sometimes brutal fashion. And those causes are almost universally anti–traditional values, pro–government intervention, and anti-war.

It has ever been thus. Since the very outset, many of television's power brokers have seen their mission as something larger than pure entertainment: they've seen it as promulgation of "progressive" social values. They were and are, after all, intelligent and principled and far-seeing men and women—artists. They weren't interested in perpetuating the vast Philistine wasteland of television. They wanted to do something better. And so they began to push the envelope of culture, consciously or unconsciously, trying to open and liberalize the American audience just a bit at a time.

Because they were crusaders who thought alike, they hired alike. Even as television creators ignored more popular conservative programming in favor of transgressing age-old taboos, their social radicalism alienated them from the very society they were busily reshaping in their image. That alienation led them to a sort of ideological nepotism: in addition to helping out relatives, like previous Hollywood dynasties (the Laemmles, Coppolas, or Barrymores), the new Hollywood leaders promoted those who hung out in their social circle. This liberal feedback loop is now self-sustaining: Past liberal luminaries help new liberal stars; new liberal stars create new liberal programming; the new liberal firmament enshrines the old liberal benefactors as everlasting contributors to "social progress."

In fact, television's development can be described as a vast social content feedback loop. Television, perhaps more than any other business, is reliant on its successful measurement of the Zeitgeist. Every night's Nielsen ratings are an exercise in social science—what are Americans concerned about? What are they looking for? This constant emphasis on "catching the wave" in terms of social trends means that executives and creators don't merely perceive themselves as artists and businessmen—they perceive themselves as barometers of public opinion. They cannot lead the public *too* much, lest they lose contact with the Zeitgeist completely; nor can they lag behind it, lest their competitors capture the commercial high ground.

Thankfully for television's biggest hitters, they control the Zeitgeist. Not wholly, of course—culture is far too complex to be led in top-down fashion by television executives and creators. But what they *can* do is identify "realistic" trends, then bring those trends to the public's attention, thereby heightening and accentuating the trend. Unsurprisingly, the trends the television executives and writers focus on are almost invariably liberal. We have been speeding consistently down the liberal slippery slope for decades.

This process is not irreversible. As the television industry morphs into an Internet/television cyborg, the market is beginning to open for non-liberal creators and executives. The process we are watching in relation to the print medium applies also to television—more and more creative minds and sponsors are being given the means and the methods to contribute by the cheapness and convenience of the Internet. The Internet is Prometheus, and it has brought fire down from the television gods. All that is left is for men and women with diverse political viewpoints to learn how to use it.

Nevertheless, the gods retain a considerable advantage in resources and talent. After all, they have a sixty-year head start. Television as it is currently structured is not going to transform overnight—remember, Brandon Tartikoff, former head of NBC, was talking about the synthesis of television and the Internet back in the late 1980s. It could be several more decades in the wilderness for conservatives before they reach the Promised Land of the Internet/television merge. As Barbara Fisher, vice president of original programming for the Hallmark Channel, told me, "This whole fear that everything is digital, that everybody's going to watch TV on Hulu or on their computer or on their iPod—again, a little exaggerated. I mean, I couldn't watch a show on an iPod."[11] The Internet age is coming, but it may take its sweet time.

In the meantime, it is vital to examine the history and current state of the television industry. Television was, is, and will remain for the foreseeable future a powerful tool for foisting messages on the American public. One of Newton Minow's successors at the FCC, the LBJ-appointed

Nicholas Johnson, expressed the power of television succinctly: "All television is educational television. The question is: what is it teaching?"

The answer is simple: It's teaching liberal messages. Art has always taken politics as its subject, but art has never been consumerized to the extent we see now. Virtually every person in the United States watched *All in the Family* during the 1970s. How many people laughed at Archie, telling themselves that his viewpoint was the conservative viewpoint? Every girl above the age of twelve during the 1990s eventually got the Rachel haircut. How many viewers picked up the *Friends* politics, too? Television brought down the Soviet Union by showing those living under the Communist jackboot the lush lifestyle of the folks on *Dallas*; television has the power to destroy fundamental American institutions in the same way.

The transformation of American culture at the hands of television's most powerful people is a story that has remained untold for decades. It is a story we must hear, because it is a story that continues every night in our living rooms. It affects adults, teens, and children. It touches everyone who touches that dial.

How did the left take over TV? How did the most important invention of all time fall into the hands of like-minded liberals with active and insidious political intent—and how did we swallow their product without noticing?

To answer that question, we must begin at the beginning.

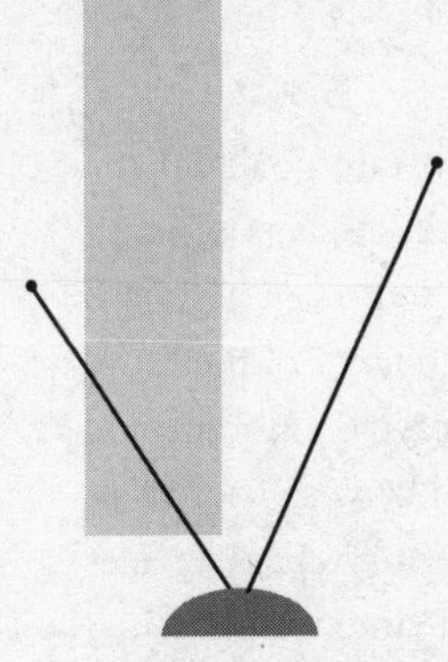

THE SECRET POLITICAL HISTORY OF TELEVISION

How Television Became Liberal

History, they say, is written by the winners. That is certainly true of television.

The story of television, as told by those in the industry, goes something like this: Television's formational years were childish and immature, catering to the lowest common denominator and afraid of controversy. That's why programming looked conservative in the old days. Over time, as America became more liberal, television began to reflect that nascent liberalism, taking new risks and depicting new realities. Liberal television was rewarded with profits and ratings, and happiness and contentment spread over the land. But it was not to last. The rise of Reagan and the Moral Majority soon ignited a battle between the creative knights in shining armor and the dastardly conservative censors. Consonance was eventually achieved by corporations, who were able to moderate television content in order to please conservatives while simultaneously allowing a limited amount of creative freedom. Overall, in this view, television has lagged behind social change, with a few notable exceptions. Television has always followed the market, never led it; television has always offered something for everyone.

It's a convenient story. That narrative achieves certain goals for the powers-that-be. First, it means that they can portray themselves as political moderates while still occasionally speaking truth to power. This version of history obscures the more conservative past in favor of the more liberal present—it castigates long-dead 1950s pioneers as ignorant and paints the sainted creators of the late 1960s and early 1970s as visionaries. As for the current crop of creators, this flattering history characterizes them as cutting-edge moderates: They haven't propagandized on behalf of liberal values, but at the same time, they've broken new ground in terms of racial tolerance and sexual orientation in particular.

Second, this narrative characterizes television as a commercial medium impervious to criticisms about content—we don't generally criticize McDonald's for providing Big Macs, even if they're unhealthy, so why should we criticize the television industry for providing liberal programming to eager consumers? Furthermore, those in the television industry can always cite business practicalities as the reason for greasing the cultural slippery slope. They can blame corporations for failures to push the progressive agenda, but take credit for any progressivism they sneak into their programming.

In short, this history is a giant version of the Oscars: a self-congratulatory event designed to cast today's creators—and certain sainted creators of yesteryear—as heroes in both artistic and political terms while utterly ignoring the achievements of those who launched the industry.

There's only one problem: This version of history isn't true.

The secret history of television is a story of how an industry was taken over by the left, through both conscious infiltration and unconscious socialization. Conservative entrepreneurs broke open the new industry—and in the name of profit, they employed the best-in-breed entertainers, who all happened to be liberals. The conservatives looked to cater to rural viewers, knowing that rural affiliates were those most likely to censor programming; they therefore got both rural and urban viewers. As the medium matured, more and more urban-based entertainment-oriented businesspeople began infiltrating the executive ranks, changing and shaping the goals of television, altering its target audience from rural to supposedly more valuable and sophisticated urban audiences. With the new target audience in hand, television consistently pushed itself farther and farther to the left, squeezing out all those who disagreed, using the tools of entertainment to forward social messaging. Now, the television industry is largely conservative-free, and the product shows it.

CONSERVATIVE BEGINNINGS: THE GRAND OLD MEN OF RADIO

Television began with radio.

The radio business, just like other businesses, began as a vehicle for creating products and services that would generate revenue. Even though FCC regulations required that radio serve the public interest, the first executives in radio were interested in profit first, last, and always. Most of them were Jewish Garment District types who launched themselves to the technological and cultural cutting edge using their newly acquired American freedoms to build their businesses from the ground up.

The consummate capitalist was David Sarnoff, the ruddy-faced, short, balding president of the Radio Corporation of America and founder of NBC. He was a Jewish immigrant from Minsk with a gift for both self-promotion and business strategy.[1] His love for television made him one of the medium's first funders and proponents. Politically, Sarnoff was right-wing. During World War II, General Dwight D. Eisenhower made him a communication consultant and gave him the rank of brigadier general, a title he carried around with him for the rest of his life. He often trumpeted "traditional" American values and the total defeat of global Communism.[2] As a product of capitalism, Sarnoff was an ardent defender of it.[3]

Sarnoff's counterpart at CBS was William S. Paley. Like Sarnoff, Paley was an enterprising Jewish kid with an ego that would make Orson Welles look amateur by comparison—as a child he added a nonexistent middle initial S. on a school application, for the prestige. If Sarnoff was a great businessman, Paley was even better—or at least, less principled. In the television industry, independently owned stations decide which network's programming they want to carry—that's how they become affiliates. Paley employed strategies designed to steal Sarnoff's affiliates, offering stations CBS programming for free, in return demanding that they play commercials sold by CBS. Paley didn't steal just Sarnoff's affiliates—he stole Sarnoff's stars. He pirated stars from other networks, including Fats Waller, Bing Crosby, Will Rogers, and Jack Benny.[4] He was, as the *New York Times* called him upon his death, "A 20th-century visionary with the ambitions of a 19th-century robber-baron."[5]

Unlike Sarnoff, Paley was a political chameleon. He was an enthusiastic opponent of Joseph McCarthy, declaring that CBS deserved credit for McCarthy's destruction. At the same time, under his leadership, CBS forced its employees to take a loyalty oath stating that they had never been members of the Communist Party. He was a lifelong member of the GOP, but he did not shy away from kowtowing to the FDR White House to maintain his broadcast licenses.[6]

Paley's programming perspective was just as mercenary—and he wasn't shy about it. As he put it, "What we are doing is satisfying the American public. That's our first job."[7] He had no interest in converting viewers and listeners to high-minded programming; CBS, he said, "cannot calmly broadcast programs we think people ought to listen to if they know what is good for them."[8] For Bill Paley, only one thing mattered: the bottom line.

The leadership at ABC thought differently—they looked to shape the audiences to meet their programming rather than vice versa. At that network, the third member of the original television executive triumvirate, Leonard Goldenson, held the reins. Like Sarnoff and Paley, Goldenson grew up in a Jewish household. Unlike Sarnoff and Paley, however, he was a liberal, born and bred.

Goldenson's family was moderately wealthy, which allowed him to attend Harvard College and Harvard Law School—a rare accomplishment for Jews of that time. After working as a lawyer at Paramount, Goldenson managed to finagle ownership of the company's theater business, which he then sold off in order to buy up the nascent American Broadcasting Company, a former subsidiary of NBC.

Goldenson remained politically liberal throughout his career. Early on, he put conservative firebrand Billy Graham on the air in *Hour of Decision* in a successful attempt to score ratings. Then he reversed himself, citing his belief in separation of television and religion. Goldenson reviled legislators' concern with sex and violence on television.[9] While he remained a businessman like Sarnoff and Paley, he did not shy away from injecting social messages into programming. During the McCarthy hearings, he ordered all 187 hours aired live, at a cost of $600,000. "I felt that if the public could see just how McCarthy operated, they would understand just how ridiculous a figure he really was," Goldenson later wrote.[10] This was not news coverage—this was coverage as commentary. Along the same lines, Goldenson considered Barbara Walters the epitome of reportorial courage for playing up to Fidel Castro.[11] His programming followed the same pattern, even though Goldenson claimed he was only catering to the market.[12]

THE WILDERNESS YEARS FOR LIBERALS: 1950–1960

The respective viewpoints of Sarnoff, Paley, and Goldenson led the networks to evolve in different directions. NBC became a semi-elitist mouthpiece geared toward informing the public; CBS became a ratings juggernaut interested almost solely in revenue; ABC focused on sex and violence.

At NBC, General Sarnoff deferred to his chosen deputy, Pat Weaver, a highly educated Dartmouth graduate. Weaver's philosophy was simple: Make money by educating the audience. Weaver wanted America to be a place in which "every man is an Athenian."[13] He dubbed his effort Operation Frontal Lobes.[14]

Weaver's strategy could only work if he broadcast—that is, attracted as many viewers at a time as possible. He shunned the idea of gearing programming toward target audiences, a trap he felt the movies had fallen into. "The advertising responsibility is to *reach everyone*," he said. He pursued that goal by programming "spectaculars," large-scale live events designed to draw in "light" viewers.[15] But how could he fund the spectaculars?

He came up with the funding in a stroke of genius that would have massive implications for the entire industry: Instead of advertisers purchasing entire shows or producing the shows themselves, NBC would produce its own shows and allow advertisers to buy *segments* rather than entire shows. This was a breakthrough for the networks—instead of having to keep one advertiser ecstatic, they could now keep seven or eight advertisers relatively happy. No longer would advertisers, the parties most responsive to the public, be able to dictate what the networks broadcast; now the networks themselves would dictate their programming, and advertisers could buy only in small chunks. Increased network control, insulated from the feedback of individual advertisers, meant more liberal control of the industry over time.

At CBS, the management cared far less about teaching America than winning the numbers battle. Dictator Paley brought on a statistics-minded second-in-command, Frank Stanton, a radio research guru with a doctorate in psychology from Ohio State University.

Stanton's philosophy was as capitalistic as his boss's, a direct contrast to the later intellectualism of Newton Minow. "Television, like radio," he said in 1948, "should be a medium for the majority of Americans, not for any small or special groups; therefore its programming should be largely patterned for what these majority audiences want and like."[16] Stanton's statistical knowledge, combined with Paley's populist programming tendencies, made CBS the leader in the ratings for much of the 1950s.

ABC, meanwhile, struggled mightily—mainly because it was the smallest, but also because it was the least conservative of the three networks. Robert Kintner, a former White House correspondent and future cabinet liaison for LBJ, led the way.

Kintner, unlike the communist-fighters at NBC and CBS, was an ardent opponent of McCarthyism. He stood up for closeted former communist Gypsy Rose Lee, braving advertiser boycotts to do it and winning a Peabody Award in the process.[17] That move demonstrated his liberal bona fides. He burnished them even more when he insisted on carrying the Army-McCarthy hearings wall to wall.

His liberalism wasn't restricted to news coverage. Kintner's programming strategy focused on the lowest common denominator—he was liberal enough to think that broadcast standards were tyrannical limits on creativity rather than traditional hallmarks of good taste. According to one of Kintner's subordinates, David Levy, he was the man behind the rise of sex and violence on television, titillating younger audiences with envelope-pushing material.[18]

There was a reason for the focus on sex and violence: Goldenson's smaller station roster created the need for a new sort of strategy. Unlike NBC, ABC could not champion its ratings; unlike CBS, it could not champion its affiliate base. ABC's affiliates were restricted largely to the major cities, and even there, they did not draw major numbers. ABC therefore needed to come up with an alternative marketing ploy that could work for advertisers.

In the mid-1950s, Goldenson's deputy, Ollie Treyz, hit on the winning idea: pushing the young urban consumer as a higher-value consumer for advertisers. The idea was simple—if ABC couldn't get older, rural viewers for its programs, it would tell advertisers that its young, urban viewers were worth more in the grand scheme of things, with or without the data to prove it. "We began programming for the young families of America," Goldenson later wrote, "and in doing so revolutionized television . . . we simply had no other choice."[19] This philosophy bore the obsession with the 18-to-49 crowd—and in catering to that crowd, television's manic obsession with sex and violence was born too.

While the political allegiances and market manipulations of the executives helped shape the industry on a broad level, on a day-to-day level, the writers, actors, and producers were shaping it in a covertly liberal direction. Most of the early prominent creators of television were Jewish kids who had found their way on the New York entertainment scene—which meant, typically, that their parents had been poor, often socialist, and that they had grown up with vaudeville, which translated exceptionally well to television.

The early years of television were replete with liberal Jews who were cutting-edge for the time (remember, this was 1950, not 1970). Milton Berle, a liberal Jew, dominated the television ratings—in fall 1948, he had an astounding 86.7 audience rating—meaning that 86.7 percent of the television audience was tuned in to Berle.[20] Sid Caesar was Jewish, liberal (his wife was a socialist), and earning a million bucks a year with *Your Show of Shows* and *Caesar's Hour.* He hired Jewish liberals like Neil Simon, Mel Brooks, Woody Allen, Carl Reiner, and Larry Gelbart—a star-studded Jewish liberal lineup that has to rank alongside the 1927 Yankees in terms of star quality. Phil Silvers was the youngest of eight children, a Jewish kid who made good on television in *The Phil Silvers*

Show and later *You'll Never Get Rich*—and in both shows, he satirized the military in a soft, gibing way. The stars who weren't Jewish were also generally blue-collar kids with poor parents (Jackie Gleason, Fred Allen, Danny Thomas), in line with the FDR-Democratic consensus at the least.

The heavy concentration of leftist Jews in early television doesn't spring from some concerted conspiracy. It springs from the fact that artists are generally alienated from society, as we've mentioned—and assimilated Jews were alienated from both their religious heritage (making them liberal) and the broader society. Jews were already restricted from many top law schools and medical schools, but they were welcome in the artistic community, which is by definition a community of outcasts. Highly intelligent, highly motivated, highly artistic, and heavily concentrated in New York, the Jewish community was a natural breeding ground for early radio and television. Naturally, as societal outsiders, the liberal Jews in the entertainment industry focused their politics first and foremost on the abolition of racism.

The creators were liberals from the get-go, but they were hamstrung by the times and the network higher-ups. They also knew their place, and their place was outside the realm of politics. They had to know their place, because this was live television, and networks couldn't take the risk of hiring off-the-wall zanies to host their programs. They had to have experienced, seasoned entertainers who knew better than to try to skirt the broadcast standards.

More than that, though, the television creators were also creatures of the time, living in an America that had just defeated Nazism, was fighting the scourge of repressive Communism, was booming economically, and was making racial progress. Soft social satire was the best the TV industry could or would do. Even the creative left in the television industry retained pride in America, the country that had lifted them from poverty and provided them opportunity and wealth.

Throughout this period, television grew exponentially. In Minnesota in 1948, TV sets were sold for the sky-high price of $300 ($2,715 in today's dollars)—and that was on the low end.[21] In 1954, according to historian James Baughman, just "20 percent of Arkansas homes had a TV set; in North Dakota, 8 percent."[22] Once the television industry realized that the best way to make money from television wasn't selling television sets but selling advertising *on* television sets, television exploded. By the end of the 1950s, 90 percent of American homes had at least one television set.[23] The television era was here—and the most powerful mass medium in world history began to test its muscles.

LIBERALS UNDERGROUND

Liberalism remained a subtle phenomenon on television in the late 1950s and early 1960s, but it was there. Hollywood types pushed consensus issues ranging from racial tolerance to a more overt role of government in the economy; all of it was relatively uncontroversial. As the decade progressed, however, television leftists began to embrace more subversive and dangerous politics. Where the liberalism of the 1950s had aspired to a better world, 1960s liberalism sought to set the world aflame, tearing down the status quo through vulgarity and shock value.

The decade didn't begin with that dark, cynical liberalism. It began with the hopeful, triumphant politics of John F. Kennedy, who wasn't far removed from Dwight D. Eisenhower or even his 1960 presidential opponent, Richard Nixon. It began with the sense that something great was in the air—that America was on the move.

Executives remained profit-driven—like their predecessors, they sprang from the corporate world. Unlike their predecessors, however, the new breed of executives hadn't started at ground level—most were highly educated in the mold of Goldenson rather than garment district salesmen in the mold of Sarnoff. Many sprang from the quasi-creative milieu of Madison Avenue, where they had been advertising executives. They were more liberal than their predecessors, as JFK babies, but they still held one value above all: the value of cash.

The pursuit of bucks meant a transition from live to taped television. Where most of the shows of the early-to-mid 1950s were live specials starring classic entertainers, shows of the mid-to-late '50s were tape delayed for rebroadcast on the West Coast. Artistically, the death of live television meant less excitement. More important, the transition to taped television actually led the way to greater television liberalism. Before the transition, network censors, whose job it was to ensure that advertisers didn't freak out over broadcast material, had to be wary of anything that could offend the audience; their motto was "if in doubt, lose it." That meant more conservative values on television. In taped television, by contrast, everything was preplanned. That meant that programmers could push the envelope more and more often, and they took full advantage, bugging the network censors and generally daring them to wield the heavy hand of censorship.

Perhaps most important, taped television also meant that programming production could move to the West Coast, since the networks didn't have to broadcast live from New York. While the programming executives remained in New York, the creative folks moved out west. Hollywood was a much smaller, more parochial community than New York—while New York was the cultural center of the world, it was also the financial center of the world, which meant that even its creative community recognized the necessity for entrepreneurship over social messaging. In Hollywood, it was a different story. The creative people ran the town, and they spent their time with like-minded creative people. An echo chamber was created, largely removed from the rest of the country.

Ever so slowly, a chasm began to form between the creative and business sides that hadn't truly existed before. While the new executives zealously guarded the capitalist nature of the system, certain creators began to see their role as something more than simply providing a product for people to consume—they were now the stewards of the culture, and the executives were bourgeois exploiters. The executives, thought the creators, wanted to make crap for stupid people; the creators, the executives thought, wanted to do Shakespeare in primetime. The stage was set for real conflict between the two groups.

The burgeoning executive-creative split forced a covert deal between executives and creators. Executives wanted to make money, so they aggressively courted audiences without worrying about cultural pretensions. Meanwhile, creators fulfilled the market for that lowbrow programming—which was often conservative in tenor and tone—with the understanding that every so often, the networks would allow them to insert highbrow messaging programs, intellectual fare, Kennedy Center–type material. A dichotomy broke out on television: Shows either became dumb attempts to win ratings or elitist attempts to score political points. There wasn't much in between.

The dominance of dumbed-down television began at ABC, which had to push the envelope merely to survive. In the late 1950s, Ollie Treyz took over from Robert Kintner—Mr. Sex and Violence—at ABC.[24] Treyz took Kintner's strategy to the next level. He greenlit programs like *The Untouchables*, a show so violent that tepid *TV Guide* observed, "In practically every episode a gang leader winds up stitched to a brick wall and full of bullets, or face down in a parking lot (and full of bullets), or face up in a gutter (and still full of bullets) . . ."[25] Next, Treyz got himself into hot water when he greenlit *Bus Stop*, one episode of which depicted the Justin Bieber of the 1960s, Fabian, playing a psychopathic killer who brutally slays an old man. Senator John Pastore (D–Rhode Island) was so incensed by the episode that he held Congressional hearings on it and dragged Treyz in to testify. After the season, the show was canceled and Treyz was fired.[26]

Treyz was merely one charter member of the ABC envelope-pushers' club—all in the name of statistics, of course. Tom Moore, who took over for Treyz, was committed to pushing the same envelopes in terms of sex and violence, since that's where the dollars were, even though as a born and bred Mississippian, he leaned conservative. Nonetheless, under his tenure, ABC picked up cutting-edge shows like *77 Sunset Strip*, *Peyton Place*, and *The Mod Squad*.

Many of these shows were the brainchildren of television craftsman Leonard Goldberg, a former ad agency executive who had originally been a research department clerk at ABC after attending the Wharton School of Business. He returned to ABC under the tutelage of Edgar Scherick, and he quickly imbibed the ABC mantra: "I had always felt that at ABC you had to do something *different* to attract an audience . . . if you're ABC, you can't just play it safe. You play it safe, you lose."[27] That translated into "some show with go-go girls and music on the beach" (*Where the Action Is*) and a competition show about a "young married couple" (*The Newlywed Game*). Goldberg's logic—"What are young women interested in? Young men. What are they most interested in? Romance"—led to *The Dating Game*. This was not *Julius Caesar*, but it did sell ad time.[28]

Because of ABC's burgeoning success, ABC's former executives filtered through the industry. Former Treyz disciple James Aubrey, who had started off in radio before becoming ABC's head of programming and talent, took off for CBS in 1958. Aubrey was widely disliked but highly successful, a nebbishy playboy with a mind for broads and a penchant for booze. Like Treyz, Goldberg, and Moore, he pursued a strategy of—in his own words—"wild, sexy, lively stuff, things that had never been done before" at ABC. He continued to pursue that strategy at CBS. Aubrey was the stereotypical model of corporate excess and tyranny. He cared nothing for politics, and he cared nothing for "quality TV." He was something straight out of *Mad Men*.

As *Life* magazine explained, Aubrey's "code was unwritten but so rigid it permitted few exceptions: feed the public little more than rural comedies, fast-moving detective dramas, and, later, sexy dolls. No old people; the emphasis was on youth." Aubrey justified his programming decisions the same way his bosses, Frank Stanton and William Paley, did: "People just don't want an anthology. They would rather tune in on *Lucy*."[29]

Aubrey programmed "rural junk"—funny, hip shows with special appeal to CBS's heavily rural affiliate base. He dominated with those programs. Still, the critics—and the liberal creators—demanded a few political sacrificial lambs, and Aubrey's CBS obliged with *The Defenders* and *East Side/West Side*. *The Defenders* was a controversial lawyer show starring Robert Reed and E. G. Marshall, tackling issues like euthanasia, abortion, and movie censorship, almost always from a liberal angle. Creator Robert Rose explained, "We're committed to controversy." When the show aired an episode entitled "The Benefactor," which uncritically parroted the pro-choice line, several advertisers pulled out. A last-minute advertiser saved the episode, though, and from then on, the show made no bones about its politics.[30]

East Side/West Side was another landmark liberal show, starring George C. Scott as a social worker dealing with kids from the wrong side of the tracks. Soon enough, Scott's character joined an idealistic liberal congressman and became his aide. Simply put, it was propaganda for the big government, Democratic agenda. Aubrey soon stepped in. He did so not because he was conservative, but because he was concerned about the fact that the show was unrelentingly depressing, gritty, and minority-oriented. "Every script dwelt on the problems of Harlem—minority groups, and so on," said Aubrey. "I went to [David Susskind, the producer] and said, 'David, look, you can have just as big a problem in Sutton Place. Let's once in a while take it out of Spanish Harlem.' They did."[31] It didn't help. The liberal show went down in flames in the ratings.

Ratings and revenue remained Aubrey's first priorities. He did rural junk like *The Beverly Hillbillies* (which garnered, believe it or not, *57 million viewers* every Wednesday night), *Green Acres*, *Mr. Ed* (yes, the talking horse), and *Petticoat Junction*. He was also responsible for *Gilligan's Island*, as well as *The Munsters* (which, incidentally, his boss, Paley, hated). Many of these programs were produced by Aubrey's personal friend Martin Ransohoff, who told me what the programming philosophy behind his shows was: "I never felt the pressure to include social content in the shows. . . . We just wanted to get in and do successful shows."[32]

It was Aubrey's personal habits, not his programming strategies, that eventually led to his downfall. He was too fond of partying and womanizing and lowbrow programs that got good ratings, and it embarrassed Paley and Stanton no end. "I don't pretend to be any saint," said Aubrey. "If anyone wants to indict me for liking pretty girls, I guess I'm guilty." In 1965, the CBS brass found him guilty and dumped him. When they did, Aubrey had brought them "the biggest profits in TV history—up from a net of $25 million a year in 1959 to $49 million in 1964." CBS led in the ratings by a whopping 9 million viewers.[33]

After Aubrey's ouster, his profit-seeking, ratings-obsessed subordinates remained atop the networks. One of Aubrey's former subordinates was Mike Dann, a numbers man like his former boss. Dann saw the numbers as the only realistic gauge of what would work and what wouldn't. "The most dangerous thing I could have done is go by my gut," he told me. "Numbers, numbers, numbers. . . . A show is good if it got numbers, and it was bad if it was canceled. It has nothing to do with quality."[34]

Unlike Aubrey, however, who greenlit highbrow liberal programming as a sop to critics, Dann did it for ideological reasons. He pushed *The Defenders*, bragging, "[it] was one of the most exciting and socially conscious shows that I ever put on television. . . . I was proud to have been a part of it."[35]

Despite Dann's continued power, Aubrey's firing was an early clue that the ancien profit-first régime was on its last legs in television. In dumping Aubrey, the television executives embarrassed by his lowbrow programming cleared the way for a far more dangerous programming ideology: the merger of gutter style and liberal substance. By throwing out a man who made them money, who really *did* cater to the market, they made clear that television would have to provide something deeper while still earning a profit. "Social meaning" would have to be married to entertainment to provide justification for that entertainment—the simple justification of the buck was no longer enough.

STARTING DOWN THE SLIPPERY SLOPE

The assassination of John F. Kennedy certainly had something to do with the ouster of men like Aubrey and the shift from so-called "rural garbage" toward "quality programming." Obviously, JFK's assassination had a major cultural impact across the country—the hopeful liberalism of the Camelot years was almost instantaneously replaced by an infinitely more cynical, pessimistic liberalism that rejected faith in American individualism and optimism. Perhaps even more than the general public, members of the Hollywood TV community were devastated by JFK's death, and they suddenly began taking seriously the criticisms he and his appointees, like Newton "Vast Wasteland" Minow, had made about television.

Larry Gelbart's paean to the dead president reflected the general feeling in Hollywood: "One way or another, he was going to win you over. . . . You could be seduced merely by a photo of him. . . . We are his forever. / We are eternally charmed." Gelbart nauseatingly described the murder as "our loss and our shame,"[36] despite the fact that Lee Harvey Oswald was a communist with ties to both the Cuban and Russian governments. James Aubrey, by contrast, was shameless. The day after the murder, he told Blair Clark, head of CBS News, "Just play the assassination footage over and over again—that's all they want to see."[37] Gelbart's view trumped Aubrey's; Aubrey found himself out of a job.

The path was clearing for open liberalism on television.

Perhaps the first executive to move television in a more openly liberal direction was Robert Kintner. The former "sex and violence" ABC head had taken over at NBC. But whereas he had programmed the most salacious shows he could find at ABC, he suddenly moderated his programming choices at NBC in favor of "quality" programming—elitist stuff in line with the Newton Minow vision of television. One example was a British import entitled *That Was the Week That Was* (known more briefly as *TW3*), a proto-*Daily Show* with a varied cast making fun of the news. In the United States, the show starred Henry Fonda and Henry Morgan, and featured regular guests like Alan Alda and Gene Hackman. Gloria Steinem and Tom Lehrer wrote for the show. Steinem, of course, was a militant feminist; Lehrer was a militant liberal satirist; Alda was tremendously liberal, as were most of the other hosts and guests. For those too young to remember Lehrer, he was a Harvard mathematician who penned lyrics like this, to his song "Send the Marines": "We send the Marines. / For might makes right / Until they see the light / They've got to be protected / All their rights respected / 'Til somebody we like can be elected." It's no wonder the teens who watched this ended up protesting Vietnam and chanting "Ho, Ho, Ho Chi Minh, Viet Cong Are Gonna Win!" The show bombed in the ratings, but it broke through the unspoken ban on open politics during entertainment hours.

Grant Tinker, who worked under Kintner (he later became the head of NBC himself) saw Kintner as "reach[ing] for something more than the ratings . . ."[38] In 1966, Kintner reached for more than television—he left NBC to join the LBJ Administration.[39] But he didn't leave without foreshadowing just where television was headed: toward the fusion of ratings-grabbing lowest-common-denominator style with ardent political liberalism. Kintner recognized that audiences did not respond to Shakespeare, *Profiles in Courage*, or *That Was the Week That Was*—they responded to *Bonanza*.[40] With that simple fact in mind, he urged that television produce programming insinuating political propaganda into entertainment programming rather than creating elitist programming that would appeal to a select few. He wanted television to "deal with more controversial social, economic, and political subjects in both news and entertainment programming."[41]

While the executive ranks at the networks were gradually shifting toward a more openly liberal stance, the creators were waiting in the wings. They were generally the same people who had made it big in the

1950s—the Jewish vaudevillians were now out on their own. Mel Brooks, the former Caesar writer, was now running *Get Smart!*; Carl Reiner, another *Your Show of Shows* graduate, was running *The Dick Van Dyke Show.* Leonard Stern, who had started as a jokewriter for Gleason, helped create *The Honeymooners*, became a force in his own right, working on *Get Smart!* and the more openly liberal and urban *He and She*. Firebrand political liberal Aaron Spelling was in town, and he was finally hitting the big time after writing regularly for *Playhouse 90*. Hardcore leftist Gene Reynolds had worked his way up from actor to director of shows like *Leave It to Beaver* and *The Andy Griffith Show* to enter the world of production.

There were too many liberal creators waiting for a political platform for their skills. If only the executives could be convinced to shift their focus to the right kind of audience, the creators would be given free rein to preach their politics. There was a sense in the industry that the dam was about to burst.

TELEVISION'S SOCIAL REVOLUTION: THE LIBERAL BREAKTHROUGH

The Vietnam War burst the dam wide open.

During its early years, Americans largely approved of the Vietnam War. When Gallup asked the public whether the United States had made a "mistake" sending troops to Vietnam in mid-1965, only 24 percent of Americans said we had. By the third quarter of 1967, 41 percent of Americans thought it had been a mistake (against 48 percent who thought it had not been a mistake), and by August–September 1968, 54 percent of Americans thought it had been mistake.[42]

On a societal level, this disenchantment with America's military foray combined with the sexual revolution, the civil rights movement, the drug subculture, and the growing socialist movement on college campuses to form a powerful counterculture. Early on, television contributed to the counterculture in relatively minor ways—the semi-innocuous emphasis on sexual liberation on television in shows like *Peyton Place* and *The Avengers* (ABC), the similarly innocent focus on race in shows like *I Spy!* (NBC), the less harmless antics of the political leftists on *TW3* (NBC). But once television picked up the current of the counterculture, it elevated it to new heights in the public consciousness; the honchos on television realized that for the first time, the counterculture had an element that received majority approval—namely, opposition to the Vietnam War—and they capitalized.

That couldn't have happened without the emergence of a new set of executives. The newer crew was college educated, literary in taste, and had grown up with television. They were comfortable with the medium. They also bridged the gap between executives and creators—rather than leaving production to the creative side, they often stepped over the line and involved themselves in creative projects. That merger between business and creative elements marked the beginning of the end of profit-only television, and the beginning of social goal-oriented TV. No longer would television be separated into lowbrow entertainment geared toward profit and highbrow programming geared toward political propagandizing—now the two would be combined into a form of lowbrow politics that would infiltrate American society from top to bottom.

At ABC, co-opting the counterculture had always been a network goal. Leonard Goldberg, who knew the value of targeting youth audiences, had taken over as head of programming. Goldberg was also a creative talent, not merely a business administrator. Later, with Aaron Spelling as his partner, he would go on to create some of the most provocative and popular shows in the history of American television. His vice president of planning, Fred Pierce, led the effort to target advertisers by spreading the message that young people were better buyers. Pierce was actually a political conservative, but he was a research maven, and targeting youth was the only way ABC could survive.[43] Leonard Goldenson expressed the ABC mind-set of the mid-1960s: "Neither of our rival networks was particularly willing to experiment with radical ideas. They didn't need to. They were already winning."[44]

ABC's programming reflected that reality. In 1965, ABC finally broke into the top ten with *Bewitched* and *The Fugitive*; both centered on action or sexy comedy (if you don't remember *Bewitched*'s use of double entendres, rent it). It wasn't until 1968, though, that ABC really started to make a dent with *The Mod Squad*, a series that relied on action and young faces and featured an openly liberal sensibility about the youth movement. Goldberg worked with Aaron Spelling, his future partner, on it.

Goldberg brought in allies to push the youth revolt. He found and recruited a couple of brilliant young minds who would go on to become dominant players in the entertainment industry: Barry Diller and Michael Eisner.[45] Diller was far more of an ideologue than Goldberg; Diller found an ideological and business ally in Eisner and brought him in with Goldberg's go-head. Both Diller and Eisner were unapologetic liberals, and they programmed as such.

As the producer of the ABC movies of the week, Diller's programming genius was utilized to promote liberal social messages, from *The Young Lawyers* (1969) to *That Certain Summer* (1972), the first television movie tackling homosexuality. *Summer*'s writers and producers William Link and Richard Levinson gave credit to Diller, who is widely rumored to be gay in Hollywood, for putting the movie on the air: "It would never have been on the air if it weren't for Barry Diller," said Link.[46]

At CBS, too, a transformation was under way. Paley was still in charge, and Mike Dann was at his side. In 1966, though, Dann unexpectedly paved the way for his own exit by giving the go-ahead to an innocuous variety show starring two musical brothers who had already failed once on television. Their names were Tommy and Dick Smothers, and they had a cute and innocent shtick playing off their sibling conflict. No big deal. It would be innocent fun.

But they didn't exactly live up to their clean-cut image. Tommy, it turned out, was politically active. He was part of the hippie movement, the antiwar movement, the drug movement. The show died when Tommy began stealing tapes of the show so the network couldn't censor them.

But the snowball was already rolling down the hill. *The Smothers Brothers* opened the eyes of the management—youth audiences could bring in huge numbers. It was one thing to trot out a sop to the kiddies; it was another to actually *win* using youth programming. And *The Smothers Brothers* had put up real competition to *Bonanza*, the number-one show on television, which was unthinkable.

Paley saw the light. Before Dann knew it, his regime was on its last legs. In 1969, Paley elevated Robert Wood to the network presidency. Wood, like Goldberg, had spent virtually his entire adult life in television. Unlike Dann and the other CBS brass, Wood wasn't addicted to numbers, whether those were ratings points or audience-testing results. "I read the reports," he said, "but I figured they should get a certain weight of importance of five percent of your thinking, or six percent, or something like that. I always felt that if you rely too heavily on testing, you were substituting [for] your own intuition, your own instincts, your own experience."[47] This reliance on gut instinct as opposed to research gave executives far more leeway in picking programming—now they could put on programs *they* liked, as opposed to programs that had charted well in testing.

And Wood was eager to apply his sensibility to programming. He proposed that CBS dump its entire rural schedule—all the successful programs like *Gomer Pyle, Petticoat Junction, The Beverly Hillbillies*—and instead slot in hipper, more urban programming targeting younger audiences. He wasn't interested in highbrow liberal programming—he wanted lowbrow material that could attract audiences.

Mike Dann called Wood's play "a massive assault on my scheduling philosophy"[48]—and it was. It was a calculated attempt to move away from reliance on rural, conservative audiences, and to cut off the burgeoning youth movement at ABC.

That nascent conflict broke into the open in a 1970 meeting that changed television forever. As Dann described it, "For Bob Wood winning the numbers was no longer enough. . . . To my horror, he even suggested that we could afford to lose the ratings if we had to, because the gain in revenues on the back of a younger audience would offset the loss."[49] Dann stood up to Wood—and Paley cut Dann dead. CBS was moving away from programming for America and moving toward programming for particular Americans under the direction of Bob Wood.[50]

Wood's deputy was Fred Silverman, another TV baby, who sported outsize glasses and a consistently wry smirk on his face. He majored in television programming and theater at Syracuse, then attended graduate school at Ohio State, where he wrote a famous dissertation on the development of the ABC network, even going so far as to interview Leonard Goldenson. By age twenty-five, Silverman was CBS's director of daytime programs.

Silverman eventually rose to become CBS vice president of programs. As a creative man rather than a numbers cruncher, his programming philosophy mirrored Wood's—he relied on what the press casually termed his "golden gut." Silverman explained his strategy to me: "There was no research in buying a script. You're basically going by your own judgment. . . . I'd say yes or no, usually based on a couple of lines of description."[51]

This left Silverman a lot of discretion, and he wasn't shy about using it. He opposed the Dann method, which acted as a barrier to change. And he *was* interested in doing socially important programming. "I would hope in some ways that we kind of led the audience," he told me, "that we didn't follow the audience, and that on some of the shows, we were at the forefront of movements."[52]

It was no wonder that during this period, CBS's programming shifted television dramatically to the left. The brass gave the go-ahead to a vulgar and shocking new show called *All in the Family*, which featured television's first flushing toilet, frequent use of racial epithets, and issue-centric episodes focusing on hot button topics. The show was introduced to the network via agent Sam Cohn, a friend of Mike Dann's—Dann and Cohn knew each other from their work with the Democratic National Committee for Television during the McGovern campaign, of which Dann was chairman. Paley hated the show, but Silverman, Dann, and Wood backed it, and they won.[53]

CBS also bit on *The Mary Tyler Moore Show*, a feminist legitimization of the single woman who doesn't need a man. CBS honchos swung into action on *M*A*S*H*, a dramatically antiwar show that captured the spirit of the times by mocking the military, religion, and traditional values. They even bought *The New Dick Van Dyke Show*, which was nothing like the original *Dick Van Dyke Show*—Carl Reiner, now fully able to express his liberal viewpoints, inserted his progressive sensibilities to the hilt, going so far as to quit the program after Bob Wood rejected a scene in which Van Dyke's screen daughter walks in on Van Dyke having sex with his screen wife, played by Hope Lange. CBS's urban renewal project paid huge dividends—they dominated the ratings for the next five years.

At NBC, a similar transformation was under way. Herb Schlosser was now heading NBC's West Coast programming (eventually, he'd take over as head of the network). Schlosser, a Princeton and Yale Law grad, was yet another political liberal, and he believed that television could be used as a message medium. In a 1974 speech, he laid out his elitist viewpoint. *"We have to strike the delicate balance between following public taste and leading it* [italics mine] by offering new forms and styles of entertainment."[54]

The most notable example of the "message medium" philosophy leaped into the public consciousness in 1967, when Schlosser greenlit a special titled *Rowan and Martin's Laugh-In*. The name of the special was a takeoff on the hippie culture be-ins, love-ins, and die-ins, vestiges of which can still be seen on today's college campuses when students need an excuse for ditching class. The special was a hit, and NBC picked it up as a series for 1968. The show was in the mold of *The Smothers Brothers Comedy Hour*, but it was far more fast-paced and visually edgy. Like *Smothers Brothers*, it was eminently political—and eminently leftist.

If the executives during the late 1960s and early 1970s were different, so were the creators. Sure, there were still the holdovers—Larry Gelbart was responsible for one of the biggest shows on television, and so were men like Leonard Stern, Gene Reynolds, and Allan Burns. But those holdovers were now able to take the risks they'd always wanted to take. "The writers were leading the networks at that point because they wanted to write stuff that was more socially conscious," Burns told me.[55] By the late 1960s and early 1970s, the networks began to catch up to the early starters like Burns and Reynolds. By the time Burns wrote *Mary Tyler Moore* along with Brooks, he could openly approach his subject with a socially conscious attitude, so long as he did it strategically: "We weren't trying to ram home messages in the show, we were trying to do it subtly."[56] Reynolds was hired to do *M*A*S*H*, where he joined Gelbart in using the program as a weapon on behalf of the antiwar movement.[57]

Perhaps the best example of an older writer who benefited from television's transition to the new age was Norman Lear. Lear was forty-eight when *All in the Family* premiered on CBS. He had written for television in relative obscurity during the 1950s—he wrote episodes of *The Tennessee Ernie Ford Show*, *The Colgate Comedy Hour*, and *The Deputy*. In the 1960s, he turned his attention to movies, writing and directing *Divorce American Style* and *The Night They Raided Minsky's*. Once *All in the Family* hit, he became not only the biggest star in the television industry—he virtually ran it. And all the while, Lear was promoting his agenda. With *All in the Family,* Lear wanted to use Archie Bunker as a repository for and caricature of all right-wing views, then mock them. His other shows followed the same leftist pattern.

The nonholdovers—people like George Schlatter and Susan Harris—were college kids who had imbibed the culturally Marxist guilt propagated by Frankfurt School intellectuals like Herbert Marcuse ("make love, not war"). They made no bones about their politics, and they were largely uninterested in telling both sides of the political story. These were militant feminists, militant atheists, militant liberals.

The transition in the creative world had started—open liberalism was in. By 1975, liberals in the industry had utterly consolidated their control, and they were programming their political viewpoints straight into the public consciousness.

But the liberals made one mistake: They overreached.

"JIGGLE TV"

By 1976, the American people were tiring of the strident and cynical liberal commentary of Norman Lear. The American people had already unleashed their pent-up rage against Richard Nixon, who was gone, and the Vietnam War, which was now over. It was a time to rebuild—and more than that, it was a time for escapism. Disco was the new thing, replacing the drug rock of the late 1960s; movies like *Easy Rider* had been replaced by *Rocky* and *Star Wars.* Politics on television largely went. The lowbrow programming stayed.

The man who saw it first was Fred Silverman, who shifted in 1975 from CBS, which had nine of the top eleven shows on television, to ABC, which had none. The reason for his shift was simple: He wanted more control over programming. And he was perfectly situated to bring his expertise to bear. "The rules that applied at CBS didn't apply at ABC," Silverman told me. "CBS was more of an upper income, a more sophisticated audience. ABC was basically working class. Quite urban—by urban, I just mean big city."[58] By urban, Silverman also meant young.

Silverman grabbed a couple of ABC's building blocks that were riding low in the ratings—shows like *Happy Days*, which had just been converted into a three-camera comedy with an audience, and *Starsky and Hutch*. He also took up *The Six Million Dollar Man* and *The Bionic Woman*, as well as *Laverne & Shirley*, a spin-off of *Happy Days*. He also greenlit a show called *Charlie's Angels*, produced by Aaron Spelling and his new partner, Leonard Goldberg. In the same mold, he gave the go-ahead for *Three's Company*, which received an outsize share of attention based on Suzanne Somers's sex-symbol status.

The emphasis for Silverman was on action and romance. The movement away from politics was obvious, and the move toward sex and violence even more obvious. The media labeled Silverman's programming strategy "jiggle TV" and condemned the exploitative nature of the programming. Silverman called such programming "the heat," and Larry Sullivan, who wrote promos for the shows, explained, "We sell the possibility of tits and ass and the possibility of violence. We present the stimuli and the response."[59] Silverman's strategy worked like magic. By 1976–77, ABC had ten of the top fifteen shows on television.

Perhaps to quiet those critics, and perhaps as an attempt to find moral worth in his programming, Silverman and his subordinates greenlit some of the most liberal shows on television too. One of his deputies, Marcy Carsey, joined ABC in 1974 and rose to become senior vice president of primetime series. She would go on to become one of the most prolific and powerful producers in television history, creating *The Cosby Show, Roseanne, Grace Under Fire, 3rd Rock from the Sun*, and *That '70s Show*, among others. Her programming strategy was vintage Silverman: by the gut. "I don't believe in research," she told me. "What I believe in is the writing on the page." She sought to create shows that carried entertainment value along with promotion of certain messages. "I don't think [entertainment and messaging are] competing," she said. "I think the more you engage somebody's gut, heart and soul, with something that they're living or feeling or something that is keeping them up at night, if you get to where their gut is, and where their heart is, then you have a hit show." She added, "I'm of a liberal bent, so obviously that's going to come out of the shows that I was involved with."[60] At ABC, the first show Carsey greenlit was *Soap*, from Susan Harris, a controversial take-off on soap operas that featured the nation's first openly gay regular character, Billy

Crystal's Jodie Dallas (who would show up in drag in the series pilot).

Meanwhile, with Silverman gone, the story quickly became grim at CBS. Just as Silverman left, so did Bob Wood, and the programming side deteriorated rapidly. By the middle of 1976, CBS had dropped behind both ABC and NBC in audience ratings.[61] CBS recovered the second-place position by the end of the 1976–77 season, but they trailed ABC by a large margin.

NBC struggled, too. They hadn't capitalized on the boom in liberal television in the early 1970s, and now they were in serious trouble. During the 1976-77 season, NBC had one show in the top 15. It got so bad at NBC that industry jokers whispered to one another, "What's the difference between the *Titanic* and NBC? Answer: The *Titanic* had an orchestra." RCA Chief Edgar Griffiths had enough and ordered Herb Schlosser, "Get us into second, or get out." It didn't happen—NBC finished the 1977–78 season with a 17.9 average in the Nielsen ratings, as opposed to a 20.7 for ABC and an 18.8 for CBS.[62] That was it for Schlosser.

To replace him, NBC brought in . . . Fred Silverman. They offered him the kingdom. He would be making $500,000 per year (in today's dollars, about $1.7 million), and he'd be running the entire network. It was "well beyond the scope of my present duties or any I've performed in the past," Silverman reveled as he accepted the job. Former assistant Michael Eisner was more skeptical: "Freddie has now met his mountain. If he climbs this one, he'll go down in entertainment history."[63] Silverman was aghast when he saw what he was stepping into. "NBC had no identity when I got there," he told me. "It was a mess. There was nothing there." He tried everything from classic extravaganzas to blockbuster disasters like *Supertrain*, which nearly bankrupted the network.

In 1980, NBC still trailed the pack by a mile. In January 1981, the RCA board kicked out Ed Griffiths, effective July 1, 1981. A week before Griffiths was finally thrown out, NBC tossed out Silverman, too. "The moment that Ed Griffiths got fired, I knew that was it," mourned Silverman. "It was just starting to click."[64]

A few made their mark with politically radical series during this period—Susan Harris's *Soap* was the best example—but most bided their time. Garry Marshall, creator of *Happy Days*, turned out hit after apolitical hit, and he continued to breed future liberal hit makers—men like

Gary David Goldberg, a late-1960s hippie living on "food stamps and welfare," and Bill Bickley, who would later create *Perfect Strangers, Step By Step*, and *Family Matters*. Earl Hamner, writer of *The Waltons*, was an FDR-type liberal, but he was working on a show that was clearly more conservative in tone and tenor than the others on television at the time—in fact, Bill Paley picked up the show as a counterweight to *All in the Family*, even if Hamner didn't intend it that way.

Liberalism on the networks was in retreat. Liberals still dominated the playing field, but the era of Big Leftism was over—it seemed, for all time.

THE RISE OF CABLE

Just as the networks retreated from their overt liberalism, cable picked up the ball and ran with it.

Cable truly got started in 1972, when a man named Charles Dolan built an underground cable system in Manhattan. That company became Home Box Office—HBO for short. The network's true focus was on breaking the rules. As a subscription service, HBO didn't have to face the FCC's scrutiny. Shock value was their selling point. As comedian Robert Klein, one of the first stars broadcast on the network, shouted, "It's subscription! We can say anything. Shit! How'd you like that? Shit!" Sophisticated content was clearly HBO's forte.

In fact, that deep concern for meaningful content was evident throughout HBO's early programming. Michael Brandman, the first director of program development at HBO, was a liberal, and he was all for pushing the boundaries of taste, even beyond what his bosses wanted. Brandman produced George Carlin's first HBO special, which featured Carlin's famous monologue, "The Seven Words You Can't Say on Radio or Television." "[W]e chose to do that show because of the freedom that paid television afforded us," Brandman told me.[65]

HBO wasn't just a content breakthrough—it was a business breakthrough. Brandman lauded "the absence of commercials, the absence of traditional standards and practices." HBO promoted freedom—freedom to be vulgar or crude or edgy, because the viewer controlled the remote rather than the advertisers.[66] Censors were unimportant because there were no advertisers—the viewers were now the only censors.

More than that, the channel *required* envelope pushing. If the networks could provide their programming free to the viewer, the only way to compete using pay-per-view was to provide programming worth paying for—programming that wasn't usually to be found on television. Hence HBO's slogan: "It's not TV. It's HBO."

As HBO began to open the market for cable, a young entrepreneur named Ted Turner took notice. Turner had grown up in Cincinnati, Ohio, son of a Republican businessman. When Ted's father killed himself, Ted, twenty-four years old, took over the enterprise. In 1970, Turner bought a local Atlanta station which he called Turner Broadcasting System (TBS). In 1976, building on HBO's successes, he decided to take TBS national, broadcasting Atlanta Braves games and old movies. By 1979, he had launched CNN.[67] Turner's ventures were bold moves that would shape television in heretofore unknown ways. As Turner became more successful, he became more liberal. Over the years, that liberalism would infect his networks.

The biggest cable player of all, though, entered the American lexicon in 1981, with the stated goal of programming liberalism to youth. That new cable channel was called MTV. It was a reaction to the 1980s Reagan Revolution, a rejection of the spirit of can-do optimism that pervaded the country after Jimmy Carter's ouster. Instead, MTV promoted a new sort of liberalism—not the idealistic liberalism of the 1960s or the angry, caustic liberalism of the 1970s, but a nihilistic, narcissistic liberalism.

MTV was the creation of Robert W. Pittman, an executive at Warner Cable. Pittman loved rock and roll—he was a 1960s baby, a former disc jockey. And he was a child of the new television, the *Laugh-In*, *Smothers Brothers*, *All in the Family* era, complete with vulgarity and quick cuts. Pittman was a spokesman for "youth"—at twenty-seven, he was creating an entire music video network. "Early on," he wrote, "we made a key decision that we would be the voice of Young America. We would not grow old with our audience . . . we laid as our cornerstone the concept of 'change for change sake.' . . . We would stay ahead of the audience—not follow the TV programming tradition of mirroring the audience."[68]

MTV embodied Pittman's postmodern politics to a T. Their slogans, bragging about their counterculture status (even as they became the mainstream culture), were legendary: "MTV: We're Making It Up as We Go Along," "MTV: Better Sorry Than Safe."[69] They followed in the footsteps of *TW3* and *The Smothers Brothers* and paved the way for Jon Stewart by promoting their liberal agenda in playful, rock-oriented news. On *This Week in Rock*, for example, MTV used the trappings of network news to promote abortion, rip Oliver North, push AIDS funding, and laugh at flag-burning.[70]

Aside from the socially libertine politics of much of MTV's music—remember Madonna writhing around in full bride-whore regalia at the MTV Awards singing "Like a Virgin"?—the honchos at MTV recognized their power, and they felt a responsibility to use that power to push the "do your own thing" ethos. Doug Herzog, who began working at MTV in 1984 as news director for music news and ended up as president of MTV productions, explained the network's political vision to me: "We're talking to young people every day, and a lot of responsibility comes with that. We kind of have superpowers . . . [we] believe that through the medium of television we try to make the world a slightly better place." For Herzog, that meant programming to the left.[71]

Herzog is proud of MTV's impact on the culture. "I think MTV has been for a long time a cultural bellwether," he told me. "[It has affected] several generations of young people. It's had enormous impact, enormous influence. . . . MTV did a hell of a lot on pro-social issues and pro-social causes, and pro-social messages." MTV, said Herzog, was designed "to be a leader and groundbreaking and first and breakthrough."[72]

NETWORKS IN CHAOS: THE REAGAN ERA

As cable grew—as Ted Turner's empire opened before him, as MTV was joined by Nickelodeon, as HBO broke new ground—the traditional broadcast networks were faced with a dilemma. These cable channels were focused on what they called "narrowcasting," a new strategy designed to seek out specific audiences that would pay subscription rates, then sell those specific audiences to advertisers. In truth, this was merely an extension of the old Bob Wood axiom that you could lose in the ratings overall if you retained the *right* audience. And it was working. While the networks were still trying to draw the broadest possible audience, the cable channels were gradually chipping away at them by parceling out programming to specific subsections of that audience.

The traditional networks were stuck in the middle. They responded, predictably, by programming in schizophrenic fashion: They embraced slightly liberal family fare in order to shore up their broader audience while simultaneously greenlighting edgy adult-oriented liberal dramas.

This wasn't just a response to the rise of cable—it was a response to the rise of the political right. Not only was Reagan in ascendance, but religious conservatives were beginning to push back against network television's dramatic shift to the left. In 1979, evangelical Christian leader Rev. Jerry Falwell founded the Moral Majority, which quickly targeted the social liberalism and political leftism of network television. Soon after, Rev. Donald Wildmon founded the American Family Association, which joined Falwell in condemning sexual and violent television content. Their moral opprobrium drew an initial public response that shocked the networks—it was the first time anyone had effectively countered the leftist domination of television.

As a solution, the networks sought compromise.

At CBS, Tom Wyman led the way with programs like *The Dukes of Hazzard*, which was basically early-1960s-style rural programming, and *Magnum, P.I.*, an action show starring Tom Selleck. Don Bellisario, the creator of *Magnum, P.I.*, was a pro-military conservative who purposefully made Magnum a Vietnam vet in order to quash the antimilitary bigotry that labeled all Vietnam vets *Taxi Driver*–type crazies.[73] CBS still carried a few 1970s holdovers like *M*A*S*H* and *Archie Bunker's Place*, an *All in the Family* knockoff—they weren't going to surrender shows that were still bringing in numbers. CBS's biggest new hit was *Dallas*, a primetime soap opera complete with all the usual sexual peccadilloes and moral complications. But as the decade progressed, it was clear that the era of openly political programming was over on the network. Detective shows like *Simon & Simon*, *Murder, She Wrote*, and largely apolitical *Dallas* imitations like *Falcon Crest* and *Knots Landing* populated the network schedule.

ABC continued its tradition of Silverman holdovers with *The Love Boat* and *Three's Company*, but most of its groundbreaking programming was relegated to movies of the week under the auspices of Brandon Stoddard. Stoddard was entertainment oriented, but he liked to insert social issues into the programming, too. "I was fascinated in my career with that [balance]," Stoddard told me. "Being able to say something but also putting something on the air that was entertaining."[74] Stoddard aired controversial movies of the week like *The Day After*, which many argued was blatantly anti-Reagan, a piece about America being nuked that drew the ire of conservatives—and drew huge ratings.

The biggest story in network programming during this era, though, was at pitiful NBC. After Silverman met his premature demise there, the network brought in Grant Tinker to take over. Tinker had been a busy man over the past thirty years. He was an old-school outspoken liberal, a man who had risen from the TV department at McCann-Erickson Advertising Agency in the 1950s to vice president in charge of West Coast programming at NBC in the 1960s. During that meteoric rise he met Mary Tyler Moore, whom he quickly married. In 1970, with Moore out of work and Tinker's career on the skids, he decided to form MTM Enterprises, using Moore as the face of the organization. After collaborating with Jim Brooks and Allan Burns to write a pilot for Moore, he got CBS to bite on *The Mary Tyler Moore Show*. He followed that success by recruiting talented writers like Gary David Goldberg, Joshua Brand, Steven Bochco, Bruce Paltrow, and others. MTM was a writer's paradise, according to everyone who worked there. "Grant Tinker was someone who really valued writers," Josh Brand told me.[75]

Tinker had always loved social messaging. "Most television (and movie) writers are somewhat left-leaning," he acknowledged. And they had an obligation to put their talents to work in favor of the common good, with the acceptance of the executives, according to Tinker. "I have considerable impatience with the maximum profit fixation of the current network owners," Tinker said.[76]

Tinker's first shows at NBC, unsurprisingly, were liberally oriented pick-ups from MTM Enterprises. He renewed *Hill Street Blues*, Bochco's gritty cop show, despite that show's dismal ratings. Then he picked up *St. Elsewhere*, a far-left show about medical school that featured a sex-change operation during the first season. The idea was to build up NBC's prestige in the industry, create programming of substance. After all,

Tinker snorted, "so little sticks to your ribs."[77] (Lee Rich, the man behind Lorimar and *Dallas*, responded to Tinker in colorful terms: "Tinker sets himself up as a god of what television should be. And what is this bullshit about sticking to your ribs?")[78]

Tinker's deputy was a young kid named Brandon Tartikoff. Tartikoff was actually a Fred Silverman holdover—Silverman had recruited the self-professed "child of television" in 1978, and Tartikoff had remained after Silverman's departure. Tartikoff's strategy wasn't numbers focused, it was talent focused, just like that of his two bosses. "Despite volumes of research," Tartikoff once wrote, "renewal decisions ultimately come down to instinct."[79] Like Tinker, Tartikoff saw an obligation to program in the "public interest." Tartikoff's favorite moments as a broadcaster included the production of *Roe v. Wade*, about the abortion case; the made-for-TV movie *Special Bulletin*, a rip-off of *The Day After*; and *Unnatural Causes*, a made-for-TV movie about crazy Vietnam vets.[80]

Tinker and Tartikoff were stunningly successful. From 1981, when Tinker took over, to 1986, NBC's profits jumped from $48 million to $400 million. That wasn't because of his prestige programming, though, even if revisionist history would tell us otherwise. Neither *Hill Street* nor *St. Elsewhere* ever cracked the top 20 in programs, and it took *Cheers* two years to crack the top 30. NBC's success was a result of two action shows in the mold of ABC, and two sitcoms with a conservative bent.

The two action shows were *The A-Team* and *Miami Vice*. But the true breakthrough came in 1984, when Tinker and Tartikoff greenlit a show produced by Tom Werner and Marcy Carsey, starring Bill Cosby. It was called *The Cosby Show*, and it had an underlying conservative feel. Building on the vast success of *The Cosby Show*, NBC moved a stalwart, *Family Ties*, into the follow-up slot and made that Michael J. Fox starrer a hit, too. While the creator of *Family Ties*, Gary David Goldberg, was vastly liberal and sought to portray conservatives as quasi-evil, the charm of Fox undermined his goals, making the show a success among conservatives.

For politically motivated writers, the 1980s was like living in exile after the free-and-easy 1970s. Susan Harris, who had created *Soap*, was now relegated to writing about older women making sex jokes on *Golden Girls*; even if she did slip in her politics on a regular basis, it was hardly on the order of Jodie seeking a sex change. Gary David Goldberg was no longer writing about hardcore politics on *Lou Grant*; now he was putting out dual conservative messages of respect for parents and capitalistic entrepreneurism (even if he was trying to criticize capitalistic entrepreneurism). Carsey and Werner, both leftists, were portraying Bill Cosby as an authoritative dad with experience and knowledge, boosting the image of the two-parent black family.

All in all, it was a quiet time for the networks. People were generally happy under Reagan, and television reflected that complacency. All of that was about to change.

HOW THE LEFT'S MOST HATED CONSERVATIVE REVITALIZED LIBERAL TELEVISION

The liberal resurgence, ironically enough, began with a conservative: Rupert Murdoch. Murdoch was born in Australia, the son of a rich newspaper publisher. Like Ted Turner, Murdoch lost his father at an early age and took over the family business, then grew it exponentially. Murdoch was from the beginning a capitalist without regard for the proprieties. After buying up London's *News of the World*, *Times*, and *Sun*, he moved his efforts to America, where he bought the *New York Post* and *New York Magazine*. Then he got himself American citizenship in order to comply with American media-ownership laws.[81]

In 1984 and 1985, Murdoch decided to get into the American film and television business. He bought up the entirety of the 20th Century–Fox film corporation, then soaked up seven major market affiliates around the country (New York, Los Angeles, Chicago, Washington, D.C., Dallas, Houston, and Boston). He called his new network the Fox Broadcasting Company. Originally, the company lost money—in 1988, $90 million, and in 1989, $20 million. But Fox began to grow once it found its programming strategy.[82]

That strategy in the mid to late 1980s resembled ABC's in the early 1960s. It had to be risk-taking to gain audience share, and it had to be low-cost to maintain profit share. That led to programs like the short-lived *Late Show* with Joan Rivers, the moderately successful *Tracy Ullman Show*—and more important, shows like *Married . . . with Children* and *The Simpsons*.

These latter two shows set the pace for the network. Sandy Grushow, who was the senior vice president of advertising and promotion when those two shows were picked up, told me that Fox went after "shows that had an alternative bent to them, that spoke to what was then, in the late 1980s, a very disenfranchised audience of young people, particularly young men, who weren't interested in watching *The Cosby Show*."

Like ABC, they programmed young. And just like ABC, that meant they skewed liberal. "I think by definition when lots of people start creating content that speaks to more youthful audiences, who tend to be more progressive, then the content is in fact going to feel edgier than the bland, banal, saccharine sitcoms," Grushow said.

Grushow later became the senior vice president of programming and scheduling, then president of the Fox Entertainment Division. Personally, Grushow was liberal when it came to programming standards—he considered the vulgar *Married . . . with Children* "bloody innocuous."[83] Grushow would later ridiculously claim that the seedy show *Temptation Island* was "not . . . about sex," but rather a dissertation "exploring the dynamics of serious relationships."[84]

The rise of Fox and the cable networks had a huge impact on the nature of the business. In 1970, the FCC had installed the Financial Interest and Syndication Rules (the so-called Fin-Syn rules). These rules accomplished two purposes: First, they prevented networks from owning an interest in any programs they put on the air beyond the original airing. Second, they stopped networks from creating syndication companies designed to sell their series. (These processes are often referred to as "vertical integration.") This limited the possibility of network profit from producing programming, creating an enormous market for independent production companies.

In 1991, as a result of Fox's rise and the growing success of cable, the FCC decided that the rules were no longer relevant—the networks were being penalized despite their decreasing market share. By November 1995, the rules were completely gone.[85]

The predictable result was the production of edgier programming on network television again. The networks could pursue the dual strategy of cutting off the cable networks' "edge" advantage by programming more radical material—at the very worst, their programming might fail, then be sold to cable networks. At the same time, the networks could produce programming independently for the cables, meaning they could now make money from their former competitors.

THE NEW GOLDEN AGE OF POLITICAL TELEVISION

The networks took full advantage. In the latter days of the Tartikoff regime (and as the Reagan era drew to a close), NBC picked up controversial series like *L.A. Law*, a Steven Bochco production. ABC, now under the full control of Brandon Stoddard, picked up *thirtysomething* and *Roseanne*, both pushing liberal social values under a patina of family wholesomeness. CBS, which was now being run by Bill Paley friend and investor extraordinaire Laurence Tisch, picked up *Picket Fences* (by a young writer named David E. Kelley) and *Murphy Brown*, which as Dan Quayle famously pointed out, stood in favor of liberal social policies, including championing the virtue of single motherhood.

The trend toward more liberal programming disguised as conservative family-friendly fare continued throughout the decade. Warren Littlefield took over from Tartikoff at NBC, and he built the famed NBC "Must-See TV" lineup, which included a little show called *Friends*, as well as *ER* and *Seinfeld*. Littlefield also picked up *Law & Order*, *Homicide: Life on the Street*, *3rd Rock from the Sun*, *Mad About You*, *Caroline in the City*, and many other hits with liberal orientations. He had an uncanny ability to pick hits—during the 1996–1997 season, NBC had the top six shows on television.

Littlefield was a committed liberal and a television addict. He had helped develop *Cheers*, *The Cosby Show*, and *Golden Girls* before supplanting Tartikoff. After seeing Michael Moore's *Roger and Me*, he called Moore in for a meeting to pitch a TV show titled *TV Nation*. Moore told Littlefield and his underlings that "it would be a cross between *60 Minutes* and Fidel Castro on laughing gas. . . . The show would be the most liberal thing ever seen on TV. In fact, it would go beyond 'liberals' because liberals are a bunch of wimps and haven't gotten us anything. This show would go boldly where no one has gone before." NBC greenlit the pilot at a cost of

$1 million.[86] The show flopped and was cancelled after one season (Fox picked it up for a second season), but not before Democrats in Congress introduced a resolution declaring August 16, 1994, TV Nation Day.[87]

At CBS, Lawrence Tisch's tenure had brought trouble. In 1986, Tisch bought 24.9 percent of CBS at the behest of Bill Paley, who hoped to save the company from hostile takeover bids (one bidder was a consortium led by Jesse Helms, who hoped to turn CBS conservative again). Tisch was a lifelong liberal who supported Democratic politicians ranging from Carter and Mondale to Chuck Schumer and Bill Bradley. Tisch's friends insisted it was "a mistake to think that he'd apply his personal views to anything as visible as his CBS position," but he did just that.[88] To run the programming side of the business, he brought in former Dan Rather–producer Howard Stringer as president of the CBS Broadcast Group. The first two people Stringer called after getting the job? Norman Lear and Grant Tinker.[89]

Stringer then brought in a like-minded second as head of programming, Jeff Sagansky, a former Tinker protégé. He refused to program anything that even hinted at religion. "The first thing you learn as a program executive," he said in 1994, "is never program anything whose content has to do with religion and God. It isn't hip."[90] Pretending to be apolitical, Sagansky told *Time* magazine, "It's the responsibility of good television to be topical, but it should not espouse any political candidacy. . . . The viewers vote for *Murphy Brown* every week, and only vote for Dan Quayle every four years."[91]

By 1992, Sagansky had brought CBS to the forefront of the ratings. But the combination of cost cutting on Tisch's part and liberal programming on Stringer's part didn't end well. By 1995, Tisch was ready to sell CBS and be done with it. He found his buyer in Westinghouse Electric Corporation. Their new man was Les Moonves, then president of Warner Brothers Television. Moonves was a programming genius, a man who greenlit both *Friends* and *ER* (both were picked up by NBC). At CBS, he grabbed graphic shows like *CSI* and family-friendly fare like *Everybody Loves Raymond*.

Moonves was a liberal, just like his predecessors. But he was old-school in that he programmed first, last, and always with the ratings and the advertisers.[92] "Earnings is what I'm judged on," Moonves said.[93]

At ABC, Brandon Stoddard's departure made way for the entry of Bob Iger. Like the other executives, Iger was a liberal—but unlike Moonves, he allowed it to influence his judgment. The first two shows Iger greenlit were the David Lynch bizarro-world *Twin Peaks*, which titillated elites but fell flat with audiences, and Steven Bochco's *Cop Rock*, which was a disaster for the network. Later, Iger greenlit *Ellen* and backed the show when Ellen decided to come out of the closet. (He'd have to backtrack in the end, canceling the show because of its constant focus on homosexuality, even as he claimed that it lost audience "primarily because of sameness. Not gayness.")[94]

But Iger's genius for cable was better than his programming selection (although he did greenlight the hits *Family Matters*, *Full House*, and *America's Funniest Home Videos*). Iger was one of the biggest proponents of changing the Fin-Syn rules, which had barred vertical integration in the industry, promising that the rules would help diversify programming.[95] Naturally, that wasn't what happened—once Fin-Syn was gone, the big-studio system reasserted itself. Iger led the way, championing the acquisition of A&E, the History Channel, Lifetime, and most profitably ESPN.[96] And once ABC was sold to Disney, that consolidation only accelerated.

The rise of Fox, cable, and the death of the Fin-Syn rules led to a new wave of liberal creators finding their way in Hollywood. Liberals largely hired liberals, and all of them worked together to create new and envelope-pushing content for both broadcast television and cable. It was a golden age of political television.

What nobody knew at the time is that the golden age of political television was also the beginning of the end.

THE DEATH OF THE NETWORKS

The profit-making capabilities of the networks skyrocketed during the 1990s with the consolidation of the industry under major corporate auspices. But with the vertical integration of the networks—networks now owned the production companies, the distribution mechanisms, and the exhibition channels—came an unexpected challenge. Now cable networks could have all the production values of the Big Four, and they could program without regard to FCC rules and regulations. The cable channels narrowcast, so they appealed to particular viewers, which advertisers found valuable. As Warren Littlefield, former head of NBC, said, "There's no concept of a network versus any other channel. Comedy Central's a channel; NBC or CBS is a channel. That's all. There's no prestige to one versus another."[97]

At this point, the networks are on their way out. And that is a problem for the political advocates in the television industry. The big money is still in network TV (aside from pay-per-view channels like HBO)—cable series pay less because they make less for the corporate behemoths—but because the networks are losing market share, they play it safer and safer on political topics for the benefit of advertisers. Not only that—reality television has supplanted scripted TV as a safer and cheaper means of drawing audiences, and the creators of reality TV are less politically driven, in general, than their writer compatriots. Mark Burnett, creator of *Survivor* and *The Apprentice*, among many other enormous hits, summed up his view of programming to me in pure and innocent terms: "Understand that the gift you're given with network television is a huge gift, and you can reach millions of people, and you have an obligation to use that gift. . . . I'm trying to do aspirational shows that are positive and that raise people up. I don't want to do shows that tear people down."[98]

Surely the post–September 11 climate has something to do with the apolitical programming shift as well. Audiences wanted less controversial fare—or if the fare was going to be controversial, it had to be promilitary and antiterror rather than domestic policy–centric, like *24*. The changing political climate combined with the changing television business model—and the synthesis became a subtler form of bias in programming. Shows like *House*, *Law & Order*, and even *Desperate Housewives* insert politics in more or less minor ways into their storylines but remain essentially crime procedurals or basic soap operas. Marc Cherry, the creator of *Desperate Housewives*, sees himself as a conservative who attempts to uphold certain traditional social values (he is a Republican).[99] Political sitcoms have largely fallen by the wayside. It is now left to shows like *Family Guy*—a cartoon!—to pick up the *All in the Family* torch.

The new demand for political blandness is reflected in the executive management. Moonves still presides over CBS, and he demands high audience numbers—but the audiences Moonves demands are, as mentioned, older. And older viewers aren't as interested in lesbian weddings or diatribes about the evils of American xenophobia. At ABC, the rigid hierarchy of Disney wants politics inserted into programming less and less. Even Jeff Zucker, the wildly liberal former head of NBC,[100] didn't do much with NBC's programming, other than inserting relatively innocuous "green" messages into all of the primetime programming and helping out motivated liberals like Tina Fey (whom he calls the "queen of comedy" due to her snarky impressions of Sarah Palin on *Saturday Night Live*).

Politics is now relegated largely to cable. Bravo is similarly left-wing, programming gay-centric shows like *Queer Eye for the Straight Guy, Workout*, and *Blueprint*. Showtime is known in town as the gay channel (sorry, Logo). CW tries to suck in teenage girls with sex-first programming like *Gossip Girl* and the new *Melrose Place*. Viacom has maintained MTV's and Comedy Central's liberal reputation, and pushed Nickelodeon's children's programming toward social liberalism as well. Even Disney has joined the fun, using ABC Family to promote single motherhood (see *The Secret Life of the American Teenager* and *Greek*).

The division between cable programming and network programming has become more and more pronounced in terms of politics. Of the top twenty rated shows on network television during the 2009–2010 season, eleven were reality shows, documentaries, or sports; only two, *Desperate Housewives* and *Grey's Anatomy*, could be said to have any deep political content. On cable, shows like AMC's *Breaking Bad* and *Mad Men*, HBO's *Big Love* and *True Blood* (earlier, *Sex and the City*), and Showtime's *Weeds* were garnering most of the media attention—and were making most of the political points. Needless to say, they weren't garnering most of the viewers—*Weeds*, on a fantastic night, might attract 1.7 million viewers; *Chuck*, an NBC midlevel show, might grab 5.8 million viewers on a terrible night. But the media attention is enough to grab advertisers, who could make those audience numbers and cheaper rates work for them.

Perhaps television's politics will change in the near future. Even cable is having trouble these days keeping up with the Internet and TiVo; Hollywood is in serious trouble, because advertisers have lost their ability to hold audiences still to watch their spots. Simultaneously, the costs of production have dropped dramatically, and the Internet makes it possible for anyone—to put a show up at any time with worldwide distribution.

Still, despite predictions of its imminent decline, television remains intensely powerful, the single largest generator of quality entertainment on the face of the planet. And it's essentially a closed circle. An in-group. A clique.

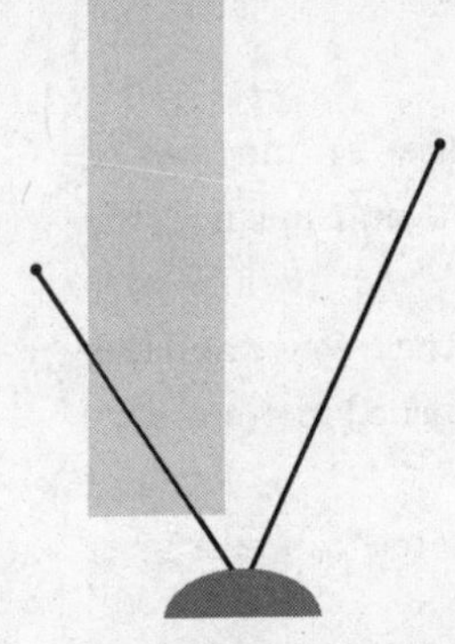

THE CLIQUE

How Television Stays Liberal

On March 3, 1991, an African-American man with a rap sheet longer than his arm sped through Los Angeles' residential neighborhoods in excess of 115 mph. The police pulled him over and asked him to exit the vehicle. When he resisted arrest, several Los Angeles Police Department officers, believing him to be high on PCP, proceeded to beat him with their batons. The whole incident was captured on tape. Before anyone knew what was happening, Rodney King was a worldwide celebrity.

But the real action didn't start until a few months later, on April 29, 1992, when the LAPD officers were acquitted by an all-white jury for their excessive use of force. That's when the entire South Central area of Los Angeles burst into flame, figuratively and literally. African-American and Hispanic residents of the gang-infested area rioted and looted in retaliation for the acquittal, causing billions of dollars in damage.

What did the Hollywood glitterati, those who fight human rights abuses around the globe and insist that minority populations are victims of a racist society, do as the city burned?

They sat and drank at the Beverly Hills Hotel, one of the most exclusive and swankiest resorts in the country. "When I got there, much to my *shock*, the whole town picture business people had decided to do the same thing!" real estate agent Elaine Young later told playwright Anna

Deavere Smith. "So basically, what happened the three or four days of the heavy rioting, people were going to the hotel. And I mean it was *mobbed*. . . .

"Everybody was talking. 'What was going on?' And 'How could this happen in California?' And 'Oh my God, what's happened to our town?' and 'These poor people . . .' "

The general feeling, Young concluded, was, "No one can hurt us at the Beverly Hills Hotel 'cause it was like a fortress!"[1]

Hollywood is like the Beverly Hills Hotel writ large. It takes an exclusive ticket to get in. It's filled with cloistered people who have little connection to the world around them. And those people revel in their wealth, even as they express sympathy for the plight of those who can't live in such lush surroundings. At least in New York, the upper-crust liberals sometimes take the subway. In Hollywood, their private chauffeurs drive them to self-aggrandizing awards parties where they all get together to wear ribbons on behalf of the homeless. Even other liberals around the country know that those in Hollywood live in their own self-enclosed utopia—but those in Hollywood are blissfully unaware of that fact.

They're stuck in their bubble, and they can't get out.

That's because if the leftists in Hollywood recognized their bubble, they wouldn't be able to live with themselves. If limousine liberals *knew* they were limousine liberals, they'd either have to give up the limousine or the liberalism. So they ensconce themselves ever deeper in the charmed reality of their own making, surrounding themselves with those who look, think, and earn like they do, so that they never have to come face to face with the fact that their lifestyle clashes with their politics.

So how do you get into the bubble?

It usually requires some help. That help almost always comes from somebody you know or somebody you're related to.

It's not difficult to look around Hollywood and see the generations-long transmission of the television lineage. Jim Burrows, for example, the incredibly successful writer and producer of shows like *Cheers*, *Will & Grace*, and *Gary Unmarried*, is the son of Abe Burrows, a comedy legend from television's early days. Tom Moore produced *Doogie Howser, M.D.* and *The Wayans Bros.*—his dad was Tom Moore, former president of ABC television. Rob Reiner, star of *All in the Family,* got his big break because his dad is Carl Reiner. Former NBC president Grant Tinker acknowledged that Hollywood was crazily insular. "It's a tiny little business," he said. "There is no question that [TV] is sort of a little closed society and very hard for the new guy to get into . . . [and] the product looks like it. It reflects that we are a limited crowd."[2] Tinker should know. When he ran NBC, it looked like a poker game among his old buddies from MTM Enterprises (not that they didn't merit their special attention). He also helped out his son, Mark, a writer on *St. Elsewhere,* by greenlighting the ratings failure for another season.

While familial nepotism remains a problem in Hollywood—Francis Ford Coppola, anyone?—most nepotism in Hollywood isn't familial, it's ideological.

Friends hire friends. And those friends just happen to share their politics. The same people who kibitz at the Beverly Hills Hotel *tsk-tsk*-ing white racism while Reginald Denny gets the tar beat out of him in South Central hire one another to work on their shows.

Just look at some of the biggest shows of the last two decades. In the early 1990s, liberal Les Moonves spotted a young, extremely liberal writing team, David Crane and Marta Kauffman, and their producer, Kevin Bright. Crane and Kauffman had worked for iconic liberal Norman Lear. Together, that group would create *Friends.* Liberal Aaron Spelling worked with a talented and liberal young writer named Darren Star to create *Beverly Hills, 90210* and *Melrose Place.* Liberal Michael Patrick King got started by working with liberal Diane English on *Murphy Brown,* then parlayed that into a writer's slot on *Will & Grace* under liberals Max Mutchnik and David Kohan, and then the creatorship of *Sex and the City.* Liberal Matt Groening was brought into primetime television by liberal James Brooks, who spotted Groening's counterculture *Life in Hell* cartoons and decided to turn them into a series called *The Simpsons.* Liberal Chuck Lorre would be spotted by liberal Marcy Carsey while writing for *Roseanne* and would go on to spawn some of the most popular sitcoms of the 1990s and 2000s, including *The Big Bang Theory* and *Two and a Half Men.* Lorre, in turn, would spot liberal Alan Ball and give him a shot in television on *Grace Under Fire*—Ball would go on to create HBO's *True Blood*, among others. Liberal Steven Bochco found liberal David E. Kelley, who would create *Picket Fences*, *Ally McBeal*, *Chicago Hope*, and *Boston Public*. Kelley found liberal Michael Nankin, who would go on to work on *Picket Fences*.

Spotting a pattern yet?

The people I met in Hollywood generally got into the business through somebody of like mind. "It doesn't hurt to know somebody," Larry Gelbart told me.[3] Susan Harris, writer of *Soap* and *Golden Girls*, said, "of course it's easier if you know somebody."[4] Abby Singer, a legend in the industry who worked as a production manager and assistant director on everything from *Gunsmoke* to *Hill Street Blues*, explained, "a lot of jobs today are from who you know. Who can help you. It's a really tough business to get into."[5] "There's definitely some truth to [nepotism in Hollywood]," said Andy Heyward, the creator of *Captain Planet*, who got into the industry partially based on the fact that his dad was a writer and producer in town.[6]

Nonetheless, many of those in Hollywood argue that the nepotism there isn't worse than it is in any other business. "I think it's like anything in this country," opined Chris Chulack, producer of *ER* and *Southland*. "I don't think there's more nepotism in Hollywood than anywhere else, it's just that Hollywood is so high-profile and a small community."[7] Michael Brandman, formerly of HBO, agreed: "Same as everything else in America."[8]

They're right, of course. When it comes to the need to know people, Hollywood's no different from any other business. People get jobs by knowing somebody who knows somebody, by calling in favors, by flipping through the Rolodex.

The difference is that the television industry is so dominated by liberals that unless you have a Rolodex filled with liberals, your chances of breaking in are relatively slim.

Carlton Cuse, executive producer of *Lost*, explained, "In entertainment . . . you're basically asking a bunch of disparate people to come together to find a shared vision, because movies and television are collaborative. So prior knowledge of work experience is really valuable in building that trust and sense of confidence with other people to work with."[9]

Michael Nankin, producer on *Chicago Hope* and *Picket Fences*, told me exactly the same thing. "People generally like to work with people they've worked with before or with whom they're comfortable. . . . And that mindset, which is entirely appropriate, makes it hard for new people to get in."[10]

It's a tiny cocoon. According to television historian and sociologist Todd Gitlin, as of 1983, "Fully half of prime-time television [was] scripted by only 10 percent of the Writers Guild's 3,000 active members." In order to get a job, writes Gitlin, desperate writers expose themselves to idea theft, throwing out scenes and scripts in the hopes that some executive will bite.[11] Today, those numbers have broadened. Still, as of 2007, just 52 percent of West Coast Writers Guild of America members are employed. Many of those work sporadically and non-union at times in the hopes that they can eventually make their way to the big time. The average salary is raised, however, by those who *do* make it to the big time. The average working WGA member takes home about $200,000 per year.[12]

Once you break in, you can live inside that warm cocoon indefinitely. Executives who make it can move from job to job without fear of unemployment. Actually, job mobility is often the best perk of becoming a high-level executive at a network: Executives are almost always paid off when they leave with production deals, first-look guarantees from studios. The perfect career path for an executive looks something like this: Get into the business through Mom or Dad or a liberal buddy, jump from a production company to a network, then get fired or quit the network and receive a lucrative severance package and first-look deal.

Ben Silverman is the textbook example of that career trajectory. His mom, Mary Silverman, worked as Court TV senior vice president of programming, as an executive at USA Network, and as head of international coproductions for the BBC.[13] Silverman went to Tufts, then worked for CBS and the William Morris Agency doing U.K.-U.S. deals (just like Mom!). Finally he started a production company called Reveille, where he turned the British hit show *The Office* into an American hit show called *The Office*, starring Steve Carrell.[14]

In 2007, Silverman took over programming for NBC as cochairman of NBC Entertainment. Silverman is a massive liberal—"I'm as liberal as Norman Lear was," he bragged to Nikki Finke of *Deadline Hollywood*—and he programmed with his politics in mind. Upon his accession to NBC's entertainment chiefdom, he proclaimed that he wanted to "layer issues with a point of view and create a dialogue," pushing "big bold TV shows" in Lear's mold. He also announced that he wanted to run for office after leaving television, and admitted his proclivity for smoking pot.[15]

Unsurprisingly, Silverman immediately helped run NBC into the ground. To be fair, he was saddled with a terrible lineup—NBC's primetime lineup in 2007 featured single-season ratings failures like *Bionic Woman*, *Journeyman*, *Life*, *Lipstick Jungle*, and *The Singing Bee*.[16] But Silverman did nothing to improve matters; in April 2008, every single new primetime show announced by Silverman was a one-season-and-out failure.[17] To strike out on twelve new shows is incredible. To do so while labeling yourself a "rock-star television executive" is unheard of.[18] No wonder Peter Mehlman, who wrote for *Seinfeld*, dismissed Silverman out of hand to me: "I was reading an article where they were talking about Benny Silverman from NBC talking about how brilliant he is adapting shows from other countries. *That's a skill now?* Come on."[19]

But proving that quality of management matters less than whom you know, Silverman retained his job until July 2009. Finally he was ousted, leaving the network to form a new company with Barry Diller, the former ABC honcho. *Time* featured his exit with the snarky headline, "Exit the No-Hit Hitmaker."[20] His replacement, Jeff Gaspin, stated, "I bought Ben's first show, *The Restaurant*. I believe I bought his second show, *Blow Out*, and, as I recall, I bought his third show, *The Biggest Loser*. . . . NBC and Ben have had a lot of success together, and I suspect Ben will want to continue that relationship."[21]

Once you get into the Beverly Hills Hotel, they have a tough time booting you out. It pays to be part of the clique. But to get in, as they say in the commercials, make sure you bring your Democratic Party membership card.

KEEPING HOLLYWOOD CONSERVATIVE-FREE

To get into the clique, you must have the right background. Generally, that means coming from New York or Los Angeles or San Francisco or Chicago. You don't want to be the hick from the sticks. If you are from a smaller town, you need to make sure you disassociate yourself from the vast unwashed from whence you sprang. You should preferably be young—after all, old coots aren't going to draw in that coveted 18-to-49 crowd. You have to be talented.

And most of all, you must be liberal.

The industry is liberal from top to bottom. Virtually everyone in town is an outspoken advocate of leftist politics. Ben Silverman's former boss at NBC, Jeff Zucker, was offered a slot in the prospective Gore Administration. Ted Turner stands loud and proud with the left, stating that pro-life advocates are "bozos," that Christianity is a "religion for losers," and that Iraqi insurgents are "patriots." He also offers helpful environmental projections, such as the notion that global warming will cause most of the world's population to die and that the rest of mankind will turn to cannibalism. Les Moonves at CBS is a committed leftist. Aside from backing President Clinton heavily during his heyday, Moonves also went with several of his friends to visit Cuba and hang out with Fidel Castro, and paid $55,000 for the privilege. At one point, Moonves even encouraged speculation that he'd use Jon Stewart as a part of CBS's Evening News.[22]

Liberal mouthpiece the Huffington Post features the political musings of more Hollywood heavy hitters than attended this year's Emmy Awards: Carolyn Strauss, longtime HBO executive who oversaw development of *The Sopranos, Sex and the City, Six Feet Under*, and *Big Love*; Haim Saban, owner of Univision and former owner of ABC Family; Norman Lear; Kara Vallow, producer for all of Fox's primetime Sunday night shows with the exception of *The Simpsons*; and Michael Patrick King, creator of *Sex and the City*, among dozens of others. It's no wonder that in 2010, ABC greenlit a pilot entitled *Freshman*, to be produced by Hollywood heavyweight Greg Malins—and Arianna Huffington.[23] Fred Silverman, former head of NBC, ABC, and CBS, sums the situation up nicely. "Right now," he told me, "there's only one perspective. And it's a very progressive perspective."[24]

More troubling, far too often, liberals discriminate against conservatives. Everyone in town knows about the blacklist, by which conservatives are banished if they get too uppity for their own good. And many liberals, sickeningly enough, openly celebrate the existence of that blacklist. Vin DiBona, producer of *MacGyver* and *America's Funniest Home Videos*, blithely informed me, "Well, I think it's probably accurate and I'm happy about it, actually. . . . If the accusation is there, I'm OK with it."[25] Nicholas Meyer, director of *The Day After* as well as the movie megahits *Star Trek II, IV,* and *VI* said the same thing when I asked him whether right-wingers were discriminated against in Hollywood: "Well, I hope so."[26] Actor Eric Roberts said, "The person who will get snickered at and picked on is the one wearing the McCain-Palin button. But that's OK. It's America. A free country. If you're going to stick your neck out, it's gonna get whacked."[27] Substitute "black" for "conservative" and these people would recoil in horror. Hell, substitute "communist" for "conservative" and these people would lecture you about the horrors of McCarthyism. But when they have the chance to confront the most blatant form of discrimination within America's cultural bulkhead, they shy away, or instead, cheer.

Fred Pierce, president of ABC-TV throughout the 1970s, stated without hesitation that conservatives were discriminated against in Hollywood. "True. That's true," he nodded. "The people who are not leaning liberal or left don't promote it. It stays underground."

Why, I asked him, did the industry lean left? "Probably they feel that since it's a very commercial business, that younger people generally in their youths have liberal ideas," Pierce said.[28] He's right—the focus on youth obviously pushes the industry left. But there's something else going on, too: a sense of entitlement that runs throughout the industry, an automatic assumption that conservatives shouldn't get work, and that barring conservatives from the industry is somehow excusable on the grounds that conservatives are racist, sexist, homophobic bigots.

Leonard Goldberg, former executive at ABC, now board member at CBS, and producer of the hit Tom Selleck series *Blue Bloods*, agreed with Pierce that Hollywood is exclusively leftist. "There's no question about that. I don't know about the content being pushed, but in terms of the thought about various matters social and political, [liberalism is] 100 percent dominant. And anyone who denies it is kidding or is not telling the truth. I can say that as an independent. There's no question what the agenda is. . . . Because that's the personal belief of the people doing the shows. . . . They consider a vote for Prop. 8 to be [worthy of being taken] into the streets and [being] tar[red] and feather[ed]."

Is conservatism a barrier to entry in the industry? I asked Goldberg.

"Absolutely," he answered. "Hollywood is unquestionably a liberal community."[29]

David Shore, creator of *House* and an unabashed liberal, sensed the discrimination, too. "I do think there is an assumption in this town that everybody is on the left side of the spectrum, and that the few people on the right side, I think people look at them somewhat aghast, and I'm sure it doesn't help them."[30] If your political position doesn't help you in Hollywood, it hurts you. There's no true in-between.

Staying apolitical isn't an option; in writers' rooms, politics simply arises too often. Silence is conservatives' sole salvation in this town. And many liberals are OK with that—they're not particularly interested in diversity of ideas.

When I asked Barbara Fisher of Hallmark Channel whether there was nepotism of values in Hollywood, she answered frankly, "I think there's definitely some truth to it. . . . I mean, I know there's truth that it is a more left-leaning industry." Fisher continued, voicing the common Hollywood advice: "I think anybody who's . . . not welcome because of their politics, they should leave their politics at the door when they're doing something creative."[31] Naturally, there is truth to this—it's true of every collaborative endeavor. You don't want to spoil a social setting by talking politics at work any more than you want to spoil a social setting by talking politics with dissenting family members. The difference is that anger over politics may result in fights with your siblings, but it can result in firings in Hollywood. The other problem, of course, is that if you articulate a radical liberal position in the writers' room, you'll be praised as a freethinker; if you laud Ronald Reagan's presidency, you'll be bashed behind your back, discredited, and smeared.

Many Hollywood creators, knowing that conservatives are often the target of discrimination, believe that television should do more to reach out to nonliberal artists. "They should get more writers into TV who are right-wing," said Tom Fontana, writer for *St. Elsewhere* and later the creator of *Oz*. Fontana believes that political diversity in the writers' room makes for interesting television product. "When I was learning how to write," he said, "I learned that nobody wants to watch a one-sided football game."[32] Unfortunately, Fontana represents a viewpoint that is all too rare in the television industry—many creators pay lip service to the notion of political debate on television, but they aren't prepared to hire a former College Republican.

Even more problematic than Hollywood's bias against conservatives is its general refusal to even acknowledge that such bias exists. Recognizing and fighting the new McCarthyism would destroy the industry's image of itself as a paradise for those of all stripes, creeds, and colors. Many of the people I talked to said flatly that television was balanced in terms of politics. "I really believe there's something for everybody on television," said Marcy Carsey. "If anything, I think that conservative shows are broadcast right now, which is fine."[33]

Michelle Ganeless of Comedy Central agreed with Carsey. "My opinion is that there's something on television for everyone, and not every show is for every person. The great equalizer [is] sort of the television ratings." Ganeless's channel, of all the cable channels, may be the most liberally biased in terms of programming—Jon Stewart acts as a comedic PR wing for the Obama Administration and, together with Stephen Colbert, forms a phalanx of anticonservative propaganda on television—but Ganeless dismissed claims of discrimination: "I doubt that people are blacklisted."[34]

Michael Brandman, formerly of HBO, also waved off such criticisms: "I sort of feel—I sort of give it the same importance that most of the right-wing rants deserve. It's right-wing rants."[35] So did Herman Rush, producer of *The Montel Williams Show*: "I don't believe Hollywood is any more liberal or conservative, it's mixed up of both people."[36]

Unfortunately, not everybody is entitled to an opinion, unless they have the *right* opinions—which is to say, leftist opinions.

THE BLACKLIST AT WORK

Even when the television industry's residents refuse to acknowledge a problem, though, the problem presents itself. Take, for example, a relatively innocuous piece by *Entertainment Weekly* former executive editor Mark Harris from April 2010. In that piece, Harris celebrated political content in various television shows, from *The Office* to *Parks and Recreation*. So far, so good—nobody is arguing that liberal content on television should be restricted. Then Harris stepped into discriminatory territory: "Take, for instance, *The Middle*, ABC's beautifully written and acted, underheralded family sitcom—and a show that, to admit my own bias, I expected to hate, since many of the political views of its star Patricia Heaton are about 8,000 light-years to my right. I'm not sure exactly how Heaton and the show's creators—veterans of the left-populist '90s classic *Roseanne*—found common ground. But what they've come up with . . . has an unmistakable ideological [left-leaning] undercurrent all its own."[37]

First off, Harris's comment betrayed a shocking lack of knowledge about how the industry works—the actors generally don't write the shows, so Heaton wouldn't be determining content. But more important, Harris's antipathy for Heaton's politics infected his estimation of her work. While he was pleasantly surprised to find that *The Middle* skewed liberal on issues like gay rights and the economy, his initial expectation was that any show with Patricia Heaton had to be some sort of right-wing diatribe—and that, by extension, it had to be terrible. Unfortunately, this is the logic of far too many in the industry, who assume that just because someone voted for Bush or McCain, their work must be correspondingly conservative and therefore awful.

The logic is not only flawed, it's repulsive. Conservatives *are* able to write in a nonpartisan fashion—even if work is conservative, that doesn't make it bad. But when liberal equals good and conservative equals bad—when you judge work based on its politics rather than its quality—quality falls by the wayside.

Harris's dislike for Heaton not only demonstrates how the left often infuses its criticism with political discrimination, it demonstrates how skewed that criticism is altogether. Harris criticized Heaton for her politics and implied that her politics would taint *The Middle*. But that criticism couldn't be further from the truth in the case of Heaton, who is not only one of Tinseltown's most skilled comic actresses, but by all accounts, a voice of reason on the set. She's far from a controversy monger.

But that hasn't stopped people like Harris from attacking her. It also hasn't stopped other television figures like vulgarian Kathy Griffin from going after her with a rhetorical chainsaw. Back in December 2006, Griffin did an interview with the *National Enquirer* in which she stated that she "used to think Patricia Heaton was funny, but now I'm just grossed out by her! . . . The whole gay issue, I gotta tell you—when I hear Patricia talking her bull—and saying it's not in the Bible that gay people should be together—those are the pieces of information that I can't forget about."[38] Of course, Heaton has never stated anything about gay marriage; this was Griffin tarring Heaton simply because Heaton identifies as a Republican. It doesn't matter much coming from Kathy Griffin—but it does matter when even a figure as publicly reasonable and talented as Patricia Heaton is attacked for her moderate-right politics. If they attack Heaton, whom won't they attack?

Conservatives in Hollywood know that they're fighting an uphill battle just to exist. The few conservatives in Hollywood who do speak out are adamant that discrimination exists on a widespread basis. They state to a man that outspoken conservatism is not to be tolerated on sets, in executive meetings, or in pitch sessions. Those conservatives who are most successful now were silent during their early days in the industry; only later did they reveal their political proclivities. That, they often say, is the only path to success as a conservative in Tinseltown. As a general rule, the conservatives who have made it in television tend to feel discrimination less than those who have not made it—but that's because, as a general rule, those conservatives who made it in television didn't do so when they were openly conservative, and many still don't consider themselves conservative on social issues.

"Are you kidding me? Of course it's true," explained Kelsey Grammer, star of *Frasier* and *Cheers* and well-known Hollywood Republican, when asked about the blacklist. "I wish Hollywood was a two-party town, but it's not." Grammer told the *Hollywood Reporter* that in his early days in the industry, he was essentially forced to donate $10,000 to Barbara Boxer and the Democratic Party to prevent a director from blackballing him. Grammer said the best strategy is to keep quiet about politics "unless you think the way you are supposed to think." Evan Sayet, who wrote for Bill Maher before going out on his own, said that while on staff at one of the comedy shows, "I was informed I could not write jokes about ebonics, global warming, or any other cause coming from the left."[39] One extraordinarily high-profile television actor who openly identifies as a conservative refused to comment publicly for this book, citing backlash from the Hollywood community and possible impact on family, friends, and media coverage.

"[Liberals] can speak very openly, even in business meetings," avers Andrew Klavan, author of the novel *True Crime* and other adapted Hollywood hits, who now does video commentary for Pajamas Media. But if Klavan speaks openly, he says, "that's pretty much the end of my sale."[40] Gary Graham, a character actor who has guest starred in *Star Trek: Enterprise*, *Nip/Tuck*, *JAG*, and *Ally McBeal*, among other shows, writes the same thing: "There are very dire consequences to being in this town, working in this industry—and speaking out against the sort of leftist agenda that is now racing through our government at every level—from city to state to federal. It pisses them off. And unfortunately for those who speak out, they control the gates to the kingdom."[41]

The blacklist, according to character actor Dan Gifford, "exists as certainly as political correctness and passive aggressiveness in Hollywood exist."[42] Anybody who has spent five minutes in Hollywood knows that PC and passive aggressiveness are perhaps the two main driving forces in the industry.

Oscar- and Emmy-nominated writer Lionel Chetwynd was similarly disparaging about the supposedly "open" nature of the industry. "Hollywood is always a liberal enterprise any way you look at it," Chetwynd told me. We were ensconced in his home in the Hollywood Hills, in a study piled floor to ceiling with books. Bagpipes blared in the background, a constant reminder of Chetwynd's military service with the Black Watch, Royal Highland regiment of Canada. That military service, which Chetwynd marked as one of the formative experiences of his life—"I'm a captain, Frazier Highlanders, so you fuck with me, you deal with guys in loincloths and blue faces"—also influenced his perspective toward the industry. When he entered the industry in the 1970s, it was dominated by the antimilitary hangover of the Vietnam War. Chetwynd immediately ran into this liberalism head-on.

In one social setting Chetwynd began telling a major Hollywood producer about his experiences in the army and how it had shaped him. "How can that be?" the producer asked him. "I mean, you're a smart guy, how can you believe that shit?" Chetwynd answered him by way of a story: the story of the Allied assault on Dieppe in 1942, a gallant but fruitless test assault on the French Coast in which 3,623 of the 6,086 men who came ashore were KIA, wounded, or taken prisoner. As Chetwynd told me the story, I couldn't help but be engrossed—it was a story of unbelievable bravery by men who knew they had to sacrifice themselves in a raid that would be mostly a learning experience for troops and commanders rather than a significant contribution to victory in Europe. The generals had to send them in order to test what a German response to an amphibious assault on Fortress Europe would look like.

The producer was similarly enraptured. "This is a movie!" he reportedly exclaimed. "Is it available? Come over and pitch my people."

Three days later, Chetwynd pitched the producer's people. "I told the story. . . . It was a suicide mission. It was Canada's coming of age [Canada lost an enormous number of soldiers]. That was the part that brought him to tears. The church bells tolled from St. John's Newfoundland to Vancouver Island. It was a dreadful national loss."

The executives were predictably enthralled, too. Then the producer said, "So you mean our bloodthirsty generals sent their own men to their death? What a story!"

"You don't quite have it right," Chetwynd interjected. "In fact the generals, if you read the memoirs, wept. It was terrible. One is believed to have committed suicide. Because of the exigencies of war, they did it."

"It wasn't the generals?" the producer replied. "Then who is the enemy?"

"Well," said Chetwynd, "Hitler and the Nazis."

And the producer's representative responded, "No, no, I mean the *real* enemy."

Chetwynd erupted volcanically. "I was pulling a cigarette out," he remembered, "and I plunged it into the glass table and broke it. I was so angry at someone who could only understand Nazism as a cipher for the evil in us. I couldn't posit it as a voracious ---- animal that's out there to destroy us. . . . [This experience was a] way station where I discovered what I was up against."

Burt Prelutsky, a writer on *M*A*S*H*, among other shows, as well as a two-term member of the Writers Guild board of directors, told me about an incident that underscored his recognition of the intolerant liberalism in the industry. As a member of the board, he had to vote on whether to give Guild money to a defense fund for a gallery owner who had displayed the pornographic works of Robert Mapplethorpe. "I spoke against them, which must have been an eye opener to the other people in the room," Prelutsky remembered. "The eye opening thing was that once they got over their shock that I was arguing against it, they almost tuned me out."[43]

Perhaps the first conservative actor to openly challenge the liberal blacklist was Michael Moriarty, then the star of *Law & Order.* Moriarty voted for Clinton—he was a liberal Democrat. But after Attorney General Janet Reno attacked television for its violent content—a ploy often used by liberals to distract from television's overt sexual content—Moriarty fought back in the press, alongside the show's creator, Dick Wolf. On November 18, 1993, Moriarty attended a meeting with Reno; Don Ohlmeyer, president of NBC programming; Wolf; Roz Weiman, an NBC censor; Betsy Frank, an advertising executive; Linda Otto, a producer; Thomas Carter, a director at the Equal Justice interest group, and a psychiatrist. At that meeting, Reno apparently suggested that the federal government control television programming from 3:00 P.M. to 9:00 P.M. As Moriarty later wrote, "I won't go into any greater detail about the meeting except to say I was feeling . . . frustration, shame and *rage* during this *travesty*, this lavish display of *contempt* for the *Bill of Rights*. . . ."[44] When Moriarty attempted to get a movement underway to force Reno's resignation, he said, he was abandoned by NBC and Wolf and hung out to dry. He ended up resigning from the show. One year later, he took out an ad in *Variety* in which he stated that he was "now a blacklisted actor." "I left my job in protest," he wrote. "I must now leave my country."[45] Moriarty told me that Dick Wolf and much of the television establishment abandoned him when it became clear that by siding with him and against censorship, they'd be standing against Clinton. He was, he said, a "foolish idealist . . . I regret none of it."[46]

Moriarty is an exception to the rule. Many conservatives *do* regret their blacklisting, and with good reason. By simply expressing an opinion, they often lose out on hundreds of thousands—even millions of dollars. What makes Moriarty's story all the more shocking is that he wasn't even standing up for conservatism per se—he was standing up against Clintonian censorship. When Democratic political liberalism comes into conflict with principled, old-style liberalism, however, even old-style political liberals lose out in Hollywood.

Dwight Schultz had a similar story to tell. When I met with Schulz, star of *The A-Team*, recurring guest star of *Star Trek: Voyager*, and prolific voice-over artist, he handed me a piece of paper—a casting call for a computer-animated 3-D film entitled *Astro Boy* (which would eventually star Kristen Bell, Nathan Lane, Eugene Levy, Donald Sutherland, Charlize Theron, and Nicolas Cage). He pointed angrily at the character description for one President Stone, the villain of the piece: "Direction: A cross between a refined, somewhat more controlled version of General Buck Turgison (George C. Scott) from *Dr. Strangelove* and Dick Cheney. . . ."

"When you're auditioning for voice-over work, cartoons, you get this in the mail," Schultz told me. "This is very typical, very mild. This is the type of thing you'll get. Or, 'He's an asshole like George Bush.' . . . You never saw it during the Clinton years. It's only conservatives. And it's every day."[47] Schultz doesn't describe the industry's discrimination against conservatives as a blacklist. Instead, he describes it as a "liberal Bastille. . . . It's a social network. . . . But the social aspect of this business is, to a large degree, everything there is."

Schultz's first honest-to-goodness run-in with the liberal Hollywood establishment, he says, came when he was reading for Bruce Paltrow, producer on *St. Elsewhere*—he was auditioning for the part of Fiscus, a part that eventually went to Howie Mandel. The episode truly led off several months earlier, when both Schultz and Paltrow were attending the Williamstown Theater Festival. Paltrow spotted Schultz praising Ronald Reagan. "Dwight," Paltrow piped up, "so you're a Reagan asshole!"

Fast forward a few months. At the *St. Elsewhere* audition, Schultz ran into Paltrow, the show's producer. "Dwight!" Paltrow called. "What are you doing here?" Schultz blanched—when the producer asks what you're doing at an audition, you're finished. Schultz told Paltrow that he was there to read for the part of Fiscus. "There's not going to be a Reagan asshole on this show!" Paltrow stated authoritatively. That was the end of that.[48]

Later, Schultz, told me, he couldn't take it anymore. "It's not worth it," he said sadly. "It's simply not worth it . . . you can't go after what they say because it becomes too personal, and then you lose your self-respect to a certain degree. So I ended up in withdrawal from Hollywood."[49]

It's outspoken conservatives like Schultz and Moriarty who fall out of favor with the Hollywood establishment. That's because the typical liberal take is that all conservatives must be raving lunatics who are honor-bound to destroy chemistry on sets and in the writers' rooms. More than that, liberals believe that conservative artists are almost literally missing a part of their hearts or brains—the part that contains empathy and social conscience, without which no great artist can operate. This is xenophobia of the highest order, but it is viewed as rational discourse in the industry.

"You know, I think for the most part, scripted television is very liberal. Because of the kind of people it attracts to it," said Michael Nankin, writer for *Life Goes On* and producer on *Chicago Hope* and *Picket Fences*, in a typical explanation. "TV writers are very literary, for the most part socially conscious artists. And that's the personality that you need to succeed in that business, that's the personality that it attracts. . . ." Liberalism, Nankin continued, was about "this very old-fashioned idea that art was meant to ennoble and lift up."[50]

"[Artists are] the intellectual community, that's why [they're liberal]," said Allan Burns, co-creator of *The Mary Tyler Moore Show* and producer on *Lou Grant*, agreeing with Nankin's derision of conservatives on television. "Writers have always had a social conscience. That's no surprise. I don't mean to sound arrogant about it, because I don't consider myself to be an intellectual, but I do consider myself to be a person who empathizes and thinks about what's going on in the world."[51] This borders on malicious—conservative works from authors such as Ray Bradbury to

George Orwell to Alexander Solzhenitsyn have captivated readers and audiences the world over. But the big-hearted leftist versus the cruel, stupid right-winger is a liberal conceit that just won't die in Hollywood.

Barbara Fisher was similarly outspoken about the perception in Hollywood that liberals are simply *nicer* people than conservatives. I asked her whether the programming tended to be more liberal at Lifetime (ex-slogan: "Television for Women"), where she had been executive vice president of entertainment, than it was at Hallmark Channel (slogan: "Make Yourself at Home"). She said that while she didn't consider the programming at Lifetime to be more liberal, "when you're sort of a pro-social place and you do get involved with public affairs, I think people immediately think it's left-leaning."[52]

This initial bias against conservatives means that conservatives must spend time infiltrating the industry before revealing their politics. They have to make friends and influence people *before* announcing their identities. In order for conservatives to come out of the closet, they must first convince those around them that in spite of their political viewpoint, they aren't baby-eating barbarians who want to use the poor for dog food.

In fact, there are many such conservatives—people who focused on career and social circle first, then revealed to a select few where they stood. These conservatives tend to talk about Hollywood in warmer language than Schultz, Klavan, Chetwynd, or Sayet. Robert Davi, star of NBC's *Profiler*, told me, "In the early career, my politics didn't come up."[53]

That didn't mean that Davi didn't run into industry bias once he did become more politically vocal. "I had different issues on different shows," he said. "It wasn't said definitively, but it was inferred that if you wanted to make a character a born-again Christian, make them a hypocrite, or a nymphomaniac . . . there's definitely a tendency towards ridicule." On one occasion, there was a party for Gore; Davi supported Bush. "There were repercussions," he recalled. Davi wanted to make clear to me that he wasn't looking for "conspiracies in Cheerios. I'm reasonable," he continued, "I have close friends who are absolutely left, who are good guys. . . . But *all work is social*. It's social networking. . . . It's the cultural milieu."[54] Davi retains his friendships in the industry, and so he gets along just fine. In 2010, Davi appeared in an episode of *Nip/Tuck*, an episode of *Criminal Minds*, and was working on several movies.

Adam Baldwin, one of the more successful character actors in television—he plays John Casey on *Chuck*, and played Jayne Cobb on the cult classic *Firefly*—is an outspoken conservative. I met him on the set of *Chuck* to discuss what it's like to be a conservative in Hollywood. Baldwin is soft-spoken and tolerant. "I have wonderful, wonderful nice friends who are very hard left," he said. "And I love them and I'm happy to know them . . . I would never want them in office."[55] Whether Baldwin's strong work record is a result of his reasoned nature or his long history in Hollywood prior to his political conversion remains an open question. But there is no question that Baldwin is correct that conservatives would do well to tone down their rhetoric when it comes to the entertainment business.

If the first type of successful Hollywood conservative is the quiet conservative—the conservative who stays in the closet, at least until he or she has already found success—then the second type of successful Hollywood conservative is the social liberal. Not all conservatives are created equal in Hollywood—it's tolerable to be antitax and pro–war in Iraq, for example. It's utterly verboten to be openly anti–gay marriage or anti-abortion.

Don Bellisario, one of television's most successful producers and the man responsible for the massive hits *NCIS* and *JAG*, said he felt less discrimination in Hollywood than other conservatives. "No, no," he said when asked whether those in the industry had criticized him for his non-liberal programming. "Hollywood *is* very liberal, very left. They always have been," he told me. But, he said, he had never been blacklisted.

How did Bellisario make it? Part of that has to do with his immense talent. Part of it has to do with the fact that he has never used his programming as a vehicle for his politics. Part of it also has to do with the fact that he's not conservative on social issues.

"The thing is, I'm conservative—I'm pro-military and I'm conservative—not a Bible thumping conservative," he explained. "I mean, I'm liberal in a lot of things. I'm liberal about the right to choose. There's plenty I'm liberal about. So I don't pick a label to put on me as just conservative."[56]

This is the acceptable answer in Hollywood. You're never an across-the-board conservative in public—you're an independent. You're never pro–traditional marriage—you're open on the question. You're never pro-life—you believe it's a woman's choice. This is the code, and everyone is expected to abide by it. That's because many in Hollywood are under the misperception that being pro-traditional marriage means being intolerant of gays or that being anti-abortion means being intolerant of pro-choice Americans. That's far from the case. But that inherent distrust of social conservatives is difficult to overcome.

Social liberals who consider themselves conservative on other grounds, like Bellisario, generally have little problem getting along in Hollywood. Marc Cherry, creator of *Desperate Housewives*, is a case in point. "Yeah, I'm an odd duck in the sense that I'm a gay Republican," Cherry told me. "On certain issues I'm very very conservative, and on other issues I'm as liberal as anyone in Hollywood."

As a gay Republican, Cherry said he has never experienced anti-conservative discrimination in Hollywood. "First off, I think it's always difficult to get work, and two, if you're really really good at your job, that comes first . . . most people didn't know what my political beliefs were starting out, and no one ever cared until *Desperate Housewives* became a hit. . . ."[57]

The fact that there is some small debate in conservative Hollywood circles—and yes, there are conservative Hollywood circles—about the depth of the discrimination in Hollywood allows certain liberal journalists in Hollywood to claim that no discrimination actually exists. These journalists defensively assert that all conservative complaints boil down to sour grapes. They establish a catch-22: If a conservative is successful in Hollywood, he has no cause for complaint; if he is unsuccessful, it must be that lack of success driving his complaint rather than actual discrimination.

One of the chief practitioners of this odious manipulation is Patrick Goldstein of the *Los Angeles Times*. "Today's conservatives are still complaining about [what] they say is Hollywood's rigid ideological slant," Goldstein wrote in a May 18, 2010, piece, "but they apparently aren't brave enough to actually name names." Goldstein focused on Jonathan Kahn (aka Jon David), a singer-songwriter who has performed at Tea Party events around the country using a pseudonym to avoid the blacklist. Kahn told the *Wall Street Journal* that he used an alias "for protective reasons. In Hollywood, being a conservative is the kiss of death." But Goldstein essentially called him a liar, since Kahn "only managed to direct one film . . . which earned lukewarm reviews and barely got a release."

"Based on that very limited output," Goldstein wrote, "it's [*sic*] seems like quite a stretch to say that Kahn's politics have held him back. But that's what all too many conservatives do. They put the blame for their stalled careers on liberal Hollywood, when lack of marketable talent might be a far more likely source for the problem. Don't get me wrong. I'm not saying that Hollywood isn't lousy with liberals. It is indeed an overwhelmingly liberal community. But it is also very much a free-market community where the best ideas, scripts and talent ultimately rise to the top. . . . If a political conservative (in or out of the closet) wrote a hot action script that looked like a global tent-pole hit, all those squishy liberals would be pushing their best friends down elevator shafts left and right trying to get the rights to it."

Finally, Goldstein implied Kahn was a coward. "If Kahn really thinks otherwise, he'd better start naming names, because this story line of shadowy Hollywood liberals squashing the careers of righteous conservatives is getting pretty old indeed."[58]

Goldstein's argument is vapid, empty-headed in the extreme. He's essentially suggesting that conservatives cannot complain about "shadowy" discrimination (even though liberals do this on a routine basis—just look at the continuing case for affirmative action) because they won't name the names of those in Hollywood who discriminate. But as we've seen above, there are plenty in Hollywood who discriminate on a regular basis, and there are even a few who openly cop to it and celebrate it. Conservatives often don't want to name names for fear of retaliation by those they expose.

Those few vocal liberals aren't the real problem, though. The real problem *is* the shadowy liberal discrimination, because it sets the bar too high. Hollywood produces a "hot action script" that becomes a "global tent-pole hit" maybe once every five years or so. Stating that liberals in Hollywood would buy such a script off a conservative is utterly uncontroversial. It's just as uncontroversial as stating that if a black man came to Bull Connor holding the Hope Diamond, Connor would be willing to buy it off of him for a few thousand dollars. That doesn't make Bull Connor an emblem of racial tolerance. It makes him a non-moron.

Nobody argues that conservatives can't sell blockbuster scripts. But just as in the Bull Connor/Hope Diamond scenario, the problem is getting through the door. High level executives don't take random meetings with one-shot-wonder conservatives. Generally, those who create hot action scripts are people who have worked in the industry a long time, who have honed and perfected their craft. In other words, to get to the level Goldstein is talking about—the level of the million-dollar script—you have to move your way up the ranks first. And that means getting jobs in writers' rooms, making indie pictures, immersing yourself in the industry.

People like Goldstein often point to successful conservatives like Joel Surnow of *24* fame and mega-producer Jerry Bruckheimer (*CSI*, *The Amazing Race*, *Without a Trace*) as examples of folks who have made it, as though their mere existence proves that discrimination in Hollywood is a fantasy. But nobody is challenging whether a Surnow or a Bruckheimer can get ahead. The true question is, Why should a conservative have to *be* Jerry Bruckheimer or Joel Surnow to get ahead? There are literally thousands of writers in Hollywood who have never written anything of quality, who make unprofitable movies on a routine basis, who create bomb pilot after bomb pilot—but who still make a living. How many of *those* people are conservatives?

Oddly, the same people who proclaim that discrimination against conservatives in Hollywood doesn't exist suggest that racial discrimination in Hollywood—for which there is substantially less evidence—remains a paramount concern. Goldstein himself wrote a column in the aftermath of President Obama's election suggesting that Hollywood segregates blacks and whites in its movies and television shows (and dismissing the stardom of Will Smith and the box office and critical success of movies like *Dreamgirls* and *Ray*). "If Hollywood really wants to show some respect for the Obama revolution," Goldstein penned, "it's time for the movie business to break some ground of its own."[59] Goldstein is far less interested in breaking ground in the area of ideological tolerance than he is in promoting tolerance for different levels of melanin.

Goldstein wrote a column in November 2009 about Universal Pictures' terrible decision to remove a black couple from the British poster for the Vince Vaughn vehicle *Couples Retreat*. "I've talked to enough frustrated black filmmakers over the years to know the real underlying issue behind these kinds of gaffes," Goldstein wrote. "The real solution to this kind of issue would be for Hollywood to find a way to hire a decent sampling of African-American executives so its decision-making wouldn't look so clueless and out of touch with the diversity in the rest of our culture."[60] Switch out "conservative" for "black" and "African-American" in that last paragraph, and Goldstein would disown his own paragraph, despite the fact that there are likely more successful blacks in Hollywood than successful conservatives of any ethnicity.

Aside from the direct evidence of anti-conservative discrimination in the business, there is strong circumstantial evidence as well. One element of that circumstantial evidence is Hollywood's emphasis on youth. The focus on the 18-49 crowd is both a result of and a rationale for Hollywood's liberalism—young people are liberal, so programmers prefer to target them, and by making the case for targeting young people, programmers justify their own liberal programming. The natural outgrowth of the focus on the liberal 18-49 crowd is age discrimination in Hollywood. Walk around any network programming or development office in Los Angeles, and you're more likely to see a unicorn than a man or woman over age fifty. If you're over age forty in this town, the chances of getting a job are significantly lessened. Not coincidentally, if you're over forty in this town, there's a far higher chance that you're conservative than if you're under forty (the same holds true for the general population).

That's why in January 2010, seventeen networks and production studios, as well as seven talent agencies, settled a class action lawsuit for $70 million based on age discrimination.[61] One of the lead plaintiffs was Burt Prelutsky. "Some might find it ironic that Hollywood's liberals, who are still inflamed over a blacklist that took place 60 years ago, not only condone it in their hometown, but practice it every day of their lives," Prelutsky wrote.[62]

Ageism isn't directly correlative with discrimination against conservatives—God knows there are scores of older writers who are liberals.

But the same emphasis on youth that forced television to the left in the 1970s forces it left today—and forces out those who are "too old" to evolve with the ever-liberalizing morality of the times.

LIBERALS: TV ISN'T TRANSFORMATIVE ENOUGH

Liberals in Hollywood tend to believe that their shows are not *transformative* of the audiences who watch them—rather, they say, they are *reflective* of prevailing realities. These creators and executives see themselves as documentarians of inarguable truths, not propagandists attempting to change hearts and minds.

This may seem bizarre to those of us who have actually met people who live in Alabama or Texas or Kansas and have a different take on life than those who sip lattes at the Coffee Bean & Tea Leaf in West Los Angeles.

But the liberals in Hollywood aren't dissembling. Their shows *do* reflect prevailing realities *as they see them*—which is to say, through the prism of their sophisticated urban liberal outlook. Their programming not only reflects big city liberalism—it transforms everybody who isn't one already into a big city liberal.

Hollywood leftists refuse to recognize this obvious truth. To the contrary, they actually believe that their shows aren't transformative *enough*—in fact, they think their shows are too *conservative*.

"I think when television is living up to its greatest potential, it would be transformative," Tom Fontana, creator of *Oz*, told me. "When it's groping for ratings, it's reflective. When it's reflective, it's trying not to offend too many people. And if you're going to try to change the world for the better, you have to be willing to offend some people."[63] Fontana, you may recall, is one of the few honest liberals in Hollywood who will admit that the industry needs more balance—but even he seems unaware that the programming on television generally reflects liberals' reality, not conservatives'. From where Fontana stands—the hard left—television seems neutral. More than that, he believes that the only truly transformative programming is that which is offensive to common standards.

"I don't think television has been a force for change," Susan Harris, creator of the massively transformative series *Soap*, told me. "I think it's reflective and I think it's behind the times. . . . You've got a Miss America contestant causing an uproar because she just believes in opposite sex marriage, and that's no longer a popular opinion," Harris continued. "So we've come that far in our social thinking . . . [but] I think it's not reflected on television."[64] Harris's opinion reflects the inside-the-bubble thinking so pervasive in Hollywood. Huge swaths of the country saw Carrie Prejean's destruction at the hands of Perez Hilton as a despicably inappropriate ambush on someone with a mainstream opinion on gay marriage. Harris saw that same incident as evidence that Prejean was wholly out of the mainstream—and even more ridiculously, she saw the Prejean incident as evidence that television, which is the culture's most ardent advocate of gay marriage, should stump even harder for it in order to keep up with the times.

Harris is uncomfortable with the "commotion" that Americans cause when they see radical liberalism on television. That commotion is generated by the vast disconnect between the world of Susan Harris and the world of middle America and the South. Despite the parochialism of the Hollywood crowd, millions of conservatives still watch their shows and disagree with the social values portrayed on those shows. In fact, millions of so-called ignoramuses often strongly object to the portrayal of rural values on television—they think that the liberals in Hollywood are out to unfairly ridicule them, as Chris Chulack, producer of *ER*, pointed out: "If [television is] done by people who grew up and only know urban values, they're the ones that are interpreting or portraying rural values as well—there's going to be a bit of a [twist]."[65] Nonurban nonliberals have a legitimate beef. But when networks react to those viewers, creators react by blaming the networks for acting as a stodgily conservative barrier to liberal programming.

Hence the viewpoint of Gene Reynolds, producer of *M*A*S*H* and *Room 222*, two of the more transformative shows in television history. "I think [television is] more reflective than pushing," he stated. "I remember getting a lecture from an NBC executive. I had shot the pilot of the *Ghost and Mrs. Muir* and I had directed the first three episodes. . . . And [the executive] said, 'I don't want to have anything new on the show. We [should] deal with issues that have already been dealt with before.' And he was a Southerner. 'But we certainly don't want to be in the *vangaaahd.*' "

Reynolds mimicked the executive's pronunciation with a long, Southern drawl "[T]hey don't want to be in the vanguard. They don't want to get into stuff that could be controversial."[66]

Fred Silverman, who ran all three of the networks at one time or another, said television was "certainly not [transformative]—it's not doing anything."[67] Likewise, Gary David Goldberg, creator of *Family Ties* and *Spin City*, stated flatly, "I think it's reflective."[68] Barbara Fisher, vice president of original programming for Hallmark Channel, lamented television's lack of transformative power. "I would like to say transformative, but I think more reflective. Because I think everybody's scared."[69] When I spoke with Marc Cherry, he stated that the transformative era in television began to wane with *All in the Family*, which he said "had an effect on millions of families in terms of how they perceived issues." Today, he said, "any progress that is being made . . . in relationship to entertainment is glacial."[70]

Leonard Stern of *Get Smart*, *He & She*, and *McMillan & Wife*, also said that television had grown less transformative due to network fear. "At times [television] leads, and very often now it follows," he averred. "Unfortunately, [the shows] follow each other, so there's so much [that's] repetitive. . . . I hold testing and research and demographics in contempt, because I feel they substitute for what used to be instinctual response, visceral go-aheads. And we were a better world for it."[71] A better world according to Leonard Stern and those who think as he does—but there are those who disagreed and who sought to promote a different set of values. And those people, too, buy dish soap. Why shouldn't the networks count their opinions?

Former HBO executive Michael Brandman agreed with Stern's view. "I don't know that there's anything I can cite nowadays that's transformational, not in the way Norman Lear's shows were transformational, or some of the television that was done in the 1980s, early 1990s where the social revolution began to be reflected on television."[72] No doubt Brandman correctly summarizes the gap between television of the Lear era and today's television—Lear's shows were far more revolutionary than what we see today. But again, that's because Lear was fighting something—and Lear won. The 1960s are over. But Hollywood can't get over it. They're the former high school football stars reveling in the touchdown of yesteryear while lamenting their beer gut. Today's Hollywood liberals are in full psychological meltdown because victory brings stagnancy—and Hollywood liberals can't afford stagnancy, because if the status quo is hunky dory, they'll have to find another way to justify their affluent lifestyles.

"I think it's rare that television is a leader in pushing anything forward," agreed Herman Rush, producer of *The Montel Williams Show*. "I think it is reflective, and I think it's reflective because our survival, whether it's the advertiser, the network, or the creative community is to be successful. And therefore to be reflective of what's going on in the society is always safer than trying to lead it. So I think few shows try to lead it."[73]

Why this emphasis on "leading" the audience and "transforming" society? Because television liberals can't accept the notion that their business is a *business*, and that their main job is to sell products so that advertisers will pay them enormous sums of cash. Hollywood's liberal elites suffer from the Michael Moore Syndrome—love your private jet, but hate the system that bought you that jet.

They therefore try to justify their participation in the economic system they profess to hate by "leading" the public—which nowadays means pushing the envelope on social and lifestyle issues. And pushing the envelope, not coincidentally, raises ratings. Cynically, they congratulate themselves for making Grandma blanch, even if the real purpose of doing so is to draw in mass audiences. If they don't make Grandma blanch often enough, they think they're not doing their job.

It's all transparently exploitative, transparently profitable, and transparently empty. And yet to these Hollywood leftists, the only material that's admirable is that which shocks the conscience of their audience. Everything else is simple Babbitry, reflective and humdrum.

THE TV LIBERALS' DISCONNECT WITH REALITY

Liberals think their programming isn't transformative enough—it's too "reflective" of the surrounding society. The rest of us laugh at that notion. We laugh because we don't live the same lives that those in the television industry do. We understand that their shows are transformative of our lives.

But to truly understand the minds of those in Hollywood, we must understand that their shows are reflective *to them*. In their world, what they put on television is just as real as what you see on the History Channel. That's because they're enshrining their own personal histories. "What makes for a great pitch?" asked Brandon Tartikoff in his autobiography. "A connection to real life."[74] Remember the old writing adage, "Write what you know"? In Hollywood, that adage is gospel—and that means that everyone is writing about their particular world, which is almost invariably liberal. And in their view, liberal is "real."

That's why Hollywood leftists cannot understand, for the life of them, why anybody would attack their programming choices. After all, they argue, Americans don't attack the Associated Press's reporting. Why should they attack Hollywood when it merely reports what's happening in the world?

Television creators' insistence on reality goes even deeper than mere reflection of the goings on in the 90210 zip code. When Hollywood liberals talk about reflecting reality, what they *really* mean is that they make shows that reflect their values. And as we've seen, to Hollywood liberals, their values aren't up for debate—they represent the one true reality. There are plenty of characters and stories and plotlines in television shows, but they almost universally reflect the same set of values—and their creators almost universally praise their concomitant "realism." Liberal values are truth to the folks who populate the high rises on Wilshire Boulevard. And that fact makes it dangerous for conservatives in town, who disagree with the fundamental "realities" liberals seek to establish and promulgate.

That's why Anne Sweeney, president of Disney-ABC Television Group and co-chairman of Disney Media Networks, justifies transitioning ABC Family from a family-friendly network to a more adult-themed network by stating, with a straight face, "The best way to resonate with your audience is to be authentic. And you're only authentic if you are holding up a mirror to your audience and saying, 'I see you.'"[75] What's so authentic about high school girls making out with one another in *Pretty Little Liars* or the beautiful sterility of teenage pregnancy on *Secret Life of an American Teenager*? Not much, on a broad scale. But leftists in the television industry see those shows as realistic in their *values*, reflective of a new strain in American morality that accepts teenage sexual exploration, teenage pregnancy, and all other forms of teenage deviance and misbehavior as a fait accompli. They mistakenly believe that this new strain in American morality exists in the audience, when it really exists mainly in their own minds. The problem is that they bring such morality to the public fore, and by doing so, promulgate it.

Similarly, Susan Harris, who hated that television was "reflective" rather than transformative of American society, praised her own show's focus on realism. "We brought it back to reality," she explained. "As crazy as *Soap* got, and we had some farcical scenes, and then the very next scene would be a very realistic one and a very emotional one."[76] The reality in *Soap*, according to Harris, was *Soap*'s typically leftist morality of multiculturalism, tolerance, and diversity.

During the shift to urban programming in the late 1960s and early 1970s, "reflecting" reality was the preferred excuse for the networks. What they were doing wasn't transforming the industry's depiction of American values—that would have been wrong. No, what they were doing was bringing television down to earth. All of a sudden, television's top executives seemed to realize that *The Beverly Hillbillies* and *Green Acres* constituted a fantastical nonrealistic universe—and that true reality was to be found instead in gritty big city liberal programming. "I think the feeling was in those that championed it that television was growing up and that it had to reflect much more the period we were living in," Fred Silverman told me. "The days of *The Beverly Hillbillies* were over. It was time to put some shows on the air that were about the real world. And thank God that they prevailed."[77] Again, Silverman never seemed to acknowledge that the values of *Green Acres* were real to the majority of Americans—they didn't reflect his reality. To Silverman, the morality of the people in Birmingham, Alabama, no more resembled reality than the values of the aliens in *My Favorite Martian*.

A few creators acknowledge that television still inherently shapes American culture; a few recognize that television by default changes people's opinions on crucial issues and critical values. Josh Brand, creator of *St. Elsewhere* and *Northern Exposure*, spoke eloquently when asked whether television was reflective or transformative of American society: "It certainly reflects culture and it certainly can transform culture."[78]

Robert Guza, head writer of *General Hospital*, believed the same. "We should reflect what we see going on in the greater society," he explained. "But at the same time we all have an obligation to try to transform it. You see wrongs, you want to try to transform it."[79]

That sort of transformation occurs with regard to politics, as Marcy Carsey, creator of *The Cosby Show*, *Roseanne*, *That '70s Show*, and many others, illuminated. "I think it's both [reflective and transformative]. . . . I would guess that something like Ellen DeGeneres with her half-hour comedy and *Will & Grace* . . . I think that had to be one factor of many that has shifted people's attitudes toward homosexuality in this country, and it has shifted quite, quite dramatically."[80] Michelle Ganeless of Comedy Central cited exactly the same shows as evidence that television has an effect on American values, then summed up, "I think it's both reflective and transformative because it can expose people, it reaches so far and wide, it can expose people and break down stereotypes and barriers, but it's also certainly a reflection of what's already happening."[81] Ganeless and Carsey are exactly correct—those shows reflected the liberal realities of New York and Chicago and Los Angeles, and they transformed everyone else. Transformative television, Marc Cherry said, "has the effect of making the unfamiliar a little bit more familiar." Familiarity, in short, breeds acceptance—an idea with which the late Senator Daniel Patrick Moynihan (D-NY), purveyor of the notion of "defining deviancy down," would surely agree.[82]

While most liberals believe that their programming reflects reality because it reflects *their* reality, some liberals are more cynical. Some know that their programming is transformative but cite "realism" as a defense to their proselytizing agenda. David Shore, creator of *House*, scoffed at such attempts. "I think there's a knee-jerk reaction from people to some extent to say, 'It's just reflective, it's just reflective, you can't hold me responsible' from people within the industry," he said. "That's a cop-out because . . . we're also thrilled by the fact that we're touching people's lives."[83]

Shore's assessment is right on the money. Television affects Americans whether we like it or not. And here's the bottom line: Television reflects those who create it and transforms everybody else. If the creators are liberal—and they are—that liberalism will have an effect on Americans. Television acts as a magnifier for television creators' liberal life experiences—those experiences now become the basis of a prevalent element in American life. Liberals' reality becomes our reality. As Barbara Fisher said, "We have a very different perspective. [When it comes to what] we find pioneering or shocking, we find very little that way. Whereas in . . . Knoxville, we call them the villes, [they think differently]."[84]

The transformative power and influence of television can be wielded for political causes, ideological causes, and moral causes well outside the bounds of mainstream America. And as we'll see in the coming chapters, television's creators and executives do just that on a routine basis.

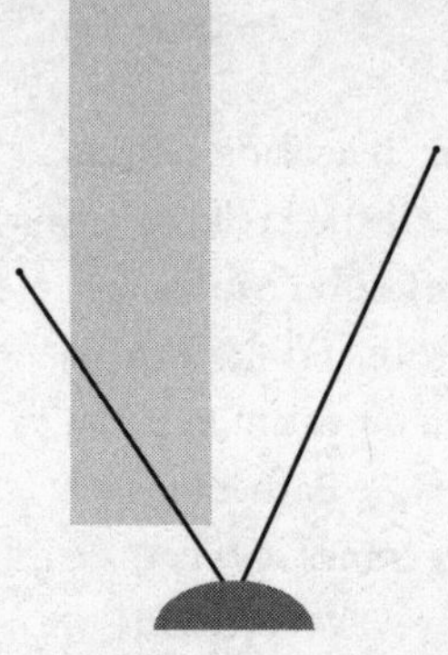

A SPOONFUL OF SUGAR

How Television Comedy Trashes Conservatism

The creators and executives who populate Hollywood are almost universally liberal. Creative output tends to reflect the beliefs and experiences of creators. Therefore, you'd expect television's major shows to be liberal. And they are. Unfortunately, we don't always notice it.

We don't notice it because the members of the television clique are immensely talented. They aim to entertain, and they hit their mark. And when we're being entertained, it's difficult to separate out the political content from the entertainment. Nobody thinks about the politics of *Friends*—we just laugh at Joey's idiocy, Ross's awkwardness, and Chandler's spastic flailing.

But the politics are there. And they influence us, the same way that Rachel's haircut influenced a generation of young women or Fonzie's leather jacket defined cool.

Traditionally, scripted entertainment has been divided between comedy and tragedy; these are the two lobes of the creative brain. Aristotle (the father of Western literary criticism) believed both genres were cathartic—comedy was designed to attack "base" or "ignoble" characters, while tragedy was designed to elevate superior characters.

Obviously, the form of comedy is well-geared toward political ends. Comedy has always been a useful vehicle for attacking customs and manners, and exposing hypocrisy for its own sake, both of which are thrusts aimed directly at the heart of the prevailing authority structure. Comedy asks a continuous stream of questions about the status quo. Such questioning is unique to Western civilization, and in a way forms the basis of democracy—Socrates' incessant questioning of tradition, the philosophical basis for open political debate, is the most serious form of comedy.

A unique problem arises, however, when there is no authority left to attack. True comedy only satisfies because in the end, the authority structure is generally validated (when it isn't validated, that's drama). That's why comedies of errors typically end with a wedding—after spending three hours watching Benedick and Beatrice mock marriage, they end up under the canopy, reinforcing the status quo. To take a more earthy example: my mom always used to laugh hysterically when my dad would clock his head on a kitchen cabinet. "I knew you weren't really hurt," she'd laugh. Now that I'm married, my wife does the same thing, with exactly the same justification. That's because physical pratfalls are only hilarious when we know that the victim isn't *really* injured.

The same is true of authority. When the authority remains generally unharmed, there is no problem—we can mock it and chastise it and laugh at it. But what happens when the authority structure abandons the stage altogether? Now comic irony has no stable target and descends into nihilism, attacking everything left standing with equal fervor. This is where we are today.

But while modern comedy has become more and more nihilistic, it remains a dominant mode on television. As Mike Dann, former CBS executive, said, "Comedy is king. There never was a time in the history of radio, and most of television—in series—that the top shows were not comedies."[1] And comedy is uniquely qualified to convince us of certain ideas. That's because humor disarms us. Laughter is infectious. We don't care when we watch *The Simpsons* that Homer Simpson abuses his children; we don't care when we watch *Family Guy* that Stewie is an incipient serial killer. They're *funny*. We laugh at them. And that makes us more inclined to accept their liberal and/or nihilistic perspectives on the world.

Sometimes that's a great thing—when we laugh at Archie Bunker's racism, for example, we're really saying that we reject his racism. But laughter can also be politically pernicious—after all, people *used* to laugh at racist blackface routines. Laughter is a weapon to be wielded, not an ultimate good.

And our comedy writers know this full well, which is why they marshal the power of laughter to their political causes. The writers and executives know that a spoonful of sugar makes the medicine go down.

Here, then, is a survey of some of the most popular comedies of all time—and what they were *really* about. This analysis is not mere speculation. It is based on the background of creators, their stated political goals in creating their shows, and the content of the shows themselves.

You will notice two particular themes that crop up over and over. The first is the steady undermining of traditional notions of fatherhood. Since Aristophanes and Plautus, comedy has always mocked fathers—fathers are familial stand-ins for the social authority structure. But television history also happens to coincide with an outright assault on the traditional family in the name of liberal values. We will see how television—both mirroring and promoting the decay of traditional moral values—traces the transformation of fathers from steady and permanent authority figures to dunderheaded morons.

The second theme is the changing treatment of blue-collar Americans. Television comedy is an excellent gauge for how the liberal movement feels about particular populations, and the rise and fall of the blue-collar worker is a case in point.

When JFK and LBJ occupied the White House, television's rural and blue-collar characters were hard-working Americans with a strong sense of family and a tendency to do the right thing. When Nixon became president, blue-collar workers suddenly became reactionary monsters like Archie Bunker—revenge by Hollywood against the real-life workers who shied away from George McGovern. That scorn for blue-collar Americans lasted until the rise of *Roseanne*, which reflected the realization by television liberals that they could woo more flies with honey than with vinegar. Since then, however, blue-collar workers have fallen totally off the radar—most of today's comic heroes are urban liberals, the type of folks you'd expect to see at an Obama fundraiser in Beverly Hills.

Certain names come up over and over in this chapter—names like Gelbart and Reynolds and Lear and Carsey. That's because, as we revealed above, the industry is actually quite small, and influential figures can generate literally decades' worth of top-notch entertainment. The most productive comic stylists are worshipped in the industry both for their creative abilities and for their willingness to push leftist politics.

This is not a criticism of the creators. Their shows are (with a few exceptions) terrific. They bring joy to millions of people. They provide us connections with others we wouldn't ordinarily have—how many people have become friends while debating the cosmic Ginger vs. Mary Ann question? They bind us to others, to our broader community.

Nor is it even really a condemnation of the insertion of politics into programming. It would be nearly impossible for creators to avoid infusing their values into their work. That's what makes the best television creators such phenomenal artists: they give us entertainment with meaning.

That doesn't mean we should take their products at face value. The entertainment provided by television doesn't absolve us of the obligation, as informed viewers, to analyze what it is we're putting in our heads. And what we're putting in our heads is what a small group of people want to put there.

YOUR SHOW OF SHOWS (1950–1954): JEWISH SOCIALIST PARADISE

When *Your Show of Shows* hit the air in 1950, America was flush from her defeat of Nazism and Japanese fascism, in the midst of an economic boom unprecedented in world history. Americans felt confident, free, and patriotic. And why not? They were citizens of the country with the best government and best military and best economy on the planet.

Your Show of Shows embraced the feeling of zany joy so many Americans felt in those days. Even as it did so, it provided a breeding ground for artists who focused far more on the dark side of America than on her tremendous strength, opportunity, and potential.

Your Show of Shows, wrote *New York Times* critic Jack Gould, was "an island of engaging literacy in TV's sea of vaudeville mediocrity."[2] *Your Show of Shows*, said Larry Gelbart, one of the writers on the show, was "pure platinum."[3] The variety show starred television legend Sid Caesar and drew enormous ratings for its entire four-year run—in fact, it was so successful that it spawned a spin-off in its wake, the eponymously-linked *Caesar's Hour* (which ran for another three years). The show masterfully combined hilarious sketch comedy with soft social satire.

The political importance of *Your Show of Shows* wasn't the show itself—it was the creation of one of the most powerful germs from which television's full-scale liberalism would eventually spread. The show's writers all came from the same milieu: They were New York Jews, outsiders who wanted to be accepted but who undercut conventional mores with ironic humor. Politically they were liberal or socialist, and their politics mixed with their vaudeville and Yiddish theater heritage to create a new brand of humor that would come to define American entertainment. In the future, these liberal comedy geniuses would mentor a whole new generation of 1960s and post-1960s liberals who pushed leftist values far more openly in their programming.

Sid Caesar himself was a mythical figure—he was a huge man physically, and on one occasion, he famously punched out a horse after it threw his wife from its back[4]—a Jewish giant from New York with a self-declared "radical-chic" socialist wife (Caesar, his wife said, was strictly apolitical).[5] Springing from that culturally Jewish, left-leaning background, Caesar tended to draw his comedic stylings from his own experiences. "In a way," Caesar wrote, "we were making Americans laugh at themselves and their foibles."[6] This is the essence of comedy, of course—by making Americans laugh at themselves, Caesar really had them laughing at their own values.

Because Caesar came from a certain milieu, his writers also tended to come from that same milieu—how else could they genuinely channel his voice? And so the writers' room on *Your Show of Shows* and on *Caesar's Hour* was soon full-up with Jewish liberals from New York: Larry Gelbart, who would go on to write for *M*A*S*H*; Mel Brooks, who would go on to create *Get Smart*; Carl Reiner, who would do *The Dick Van Dyke Show* and *The New Dick Van Dyke Show*; Mel Tolkin, who would be a story editor on *All in the Family*; Woody Allen—yes, that Woody Allen; Lucille Kallen, one of Hollywood's first successful female writers; Sheldon Keller, who would work on *The Dick Van Dyke Show* and *M*A*S*H* and produce the television version of *The Odd Couple*; Gary Belkin, who would write for

The Carol Burnett Show; Michael Stewart, who would write the book for the Broadway musicals *Bye Bye Birdie* and *Hello, Dolly!*; and future legendary playwright Neil Simon.

The writers' room was a repository of New York Jews: "I don't think there was ever a group so aware of their own psychological problems and others', and that awareness found its way into the writing," Gelbart explained. "We zeroed in on the rough spots in life—there's no fun in happiness. Bliss is boring. Fortunately, none of us had that in abundance. One of the great engines for comedy is ambivalence, where you attack parts of something—or somebody—the worst parts of the human experience which, in total, you really love."[7] Here Gelbart lays bare the truth about comedy—in order for comedy to work, you have to love the target of the comedy.

That ambivalence toward the human experience—and toward certain basic American principles—would later lead many of these writers to become instrumental critics of the status quo, infusing their programming with openly political messages designed to subvert the social structure. Growing up unhappy in small, cramped tenement houses in the Bronx tends to leave a significant imprint on people. It certainly did on these creators. It would leave an even bigger imprint on the next generation.

THE HONEYMOONERS (1955–1956): BLUE-COLLAR CLASS CONFLICT

I met with Leonard Stern, the creator of *The Honeymooners* and producer of *Get Smart*, in a penthouse apartment off of Wilshire Boulevard. This is expensive territory, and his apartment looked it—he had letters by Jefferson and other founding fathers framed and posted on the walls. Stern, a distinguished-looking elderly gentleman with a white goatee, greeted me warmly, then handed me a copy of *Mad Libs*—the fill-in-the-blank word game he invented—as well as a copy of a book of idiotic network censorship letters playfully titled *A Martian Wouldn't Say That*.

Stern was born in New York and attended college at NYU. While he was there, he started writing jokes for Milton Berle, who embraced the young student. Soon, Stern was writing stand-up for comedians all across

New York, even writing a movie for Abbott and Costello. He then moved west to California to pursue opportunities as a screenwriter.

Stern was a victim of his own success, however. Berle's incredible drawing power put a significant commercial dent in the Hollywood moviemaking industry—people wanted to stay home and watch Berle rather than go out to the flicks—forcing the moviemakers to cut back production until they were virtually at a standstill. "I couldn't get any work out here," Stern recalled. Then his agent informed him that he could get a slot as a staff writer for *The Jackie Gleason Show*.

Stern already knew Gleason. "When I first started," Stern told me, "I was a joke writer, and Jackie was one of the many comics in New York always looking for material and meeting with writers." They met in Los Angeles. That social relationship paid dividends (as it so often does in Hollywood). Stern stayed on the show for four years, where he introduced the long-form television sketch-cum-show, *The Honeymooners*, which ran a grand total of thirty-nine classic episodes in 1955 and 1956.

The Honeymooners centered on Ralph and Alice Kramden (Gleason and Audrey Meadows), a bus driver and his wife. Ralph was a victim of capitalism, a guy always attempting to get rich quick. Alice was a tough wife, willing to take Ralph's rage but also willing to give it back to him double. The Kramdens' upstairs neighbors, the Nortons, were better off. Ed Lillywhite Norton (Art Carney) was a sewer worker and Ralph's best friend; his wife, Trixie (Joyce Randolph), was Alice's best friend.

Of all of Gleason's sketches, why did Stern choose to expand *The Honeymooners*? "First of all, family set up. Husband and a wife. And another couple. It was more traditional," he said. So far, no surprises. Then Stern explained why the Kramdens really appealed to him. "It had enormous, to me, potential because there was no working-class show on television."

Poverty on television was, Stern believed, a necessary component of reality that simply wasn't being reflected. "I didn't think there was anything representing reality of most of the watchers," said Stern. "Focus on the working class always appealed to me."

Stern particularly disliked television's initial elitist focus. "Television was infinitely esoteric in the beginning," he averred.[8] That certainly wasn't what Stern and Gleason were looking for. "In my part of Brooklyn," said Gleason, "we had a million Ralph Kramdens."[9] That was reality.

"*The Honeymooners*," Stern summed up, "was a class distinction."

Stern's class distinction in *The Honeymooners* paved the way for an entire line of comedies focusing on blue-collar workers: *The Honeymooners* turned into *All in the Family*, which turned into *Roseanne*. The evolution of the blue-collar comedy demonstrates the liberal attitude toward the lower-middle class: Stern treated them sympathetically in *The Honeymooners*; Lear treated them with acidic derision in *All in the Family*, since the left perceived such urban dockworker types as racist homophobes in the 1970s; and by the late 1980s, the left was attempting once again to reach out to blue-collar workers in an attempt to convert the newfound Reagan Republicans.

THE DICK VAN DYKE SHOW (1961–1966): THE PERFECT KENNEDY LIBERALISM

The Dick Van Dyke Show is perhaps the most perfect sitcom ever broadcast. Dick Van Dyke as Rob Petrie and Mary Tyler Moore as Laura Petrie are the most captivating sitcom couple in television history. The program is easily the most universally worshipped comedy out there among television's creators. But there was more at work with *The Dick Van Dyke Show* than simple laughs. If one show ever embodied an entire era, this was it.

While *The Dick Van Dyke Show* is now perceived as a conservative show, it was in fact quite liberal for its time. It took the liberal (and morally praiseworthy) position on race relations; it reflected the nascent feminism of the time. It gleamed with that Kennedy-era optimism.

Rob wore a perfect JFK hairdo. Laura wore a perfect Jackie Kennedy hairdo. Rose Marie played Sally Rogers, a single career woman who, along with obviously Jewish writer Buddy Sorrell (Morey Amsterdam), constituted the multicultural writers' room for a Sid Caesar knockoff (played to hysterical effect by Carl Reiner).

The moving force behind the show was Carl Reiner, who was both a star and creator of the show. Reiner was another Bronx-born Jew who got his break in Sid Caesar's writers' room. Reiner grew up in a lower-class neighborhood; his parents paid $22 a month in rent, and moved when the rent went up to $33 a month. His father, who was a watchmaker, was a self-made man in the traditional American mold; "my father would have killed himself rather than go on [relief during the Great Depression]," Reiner said. Reiner himself graduated from high school, then began working in a machine shop.

He broke out of that rut by taking acting classes with FDR's Works Progress Administration (WPA). Unlike his dad, he was perfectly willing to take advantage of government aid. That willingness launched his career.[10] "I owed my show business career to two people," Reiner later wrote. "Charlie Reiner, who prodded me to sign up for the free drama class, and Franklin Delano Roosevelt, who established the NRA, the National Recovery Act, and the WPA."[11]

One particular episode was deliberately and hilariously geared toward liberalism on racial issues. The third season of the show opened with an episode titled "That's My Boy??" which centered on Rob's paranoid belief that his newborn child may in fact have been switched at the hospital for the baby of Mr. and Mrs. Peters. Sheldon Leonard, producer of the show and another New York–born Jew, insisted that the payoff at the end of the episode would have the Peters walking through the door—and they would be black. Bill Persky, a writer on the show, later reflected, "We didn't think it would be possible." The NAACP took a look at the script before it aired, and signed off on it. Procter & Gamble, one of the show's key advertisers, didn't. George Giroux called up Leonard and told him, "We're frightened." Benton & Bowles also called up and tried to nix the script. Leonard talked them back from the ledge. Finally, CBS tried to reject the script wholesale. Leonard told them to shove it.

When it came to the climactic scene, the creators had to decide how to play it. Director John Rich hit on the strategy: "We felt the only way the show would work was having Rob give control of the situation to the black man. What scared us was having Rob ask the black man, 'Why didn't you tell me on the phone?'—the exact question the audience would ask. The answer was, 'And miss the expression on your face?' That was the key. It gave control of the moment to the black man." Rich wanted to make the black couple look good, so he held out for the best-looking couple he could find. He told them to stand and wait when they entered the Petries' home. Mary Tyler Moore recalled, "The audience went crazy." Van Dyke said it was the biggest laugh in the history of the show.[12]

It wasn't just Leonard who wanted to push boundaries. Mary Tyler

Moore decided to take a stand with regard to her attire. "I immediately caused a stir in my style of dress. I wore pants," Moore wrote in her autobiography. "TV wives didn't do that . . . here again, television hadn't quite caught up with the times."[13] It was while working on *The Dick Van Dyke Show* that Moore met and married Grant Tinker, the future NBC head and cofounder of MTM Enterprises, which would be responsible for many of the biggest shows of the 1970s and 1980s.

As always, those involved in the making of the show cited its realism. "I was writing about what I *knew*," said Carl Reiner. That was especially true with regard to including Rob Petrie's work life in the show, a new and fascinating television development. "I was breaking ground without knowing it. But that's why it probably worked, because it was one person's reality. And if you do one person's reality, there's a pureness about it."[14]

Reiner's focus on reality forced him to bump up against the censors repeatedly. The censors decided to crack down on one episode, titled "Where Do I Come From?" in which Rob and Laura's son, Richie, asks the grave question. "They wouldn't accept the fact that when the son asked, 'Where did I come from?' they actually told him, 'You come from Mama's belly,'" fumed Reiner. "And I heard: 'No, no, no, no.' I argued for days, and if I'd had -----*you money*, I would've left, I was so mad."[15]

This was the early 1960s, so Reiner lost; his vanguardism went unappreciated. But the rage he displayed at that relatively meaningless incident of censorship forebode the future of politics on television: When the gates opened, strident liberalism would come marching through.

GET SMART (1965–1970): THE STUPID INTELLIGENCE COMMUNITY

Mel Brooks started off as a young writer on *Your Show of Shows*. A poor Jewish kid in New York, he made good by using a key schmatta salesman technique—bugging people until they buy something from you. He met Sid Caesar through a mutual friend, then shadowed Caesar everywhere. "He was funny and ingenious and he liked my type of humor, so he hung around me," Caesar remembered.[16] Soon, Brooks was hired.

Like everyone else at *Your Show of Shows*, Brooks was a liberal. He brought that liberalism to bear when he created *Get Smart* (1965–1970), a parody of James Bond spy agencies, starring Don Adams as Agent Maxwell Smart—the kind of guy who has a phone in his shoe. According to Brooks, the theme of the show was "the earnest stupidity of organizations like the CIA. I would say honest and earnest stupidity. They want to do a good job. But they don't hire enough [multicultural people]. They hire too many WASPs and they get too much white-bread thinking." Naturally, he followed up that revelation with a string of invective against the current CIA: "They're still out of touch. In a strange way, they're still kind of supermen, kind of SS troops: We're blond and the best and everyone else should be incinerated. . . . They don't know right from wrong. That's what makes a satire of these government bureaus really funny."[17]

Brooks said that *Get Smart* was supposed to channel feelings of rage against the government over the Vietnam War into laughter at the government. Buck Henry, cocreator of the program, agreed; the idea, he said, was that audiences could "see government espionage for what it really is, an idiotic enterprise glamorized by Hollywood."[18]

Dan Melnick, the cofounder of Talent Associates, a production company responsible for the leftist social-issue drama *East Side/West Side* starring George C. Scott, originally came up with the idea for *Get Smart*. Melnick wanted the show to be a social satire. ABC was so put off by the pilot—one executive reportedly stated that it was "dirty and un-American"—that Melnick, along with Brooks and Henry, had to go back to the drawing board.[19] What they came back with was much more innocuous. It was so innocuous, according to producer Leonard Stern, that Melnick brought back a revised draft with the statement, "If you don't like this, you can have your money back." ABC hated it, and Melnick gave the money back. Eventually, NBC picked it up.[20]

When I spoke with writer Allan Burns, who worked on the show before getting his biggest breaks with Leonard Stern at *Room 222* and then *The Mary Tyler Moore Show*, he chuckled at Brooks's interpretation of the show as true social satire. "Obviously it was a CIA-type organization which is very inept, but if anybody had ever said, 'This is a parody of the ineptness of the CIA,' I would have been surprised because that's sort of post-show thinking. I think Mel sounds like he's trying to make it a little smarter than it was."[21] Rather, the show was supposed to parody the country's obsession with spies in shows like *The Man from U.N.C.L.E.* and *I Spy.*

Stern was even more forgiving: "It may have evolved into [a Cold War parody], yes. I thought it originally was a spoof of James Bond, and that's why it didn't work well initially in England, because they considered James Bond a spoof."[22]

Whether or not Stern believed there was social messaging inherent in *Get Smart*, his own shows were chock-full of such messages. *I'm Dickens, He's Fenster,* a series about two construction workers that lasted for one season on ABC, "had a lot of social content," according to Stern.[23] Stern's next show, *He & She,* was a precursor to the urban shift of the early 1970s—but Stern hit a bit early with it, in 1967. The show starred Richard Benjamin and Paula Prentiss as a married couple; he was a cartoonist (as was Stern in real life), and she was a social worker. They lived in a New York apartment, and the upper-middle-class urban milieu and attitudes were purely Democratic. The pilot of the show opened with Prentiss trying to stop the immigration service from deporting an old man; naturally, she succeeded.

"I think it was one of the most enjoyable experiences I had, a very rewarding show that did well," Stern recalled, "but we came after *Green Acres*, and we were totally incompatible."[24] Allan Burns, who wrote on that show, too, remembered that the show was killed by its urban sensibility and rural timeslot. "It was such a good show, and we couldn't understand how a show of this quality could be canceled after a year."[25]

THE SMOTHERS BROTHERS COMEDY HOUR (1967–1969): 'NAM AND 'SHROOMS

Take two clean-cut brothers with a comedy act and give them a variety show. What could go wrong?

Everything.

Tommy and Dick Smothers were a pair of liberals who decided to use their newfound slot on television to press the liberal agenda in a way nobody had ever tried before. The show got on the air because Abe Lastfogel of the William Morris Agency approached CBS chairman Bill Paley and told him he needed to target younger audiences. Paley bought it, and bought the Smothers, two of Lastfogel's clients. Of course, CBS's desperation had something to do with it—*The Smothers Brothers Comedy Hour* was a last-ditch attempt to counter the juggernaut that was *Bonanza*.[26]

Originally, according to writer and producer Ernest Chambers, Tommy, who would become the more vocal of the two brothers on politics, "knew nothing about any social issues . . . he was a pothead folksinger." But the writers began to educate him. Smothers himself told author Allan Neuwirth, "We didn't become politically conscious until that show happened, during the mid 1960s. . . . When we got the greenlight for the variety show, we wanted to be *relevant*." Allan Blye, one of the key writers on the show, helped push the show to the left: "They didn't just do political satire—they satirized the right by *exhibiting* the right."

Soon enough, the brothers were embroiled in a censorship battle with the network. They wanted to push the envelope further and further in terms of content. Their first full-scale run-in occurred when the brothers wanted to host Communist songwriter Pete Seeger, who would sing "Waist Deep in the Big Muddy," a criticism of the Vietnam War. Prior to the show, the network received five thousand letters of protest. They censored the song but let Seeger on the program.[27]

Things only grew worse from there. The show embraced the drug culture; they hired a comedienne named Leigh French to host a recurring sketch called "Tea With Goldie," in which French played Goldie O'Keefe, the host of a pre-Oprah talk show. In that role, she openly pushed the Haight-Ashbury pot lifestyle. She opened the sketch with the pun, "Hi! And glad of it." She told audiences that she had gotten rid of "unsightly roaches"—then said thank you to audience members who had sent her their roaches.[28]

In the end, it wasn't the drugs that did in *The Smothers Brothers*—it was their vocal opposition to the Vietnam War. As they got bigger, they got more and more strident. Said Blye, "At one point I said, 'God, here we are. We're number one.' And Tommy said, 'Yeah. Well, now we've gotta start hitting a little harder.' Then it became less disguised, let's put it that way. And more on the nose . . . and being on the nose was less effective, in my eyes."[29] Their sketches were anything but subtle. When radical leftists rioted at the 1968 Democratic National Convention and were beaten back by police, *The Smothers Brothers* ran a sketch with Harry Belafonte singing "Don't Stop the Carnival" as they showed footage from the riots.[30]

Mike Dann, VP of programming at the time at CBS, told me the show was "very sophisticated stuff for teenagers, and very dirty, a dirty show . . . the kids just exploded for it." Dann also said that he had to cancel the show because of pressure from President Johnson. "I was forced to cancel *The Smothers Brothers* at one point because they were so anti-Vietnam,"[31] he told me.

The show was short-lived—it only lasted from 1967 to 1969—but it opened the door to what would come next: the era of open leftism masquerading as entertainment.

LAUGH-IN (1968-1973): SOCKIN' IT TO THE RIGHT

George Schlatter is a jolly fellow, a comedian among comedians, with offices off of Beverly Boulevard in Beverly Hills. Walk inside, and you're in showbiz central. There are signed pictures of every conceivable celebrity, a framed invitation to Nixon's inauguration, pictures of Schlatter, solidly built and wearing a thick Vandyke, alongside stars like Goldie Hawn, mugging it up with the cast of his show, *Laugh-In*. It isn't tough to tell Schlatter's politics—he's got books by Al Franken and Chris Matthews lining his walls—and one of Ann Coulter's books. On his desk, he's got a "Bushisms" calendar, as well as an unopened "Bush in a Box" set of Bushisms.

If his office didn't tell me where Schlatter stood on politics, the man himself wasn't shy. "I miss political commentary on television," he told me. "When the funniest thing on television is Sean Hannity and his impression of Gilbert Gottfried, you realize what a sad state we're in. And some of the funniest stuff now is news. Bill O'Reilly, the loofa king, sexually harassing an employee on the phone at two o'clock in the morning, offering to bring his bony ass over there and play in the shower with a loofa, that's as funny as anything I ever did. Rush Limbaugh, this balloon buffoon, who should have a cable up his ass being floated over the Macy's day parade, taking this moral position as the head of the Republican Party, I find that to be hysterical. You have this man, this convicted junkie, who sent his housekeeper out to score pills, is a moral leader of the Republican Party? Just stop it. I find Rush Limbaugh funny. And Ann Coulter, of course. We would have no need for the c-word without Ann Coulter. That word would fade out of existence. And Laura Ingraham I like a lot—how a woman can live with no lips? I know them. I find them all amusing. You know Michael Savage? You know what his real name is?"

"Michael Weiner," I answered.

"Not Weiner, *Weener*," he guffawed. "Michael Weener. And now you have Glenn Beck, with these two bright blue contact lenses that give him these blue kind of deer-in-the-headlight surprise look, I find him really amusing. It's almost too easy to make fun of them. Making fun of Sean Hannity is like making fun of a cripple in a crosswalk. And Rush Limbaugh? Come on. I picture someone behind him with a pump, stick a fork in him and he'd deflate." Schlatter came back to Coulter, who he obviously found fascinating: "Ann Coulter could be one of the main reasons we should legalize abortion but make it retroactive. This salesperson for bulimia, who can open a beer can with an elbow, she only weighs nine pounds—I'm all for freedom of speech but I draw the line there."

Schlatter's politics were no different when he produced *Laugh-In*, a hit variety show that revolutionized both political content and style on television, holding down its slot on NBC for five seasons and finishing number one for the first two seasons. The show, starring Dan Rowan and Dick Martin, a pair of comedians, was a quick-cut festival, with sketches running one after another, *bam-bam-bam-bam*, with no letup. "*Laugh-In* was a pure television show," Schlatter related. "It was a combination of burlesque, of vaudeville, of theater, of motion picture, of circus, of carnival."

It was also a political festival. "The sixties was the Vietnam War, the pill, the Beatles, and *Laugh-In* . . . you could take the sixties in rewind and say that's what shaped the sixties," said Schlatter. "The pill changed everything; the war changed everything and made us aware of our vulnerability and made us aware of our guilt for having gone in there and destroyed a nation just because we could. . . . If we were on the air now, boy, we would be cutting it up real big, the fact that we never learn. This monosyllabic brain donor took us into a war in Iraq and we bought it. We've got to defeat them, right? Weapons of mass destruction. He was the weapon of mass destruction." It's difficult—and useless—to attack this much fatuity piece by piece. But this monologue gives an idea of how *Laugh-In* was structured: it was so much, so fast, that no matter how much was unfunny or offensive, the sheer volume overwhelmed the senses.

Schlatter insisted that the show was balanced in its politics. "Jokes on the left and then on the right." Evidence of that supposed balance was the presence of Paul Keyes, one of Nixon's joke writers. "We did not agree with Paul Keyes at all," Schlatter said, "but he was a very effective writer . . . he gave us that serious right-wing point of view that we would use to balance the political comment on the show." Keyes's greatest triumph was Schlatter's biggest regret—Keyes got Nixon to come on the show during the 1968 election in an attempt to cast off his stodgy image. Nixon appeared for approximately four seconds, questioningly uttered the show's catchphrase—"Sock it to meee?"—and that was that. But the appearance apparently had a major effect on the course of the 1968 election. "They said it elected him," Schlatter lamented, "and I've had to live with that ever since."[32]

ROOM 222 (1969–1974): THE LAUGHLESS COMEDY

"You must be Ben," said Ann Reynolds as she welcomed me into her home. "Gene will be back any second." Gene Reynolds's house was a cozy one-story colonial-style home in the Hollywood Hills off Sunset Boulevard. As we waited for Gene to return from a lunch with some of his business friends, his wife regaled me with stories about Gene's television career—and colorful commentary about her strong dislike for the Bush administration.

When Reynolds returned, he brought out a folder of pictures from his early days in Hollywood. Reynolds had been around since the beginning—the *beginning* of the beginning. After starring in several films as a child actor, he began to work on the other side of the camera. He eventually landed a job in casting at NBC, then parlayed that into a directing slot.

The idea for *Room 222* came from a program instructor he had at Poinsettia Playground in Los Angeles. "I made him a history teacher at a high school that was integrated, and that he would be black," Reynolds told me. "And it would be the first time not in a comedy show or a cop show that you had a serious lead who was black."[33]

The time was ripe for this sort of television show. A spate of movies about urban schools—many of them with black leads—had exploded onto the American landscape, asking challenging questions about race and the efficacy of the educational system (*To Sir, with Love* with Sidney Poitier being the most obvious example of the genre). The Kennedy glow had dissipated with his assassination, and liberalism had moved into heavier and darker territory. Race relations was the issue of the day.

But race relations was no laughing matter. That's why unlike prior comedies, *Room 222* was a dramedy, perhaps the first of its kind. There weren't many open laughs. There also wasn't any interracial sexual tension on the show. There were, however, lots of topical issues covered, from Vietnam to gender roles to racism. All were covered from a typical Democratic perspective—tolerance, understanding, and multiculturalism always won the day.

Reynolds worked with two of the people who would become heavy hitters in the industry: James L. Brooks and Allan Burns. Burns signed on as a writer after Brooks recruited him and ended up running the show after Reynolds was ousted. "We put on a show that had an equal number of blacks and whites," said Brooks. That, Brooks said, was a priority.[34] The network's big problem with the show sprang from its take on race—its sincerity made it unfunny. It had to be that way—Reynolds felt that "because [the main character] was black, it was important that we didn't make him a clown."[35]

"The networks weren't [looking for social content]. The writers were," Burns explained. "The writers were leading the networks at that point because they wanted to write stuff that was more socially conscious. . . . You really had to fight them on it."[36]

Despite the network battles, Reynolds drew enormous pride from the product. "I know that *Room 222* turned a corner," Reynolds said to me.[37] In racial terms, it clearly did. More than that, it emboldened the creators of the show for their next steps: *M*A*S*H* for Reynolds, and *The Mary Tyler Moore Show* for Brooks and Burns.

ALL IN THE FAMILY (1971–1983): FLUSHING CONSERVATISM DOWN THE TOILET

The opening episode of *All in the Family* featured a warning from CBS: "The program you are about to see is *All in the Family.* It seeks to throw a humorous spotlight on our frailties, prejudices, and concerns. By making them a source of laughter we hope to show, in a mature fashion, just how absurd they really are." Then the warning disappeared as, for the first time on network television, the audience heard a loud and sustained toilet flush.[38]

"In the beginning—of television comedy—in the beginning was the word," Larry Gelbart later wrote, celebrating *All in the Family.* "And the word was *Don't.* Don't show life as it is, don't show people as they are, and don't, under any circumstances, allow anyone to talk in any way that resembles how anyone actually talks. Polish 'em up, button 'em down. The less human, the better. . . . And then it happened. One amazing night, Archie Bunker went to the can. And from off-camera—could it be true?—we heard him flush! The gurgling of the plumbing at 704 Hauser reverberates to this day; flushed with a vengeance forever were network and sponsor timidity about human imperfection and all manner of hypocritical detritus. The seat went down and the lid was off."[39]

Never before or since has a show so clearly stated its objective: the mocking of traditional values, the shocking of the bourgeois, the full frontal attack on authority. And never before had a show so quickly established its style: loud and vulgar.

If that wasn't enough, *All in the Family*'s theme song, "Those Were the Days," made the target of the show even more obvious. "Girls were girls and men were men," Archie Bunker and his wife, Edith, warbled every week. "Mister we could use a man / Like Herbert Hoover again. / Didn't need no welfare state, / Everybody pulled his weight / . . . Those were the days." This has all the subtly of a frying pan in the face. The theme song clearly suggests that conservatives live in the past. It suggests that conservatism is backward-looking, nostalgic, fearful of change, and unintellectual in the Lionel Trilling sense—a series of "irritable mental gestures which seek to resemble ideas." It is scornful, caustic, a liberal's gritty picture of what conservatism constitutes—and it set a pattern for portrayal of conservatives on television that continues to this day.

All in the Family was a liberal breakthrough, and it was meant to be. Archie Bunker was the stand-in for conservatives, a moron with a loud mouth and prejudices up the wazoo. His son-in-law, Meathead, was the stand-in for liberals, a stand-up guy who fought Archie's narrowmindedness at every turn. Only rarely would Archie score a point—and even then, it was usually at the expense of Meathead's laziness or loafing, not his politics. *All in the Family* was a new kind of show for a new time. It was a seminal point in the launch of the hip, urban programming toward which television had been aspiring. When CBS greenlit *All in the Family* in order to reach out to supposedly more valuable urban audiences, it opened the door to the total takeover of liberal television.

The show also recast the television vision of the blue collar worker. In *The Honeymooners*, the blue collar guy had been the hero, the Don Quixote in search of the buck. In *The Beverly Hillbillies*, the hicks had been the protagonists, and their lifestyle was contrasted favorably with the rich and famous lifestyle surrounding them. Now, for the first time, the blue-collar guy was the villain, and his son-in-law, the aspiring graduate student, was the hero. While *All in the Family* had the trappings of the lower-class comedy, it was actually an elitist approach to politics.

There was a reason for this. In 1968, poorer, blue-collar workers voted disproportionately for George Wallace and Richard Nixon, in contravention of their history of voting Democrat. By the time *All in the Family* hit the air, liberal anger at the lower-class voter was rising to the surface; the true liberals, in this new view, populated the college campuses, as Mike did. This was a groundbreaking shift, and it paved the way for hostile depictions of lower-class whites for the next two decades, until *Roseanne* broke the barrier again.

The show clearly reflected the politics of those who created it. Norman Lear, who ran in the same social circles as the liberals who populated the comedy writers' rooms of shows like *Your Show of Shows*, was a product of his background. He experienced anti-Semitism in the army, and he was reflexively interested in infusing his social responsibility in his programming. *All in the Family*, he said, gave him the opportunity to infuse social messaging, and he took advantage—just as he did in all of his work. "They all had a great deal of social awareness," he said of his shows. "I'm a serious man. . . . Life is a serious matter. But I see it through a prism that finds comedy in anything. A gift from the universe."

Comedy, in other words, was a vehicle for Lear's politics. That comes through in almost every episode. One of Lear's favorite episodes was "The Draft Dodger." "The Vietnam episode was a Christmas episode," Lear recalled. "[Archie] invited a friend, and Mike invited a friend. Mike's friend had gone to Canada to escape the draft, he was a draft-dodger. And when Archie learns this at the dinner table, he wants him out of there. . . . There was an explosive scene."[40] The scene in question is indeed explosive—and as always, it puts Archie squarely in the wrong. "He owes explanations to the Army, the Navy, the Marine Corps, the Commander in Chief, the President," Archie shouts at the draft-dodger.

"Will you put the flag away?" shouts Meathead (Rob Reiner). "It's Christmas, not the Fourth of July."

"I wrote to the president about it, Mr. Bunker," says the draft dodger, David. "He just couldn't come up with as many reasons for killing people as I could for not killing them."

"Well, what do you know about that?" asks Archie.

The draft dodger offers to leave. "Certainly he's gotta go!" says Archie.

"Look, Arch," yells Meathead, "what David did took a lotta guts. When the hell are you gonna admit that the war was wrong?!"

"I ain't talking about the war. I don't want to talk about that rotten, lousy war no more. I'm talking about something else! And what he done was wrong. Certainly he'll go! What do you think, the whole people in this country can say whether or not they wanna go to war? You couldn't get a decent war off the ground that way." The audience laughs at Archie's stupidity, but Archie keeps going. "If all the young people would say no . . . sure they would, cause they don't wanna get killed. That's why we leave it to the Congress, cause them old crocks ain't gonna get killed. And they're gonna do the right thing and get behind the president and vote yes."

It's obvious how the scene is going to turn out. Archie has made the dumbest possible case against draft dodging. He has not spoken of the duty of citizens of the United States to follow the law. He has not defended the war. He has not talked about the duty of soldiers to one another. He has instead presented the liberal case—that young people are dying for selfish old people, and that the war is wrong.

And that's precisely how the scene turns out, of course—in particularly contrived fashion. The Gold Star father pipes up. "I understand how you feel, Arch. My kid hated the war, too. But he did what he thought he had to do. And David here did what he thought he had to do. But David's alive to share Christmas dinner with us. And if Steve were here he'd wanna sit down with him. And that's what I wanna do." Then he shakes the draft dodger's hand.

Archie is not an unsympathetic character in this scene, which is a testament to Carroll O'Connor's achievement as an actor. While Archie is never wholly sympathetic, he is at least partially sympathetic, since he does have a heart when it comes to his daughter and his wife. But he is the villain of the piece, and he is an ignorant villain. Ultraliberal O'Connor deliberately played him that way: "Writing and rehearsing and performing a TV episode in which Archie Bunker confronted a defector from the Vietnam War, I was able to satirize, albeit grimly, the mixed emotions of that uptight majority. Archie was a prototype: his variants were, and are, on all levels of American life, the highest, the lowest and the in-between. They are all bound to the heroic vision of America, though not as Duke Wayne was bound to it in perfect belief; they are all bound by a fearful apprehension about national life: that to analyze its weaknesses and contradictions is to destroy it, to gaze steadily at the mythology of it is the only way to preserve it. Nothing new in this; it is known as patriotism."[41]

Archie's foil on the show, Michael Stivic, whom Archie not-so-affectionately terms Meathead, is a righteous liberal living off his conservative father-in-law. The role of Meathead was filled by Carl Reiner's son, Rob, who was just as liberal as his pop. Rob got his start in the business as a writer for *The Smothers Brothers*, then got his job on *All in the Family* because of his dad's reputation in the business. Rob would go on to direct the liberal fantasy *The American President* (written by *The West Wing* author Aaron Sorkin, whom we'll discuss shortly), as well as hits including *This Is Spinal Tap*, *Sleepless in Seattle*, and *The Princess Bride*. Reiner is the definition of a Hollywood limousine liberal—in a *Vanity Fair* piece on Hollywood/Democratic Party bigwig Stephen Bing, Reiner remarked on Bing's obviously down-to-earth sensibilities: "Name anyone else with his wealth who has only one maid. You'd be hard-pressed."[42] He'd also go on to use his position in Hollywood as a club to wield against conservatives across the country; in October 2010, just before the historic Tea Party wave, Reiner appeared on Bill Maher's show, ranting, "They're selling stupidity and ignorance. . . . My fear is that the Tea Party gets a charismatic leader, because all they're selling is fear and anger, and that's all Hitler sold."[43]

The politics of the show are clear, and they reflect the viewpoints of its creators and stars: it is unswervingly liberal, and perverts the conservative position in order to reach the conclusion it seeks. That's how Lear tackled almost every issue, from homosexuality to abortion to race. Only *All in the Family* could dare portray Archie as a boob for dressing in a suit to write a letter to the president of the United States. The hatred for Archie's positions drips from the screen; in fact, as Archie became more popular, his character was moderated to accommodate his popularity.

"I think it's remarkable that it was able to touch forbidden topics at the time," the show's longtime director, Paul Bogart, told me. "When Carroll said something outrageously stupid, Rob would sound a reasonable reply. So it was very balanced. . . ."[44] Balanced from a leftist point of view—the left always won.

And the show had reach and impact because it was a comedy. Bud Yorkin, the co-creator of the show along with Lear, put it well, "People, in my opinion, if you lecture to them about what abortion is, or what gay is, nobody's going to watch that. When they're *laughing* . . . when it's all over, they'll say, 'Gee, I guess the change of life is not a bad thing. I can go home and make love to my wife.' "[45]

The proof of the show's liberalism is in the pudding. In 1999, Bill Clinton gave Lear the National Medal of Arts, stating, "Norman Lear has held up a mirror to American society and changed the way we look at it."[46] Clinton had a lot to thank Lear for. After all, it was Lear who helped legitimize draft dodging.

THE MARY TYLER MOORE SHOW (1970–1977): LIKE A FISH NEEDS A BICYCLE

A once-divorced out-of-work actress. Her once-divorced television honcho husband. Two of television's top writers. Put them together and what do you get? Television's most vocal feminist show.

Launched at the same time as *All in the Family*, *The Mary Tyler Moore Show* was a phenomenon. It followed in the footsteps of *He & She*, which was a protofeminist liberal program, but it went one step further, embracing the memes of the radical feminist movement. Women no longer needed to be married. They no longer needed children. They merely needed an occasional boyfriend and a solid job to find fulfillment.

The show's generation began when Grant Tinker approached James L. Brooks and Allan Burns while they were working on *Room 222*. He wanted to create a show for his wife, Mary Tyler Moore. Moore had been out of television for some time, focusing on her failing film career. Tinker thought she ought to get back into the medium. Together with his wife, he formed MTM Enterprises, which would go on to produce many of the biggest comedies and dramas of the 1970s and 1980s, including *The Bob Newhart Show, Lou Grant, Hill Street Blues, Remington Steele*, and *St. Elsewhere*.

Brooks and Burns were the perfect choices for MTM's Moore-starring launch project. Tinker had worked with them on *Room 222* as a production executive, so he knew them—they were part of the liberal clique. Tinker knew that they were of like mind creatively and politically. Burns got his start in the industry, after attending the University of Oregon, when he came back to Hollywood and got a job as a page at NBC. He worked on shows ranging from Steve Allen's show to *The Colgate Comedy Hour* (where he met a young writer named Norman Lear). After a series of career maneuvers, he ended up writing greeting cards for Hallmark, Gibson, and American Greetings. One day, Burns was watching television and saw *The Rocky and Bullwinkle Show*, and decided he could do that. He walked into Jay Ward's studio, happened to bump into him, and his career was on its way. (He actually invented the character Captain Crunch, but had no rights to it—"I weep every time I go past a display of General Mills food," he told me.) Burns worked his way up the ranks, working with Leonard Stern on *He & She* and *Get Smart* and working with Brooks and Reynolds on *Room 222*. That's when he met Tinker.

Burns is openly political. "I think television can be a little ahead of where social values are," Burns told me. "I don't mean to sound overly poetic about it, but I do think that the consciousness of people writing and producing television kind of sets the standards for the moral values of the country."[47]

Brooks is as liberal as Burns. He is an outspoken opponent of big business, small towns, and a huge fan of New York.[48] His career path was similar to Burns's; he started off as an usher at CBS, then moved to Los Angeles. He met Burns on *Room 222*, then Tinker. Unlike Burns, however, Brooks says that he attempts to avoid channeling his politics into his work. "I'm very wary of a social conscience being what is behind the writing," he told an interviewer in January 2003.[49] Regardless of whether Brooks tries to inject his politics into his work, he clearly does—his television résumé is a who's-who list of liberal shows.

Tinker and Moore, along with Brooks and Burns, decided that the show would center on a divorced woman working as a journalist in Minneapolis. "I think every comedy writer wanted to do a show about divorce," Burns told interviewer Allan Neuwirth, "because probably two thirds of the comedy writers in town had *been* divorced, and wanted to write about their own experiences. . . . We were *just* ahead of the wave that was going to become feminism—*women's lib*, as they called it in those days—where women didn't feel the need to apologize for not having been married."

But when they pitched the show idea to CBS, the network balked in colorful fashion. "Well, we sat there," Burns said, "in a room full of divorced New York Jews with mustaches and heard them say that there are four things Americans don't like: New Yorkers, divorced people, men with mustaches and Jews. . . . At that point Jim and I really did want to quit the show."[50] They didn't quit; they just changed the premise. Now Mary had almost been married, but broke up with her boyfriend.

The network presentation went well. This time, Brooks and Burns created a written presentation for the decision makers. "The whole presentation runs twenty-one pages," Tinker wrote, "and ends: *This series . . . is clearly about* one *person living in and coping with the world of the*

1970's . . . tough enough in itself . . . even tougher when you're thirty, single and female . . . [when] you find yourself the only female in an all-male newsroom."[51]

The concept, in short, was unmitigated feminism. And that's how the series turned out. Mary stayed single for the entire seven-year run of the show. Explained Burns, "I know it meant a lot to women. That it was OK for a woman to be wanting a career, OK for a woman to be over thirty and unmarried . . ."[52]

Mary Tyler Moore was the first mainstream show to allow the new, sexually liberated woman out of the closet. In one episode, Mary's parents stay with her for a night, and she stays out; when they ask her where she's been, she tells them it's none of their business. Valerie Harper, who played Mary's best friend, Rhoda (and eventually achieved her own spin-off, *Rhoda*), took the show's messaging perfectly seriously—and she was the perfect feminist to channel that messaging. "I had been doing a lot of reading through the 1960s of Steinem, and Germaine Greer, the Australian feminist—*The Female Eunuch*—but really, the mother of us all, Betty Friedan," she told Neuwirth. "That *Feminine Mystique* was so wonderful, and so earth-shaking. . . . The writers felt it was very important. I think that's why the show has a real resonance about it."[53]

Ironically enough, Moore, the mother of television feminism, later came to regret her own life choices. "I was, like most working mothers, eager to join the movement and proclaim our right and our need to express ourselves, to be fulfilled and happy knowing that every ounce of our creativity was being used," she wrote in her autobiography. "And that it was possible to raise children at the same time. I no longer believe that."[54] That certainly wasn't the message promoted by *Mary Tyler Moore*.

The show's liberalism wasn't restricted to feminist issues. Many of its stars became powerful liberal spokespeople. Radical left actor Ed Asner, whom we'll discuss in the context of *Lou Grant*, gained his voice in *Mary Tyler Moore*. Betty White, who has been a screen icon for decades and who called Sarah Palin a "crazy bitch" in 2010, gained prominence on *Mary Tyler Moore*. Cloris Leachman, who recently posed in a 2009 People for the Ethical Treatment of Animals campaign wearing only lettuce, met the public gaze in *Mary Tyler Moore*.

Mary Tyler Moore is television's first modern comedy. *All in the Family* seems dated now, tied to the issues that were hot and the debates that raged during its tenure. *M*A*S*H* is inextricably intertwined with the Vietnam era. But *Mary Tyler Moore* was the first show to truly take advantage of its likable characters to infuse social messages that could convert viewers. If you liked Mary, you had to accept her active sex life. If you liked Rhoda, you had to accept the fact that she was thirty and unmarried and fine with it. There is a direct and purposeful line between *Mary Tyler Moore* and *Friends* and *Sex and the City*.

*M*A*S*H* (1972–1983): "THE WASTEFULNESS OF WAR"

*M*A*S*H* was one of the most successful series of all time, running an incredible eleven seasons, from 1972 to 1983. Its finale rated the highest of any episode of television in history, drawing an unbelievable 106 million viewers.[55] The show was far more of a drama than a comedy, though it obviously had its comedic moments; the creators of the show fought with fanatical if unsuccessful fervor to stop the network from inserting a laugh track in the show.

The show was based on a book by Richard Hooker and a movie based on the book, starring Donald Sutherland and Elliot Gould. The network offered Gene Reynolds the opportunity to produce the pilot of the series-to-be, and he leaped at it. The first writer he thought of was Ring Lardner Jr., who wrote the movie; Lardner wasn't available. Then Reynolds thought of one of his friends, who was living in Britain at the time: Larry Gelbart.

Gelbart, you'll remember, got his start in the writers' room at *Your Show of Shows*. I met him at his home in Beverly Hills—the front of the house was modest, but it stretched back seemingly forever, a testament to the successes television can bring. His father had been a barber, an immigrant from Latvia. At age fifteen, Gelbart came to California—and by fortuitous coincidence, his father ended up cutting Danny Thomas's hair. Thomas was a radio figure at the time (he would later go on to star in *Make Room for Daddy*), and Thomas met the young Gelbart, then hired him to write for his radio show. The rest was history. The bottom line: Gelbart grew up in the Los Angeles milieu, a full-throated liberal.

And he was the perfect pick to write *M*A*S*H*, since he had served in the army during the Korean War—as a member of Bob Hope's writing staff. "My memories of the place stood me in good stead when fate (and Fox) gave me the chance to tackle *M*A*S*H*," Gelbart wrote in his autobiography.[56]

Reynolds visited London and asked Gelbart to take on the project. "It was summertime or spring, and it was light late, so we'd go off to the park and sit on the benches in Highgate and dream up something happening in Korea about twelve thousand miles away."[57]

Reynolds and Gelbart were able to find a cast quickly, but they ended up short while looking for the man to play Hawkeye. An agent suggested Alan Alda, an idea at which Reynolds leaped. Gelbart and Reynolds and Alda sat down in the Beverly Wilshire Hotel bar. "So he came down and he met us, the day before we were going into rehearsal," Reynolds related. "And we talked for about an hour or two hours and he realized where our minds were: that we wanted to point out the wastefulness of war. And that was our signpost throughout all the time we did the show: the wastefulness of war."[58] This is one hell of a simplistic signpost—if wastefulness were the sum total of war, everyone would be a pacifist. But it's the kind of bumper-sticker liberalism that often animates television programs.

Alda was a perfect pick for Reynolds and Gelbart. Born Alphonso Joseph D'Abruzzo in the Bronx, his parents were both involved in show business (his mom was a former Miss New York). He was a member of the younger generation of liberals—he was born in 1936—and he embraced the new feminist and antiwar movements. Early in his career, he appeared on the hard-left variety show *That Was the Week That Was*. Later, he became a major supporter of the Equal Rights Amendment, winning acclaim from a *Boston Globe* columnist who called him "the quintessential Honorary Woman: a feminist icon."[59]

Much of the show's beauty sprang, no doubt, from the creative and political cohesion of the men behind it. Reynolds talked about the ease of "working with Gelbart and with my own sense of what the show wanted to say—and Gelbart had a very strong sense of ethics and morality and so forth—and so did Alda. . . . It would become the whole theme of a show or an episode."[60]

Gelbart described the mission of the show in exactly the same terms as Reynolds did: to point out that "the war was wasteful." His goal with the show, Gelbart told me, was to "make 'em think more than make 'em laugh. . . ."[61]

Richard Hooker (aka Richard Hornberger), the author of the original *M*A*S*H* bestseller, hated the show because he believed it had twisted the book into an antiwar diatribe. Gelbart admitted the validity of the criticism in his autobiography: "A writer once described the series as 'shrouded in a serious-minded liberal gloom.' We certainly tended to be more serious than the film."[62]

That serious liberalism came across in almost every episode. In the pilot episode, Hawkeye jokes, "Throw away all the guns and invite all the jokers from the North and the South in here for a cocktail party, last man standing on his feet at the end wins the war." In season three's "O.R.," Hawkeye is even more on the nose: "I just don't know why they're shooting at us. All we want to do is bring them democracy and white bread. Transplant the American dream. Freedom. Achievement. Hyperacidity. Affluence. Flatulence. Technology. Tension. The inalienable right to an early coronary sitting at your desk while plotting to stab your boss in the back. That's entertainment." Or try season six's "Fallen Idol," where Hawkeye shouts, "Don't you know how much this place stinks? Don't you know what it's like to stand day after day in blood? In the blood of children? I hate this place."

Reynolds cited as one of his favorite episodes "Sometimes You Hear the Bullet," which ran during the series' first season. In that episode, Hawkeye's buddy, reporter Tommy Gillis (played by James Callahan), shows up at the M*A*S*H unit because he wants to see war from the inside. Gillis is charming and light-hearted—one of his first acts is to kiss Henry Blake (McLean Stevenson) full on the lips. Gillis visits the front to write about war, and predictably enough, is killed. Hawkeye is distraught, naturally.

The creators loved this episode. "It was the first indication that a mixture of laughter and tragedy might be possible, without any heavy-handed manipulation of the audience's emotions," wrote Gelbart.[63]

"We loved the goddamn episode," Reynolds said, "so we continued with an eye out toward having some kind of substance with a little more courage . . . we were always looking out for hypocrisy among politicians, because we said often that the war was caused by the failure of politicians. And that's really where it's at. This thing where 'they stepped on us, we've got to step on them,' the tit-for-tat kind of, the nationalism, meaning, 'you insult us, we go to war,' or we don't speak to you anymore if you don't do what we say, which is a policy we've been suffering under for a long time."[64] If the liberal view of war had to be boiled down in a nutshell and then preserved in amber, Reynolds's remarks would suffice. This pacifistic attitude is rooted in the liberal meme that all people are good, and that all conflict is bad, and that all war is rooted in the failure of petty people rather than in significant ideological differences. The rejection of nationalism is a hallmark of the Hollywood internationalist's mentality—artists often consider themselves world citizens rather than citizens of their country. Essentially, the Reynolds ideology here is no different from the John Lennon ideology in the mindlessly blithe "Imagine": "Imagine all the people / Living life in peace." Light up a doobie and sing along. That's the *M*A*S*H* philosophical underpinning.

*M*A*S*H*, more than any other piece of entertainment, brought forth the modern liberal antiwar movement—not the 1960s antiwar movement, which said that the troops were butchers and that Ho Chi Minh was gonna win; the modern movement, which opposes America's involvement in war on principle and sees the troops as victims. "Our characters were heroic at a time when America was woefully short of heroes," Gelbart wrote. "The series was antiwar. That was our intention from the beginning. But we were not anti the more than thirty-three thousand U.S. troops killed above and below the Thirty-eighth Parallel. . . . They, all of them, not as statistics, but as human beings, were surely antiwar as well. . . ."[65]

But *M*A*S*H* was about more than war. It also pushed the network into allowing material on homosexuality in the military, transvestism, interracial marriage, impotence, adultery, and other controversial issues. The show pushed the envelope. But that's what success does—it allows networks the freedom to give creators political leeway. And what better way to use such leeway than to cover it with comedy? Why bother with drama? As Gelbart told me, "It's far more fruitful to take a very serious subject and worry your way out of it with laughter."[66]

HAPPY DAYS (1974–1984): VIETNAM WAR ANALOGY?!

If ever there was an innocuous show, it was *Happy Days* (1974–1984). The story of a small-town family consisting of son Richie Cunningham (Ron Howard), daughter Joanie (Erin Moran), father Howard (Tom Bosley), and mother Marion (Marion Ross)—and one iconic outsider, Arthur "The Fonz" Fonzarelli (Henry Winkler)—was immensely popular for a decade, until it literally jumped the shark (the show coined that term after Fonzie jumped a shark while water-skiing).

But the creators behind *Happy Days* were anything but apolitical. Garry Marshall, one of television's most consistently excellent writers and producers—he is responsible for TV hits like *The Odd Couple*, *Mork & Mindy*, and *Laverne & Shirley*—is a down-the-line liberal. He's anti–big business, which he sees as linked to both government and organized crime. He's anti–small towns—he told Ben Stein that "There are a lot of dumb, violent people in small towns." He's got socialist leanings ("For some people to be poor, others have to be rich. The poor are taken advantage of by the rich").[67] He was a major supporter of President Obama's 2008 run, creating a thirty-second ad on Obama's behalf targeting the Jewish community, costarring Carl Reiner, Larry Gelbart, Danny DeVito, Rhea Perlman, and Valerie Harper.[68]

Marshall's liberalism runs along family lines, too. His sister, Penny Marshall, who starred in *Happy Days* and *Laverne & Shirley* before going on to direct and produce films like *Big*, *Awakenings*, *A League of Their Own*, and *Cinderella Man*, holds the same beliefs as her brother. Her idea of perfect happiness, she joked, is "multiple orgasms and the veal at Ago." The most overrated virtue? "Chastity."[69] She was married to Rob Reiner for several years.

Marshall's personal liberalism didn't play into his shows as much as it played into his hiring practices. He mentored writers ranging from Susan Harris (*Soap*) to Bill Bickley and Michael Warren (*Perfect Strangers* and *Family Matters*), the vast majority of whom were liberal in their politics.

Notwithstanding his own politics, Marshall wanted *Happy Days* to be innocent. That's what the network wanted—they wanted to counterprogram against *All in the Family*. And that's largely what it was, with a few notable exceptions, including a couple of first-season episodes featuring

Richie's libido (he ogles strippers in "Richie's Cup Runneth Over" and "The Skin Game"), and the addition of the Fonz, who was a concession to the 1960s rebellion.[70]

Hilariously enough, one of the staff writers on the show, Bill Bickley, told me that there *was* a liberal message on the show that nobody has ever detected. Bickley, who wrote episodes for *All in the Family* and *Room 222*, two of the most socially conscious shows on television, as well as *The Partridge Family*, one of the least, knew how to write subtext. And he had a particular subtext for *Happy Days*.

"I'm this English major that took everything seriously," Bickley told me. "*Happy Days*—I had a whole subtext for *Happy Days*. It was a literary approach that if you really look for it, you can find it. . . . I had Vietnam in there. I said, 'We know Vietnam is going on now, but they didn't then,' so I had Howard and Marion sitting in the living room as you're hearing the boys playing outside and [Howard and Marion are] talking about 'Thank God our kids will never have to go to war,' and I was thinking, 'Yes, we're going to [war], see Vietnam!' "

Vietnam? In *Happy Days*? Seriously? "I was into all that kind of masturbation," said Bickley. "But I think a lot of times, our unconscious puts the structure [into] things, and actually some shows that are actually pretty light where we had no intention other than getting the next episode done, can have some stuff there . . ."

Bickley's explanation of *Happy Days* provides a valuable window into the creative mind—the same kind of writer who can attempt to add subtext about Vietnam in a show about greasers and bobby-soxers can also add depth of characterization to a breakout character like the Fonz. Bickley saw the Fonz as "a tragic figure. . . . Fonzie was an anachronism . . . time would move on, and Fonzie would stay stuck where he was. And that was the underpinning of the story. . . . I took it very seriously."[71]

Can you spot Vietnam in Richie Cunningham's Milwaukee? Probably not. But it's there—and the fact that it's there means something, even if this particular political infusion doesn't have much impact at all.

THREE'S COMPANY (1977–1984): T&A . . . AND MOLIÈRE

Four bouncing boobs and John Ritter. That's *Three's Company* in a nutshell. If ever a show was designed with the male viewer in mind, it was *Three's Company*, the hallmark show for the T&A movement. And it worked beautifully. For seven riotous seasons, this comedy entranced America and ticked off the religious right, based almost completely on John Ritter's capacity for physical humor and the writing staff's capacity for sexual double entendre.

The show's premise was simple: two hot girls living in an apartment with a straight male friend (Ritter). The two girls (Suzanne Somers and Joyce DeWitt) aren't involved in anything sexual with the guy, but the rest of the world naturally assumes that they are. To demonstrate to the landlord that nothing is going on, the straight male friend plays gay. The premise alone was a shocker for Americans used to the separate beds of Dick Van Dyke and Mary Tyler Moore. Sears withdrew its sponsorship from the program after Donald Wildmon fomented ire against the show,[72] but that didn't stop the network from running it.

The show was another import from Great Britain (the original British title: *Man About the House*). But despite its apparently straightforward premise and lowbrow humor, the pilot's original author was . . . Larry Gelbart. Fred Silverman, who greenlit the show as president of ABC, described it to me at his palatial estate off of Sunset Boulevard: "That damn thing was number one . . . [it] was universally condemned."

When I asked Silverman if *Three's Company* was making any social statement by promoting a ménage à trois, American style, he denied it strenuously. "The fun of *Three's Company* is that everybody, starting with Mr. Roper, thought that there was something going on. And there really wasn't. . . . It's kind of like French farce. I once got criticized for comparing it to Molière at the Writers Guild. I'll never hear the end of that."[73]

Of course, Silverman left unspoken the understanding that Molière was not merely a writer of French farce—he was a satirist of French society. And in many ways, *Three's Company* satirized American society in the same vein. It substituted friends for family; it substituted liberal living arrangements for more traditional ones. And it made us laugh. On the other hand, Molière was a serious moralist. *Three's Company* wasn't serious in any way, shape, or form.

So Silverman wasn't far off—*Three's Company* is more Molière than *Three Stooges*.

SOAP (1977–1981): A GAY ROMP

Susan Harris is a uniquely talented writer, a sparkling and witty artist, and an ideologue. I met Harris at her large, modern-style home off Sunset Boulevard, a sparkling clean white gem in the hills. At sixty-nine, she is still a beautiful woman.

"In the late sixties," she told me, "I had a two-year-old, and my husband and I had split up, and I had to earn a living. And one night I was watching television, truly, and I said, 'this is so terrible, anybody could do this.' . . . Well, it turned out I *could* do that. I wrote this script on spec, and then sold it. And that started it." Harris quickly fell in with Garry Marshall—Bill Bickley, who worked with Marshall at the same time, remembered "Susan with her hot tits and long legs"—and then ended up working on a couple of episodes of television with Norman Lear.

Writing for Lear, she said, had a strong influence on her. "Prior to what Norman did, the people on sitcoms had completely unreal lives. . . . It was completely idiotic," she explained. "And what Norman did, thankfully, was he brought the real world into television. That's always what I wanted to do, and then was able to do."

While writing for Lear, she penned one of the most famous episodes in television history: the abortion episode on *Maude*.

Maude, starring Bea Arthur, was a highly successful series that ran six seasons in the Lear heyday, a spinoff of *All in the Family*. Arthur was a dyed-in-the-wool liberal, a Jewish girl who had experienced anti-Semitism growing up in the South. Predictably, *Maude* was an ode to the leftist vision of feminism—the title song proclaimed Maude the equal of Joan of Arc and Isadora ("the first bra-burner")—and it was militant in its politics. Maude herself was on her fourth marriage when the series began. Like many in Hollywood, Maude was also a limousine liberal; she had a black maid from whom she would continually solicit approval. The series ended with Maude being appointed to Congress as a Democrat.

Arthur mirrored Maude in real life. She declared that her character was great because she "looked real . . . [she] said what she felt and could tell her husband to go to hell." Personally, Arthur went through a metamorphosis with regard to militant feminism. Early in the show's run, she said openly that she "never felt that being a wife and mother isn't enough," but over the course of the show, she became more and more rigid in her feminism, finally divorcing her real-life husband and declaring, "I don't think I ever truly believed in marriage anyway . . . I guess marriage means that you're a woman and not a . . . person."[74] The Harris/Arthur marriage was more successful than Arthur's actual marriage; Arthur would later team up again with Susan Harris to star in *Golden Girls*, the show on which *Desperate Housewives* creator Marc Cherry got his start.

Maude's most famous moment, though, was the title character's abortion. In 1972, just before *Roe v. Wade* was decided by the Supreme Court, Maude, then forty-seven years old, decided to abort her fetus. The episode was a two-parter. At the end, Maude has a crucial exchange with her husband, Walter.

"Just tell me, Walter, that I'm doing the right thing not having the baby," she says.

"For you, Maude. For me. In the privacy of our own lives. You're doing the right thing," he replies.

Harris was just getting started. Her first successful series creation was *Soap*, quite possibly the most controversial series in television history. It started from Harris's desire to write a serialized comedy rather than the self-contained half-hours television had always embraced.

"It really wasn't a satire on soap operas," she continued. "It was called *Soap* because it was a good title and had the form of a soap opera, which was, you know, hooks and cliffhangers and not knowing where the story was going to go."[75]

While the series did satirize soap operas in a soft way, it was far more about character and politics. In keeping with the prevailing liberal sensibilities of the time, it focused on upper-crust liberals rather than downtrodden ones; since the Nixon Administration, liberals had shunned the non-minority lower classes.

The series' first true political breakthrough came in the form of Jodie Dallas (Billy Crystal), an openly gay man who makes a plea for tolerance of his sexual orientation in the third episode of the first season (after he shows up wearing a dress in the second episode). He confronts his stepfather, Burt: "You hate me because I'm gay, right?" Burt assents. To which Jodie responds: "Look at me, I'm a person . . . Burt, just think of me as a person, that's all. That's all I am, I'm a person sitting here. Burt, look at me, I'm a person . . . who happens to like men!" Burt balks, then finally accepts Jodie for who he is.

Crystal started the trend of "playing gay," which has become a must-do for so many television and film actors as a mark of artistic credibility. But it wasn't easy. "I was Jackie Robinson for a while," he told the *New York Times*. "It was very creepy at the beginning." But Crystal's presence on the show did exactly what its creators thought it would do: it warmed the audience up to the gay agenda. Near the end of the show, Jodie became embroiled in a battle over the custody of his love child. "The mail was three to one that I should get the child," Crystal said, "and I thought that was the biggest victory of all."[76]

This kind of stuff went over big at the network. Marcy Carsey, then an executive at the network (and a woman we will meet in depth when we discuss *The Cosby Show*), recalled, "When they made me a vice president, the first thing I bought was a show called *Soap*. . . . We also got all sorts of pressure from advertisers and even from some affiliates. They did not want us to put it on. In the spring of 1977 we screened our pilots for upper management. That's when they decided what to put on in the fall. When I screened *Soap*, I was so nervous I had a tummy ache. It was a landmark show, it broke taboos. And that, by definition, is potentially a hit. So I introduced it by saying something snippy, as usual: 'You guys are going to love this or hate it. I don't care how you feel about it. Just put it on the schedule.' There was silence after the pilot. Leonard Goldenson was the first to speak, and he said, 'We have to put this one on.' "[77] Carsey told me that putting *Soap* on the air was one of her proudest accomplishments. "I mentioned that *Soap* was one of my favorite shows that I ever put on the air . . . it dealt with homosexuality when nobody was, it dealt with all sorts of stuff that you just couldn't do on television but we did, and I thought that was a great thing to do."[78] Fred Silverman was similarly proud of his role with *Soap*: "We did *Soap*, which was groundbreaking. One of the smartest comedies that has ever been on the air."[79]

From there, the rest was history. Despite the fact that *Soap* lost money, the network stuck with it. "We had no advertisers at all," said Harris, "I think that ABC was very courageous in putting *Soap* on the air and sticking by it for four years when they lost money every single year. . . .

"*Soap* did everything," Harris proudly remembered. "We had the first gay character who was a real person. Gays have thanked us for that and still do."[80] *Soap* wasn't the first mainstream television depiction of a gay man—that was *That Certain Summer* in 1972. But Billy Crystal did what Hal Holbrook couldn't: he made homosexuality palatable to a mainstream audience through the power of laughter.

It wasn't just the politics of homosexuality that drove controversy. *Soap* had episodes dealing with impotence, adultery, and incest, among other hot (and fringe) topics. All of them pushed the audience left.

CHEERS (1982–1993): BLUE-COLLAR ELITISM

It's difficult to find a more ubiquitous triumvirate than Charles-Burrows-Charles on television reruns. That's because when you watch reruns, there's a solid chance you're watching *Cheers*, one of NBC's greatest success stories. Despite early failures (the show ranked seventy-seventh in the ratings during its first year), *Cheers* eventually became the third most popular comedy on television, after *The Cosby Show* and *Family Ties*.

Its initial difficulties sprang from its elitism. The first season featured jokes about Schopenhauer. But that shouldn't have been a surprise from the highly educated Charles brothers, Les and Glen, who wrote the show. Glen was a former lawyer who quit his job to work in television; his brother was a former public school teacher. James Burrows, who combined with the two to form the production company for *Cheers*, was an industry baby—his dad, Abe, had been a major Hollywood figure. All three had worked with Grant Tinker at MTM Enterprises. None of them are overtly political, but all three are liberal. "I can tell you," said Burrows, "not only for myself but my two partners, all we did was try to make the most funny show and characters you could identify with."[81]

Cheers is a show with which we can identify.

Still, there's no question that *Cheers* is a liberal show. *Cheers* was set in a Boston bar, but it was truly a soft culture clash in the mold of *All in the Family*, although it was far more sympathetic to blue-collar sensibilities. Sam Malone (Ted Danson, a major liberal in his own right) is a dog, a feminist caricature of men. "He's a spokesman for a large group of people who thought that [the women's movement] was a bunch of bull and look with disdain upon people who don't think it was," explained Glen Charles.[82] Diane Chambers (Shelley Long) was the conscience of the show, a liberal woman and solid feminist who constantly won the morality game with Sam and the rest of the boys, even if she was mocked during the process.

Episodes pushing the liberal agenda in a soft and funny manner peppered the first season. The episode "The Boys in the Bar" centered on the breaking news that one of Sam's old teammates—a former roommate—had come out of the closet in his autobiography. The regulars at the bar encourage Sam to reject his former roommate, fearing that the bar will turn into a gay hotspot. Sam comes out in favor of his roommate, and a gay couple shows up at the bar. Norm (George Wendt) and Cliff (John Ratzenberger) try to chase the gay couple out, but target the wrong couple. The gay couple ends up kissing Norm on the cheek at the end of the episode, demonstrating just how wrong and silly he is.

The co-writer of the episode, Ken Levine, told an illuminating tale about the filming. The network hesitated, but, "To their credit, the Charles Brothers and Jim Burrows did not back away." The cast loved it; Ted Danson told Levine not to change a word. During the run-through, the crew laughed hysterically. "And by far the biggest [laugh] was the last joke where the two guys flanking Norm kiss him," Levine recalled. But when it came time for the live filming, "Silence. Dead silence. You could hear crickets. It wasn't like some people got it and others didn't. *Nobody* laughed. Not a single person. . . . No one had an explanation."[83] Of course, the explanation was simple: The last laugh was simply too awkward for the general public. But in the world of Hollywood, if your buddies get you, everyone else must, too.

The fact that the show was always about the clash of low and high culture, represented by Diane and Sam respectively, and that high culture generally won out in terms of prevailing morality, meant that the *Cheers* universe skewed left. Nonetheless, there were clear rumblings in the *Cheers* universe that something was amiss in the lower-class conservative vs. elitist liberal universe. The show's angst about Diane's education and her tendency toward looking down her nose at Sam presented the first inkling of the yuppie conundrum that would haunt liberals throughout the 1980s. The 1960s generation that had rejected capitalism as exploitative was all grown up, and they were suffering from the cognitive dissonance of wanting monetary success. This was the same conflict that would permeate television throughout the decade in shows ranging from *thirtysomething* to *Family Ties*—how could the left, with all of its socialist tendencies, reconcile its proletariat principles with its elitism? The answer on *Cheers* lay in the synthesis of Sam and Diane. She eventually began to outgrow her disdain for Sam and to learn from his blue-collar authenticity, and he began to respect her intelligence as well as her beauty.

As early as season one, the synthesis was taking place. Take, for example, the season-one episode "No Contest." The episode concerns the Miss Boston Barmaid contest, a beauty competition among Boston waitresses. "These contests perpetuate the attitude that women are mere objects to be judged and ranked in respect to how well they serve men," Diane says. Sam secretly nominates Diane, and Diane decides to take part only if she can push the feminist agenda by winning. When Sam discovers what she's doing, she tells him, "Sam, some day, you will realize that I am doing the right thing." "Why do you always have to do the right thing?" Sam replies. She wins the contest and a bevy of prizes, including a trip for two to Bermuda. She gets so excited she forgets to make her speech. But never fear, she gets to moralize: "I sold out womankind for a trip to Bermuda," she laments, before realizing that she has also been able to shake herself out of the uptight sexuality she normally inhabits. At the end of the episode, Sam proposes that Diane take him with her to Bermuda; she's hot on the idea until he pledges to be a gentleman. It seems that he's taught her too well—she's now the sexualized feminist, the liberated woman.

This episode teaches us something about the nature of television liberalism in the 1980s. By this point, television creators were beginning to see blue-collar people as working-class heroes, so long as those dockworkers and barmaids embraced the liberal agenda (think of Martin Sheen in *Wall Street*); elitists, by the same token, could be liberal heroes by smoothing out the rough edges of the blue-collar workers. This is a view of politics that persists to this day: liberals often tend to think of lower-income people as rough material waiting to be shaped, and they think of themselves as limousine liberals waiting to be dirtied by the soot of the underclass.

"I would say that television has produced one comic masterpiece, which is *Cheers*," said far-left author Kurt Vonnegut. "I wish I'd written that instead of everything I *had* written. Every time anybody opens his or her mouth on that show, it's significant. It's *funny*."[84] Even if the creators didn't mean to overtly insert Vonnegut's kind of politics, they did.

FAMILY TIES (1982–1989): REAGAN'S CHILDREN OF THE CORN

Gary David Goldberg, creator of *Family Ties* and *Spin City*, greeted me warmly at the Coffee Bean & Tea Leaf on Santa Monica's trendy Third Street Promenade. It was midday on a weekday, and he was dressed in sweatpants and a windbreaker. Goldberg is an unapologetic liberal—he counts Barbara Boxer and Chuck Schumer among his personal friends. During our interview, he told me that he had gone to an Al Franken fundraiser the prior night—"I think [he's] going to be great"—and that he and his daughters had worked for the Obama campaign.

Goldberg got into the industry by accident, he told me. He was a 1960s-era hippie. "[In] the 1960s I went out of my mind, just crazed. [I'm] still running into people going, 'We lived together! How can you not remember?' " he laughed. After getting married, he and his wife moved to San Diego so that she could pursue her PhD. They were living on food stamps and welfare at the time. Because he needed college units, Goldberg took a writing course with a past president of the Writers Guild and former Oscar nominee. When his professor read his writing, he told

Goldberg to head to Hollywood—and his professor set up meetings with agents and showed him script forms. Soon enough, Goldberg was writing for television.

It wasn't long before the honchos in the industry took notice. At an interview with Nichols, Ross, and West (the same folks who produced *Three's Company*), they suggested that he join up with MTM Enterprises. After working on several shows, Goldberg had the idea for *Family Ties*.

"It really was just observation of what was going on in my own life, with my own friends," Goldberg told me. "We were these old kind of radical people and all of a sudden you're in the mainstream . . . but now you've got these kids and you've empowered them, and they're super intelligent, and they're definitely to the right of where you are. They don't understand what's wrong with having money and moving forward."

As Goldberg describes, *Family Ties* riffed on the angst of the 1960s generation at the Reagan Revolution. It also reinforced the nascent yuppie upset so evident in shows like *Cheers* and later, *thirtysomething*, questioning how the rebels of the 1960s could preserve their radical values while becoming bourgeois parents and business owners benefitting from the capitalist system.

But *Family Ties* wasn't designed to be an evenhanded riff on Reagan-era politics or even 1960s-liberal angst. It was designed to target conservatives. Alex P. Keaton (Michael J. Fox) was the stand-in for conservatives. He was brilliant and witty and serious-minded—and totally amoral, Gordon Gecko at age seventeen. The whole point of the show was that Alex was always wrong. Only the panache of Michael J. Fox made Alex palatable. "The interesting thing with Alex, and to the same extent with Archie Bunker, and if you go back to Norman and ask him, he'd say he did not think he was creating a sympathetic character," said Goldberg. "But all the sympathy went to Archie. It was crazy. With Alex, I did not think I was creating a sympathetic character. Those were not traits that I aspired to and didn't want my kids to aspire to, actually. . . . But at the end of *Family Ties*, when we went off the air, the *New York Times* had done a piece and they said 'Greed with the Face of an Angel.' And I think that's true. . . . [Michael J. Fox] would make things work, the audience would simply not access the darker side of what he's actually saying."

A few examples. After being told in season three by his younger, innocent sister that there's more to life than just getting rich and that "people who need people are the luckiest people in the world," Alex replies, "Jennifer, people who have money don't need people." Another season-three episode has Alex telling his pregnant mother that she shouldn't fly. "Alex, you know, if you had it your way, Mom would be locked in her room for nine months wearing a veil," sister Mallory snipes. "Oh come on, that's not true," says Alex. "I see no need for a veil." Alex is constantly putting his foot in his mouth this way, ironically poking at and caricaturing conservative positions—and he gets a laugh because he's so charming.

In fact, Alex became so much of a hero that even liberals didn't understand when he lost battles. "Steven Spielberg was a huge fan," Goldberg recalled, "used to come to all the tapings, and was a close friend and he'd come Friday nights, and one night we did a show where Alex lies to this girl and completely disses the [Equal Rights Amendment] and everything it stands for and pretends to be a feminist, and at the end, she tells him off. . . . So after, Steven comes over and I said, 'How did you like the show?' He said, 'Well, it's all right.' And I said, 'What's wrong?' And he said, 'Alex didn't get the girl.' And I said, 'Yeah, but he lied, he cheated,' and he said, 'But it's Alex, you want him to win at the end.' "

But Alex rarely won, because Goldberg and the writers' room didn't want him to win. In fact, Goldberg said, "We actually had this structure that we'd inherited from Jim Brooks and Allan [Burns], which was six scenes and a tag. . . . And then the last scene became Alex apologizes, in every show, we just left it up. Alex apologizes. Some version of it."

For example, in the season-one episode "The Fifth Wheel," Alex is supposed to babysit younger sister Jennifer. As always, his desire for cash gets the better of him. He decides to take Jennifer with him to a poker game, justifying his actions with an appeal to pseudo-conservative masculinity. "In this industrial society of ours, there aren't a lot of battles for a man to fight. There aren't a lot of opportunities to go one-on-one with another man. There aren't a lot of tests of one's courage and stamina, do you know what I mean?" he says.

Naturally, things get out of hand—Jennifer walks out of the game and gets lost. Later, she shows up at home after taking the bus. Alex gets into trouble, then promises his parents that he'll take better care of Jennifer from now on: "Yeah, we'll keep her happy, we'll make sure she gets out every now and then, we'll feed her, and keep her clean." Finally, he apologizes, blaming his own self-centeredness and his lack of sensitivity. This is a more subtle episode than some of the earlier ones, but it is just as effective: money is the root of all evil, and Alex is the greedy Reaganite who loses the child.

This show format, repeated over and over again—Alex has a conservative/greedy idea, Alex screws something up, Alex apologizes—exposes just what Goldberg and the 1960s-era creators thought of the Reagan generation. The show always ends with Alex needing to be reaccepted into the family, after attempting to individuate, to be himself. The liberal assumption is that Alex's political choices are merely teenage rebellion, and that reunification will inevitably occur once Alex comes to his senses. For that reunification to occur, however, Alex must subordinate his principles—which aren't true principles but greed manifest in a false facade of principles—to his need for communion with his family.

Goldberg makes that clear in the pilot episode. In that episode, Alex wants to go out with a hot, blond, rich cheerleader-type named Kimberly. She takes him to a "restricted" country club—it bans blacks, Hispanics, Jews, and anyone who didn't "come over on the Mayflower," as Elyse puts it. Steven stands up against Alex, but Alex goes anyway. Later, Steven shows up at the country club, humiliating Alex. Alex reams Steven when he gets home.

"I was wrong to go over there like that," says Steven, "but I hope you understand why I felt so strongly about your being at a restricted club."

"I do, Dad," replies Alex, "but I'm seventeen years old. When I see Kimberly Blanton in a strapless evening gown, I don't look past her for the Bill of Rights."

"I was seventeen myself, once," answers Steven, "but I had principles, I had beliefs." The pattern is set: Alex, despite all his talk of principle, is unprincipled; Steven and Elyse are the principled heroes of the piece. Alex's rebellion is simple Freudian psychodrama. (By contrast, Meathead's rebellion in *All in the Family* is principled opposition to conservative bigotry.) What Goldberg did not expect, of course, is that by allowing Alex to mock liberal values, he was unwittingly undermining them.

Goldberg made no bones about the fact that he infused politics into the show—but he learned early on that he couldn't simply do it in Norman Lear's obvious fashion. "That's a tension [between messaging and entertainment] we welcomed. . . . What you can't do is 'a very special episode of,' where you do this show and there's no jokes. . . . The shows we did earlier in the season were the ones we buried, because I was completely wrong about what I thought the show was going to be: nuclear war, gun control, climate change, death. And so you had to put it in a different package . . . it had to come out in a different way."

And *Family Ties* did do it in a different way. There *were* episodes about nuclear war—one in particular in which Alex learns to get along with a Russian kid at a chess tournament—and episodes about sex and episodes about the evils of capitalism. But they were covered over in a brilliant display of hilarity. It's no wonder that Ronald Reagan said that *Family Ties* was his favorite show.

Like *Cheers*, *Family Ties* was a slow starter out of the gate, but the network stuck with it. And like *Cheers*, it eventually became a massive hit when it was placed behind *The Cosby Show* in 1984, running for seven seasons.

Goldberg's other big show came years later, when he brought back Michael J. Fox for *Spin City*; Goldberg wrote the show with partner Bill Lawrence (who would go on to create *Scrubs*). That show cast Fox as the deputy mayor of New York, and was even more political than *Family Ties*. Fox was still playing Alex Keaton, but this time Keaton was grown up and a Democrat. He was just as Machiavellian, just as manipulative, but this time, he was good-heartedly trying to ram through the liberal agenda. His liberal conscience was Carter (Michael Boatman), a gay man who made sure that Michael didn't lose his leftist principles. Boatman's character ardently pushed the gay rights agenda, including same-sex marriage (one episode featured Boatman staging a marriage to one of the straight employees at the mayor's office as a political statement, then canceling the wedding when it became clear that he had too much respect for the institution of marriage generally). "Carter came about in the pilot," Goldberg told me. "We decided that was really a one-shot, but we just fell in love with Michael Boatman and what that character represented, so after that we made a deal with him to put him in as a regular, bring him in." Carter, Goldberg said, was "basically a saint."

I asked Goldberg why there didn't seem to be any real debate about politics on television anymore—why everyone simply assumed that the far-left position was correct, and that the only real question was whether that position was practical. At least in *All in the Family*, I said, the conservative position was articulated, however badly, and then knocked down. Modern television doesn't even bother articulating the conservative position. "If I was writing now I wouldn't be having those debates, either," Goldberg said. "Because I think it's great we've moved beyond that."[85]

That's certainly arguable—we're still debating gay marriage, the morality of which *Spin City* took for granted. But if we've begun to move beyond such debates, it's due in large part to the success of writers like Goldberg, who have made the leftist position so palatable to a broad swath of Americans simply by presenting likable characters who promote liberal politics as tautologies.

THE COSBY SHOW (1984–1992): THE FIRST BLACK PRESIDENT

In essence, there's no difference between *The Dick Van Dyke Show* and *The Cosby Show*, other than the color of the main character. But that's quite a difference, according to the left—which is why *The Cosby Show* made it onto the air.

Marcy Carsey, who brought *The Cosby Show* to the air along with her partner, Tom Werner, grew up in Massachusetts, the daughter of moderate Eisenhower Republicans. She moved to New York to pursue a career in television and started off as a tour guide at NBC. When she moved to Los Angeles with her husband (who wrote for *Laugh-In*), she got a low-level position at ABC, then began moving up the ranks. As one of the only women in the executive arena at the time, she remembers the kindness of Michael Eisner, who hired her despite the fact that she was three months pregnant.

She left ABC and started her own production company with Werner, and for the first few years, they had difficulty keeping a show on the air. Then, in 1984, they "talked Bill Cosby into doing a series." What appealed to Carsey? "His message was so powerful for the time. You don't think of Bill Cosby as having a revolutionary message, but he really did. . . . He was talking about the parents taking back the household from the kids.

And he was talking about men and women and how they are together and how they live together." Carsey didn't see these messages as conservative, of course—that would have been taboo. But the messages were conservative nonetheless.

Of course, he was also black. Cosby was iconic—he had been the first black television star in *I Spy*. "We were very aware of that. One of the first discussions we had with Bill . . . we had to talk him into doing a half-hour comedy. . . . And he said OK, if he was going to do a half hour, he wanted to be under the gun with not enough money, with too many kids. . . . I just kept saying to him, 'You can't do that. You can't do that.' . . . You've got to be the first guy to do a comedy about black Americans that has nothing to do with poverty, with drugs, with problems like that. . . . We absolutely knew how important it was that that be the case."[86]

The Cosby Show was, in many ways, a conservative show. In the show's pilot episodes, Brandon Tartikoff recalled in his autobiography, Dr. Cliff Huxtable (Cosby) has a chat with his son, Theo (Malcolm-Jamal Warner), about Theo's report card. After Cliff reams him and asks whether he thinks he can get into college with such terrible grades, Theo reveals that he's not going to college. "Then Theo ends his little I-gotta-be-me speech by asking Cliff why a father can't accept and love his son simply for what he is," remembered Tartikoff. "The kid has stood his ground, and stated his position well. Everyone at the taping applauded wildly. Your standard sitcom would have stopped dead right there to bask in the audience reaction. Instead, after one or two beats, Cosby speaks up. He tells Theo that he's never heard anything so stupid—that being afraid to try is about the dumbest possible approach to life. His boy, Cliff says, is *going* to try. Why? Because I am your father and I say so, that's why. The audience, having already applauded, could only cheer even louder. The cast, crew, and executives knew instantly that they had created something that worked. A Magic Moment. And—lest we forget—a 48 share in the overnights."[87] Not quite the hippie-dippy liberal message of the 1960s.

But *The Cosby Show* wasn't simply a conservative take on family life. The Huxtable conservatism was deliberately infused into a black family in order to combat stereotypes about the black community more broadly. That was purposeful. Harvard psychiatry professor Dr. Alvin Poussaint redlined scripts for the show, recognizing that "TV shapes the perception of Black kids who watch these shows . . . [it shapes the] perception of White children who might think that all Black children are comedians who conform to racial stereotypes."[88]

Because the main character was black—and because he was an obstetrician and his wife a lawyer—it provided a certain happy thinking at odds with reality. "Of course, once the show made its debut, many people thought we overdid it—that the Huxtables had much too lush a life," Brandon Tartikoff admitted. "I understand the logic, but I don't agree with it at all. I think *The Cosby Show* made people feel good. And I believe the show worked because it was more realistic than most other sitcoms. . . ."[89] Tartikoff's right when it comes to the warm and fuzzy feeling generated by *Cosby*. He's wrong when he says the show is realistic.

The Cosby Show can be taken one of two ways. First, it can be construed as a wholly conservative show, a show focused on inherent equality of the races, the opportunities America provides, and the benefits of a solid family structure. Second, it can be taken as liberal happyspeak ignoring the basic problems in the black community (single motherhood, lack of education, low income, etc.). In this second view, middle-class blacks often face a problem similar to that of the 1960s radicals *cum* 1980s yuppies; they struggle with status anxiety, the feeling that they are losing their roots by buying into the system. The Cosby family wears nice sweaters, lives in a comfortable home—and demonstrates no conflict whatsoever on this point.

The more realistic Cosby family would look like the Obamas: highly educated, affluent, successful products of an affirmative action project who are clearly haunted by racial anxieties and fears that they have forsaken their roots in pursuit of power and prestige. We thought the Obamas were the Cosbys—that they were black Americans who had climbed the ladder to success rung-by-rung, and that they were silently grateful to be part of a system that made that success possible. We forgot that the Cosby family isn't real. In fact, when Bill Cosby came out much later and stated that the black community needed to emphasize education and self-respect, crack down on crime, and set up new social standards promoting achievement, liberals raked him over the coals. Cosby, said Georgetown University sociology professor and race-baiter Michael Eric

Dyson, had "betray[ed] classist, elitist viewpoints rooted in generational warfare," was "ill-informed on the critical and complex issues that shape people's lives," and had "reinforce[d] suspicions about black humanity." Cosby, Dyson continued, "has famously demurred in his duties as a racial representative . . . flatly refused over the years to deal with blackness and color in his comedy." Dyson labeled Cosby a "racial avoider."[90]

In truth, what drew Americans to the show was the Cosby view of the family, the papered-over conservatism of the show. Americans loved *The Cosby Show* for the same reason they would later love *Everybody Loves Raymond*—the American people are rarely presented with a traditional family embodying conservative entrepreneurial values. That's why the show ran for eight seasons and was number one for six of those eight seasons. Carsey acknowledged that: "If you get to where their gut is, and where their heart is, then you are a hit show."[91]

Conservatism can be a hit—even when liberals don't know they're making conservative programming.

ROSEANNE (1988–1997): RED STATE LIBERALISM

Carsey's commercial success is no doubt related to the fact that unlike many liberals in Hollywood, she understands the conservative position. "You know, I'm of a liberal bent, so obviously that's going to come out of the shows that I was involved with," she told me. "I was raised in a moderate Republican, Eisenhower Republican family. I'm very much a Democrat, but I understand people that have that kind of a bent."[92] It is a rarity in Hollywood for anyone even to admit that they *have* conservative friends.

But that doesn't mean that Carsey doesn't embrace her liberalism in her programming. If *The Cosby Show* was about what it was like to handle a family, *Roseanne*, one of the biggest hits on television from its premiere in 1988 to 1997 (it was in the top ten seven times during that span, and in the top five for six seasons), was about what it was like to be a working woman.

"When we did *Roseanne*," Carsey stated, "the intent was to do a show about the millions, the 85 percent of households out there where the woman had to work, not an upper-class or upper-middle-class choice to work, but where the woman *has* to work. . . .

"This woman should be undereducated, should be not wealthy, should be natively smart. . . . A working-class heroine to represent the difficult lives that so many millions of women were leading."[93]

NBC rejected the initial concept—"She's a fat woman nobody's going to want to watch," they said of Roseanne—so Carsey brought it to ABC. The chief backer of *Roseanne* at ABC was Brandon Stoddard. "God," he marveled, "I'll never forget this as long as I live. I showed the pilot to the affiliates, there were a thousand, and the wives. And I'm scared to death. I mean it was risky, really risky. It was against the grain. . . . I also needed a hit *really* bad. And I thought, this could be it. And I was standing in the back of the room there with 1,000 people. And the women are invited to watch it and the thing is playing and they're laughing, laughing, laughing.

"And she makes a speech somewhere about 'I'm a mom, but I'm supposed to be a lover, and I'm supposed to be a friend, and I'm supposed to take care of the teacher, and I'm handing out food tonight.' . . . she does the confused, who-am-I role, which Roseanne did brilliantly, and there was audible reaction by the women in the audience. Audible! They were like, 'Yeah.' . . . And I went, '---- A, we've got a hit, man.' . . . They completely got it . . . because we were real."[94]

Roseanne's brilliance lies in its appeal to working-class Americans. But the values of *Roseanne* are not the real values of the typical red-state working class. There's copious vulgarity, of course. In one episode, Roseanne tells her daughter, Darlene, to use birth control, even though her daughter isn't yet having sex; in another, Darlene admits to using pot, speed, and acid. One tagged segment to an episode in which Roseanne's son has an erection has Roseanne laughing at the network censors, asking them which euphemisms for achieving an erection she can use: "What about pitching the trouser tent? Bootin' up the hard drive? Charming the anaconda? Raising the drawbridge, popping a wheelie, standing up for democracy? Waving to your chin?"[95]

This wasn't vulgarity for vulgarity's sake, though. It was vulgarity for liberalism's sake, as *Roseanne* made clear in its most famous episode,

"Don't Ask, Don't Tell." In that episode, Roseanne visited a lesbian bar with her friend Nancy, then was kissed by Nancy's girlfriend, Sharon (Mariel Hemingway, who makes a living off this sort of stuff). Frank Rich of the *New York Times* praised the episode as a step forward for gay rights. *Roseanne* didn't stop there. In 1995, it hosted a gay wedding. In season seven, Roseanne considered an abortion, telling her young son, "No man has any right to tell any woman what she should do in a situation like this." The combination of the blue-collar feel of the show and its down-the-line liberal messaging was terrifically effective.

The liberalism of the show evidenced itself in the relations of the family, too. Despite Roseanne's blather about her role as a wife in the pilot episode, it is clear throughout the program that she wears the pants in the family—and that her husband's pants keep falling off. John Goodman's butt crack is prominently featured on this show, a subtle reminder that he is a nincompoop and that she is the heroine, setting a standard that would soon be surpassed by the liberalism of *The Simpsons*. *Roseanne* is a landmark show in terms of shaping the view of the father on television—even *Family Ties* and *The Cosby Show* and *All in the Family* promoted the notion that fathers were important, even if they were wrong. If John Goodman had disappeared from *Roseanne* overnight, few people would have noticed. He was merely a foil to show Roseanne's strength.

Roseanne set new standards in terms of class warfare, too. Whereas previous shows had either ignored blue-collar workers altogether (*Family Ties, The Cosby Show*) or praised them as simple-minded folks who could be taught the virtues of liberalism (*Cheers*), or ripped them outright (*All in the Family*), Roseanne portrayed working-class people as innately liberal. *Roseanne* revolved around the self-flattering image of the Democratic Party as the working-class party. Roseanne is the kind of woman you'd expect to see at the Democratic National Convention as a delegate of the Service Employees International Union (or at least throwing eggs at Tea Party buses). *Roseanne*, along with *The Simpsons*, represented the last television gasp of the liberal FDR myth that working-class people are interested mainly in unionization and universal health care. Bill Clinton represented the *Roseanne* ethic gone presidential—the white-trash, trailer-park liberalism of *Roseanne* found its outlet in the Man from Hope. Soon, however, the myth would be washed away forever, both politically and on television; *Roseanne*'s liberalism would make way for the liberalism of *Friends*, and Bill's down-home liberalism would make way for the liberalism of Hillary and the Obamas.

Later, Carsey would go on to helm liberal shows like *Grace Under Fire* and *3rd Rock from the Sun*, as well as *That '70s Show*. All of them promoted a certain social agenda—as Carsey said, they reflected her politics. But all of them also reflected her ability to craft mainstream characters with partisan perspectives.

THE SIMPSONS (1989–PRESENT): SUBURBIA SUCKS

He attended his first anti-war demonstration at age twelve. He became "fascinated by ideas about progressive education and put them to the test when it came time to go to college," attending Evergreen State College in Olympia, Washington. The college had "no grades and no required courses." Famous alums of Evergreen include Rachel Corrie, the radical pro-terrorist Palestinian sympathizer killed by standing in front of a bulldozer in the Gaza Strip trying to defend a terrorist-infested area; Michael Richards, better known as Kramer on *Seinfeld*; and porn star Noname Jane. The college recently became one of the first in the nation to install gender-neutral campus housing specifically designed for lesbian, gay, bisexual, and transsexual students.

After college, he migrated to Los Angeles, where "the counterculture was *dead*," and began writing freelance pieces for the weird alternative universe of *LA Weekly* and the *Los Angeles Reader*. Then he created a comic strip called *Life in Hell*. Thirty years later, he is the most successful sitcom creator in television history.

His name is Matt Groening, and he's as liberal as they come. And his show is *The Simpsons*.

Groening got into the business via producer Polly Platt, former wife of Peter Bogdanovich and art director of *Terms of Endearment*, who was a fan of *Life in Hell*. She just happened to be close with James L. Brooks (of *Mary Tyler Moore* and *Room 222* fame). Brooks dug Groening's cartoons, and soon he was using them on *The Tracy Ullman Show* on the nascent Fox network.

The Simpsons certainly reflects Groening's continuing sense of rebellion so carefully cultivated in the alt-weekly world of Los Angeles. "Definitely, the struggles and the rebellion I experienced growing up are a main part of my creative output." He sees himself as a counterculture hero who has infiltrated the mainstream. "My underground pals and I used to sit around and talk about sneaking into the media, trying to see how far we could push our ideas," he told interviewer Robert Kubey.[96]

"I may be biting off more than I can chew," Groening told *Mother Jones*, "but with *The Simpsons* . . . what I'm trying to do in the guise of light entertainment, if this is possible—is nudge people, jostle them a little, wake them up to some of the ways in which we're being manipulated and exploited. And in my amusing little way I try to hit on some of the unspoken rules of our culture. . . ." Groening is the representative of pure vanguardism—he tries to shock Americans and he tries to use comedy as a spear to lampoon all manner of political enemies. Groening characterizes his political beliefs as progressive, and idolizes execrable cartoonist Ted Rall—the man who called fallen soldier Pat Tillman an "idiot" and a "sap."

"*The Simpsons*'s message over and over again is that your moral authorities don't always have your best interests in mind . . . I think that's a great message for kids," Groening laughed as he spoke to the far-left magazine. "I don't understand why William Bennett has such a problem with us . . . right-wingers complain there's no God and religion on TV. Not only do the Simpsons go to church every Sunday and pray, they actually speak to God from time to time. We show him, and God has five fingers. Unlike the Simpsons, who only have four." Groening admits that he gets away with this sort of subversive messaging because his show is a cartoon. "Yes. Of course. We always hide behind 'It's just a cartoon!' "[97] It's no wonder that in 1992, then-President George H. W. Bush stated, "We need a nation closer to the Waltons than the Simpsons. An America that rejects the incivility, the tide of incivility and the tide of intolerance." In typically hilarious fashion, *The Simpsons* responded with Bart watching Bush's speech on TV, then quipping, "We're just like the Waltons. We're praying for an end to the depression too."[98]

Al Jean, executive producer of the show, admitted that the writers and producers "are of a liberal bent." He felt, though, that the philosophy of the show is "probably nihilism."[99] *The Simpsons* does make fun of both sides (Lisa's starry-eyed liberalism is often the butt of jokes—her moral crusades usually fall short due to the stupidity of the local population). But its prevailing sentiment, as Jean said, is nihilism. The nihilism of *The Simpsons* is based on the failure of liberalism's aspirations—the war on poverty has failed, the war on drugs has failed, the war on homelessness has failed. When liberalism fails, it turns not to conservatism but to nihilism, the sense that all is useless and lost. Satire fits perfectly within this worldview—making fun of everything is easier than building anything up or backing specific provisions.

The Simpsons reserves its harshest criticisms for conservatives, however. The nihilists who create *The Simpsons* are not true nihilists—they're liberal nihilists, only roused from their bleak stupor by the benighted hogwash of conservatism. Just look at Rev. Lovejoy, Ned Flanders, and Mr. Burns, Springfield's resident conservatives, all of whom are portrayed as ignoramuses, killjoys, happy idiots, and/or evil. Lisa is vulnerable on *The Simpsons* because her starry-eyed schemes are doomed to failure, but she is in the main pure, good, and uncorrupted; Rev. Lovejoy and Ned Flanders are vulnerable because they are stupid, ignorant, and worthy of consistent mockery.

If *The Simpsons* has debased one element of traditional values more than any other, it is the traditional family structure. Homer is a garrulous goof-off; Bart is a juvenile delinquent. Marge is the long-suffering wife and Lisa the good-natured and idealistically brilliant liberal. Sound familiar? It should. It's a good deal like *All in the Family*.

Unlike *All in the Family*, however, the father figure cares little or nothing about his wife and children, except on deus ex machina occasions when such care is called for by the storyline. Homer is inconsiderate, insanely stupid, and brutishly loathsome. He is a drunken boor who belches, farts, and knocks around the kiddies. He is the image of the Ugly American so often invoked by the Europeans.

Following the line of fatherhood on television is a striking study in liberal annexation of the medium. Start with *Father Knows Best*, where father actually knew best; move on to *The Dick Van Dyke Show*, where Dick, for all of his goofiness, rules the roost and brings home the bacon. As the decade progresses, father figures—and male figures in general on television—morph into genial fools who maintain titular control (on *Bewitched*, for example, Samantha, who is obviously more powerful than her husband, leaves him the illusion of power). With the urban television shift, the image of fathers begins changing, slowly becoming even more negative—the 1960s-era youngsters' image of authority figures translates into the adolescent hallmark of the unlikable but powerful father figure (e.g., Archie on *All in the Family*). Finally, in the modern era, fathers have become absolutely hapless at best and massively horrible at worst. They are accoutrements to a family, not innate and vital parts of it. It's no wonder so many Americans now grow up thinking that fathers are superfluous or even detrimental to a happy and functional household.

One unspoken problem with *The Simpsons* is that its audience skews young. Sandy Grushow, a Fox executive throughout much of *The Simpsons'* tenure, including inception, stated, "*The Simpsons* was the huge stake in the ground."[100] Groening felt that the youth-centric audiences was one of the key components of the success of the show: "Cartoons are characterized as a kiddie medium and kids are not trusted to delineate between good behavior and bad behavior. I personally think that kids appreciate the fact that they're not being condescended to."[101]

Of course, this is deeply problematic—kids are generally unable to tell the difference between satire and well-founded criticism. They're kids, even if liberals prefer to think of them as adults who are just far away. But that's the point: *The Simpsons* is a tremendously liberal, tremendously entertaining recruitment tool to cynicism. Which doesn't mean it isn't an amazing show. It is. That's what makes it so effective and so addictive.

MURPHY BROWN (1988–1998): HUNTING FOR QUAYLE

The 1992 Bush campaign couldn't stay away from ill-advised cultural references. If it wasn't Bush himself getting smacked down by the liberals on *The Simpsons*, it was Dan Quayle famously having his lunch handed to him by Diane English and the crew at *Murphy Brown*.

English got her start in the industry after working as a high school English teacher and a journalist, when she and her husband began writing teleplays for public television. She wrote several television movies, then finally found her big break with *Foley Square*, a CBS show that was cancelled after fourteen episodes. But that started her on her way. In 1988, CBS picked up *Murphy Brown*, starring Candice Bergen as a single TV reporter with a drinking problem.

The show was almost a mirror image of *Roseanne*. Where *Roseanne* focused on the downtrodden blue-collar feminist, *Murphy Brown* focused on the upper-class feminist, the new and modern woman every woman wanted to be: glitzy job, beautiful friends, posh lifestyle.

The show took on politics, almost invariably from a liberal perspective—in one episode, broadcast at the time of the Clarence Thomas hearings, Brown appeared before a fictional Senate committee and bashed their "grandstanding and shameless self-promotion." (This wasn't even close to the most direct television bash at Thomas—that was reserved for *Designing Women*, an episode of which featured one of the main characters donning a T-shirt reading, HE DID IT and stating, "I don't give a damn anymore if people think that I'm a feminist or a fruitcake."[102])

But things got particularly nasty when English decided it was time for Brown to get pregnant out of wedlock. This was no doubt a reaction to the rise of the Moral Majority and the religious right; the Hollywood left responds to conservatism with outrage and dismay, usually combined with an in-your-face display of extreme liberalism.

Dan Quayle denounced the show on the campaign trail while speaking about the problem of poverty and single motherhood in the African-American community, stating, "It doesn't help matters when primetime TV has Murphy Brown—a character who supposedly epitomizes today's intelligent, highly paid, professional woman—mocking the importance of fathers, by bearing a child alone, and calling it just another 'lifestyle choice.' "[103]

English responded in a statement released from Hollywood: "If the Vice-President thinks it's disgraceful for an unmarried woman to bear a child, and if he believes that a woman cannot adequately raise a child without a father, then he'd better make sure abortion remains safe and legal." Murphy Brown herself responded on the show: "Glamorize single motherhood? What planet is he on? Look at me, Frank, am I glamorous?"[104] Actually, she said even more than that: "I doubt that my status as a single mother has contributed all that much to the breakdown of Western civilization. . . . In a country where millions of children grow up in nontraditional families . . . it's time for the vice-president to expand his definition, and recognize that whether by choice or circumstance, families come in all shapes and sizes."[105] Brown's second speech, of course, trumped her first—it's difficult to say that you're not glorifying a choice when you then go ahead and glorify it.

Another character on the show, Corky, was more direct: "I was raised to believe that if you had a child out of wedlock you were bad. Of course, I was also raised to believe a woman's place was in the home, segregation was good, and presidents never lie."[106] This is absurdly slanderous, implying that all those who oppose single motherhood are sexists, racists, and idiots.

Quayle's whole point was that the show was making single motherhood seem a common and acceptable choice (and for the record, Quayle wasn't suggesting abortion but marriage as the solution for single motherhood). And he was right. But English got the last laugh—the Quayle controversy drove ratings for years, and Candice Bergen thanked Quayle in her Emmy acceptance speech that year.

She also got the last laugh societally—though the perspective she pushed has caused more tears than laughter. Single motherhood has become an accepted and highly-praised addendum to the definitional family. Since Murphy was a white middle- to upper-class female, let's look at the statistics with regard to white middle- to upper-class females. From 1980 to 1990, the illegitimacy rate for white women with family incomes over $100,000 was 1.7 percent; by 2007, it had more than doubled to approximately 4 percent. Even more significant, from 1980 to 1990, the illegitimacy rate for all white women was 4 percent; by 2007 it had quadrupled to about 20 percent.[107]

Culture isn't the only factor here, of course, but it's an important one. The single-motherhood controversy is a perfect example of how Hollywood believes it is reflecting life when it is in fact transforming viewpoints across the country. While single motherhood among upper-class and middle-class white women was a major issue in Hollywood in 1992, it was not a major issue in vast swaths of the country at the time. In retrospect, even Candice Bergen essentially apologized for pooh-poohing Quayle's comments. "I never have really said much about the whole episode, which was endless," she said ten years later. "But his speech was a perfectly intelligent speech about fathers not being dispensable and nobody agreed with that more than I did."[108]

That's not what Bergen said at the time. "On this show," said Candice Bergen, "we all have fairly common political and social concerns and we get to express them. It's not only a success in terms of quality and ratings, but also [in terms of] ideology, . . . we always have a point of view even when we don't have a political message. We get to bash Democrats and Republicans alike. . . ."[109] Mostly Republicans.

SEINFELD (1990–1998): NIHILISM CHIC

Seinfeld, so often described as a show about nothing, lives up to its name. It is a show without principle, without heart, and without remorse. That's what makes it funny. It is not, however, a show without politics.

Larry David, the creator of *Seinfeld*, is an outspoken liberal. In the mold of Larry Gelbart and Woody Allen and the great Jewish creators of the pre-1970s television explosion, David was a New York kid who grew up in Brooklyn. After attending the University of Maryland and serving in the U.S. Army Reserves during the Vietnam War, David started working as a stand-up comedian, working several low-paying jobs to support himself. He eventually landed a writers' slot on *Saturday Night Live*, and the rest was history.

He often posts his thoughts at Huffington Post—thoughts like "Rove . . . God, I hate that man. . . . The only thing that bothers [conservatives] are fetuses. They love that fetus. The fetus and Jesus. Sounds like a comedy team. 'Ladies and gentlemen, give a warm welcome to Fetus and Jesus.' . . . I like how if you criticize the war, you don't support the troops. You're the ones sending them over to die, so how is it I don't support them?"[110] This is what passes for intelligent commentary at the Huffington Post.

Seinfeld came about in 1989, when NBC decided to try to build a show around Jerry Seinfeld, a comedian who had been appearing on Leno and Letterman. The show's research was awful. Audiences hated the show, hated Seinfeld, hated George, and hated Kramer. But NBC stuck with it anyway, despite initial low ratings and NBC president Brandon Tartikoff's misgivings ("It's too New York and it's too Jewish," he famously said, in an unintentional homage to the original rejection of *Mary Tyler Moore*). The result was a show that many consider the finest ever broadcast on network television.

The show's milieu was a throwback to the early days of television: It was New York shabby chic. Seinfeld himself epitomized the liberal urban sensibility, wearing ironed blue jeans. It was a far cry from John Goodman in *Roseanne*.

The philosophy of the show was purely nihilistic. In order to better reflect that nihilism, Seinfeld's character actually underwent a transformation in the first season, said *Seinfeld* writer Peter Mehlman. It happened by accident. "In the episode with the junior mint when Kramer is bugging him to come see this operation on Elaine's overweight boyfriend, during a run-through," Mehlman remembered, "Kramer was telling him, 'Come on, Jerry, come on, we can sit in the observation theater, come on.' And Jerry totally ad libs . . . 'All right, let me finish my coffee and we'll watch 'em slice this fat bastard up.' . . . The laugh was so thunderous that we said, '--- it, we'll go with it.' And that one line kind of opened the floodgates to him being . . . not an asshole, just edgy."

Mehlman told me that philosophy reflected Larry David's sensibility. "*Seinfeld's* not messaged at all," said Mehlman. "If it's anything, *Seinfeld* is pointedly *un*messaged. We'd really look at each other and say, 'What do I have to tell anybody about the world?' . . . So we don't really have anything to say other than to peck at people who do think [they know something]."

That wasn't *entirely* the case, though. *Seinfeld*'s general liberal messaging came out in its characters, who are all Upper West Side Manhattan Jewish liberals (even George acts far more Jewish than Italian). Take, for example, the season-six episode "The Couch," which Mehlman wrote. In that episode, Elaine dumps her boyfriend when he reveals that he's pro-life. "One of Larry's great, great ideas was having the boyfriend who might be anti-abortion. . . . Are you going to break up with a gorgeous guy because he's not pro-choice?" That isn't deep political commentary. But it's political commentary nonetheless, because we *like* Elaine, so we take what she says at face value: Only ugly people are pro-life.

The show clarified its scorn for traditional moral standards in its famous season-four episode "The Contest," in which the four main characters compete to see who can go the longest without masturbating. The show is replete with euphemisms for masturbation, of course, and it won Larry David an Emmy and a Writers Guild of America Award. *TV Guide* went so far as to name the episode the best television episode of all time.

Why in the world would the television industry so celebrate a puerile high school joke extended for thirty minutes? Because shock value is paramount to the Hollywood liberal nihilist. This is the bobo ideology at work—the notion that in order to justify their immense success, Hollywood liberals must freak out the middle-class masses. Larry David and many of his ilk, growing up as they did during the 1960s, are far more rooted in bohemianism, and they still revel in *épater les bourgeois*. They find their meaning by clinging to the distorted image of themselves as courageous bohemians challenging America's stodgy, prejudiced middle class. They don't attack the elite social and political consensus in America, which became largely liberal during the 1960s and 1970s; instead, they feel important because they shock for shock's sake. They aren't in the political vanguard—they're acting out their post-1960s, *thirtysomething*-type angst at living in a liberal world that for some odd reason isn't a utopia.

How does all of that crystallize? In celebrating a show about masturbation.

At the same time, what makes *Seinfeld* great is the same thing that makes *The Simpsons* great—they *do* bash both sides, though they revel more in bashing conservatives than liberals. A classic example is Mehlman's episode "The Sponge," in which Kramer refuses to wear an AIDS ribbon for the AIDS walk and gets "beaten up by gay thugs. And we're not saying anything about AIDS or support of AIDS or anything like that; we're saying something about wearing an AIDS ribbon."

The show, Mehlman said, was designed to "shine lights on people's hypocrisies. Like the whole 'not that there's anything wrong with it.' The amazing thing about that episode is that they're saying 'not that there's anything wrong with it' like five times, and the last time they're practically in tears, and the show wins a [Gay and Lesbian Alliance Against Defamation] award. Obviously they're saying there's something terrible about it."[111] This is the oddest thing about today's comedy world—the funniest material springs from liberals bashing other liberals. But liberals can't even recognize when other liberals are bashing them.

The good news for conservatives is that the newfound nihilism of the television cadre means that they sometimes make fun of liberals, too. Still, overall, nihilism tends to reflect liberalism far more than conservatism, simply because conservatism tends to promote lifestyle standards whereas liberalism does not—and it is far easier to point out "hypocrisies" among those who actually have lifestyle standards. While *Seinfeld* wasn't a liberal show, then, it *was* a rip on traditional mores. Not that there's anything wrong with that.

FRIENDS (1994–2004): AN OBLIQUE "--- YOU TO THE RIGHT WING"

Marta Kauffman has offices at the Burbank Warner Bros. lot in a bungalow that reads like a who's who of the Hollywood writers' set: the same site hosts David E. Kelley, as well as Chris Chulack and others. Kauffman is warm and gregarious, entertainingly honest and open.

"You know, David Crane and I started out doing musical theater in New York," she told me. "And the woman who's our agent today came to see the show during the time, called *Personals*. It was off-Broadway, and it was about single people looking for love. And she said, 'Why aren't you guys doing television?' And we went, 'I don't know.' "[112] She and Crane moved out to L.A.

Kauffman got lucky—a pilot she wrote with Crane titled *Dream On* was picked up. The show was a racy comedy that ran for six seasons on HBO. It was one of the first series on television to use nudity and cursing uncensored. It was also decidedly liberal. The show actually changed the complexion of HBO's subscribers, Barbara Fisher, who ran Universal Television at the time, told me: "Suddenly people were subscribing to them to get *Dream On*."[113]

Soon afterward, Kauffman got a job developing television for Norman Lear. This made sense—Kauffman is a self-proclaimed liberal, and her shows have strongly political tendencies. She worked on Lear's short-lived series *The Powers That Be*, a highly polarizing political show about a good-hearted liberal Senator with an unfortunate penchant for the ladies.

But Lear didn't like her work. "He didn't like our approach to TV. We wrote a pilot . . . after he read the pilot, and he took my hand and he said, 'You know, it's just shallow.' And he took David's arm and he said, 'It's superficial.' . . . We [jokingly] called ourselves Shallow and Superficial for ages."

This, too, made sense—Lear's shows always took political issues head on, whereas Kauffman's shows put politics in the context of character development, tackling such issues obliquely and softly. "They did issue shows," said Kauffman. "They did it before everybody else did it. . . . We didn't do issues. We did stories."

I asked Kauffman if the difference between her shows and Lear's shows was a change in the political nature of the times—a broader movement toward acceptance of liberal values—or a change in creative temperament. "In terms of changes in time, God, I hope so," she said. "But . . . I think it is also a reflection of difference in [national] temperament."

Friends came about a couple years after Kauffman began working for Lear; she and Crane wanted to write a show that reflected their lives. And because both Crane and Kauffman sprang from the New York theater scene as well as the Los Angeles television scene, their lives were unswervingly liberal. "It's about six friends who [embodied] . . . the stuff we dealt with," she said. The six friends were, of course, Rachel (Jennifer Aniston), Ross (David Schwimmer), Monica (Courteney Cox), Phoebe (Lisa Kudrow), Chandler (Matthew Perry), and Joey (Matt LeBlanc).

The central social transformation of *Friends* was replacement of family with friends. "That's what we do," said Kauffman. "We leave our parents' homes. We go to college or not. We move into areas where we make friends. . . . What we were trying to do was talk about that time in your life—and that was the phrase that we used when we pitched the show—'when your friends are your family.'" Of course, this is what *liberals* do. And they used to restrict this sort of thing to Greenwich Village, where they were aware that they were leading a rebellious lifestyle. They knew that to shock the bourgeois, they couldn't *be* bourgeois. But for Kauffman and company, Greenwich Village was everyone's village, and every American eventually substitutes friends for family.

The show was also about the fluidity of the friend-lover relationship. "I think there's truth in that," Kauffman said. "I think that when you put a group of people together and some are men and some are women and they're heterosexual, there's going to be a blurring of the lines." This is inherently liberal. In conservative thought, there has always been a sharp break between friends and lovers; the idea is that lovers are the people you marry. By blurring the lines between friends and lovers—today you're friends, tomorrow you're lovers, the day after, you're back to being friends—liberalism suggests that sex can be separated from true commitment. Conservatives understand that some friends do become lovers, but the idea is that once lovers, they stay lovers. The notion of free flow between platonic love and sexual love is foreign to conservatism. On *Friends*, however, the father of your baby can be your friend, while your friend can become your lover (just ask Ross, Rachel, and Joey). Any babies resulting from these relationships, by the way, are disposable commodities that can disappear for seasons at a time.

Because the lives of the six friends mirrored the lives of their creators, that translated into substantial coverage of issues like gay marriage. In the first season of the show, Kauffman and Crane wrote in a lesbian wedding between Ross's pregnant ex-wife and her girlfriend. "You know, as far as we were concerned, gay marriage was not an issue; it was just something that was happening," Kauffman explained.

I asked Kauffman about the development of the lesbian story line, which seemed far less comedic than it did dramatic. For example, in the episode in which Ross's pregnant lesbian ex-wife has his baby, Ross is understandably upset. Phoebe tells him that he should see his wife's lesbian lover as a fringe benefit for the kid.

Kauffman laughed recalling the episode. "Hah. I love that. My favorite part of that is not just her speech, . . . it was Ross's comment, 'Every day is the Lesbian Lover Day.' . . . Our purpose in doing it was not to get people to be more aware of lesbian relationships or, you know, fathering and moving on. It was really fun drama."[114] (Peter Mehlman was more critical of *Friends*' reliance on interpersonal drama: "You always think about the year *Friends* won the Emmy for best sitcom; that was the year they were promoting every episode with that tune from Enya. Every promo had that mournful Enya music, like 'They're having the baby.' Put it on at two in the afternoon already, what are you waiting for?")[115]

It didn't hurt that Kauffman had a close personal friendship with a lesbian couple. In one interview, she explained how proud she was of the lesbian storyline based on those friends: "We have friends—two women. They have a little girl, who never got to see the show last year because it was on too late. Now that it's on at eight o'clock, she got to see it. And she saw one with the two moms, and she turned to her mother with these big eyes and said, 'Mommy! A family like ours!' *That's* what we should be doing."[116] David Crane, Kauffman's producing partner, agreed. "It was always important to us that Carol and Susan [the lesbian couple] be three-dimensional," said Crane, who is gay. "It's very significant that when you watch the show, you get the feeling that these two women are going to be good parents—and that you see there's an extraordinary amount of love between them. And I think that comes through."[117]

I asked Kauffman whether it was legitimate to criticize the politics of the show as one-sided. She answered truthfully: "I mean, you have a bunch of liberals running the show. . . . [When we did the lesbian wedding, we knew] there was going to be some controversy. But it didn't feel to us that we were preaching anything," she continued. "Although, I have to say, when we cast Candice Gingrich as the minister of that wedding, [was there] a bit of '--- you' in it to the right wing directly? Yeah. I mean that was a choice, and it was an exciting choice, and she made a statement during the wedding where she says something about nothing makes God happier than to see any two people together in love. . . . We felt that was honest." Of course, it's not honest—the definition of "two people together in love" would include consensual incest, which even liberals reject. But for liberals, it's *emotionally* honest, even if it's politically dishonest.

Kauffman evidences a nonobjective view of the political debate. Nowhere is that more clear than in her retelling of one of her favorite episodes, "The One Where Dr. Ramoray Dies." In that episode, Rachel and Monica, who are roommates, are both looking to have sex with their then-boyfriends. There's only one condom left. They fight over the last condom. The episode caused a stir when Senator Joseph Lieberman (D-CT) protested that it was inappropriate for primetime television.

Kaufmann couldn't understand why Lieberman was upset. "Wait a minute, I'm sorry . . . two women are arguing over who's going to get to have sex because only one of them will get a condom is irresponsible?! As far as I was concerned that was extremely responsible. . . . If you don't like what you're watching, forget the V-chip, just turn it off." Of course, Lieberman wasn't truly arguing with Kauffman that sexually active people shouldn't be using condoms; he was arguing that showing promiscuous sexual activity on television was a problem altogether. But because such behavior was considered common in New York and Los Angeles, and the only true issue regarding sexuality in those communities was the issue of AIDS, Kauffman felt that the episode was tremendously socially responsible.

Similarly, Kauffman felt one of the best messages the show tackled concerned information about the risks associated with condoms. In one episode, Rachel and Ross talked about how she got pregnant despite his condom use, Rachel informing Ross that condoms aren't 100 percent effective. Ross freaks out. Kaufmann was proud of the sequence: "People actually paid attention to that and they heard that in a way they hadn't heard it in the classes they took in high school. Or even more important, the high schools that weren't given classes. . . . It had a huge effect, which I'm very very proud of. I'm really proud that there's a generation of kids that are highly aware. It's not why we did it, but it's a fantastic added bonus."

So I asked, it was important to you that the show be both entertaining and socially responsible? "Absolutely," Kauffman answered. "I tend to be the one who's more politically active. There are a few of us in that group that were fairly politically active. . . . It's not why I did it, but I'm very proud that that's one of the things that *Friends* was able to do."[118]

Friends is popular because the writing is sparkling and the drama is human (you couldn't have a more obvious case of "boy finds girl, boy loses girl, boy gets girl" than Ross and Rachel). That's the reason the show ranked in the top five for nine of its ten seasons. It's not popular because of its politics. But because *Friends* was so popular, its politics became more popular, too.

ELLEN (1994–1998): OUT AND DOWN

The creators of *Ellen* had stellar credentials: Carol Black and her husband, Neal Marlens, had created *Growing Pains* and *The Wonder Years*; their co-creator, David Rosenthal, went on to become a showrunner and producer for *The Gilmore Girls* and *Spin City*. But when they ran into Ellen DeGeneres's ardent desire to come out on national television in the middle of their sitcom, even they couldn't save the sinking ship.

In 1993, the show premiered to generally good reviews; by its second season, it was rated thirteenth on television. The show could have continued its climb if Ellen had abided by the hallmarks of comedian-centric television shows: Be funny. It worked for Seinfeld, Paul Reiser on *Mad About You*, and Tim Allen on *Home Improvement*. *Ellen* hit the air right in the midst of the craze for television comedians, and the network had to figure that her success would be a no-brainer.

They should have thought it through. By season three, Ellen's total inattention to the standard sitcom plot device of dating was obvious. The ratings began to decline. By the time season four came around, the producers knew they had to come up with something.

They should have been more specific.

Between seasons three and four, Ellen and the show's writers decided that Ellen should come out on the show. Finally, during sweeps week, the show broadcast the famous "Puppy Episode," in which Ellen declared her lesbianism publicly. Ellen co-wrote the episode herself. The episode featured myriad lesbians in cameos (k.d. lang, Melissa Etheridge, Jenny Shimizu, among others). In the episode, it is—unsurprisingly—Oprah Winfrey who convinces Ellen's character to come out. The next few episodes grow progressively more lesbian-centric and serious.

The show limped on for another season, but it was a zombie, living dead. "As the show became more politicized and issue-oriented," admitted Stuart Bloomberg, chairman of ABC Entertainment, "it became less funny and audiences noticed."[119]

Still, *Ellen* broke new ground by featuring a main character who was gay, and writers and executives cited the "Puppy Episode" as one of the single most important episodes of television in the medium's history.

The message that Hollywood took from *Ellen*, counterfactually enough, was that American audiences were eager to see more homosexuality on screen, not less. *Ellen* left the air in June 1998. Three months later, NBC picked up an even more groundbreaking series.

WILL & GRACE (1998–2006): EVERYONE HAS A GAY FRIEND

"The more the show is talked about, the better it is for everyone." That was the perspective of Jim Burrows, who directed and produced *Will & Grace*. And it worked wonderfully; the attention *Will & Grace* garnered outstripped its ratings. The show received seventy-three Emmy nominations despite finishing outside the top forty in four of its eight seasons.

The creators of the show, David Kohan and Max Mutchnick, have been friends since high school. Mutchnick is gay, and Kohan is straight. They write all of their shows together, and broke into the business working for HBO's *The Dennis Miller Show*. From there, they worked with Carol Black and Neal Martens on *The Wonder Years* and Marta Kauffman's *Dream On*, then had their first show, *Boston Common*, picked up. Both are liberal.

The show's central focus on a gay man (Will) living with a straight woman (Grace) came directly from the network. Warren Littlefield of NBC made the decision that those two characters, out of a group presented by Mutchnick and Kohan, were the ripest for a full sitcom; Littlefield, you may remember, is the fellow who thought that Michael Moore's *TV Nation* was hilarious. And Littlefield made clear that the network would allow Mutchnick and Kohan to go as far as they wanted. "We don't have a lot of absolutes," Littlefield told the *Advocate*. "Things are always changing. . . . On *Seinfeld* we had an entire episode about masturbation. There's not a lot you can't do."[120]

Mutchnick gives Kohan the credit for "making sure that we told a gay love story," but he takes credit for making the show mainstream. "The pilot had been picked up for *Will & Grace*," Mutchnick told the gay website AfterElton.com, "and now it was all about casting. And I was sitting in the Bel Air home of a very famous gay director. And when I told him about the script, he said: 'Just make sure you don't make it too butt-f***y.' And I said: 'What does that mean?' And he said, 'You never want the

American public to have to think about butt-f***ing.' And it could not have been better advice. . . . I *chose* to not do explicit stuff, and edgy, edgy gay stuff. Because I wanted people to stay with it, get comfortable with it. David and I said to each other, we'll have won if by the time this show is over the audience wants Will to be in love, wants him to be in a relationship." The idea, said Mutchnick, was to lead off with the premise that the show was gay, then allow the audience "to absorb it and figure it out and get comfortable with it. And realize that we're the same as everybody else in the room."

Mutchnick and Kohan were highly successful in that attempt—and for good reason. If a viewer tuned in to *Will & Grace* without knowing the premise, he or she could watch fifteen minutes of the show before discovering that Will is gay—unlike Jack, who is far more flamboyant, Will is portrayed by Eric McCormack as an openly but not overtly gay man. McCormack himself is straight, whereas Sean Hayes, who played Jack, is gay. (For the record, the vast majority of actors who play gays and lesbians on television are straight; very few gays and lesbians play straight on television, by contrast.)

Alongside *Ellen*, *Will & Grace* is often cited as a transformative show in American culture. There is no question that Mutchnick and Kohan helped forward the gay rights cause, even within Hollywood. Mutchnick acknowledges that in Hollywood, there is no longer discrimination against gays and lesbians. "There's no oppression," he said. "The fact of the matter is that the straight people that are working in these positions of power, not a one of them that I've come into contact with in my professional dealings has felt reluctant or homophobic or disinterested in this subject matter. Not once."[121]

SEX AND THE CITY (1998–2004): THE NEXT STEP IN WOMEN'S LIB

"That's the show," said Marge Simpson in one episode of *The Simpsons*, "about four women acting like gay guys." Marge wasn't the only one suggesting that interpretation. "It *is* a show with a very gay sensibility, definitely," admitted Willie Garson, who plays Carrie Bradshaw's (Sarah Jessica Parker's) best friend on *Sex and the City*.[122] Critics across the spectrum recognized that same gay sensibility in a series about four women who constantly discuss dildos, anal sex, rim jobs, and other fringe sexual practices in graphic terms (leaving aside the overdone and flamboyant gay wedding that opened *Sex and the City 2*).

Where does that sensibility come from? The two head writers on the show, Darren Star and Michael Patrick King, are gay. Star has championed promiscuous sex in virtually all of his shows dating back to *Beverly Hills, 90210*, when he wrote Brenda celebrating her loss of virginity (the network forced Star to write in a pregnancy scare soon after that).[123] In *Sex and the City*, he tried to take that celebration of sex to the next level by turning women into sexual predators. "We were very consciously turning the stereotype on its head," Star told *Macleans*. "Women have always been objectified by men, and in this case the women were objectifying men. The men had names like Mr. Big, Mr. Whatever; they weren't even referred to by name." As with most television creators, Star believes that such behavior reflects reality, even if there aren't many women who parade around New York looking for Manolo Blahniks and big penises. "*Sex and the City* was a reflection of the experience a lot of urban women were going through," said Star.

The message of the show, Star said, channeling Allan Burns of *Mary Tyler Moore*, was "that you don't need to get married. You don't really need that love to be fulfilled. . . . I think these women have each other."[124]

In other words, sex without commitment is a requisite component of a healthy life. That's certainly how Samantha lives her life; the *Sex and the City* website describes Samantha as "Forget wedding dreams; Samantha takes lust over love any night, and she's proud of it. Once, she even experimented with lesbian love, but when her 'girlfriend' demanded more intimacy, Samantha knew it wasn't going to work out."[125]

Michael Patrick King, who is also gay, started off his career with Diane English on *Murphy Brown*, then wrote for various shows, including *Will & Grace*, before Star brought him in on *Sex and the City*. King explained why gay men loved *Sex and the City*: "I think anyone who's ever been an outsider, whether it be due to your sexual orientation or your anything—your gender, your race, your anything—these four girls have moved through the world trying to claim themselves . . . I think that the villain, in any great story you need one, and I think ours is still society. I think society tells you to be some way and the individual always pushes through that bag, punches their way out."[126]

King's remarks recall the bobo mentality yet again—he's rebelling against society as a whole as the obstacle to true happiness in a bizarre sort of Rousseauian "back to nature" way. *Sex and the City* likes to push the notion that finding one's identity revolves around overcoming society's demands by embracing biology. Samantha is the most liberated of the women, and she's also the most carefree; Charlotte, by contrast, is the most rigid, and therefore the most worried, someone to be pitied for her WASPy cultural background. Miranda fights society but runs up against the strictures of the male-dominated capitalist system. *Sex and the City* takes the position that it's biological to want sex, it's biological to want a baby, it's biological to want relationships, but it is *not* biological to want a long-term monogamous relationship—even though by the end of the show, all of the women end up in long-term monogamous relationships (although Samantha later breaks off her relationship in the first *Sex and the City* movie).

The ending of the show is ironic: all of these supposedly strong, independent women end up married or in committed relationships. This is odd because it so closely follows the traditional comedic pattern: Characters engage in a misguided pursuit of wrong desires, then finally find happiness. The ending of *Sex and the City* undermined the entire premise of the show, suggesting that these women had been wasting their time for the past few years, and that if only they could have found love and settled down earlier, everything would have been hunky-dory. Even though the audience for *Sex and the City* supposedly loved the promiscuous sexuality of the main characters, in the end they demanded the age-old comedic conclusion: a wedding.

Nonetheless, *Sex and the City* has dramatically changed American perceptions of female sexuality—and as with all of the other comedies, it did so with witty writing and likable characters. But is that perception of female sexuality more or less accurate than it was before we had women openly chatting about testicle size on national television?

FAMILY GUY (1998–2001, 2004–PRESENT): HATE MAIL TO RED-STATE AMERICA

Family Guy, the highly successful animated Fox comedy helmed by Seth MacFarlane, takes no prisoners when it comes to politics. Episodes of the show have depicted God as an old man having sex with a prostitute, a Nazi wearing a McCain/Palin 2008 pin, a mentally retarded character based on Sarah Palin's son Trig, a mock musical about Terri Schiavo (sample lyrics: "the most expensive plant you'll ever see . . . her mashed potato brains"), and frequent bestiality and pedophilia, as well as depictions of Jews bordering on the anti-Semitic. And that's the mild stuff. The show's satire is often hysterically funny (who else makes random references to "Shipoopi" from *The Music Man*?), but the show has never found a conservative sacred cow it wasn't willing to skewer—or a liberal sacred cow it *was* willing to skewer.

The show's liberalism springs from the mind of creator MacFarlane, who is as of this writing the world's highest-paid television writer (he signed a contract for $100 million). MacFarlane grew up in Connecticut, where his parents sent him to a series of boarding schools. His favorite show growing up was *All in the Family*. (That love can be seen in *Family Guy*'s opening credits, with Peter and Lois singing together at the family piano à la Archie and Edith; similarly, MacFarlane labels *American Dad!* "a current-day *All in the Family* that is more political than *Family Guy*.") After working as an animator in Los Angeles, he finally got *Family Guy* on the air. Now, MacFarlane presides over the largest block of programming since the days of Norman Lear and Aaron Spelling, *Family Guy* being accompanied on the air by *The Cleveland Show* and *American Dad!*[127]

MacFarlane is a down-the-line liberal—and a supremely militant liberal at that, at least in his public rhetoric. He has compared Arizona's immigration policy to Nazi Germany.[128] He is supremely intolerant of anybody who doesn't believe in same-sex marriage: "Why is it that Johnny Spaghetti Stain in ----- Georgia can knock a woman up, legally be married to her, and then beat the shit out of her, but these two intelligent, sophisticated writers who have been together for twenty years can't get married? . . . I have arguments with people where I get red in the face, screaming at the top of my lungs."

MacFarlane rejects any right-wing mail he receives that criticizes the show. "That's like getting hate mail from Hitler," he told the *Advocate*, referring to Parents Television Council. "They're literally terrible human beings. . . . They can suck my dick as far as I'm concerned."[129]

MacFarlane says he does have limits—"It's a case-by-case thing. . . . There have been jokes pitched that seemed too mean to specific people"[130]—but he has yet to demonstrate them, except when it comes to gay rights. On the issue of homosexuality, MacFarlane seeks input from a gay censor at the network's broadcast standards department, "making sure that we're handling it in the right way."[131] The network broadcast standards officers, as we'll discuss later, have stopped protecting the public from objectionable material and now focus on protecting minority interest groups; MacFarlane's preapproval by a gay censor represents yet another in a long line of moves by Hollywood to appease particular liberal activist groups.

TWO AND A HALF MEN (2003–PRESENT): CONSERVATIVE LIBERALISM

In 2008, entertainment website Gawker.com labeled *Two and a Half Men* one of the most conservative shows on television.[132] The website didn't give a reason. It simply put that contention out there, assuming that because *Two and a Half Men* isn't openly liberal, it must be conservative.

Of course, the show isn't conservative. It features boatloads of sex and drug jokes, masturbation, threesomes—the works. But because the show doesn't feature a regular openly gay character, episodes revolving around abortion, or pregnancy out of wedlock, it's considered a right-wing show.

Chuck Lorre, the creator of the show as well as its sister hit *The Big Bang Theory*, has spent his career building well-crafted moneymaking hits like *Roseanne*, *Dharma & Greg*, *Grace Under Fire*. Like many in the television industry, he grew up Jewish in New York (his real name is Charles Levine), a member of the lower-middle class. He went to college at SUNY Potsdam, where he "majored in rock & roll and pot and minored in LSD." A decade later, he broke into the television business with Carsey and Werner.

As that résumé should suggest, Lorre leans heavily to the left on politics. He critiques network censors: "You can show maggots crawling out of a bullet hole, but God forbid we should talk about human sexuality!"[133] He tacks a text-heavy placard at the end of every episode of *The Big Bang Theory*, and they're often political. His most inflammatory placard, which appeared on the screen for two seconds but was preserved for posterity at his website, ripped Fox News by implication:

> Control of the media equals control of the populace. I am endowed like a stallion. And also why a state run television news channel is so very dangerous. I am endowed like a stallion. Now there are those who would argue this has already happened and that a certain cable news channel is actually a covert extension of our government. I am endowed like a stallion. The fact that the channel is run by a high-ranking party official, an anchor person from the channel became a White House spokesman, and another top-ranking party official became an on-air news commentator is often used to make this argument. I am endowed like a stallion. Of course, this fact would be entirely inconsequential if the oft-repeated falsehoods they attempt to imbed into the Zeitgeist were simply amusing, or at worst, inane. I am endowed like a stallion. But, unfortunately, that is not the case. I am endowed like a stallion. The heavy repetition of lies and smears for political gain are by no means inconsequential. I am endowed like a stallion. Which is why each and every one of us must use whatever resources we have at our disposal to disseminate the actual truth.[134]

Lorre has no problem using the resource of his shows to disseminate the truth as he sees it. And his methodology is an effective exposé of how Hollywood promulgates messages—they stack their politics between sex jokes and hope to distract us long enough to shovel their ideology down our throats.

30 ROCK (2006–PRESENT): LIBERAL HOLLYWOOD LOOKS IN THE MIRROR

If the history of comedy on television shows anything, it is that seriousness is no fun. Thank God, then, for *30 Rock*, which makes fun of both sides of the political spectrum. Sure, it's a liberal show. But it's a show that doesn't take its own liberalism too seriously.

Tina Fey, the creator of *30 Rock*, started her career at *Saturday Night Live*. As a member of *SNL*'s Weekend Update team, she admitted, "I think a lot of young people don't just watch comedy shows to stay informed. They also want to be guided on how they're supposed to feel. I guess that's what we do, to some extent. We have a liberal bias, obviously, and that's very much the tone of Update."[135] That same liberalism obviously played a role in Fey's dead-on impersonation of Sarah Palin during the 2008 election campaign (she said during that cycle, "If she wins, I'm done. I can't do that for four years. And by 'I'm done,' I mean I'm leaving Earth").[136]

She brought that liberalism to *30 Rock*, which was supposed to be a parody of *SNL*. Her character, Liz Lemon, is a thinly veiled parody of herself, a liberal do-gooder trying to head up a show full of crazy people. Her boss, Jack Donaghy, is a conservative executive (creators in Hollywood tend to see executives as conservative, no matter what the executives' actual political streak). But strangely, Lemon's brand of liberal politics doesn't trump Donaghy's conservatism. In fact, Lemon's politics is often depicted as pie-in-the-sky, while Jack's conservatism is often portrayed as common sense.

In one of the show's more hilarious episodes, "Rosemary's Baby," Liz decides to stick it to the Man by following Rosemary Howard (Carrie Fisher), a '60s-era comedy writer, out the door after Jack nixes some of Howard's skits. Lemon soon realizes that she's signed on with a loon, and goes back to Jack to beg for her job. In a parallel plotline, Jack has to deal with star Tracy Jordan (Tracy Morgan) and his bad decision making. When Tracy attends therapy, Jack role-plays Tracy's entire family, channeling characters from *Good Times* to do so—and Tracy is cured. It's a hysterically funny bit, taking on stereotypes and showing them to be ridiculous even as we laugh.

Lately, though, Fey has become even more strident in her anti–right wing rhetoric. Upon accepting the 2009 Mark Twain Prize for comedy, she exclaimed, "For most women, the success of conservative women is good for all of us. Unless you believe in evolution. You know, actually, I take it back. The whole thing's a disaster."[137] Fey's rhetoric here isn't funny, let alone balanced.

Unsurprisingly, the show has slid to the left in the past few seasons. Most recently and most egregiously, the season-five episode "Brooklyn Without Limits" featured Stephen Austin (John Slattery) playing a nutty candidate who is obviously of the Tea Party persuasion. "I don't believe in parties, and I don't get invited to them," says Austin. What does Austin believe in? An American renaissance. "Renaissance means rebirth," Austin explains. "I want to usher in the rebirth of this country, that's why the theme of all my campaign commercials is: I'm a Baby." Austin continues: "The government shouldn't interfere in anything. What happens inside a man's own rain poncho at a minor league baseball game is his own business." In Fey's world, all Tea Partiers are nutty sexual perverts who don't understand basic concepts of government or constitutionalism. Fey's scorn is palpable with regard to Americans who want smaller government and believe that President Obama has led us astray from founding principles.

It's not that this is biased, though it is. It's that it's utterly unfunny unless you happen to think Barack Obama is Jesus. No wonder *30 Rock*'s viewership continues to decline along with its humor standards. The show used to demonstrate that nonpartisan political comedy could be done right by liberals. All it took was a commitment to self-effacing humor and the humility to write funny instead of merely targeting political enemies. Sadly, it looks as though Tina Fey has moved beyond nonpartisanship and is now doing what so many of her colleagues do: targeting those on the other side of the aisle with as much acidity as humanly possible.

LEFTIST LAUGHTER

The history of leftism in television comedy is a history of American liberalism, preserved for all time in film. It is a history of major figures biasing their programming to satisfy their consciences, which had been tarred by the stain and stigma of monetary success. It is a history of motivated people consciously and unconsciously infusing their values into America's entertainment, shocking the bourgeois in order to normalize ever more radical moral systems.

It is a history of class conflict. Following the leftist perspective on blue-collar workers from *Your Show of Shows* through *30 Rock* shows Hollywood liberals' reactivity to the middle and lower classes' political persuasions—when blue-collar workers vote Reagan and Nixon, Hollywood despises them and focuses instead on upper-class elites; when blue-collar workers vote Carter, Hollywood loves them and paints them as ignorant heroes.

It's a history of sexual conflict. Tracing the leftist perspective on homosexuality, fatherhood, and feminism shows the total allegiance in the television community to the anti-traditional-family-structure agenda. Their ability to infuse programming with their bohemian mentality accelerated with the shift toward urban programming in the early 1970s, but it had been latent long before that. Now, it's out in the open, and over the course of decades, it has shaped our perspective on who should have children, who should get married, and the very nature of sexual relationships.

It's a history of generational conflict. When conservatism dominates the older generation, the older generation is portrayed as villainous, as on *All in the Family*. When conservatism dominates the younger generation, the younger generation is depicted as foolishly rebellious and in need of life lessons, as on *Family Ties*. Eventually, when liberalism exhausted itself in the failures of the Great Society, Hollywood settled on liberal nihilism, lashing out occasionally, like a rattlesnake, at any upswing in strong conservatism among Americans at large.

Most of all, the history of television comedy is a history of laughter. Liberalism has dominated the world of television comedy for decades.

Virtually every major comedy has been messaged in leftist fashion—and when it's done right, it's tremendously effective at changing hearts and minds. Far more than we do in dramas, we identify with the characters in comedies because we *wish* we had friends that funny, that witty. We spend time with comedy characters because we like them.

And that enables them to propagandize without our even knowing that we're watching propaganda in the first place.

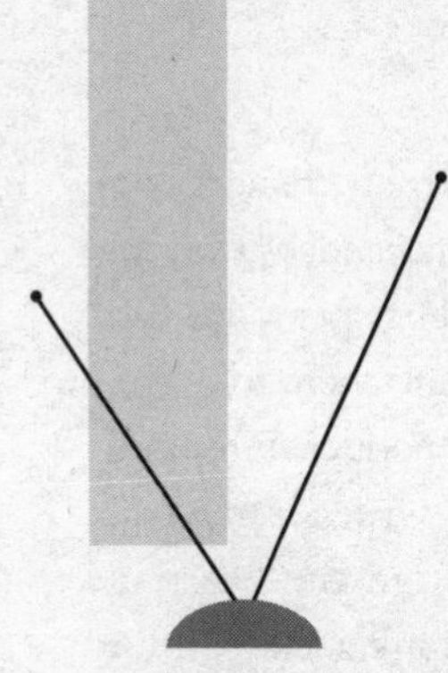

MAKING THE RIGHT CRY

How Television Drama Glorifies Liberalism

If laughter can edulcorate liberal politics to the point where we no longer even taste them, drama can serve to sear liberal politics into our consciousness. While laughter attacks, drama converts, pulling our heartstrings, manipulating our emotions. If the philosophy of the political comedian is to make innocuous that which seemed offensive, the philosophy of the political dramatist is to make offensive that which seemed innocuous. Comedies are anti-morality crusades; dramas are morality tales. The question in drama is always which morality is being promoted.

The beauty of using drama as a political vehicle lies in the set-up: by stacking the characters and facts on one side or another, creators can drive audiences' emotions. Think about *The Godfather*, for example. In that brilliant drama, the main character is a murderer and a bootlegger; his father is an extortionist and a murderer as well; his oldest brother is an adulterer and a violent hothead. We like all of them, because Mario Puzo, Francis Ford Coppola, and Robert Towne weight the situation to their benefit: Michael Corleone becomes a murderer only because his father is unjustly threatened and his wife is murdered—and he only murders corrupt cops and drug dealers; Don Corleone extorts a pedophile; Sonny cheats on his wife but defends his sister from her abusive husband. The ease with which brilliant dramatists can twist and turn our morality is truly astonishing.

As in comedy, the most successful dramatic television creators comprise a small group of committed liberals. We will meet them over and over again. Their talent is undeniable, but their politics pervades their work, which is one of the reasons the industry worships them so.

And as in comedy, the long tradition of infusing politics into drama started from the beginning. Whereas many comedy writers came from vaudeville and radio, many drama writers came from the 1930s and 1940s theater scene, a milieu dominated by socialist thinkers like Clifford Odets and the Russian-influenced artists of the Stanislavski school. The dramatic television creators brought those sensibilities to their work, infusing social messages wherever they could. As with comedy, pushing the envelope quickly led to further pushing the envelope.

That evolution is evident in all of the major dramatic television templates: the cop show, the medical show, the legal show, and the soap opera (both daytime and primetime). Over time, cop shows moved from the outright worshipfulness of *Dragnet* to the cynicism of *The Wire*. Medical shows shifted their focus from doctors working to heal others within a functional medical system in shows like *Dr. Kildare* and *Ben Casey* to doctors struggling with the injustices of society in *St. Elsewhere* and even *ER*. Legal shows changed from the aspirational *Defenders* to the dark and gritty view of lawyers in *Damages*. Soap operas started as simple interpersonal dramas and shifted to encompass controversial storylines.

The liberal leanings of particular dramas do not in any way diminish the brilliance of the dramatists. One of the most challenging tasks for any artist is infusing beauty and feeling with meaning. Certainly no one can blame the creators for infusing their ideologies into their dramas—that's what creators do. Still, we must open our eyes to what we're watching. Drama tells us what is moral and what isn't. It ponders deeper questions than comedy, and invariably skews the storyline in order to reach conclusions the creators want us to reach. As viewers, we must be aware of how our emotions are manipulated so that we can embrace Hollywood's pecular brand of liberalism.

PLAYHOUSE 90 (1956–1961): WHEN MAINSTREAM LIBERALISM WAS RIGHTEOUS

Without question, *Playhouse 90* was one of the finest television programs ever produced. A series of ninety-minute made-for-television movies, the show ran from 1956 to 1960 on CBS and broadcast the combined talents of the world's best writers and directors. Those who contributed to the show included Abby Mann (*Judgment at Nuremberg*), William Gibson (*The Miracle Worker*), Horton Foote (*To Kill a Mockingbird* and *Tender Mercies*), and Frank Gilroy (*The Subject Was Roses*). John Frankenheimer directed the vast majority of the episodes, though Franklin Schaffner, Sidney Lumet, George Roy Hill, and Arthur Hiller, among others, also directed episodes. As for the stars—well, let's just say that there wasn't a star in the pantheon who didn't once appear on the show.

These were heady days for television—days when dramatists were given relatively free rein to pursue their art. That freedom was partially due to the fact that television had not yet entered all American homes; only the rich could afford them, and the rich preferred deep and abiding entertainment. The artists took advantage with alacrity.

In American society more broadly, it was a time of relative tranquility. Under President Eisenhower, Americans reached the Cold War consensus: strong anti-Communism and enthused pro-capitalism. At the same time, tensions bubbled beneath the surface, particularly with regard to racial issues. Creators at *Playhouse 90* embodied these differing strains, simultaneously taking part in the Cold War consensus while pushing, correctly, for the liberalization of the country on racial issues.

Two young writers in particular came to prominence on the show: Aaron Spelling and Rod Serling. It's difficult to overstate the impact Spelling's career had on television drama—his shows dominated the industry for decades. He coined the modern action genre, the modern primetime soap opera, and the teen and young adult sexy genre of the 1990s. He started at *Playhouse 90*.

Spelling grew up in Texas, the son of a poor Jewish salesman and an overworked Jewish mother. "To the day Dad died," Spelling recalled, "I don't remember him ever making more than $45 a week." Spelling's parents were both politically liberal—and they were both brave. Spelling's dad befriended a black man, Spelling remembered, and brought him over "to join us on holidays. Whites and blacks didn't spend time with one another back then in Texas, but that never meant anything to my dad."[1]

Spelling, like many of his Jewish compatriots, experienced tremendous discrimination, which affected his view of politics for his entire life. "I grew up thinking 'Jew boy' was one word," he wrote. "You never saw so many rednecks in your life." He also saw racism's cruel and insidious effects time and again. When he directed *Native Son* at the Edward Rubin Playhouse, his father was immediately fired from his job as a tailor for Sears. "He wasn't given an explanation, but the answer was obvious to all of us," said Spelling.[2]

When Spelling arrived in Hollywood, he tried to make it as an actor, playing character roles in *I Love Lucy* and *Dragnet*. He soon realized that his true calling was writing. On *Playhouse 90*, Spelling got a chance to play out his politics on the small screen—and as with many artists, he also got a chance to channel his demons into creativity. "In my early writing career, I felt everything I wrote should really say something," he later wrote in his autobiography. "Why was I so interested in man's inhumanity against man? Because I grew up in a neighborhood that was full of it. When you get your ass kicked every day as a child and have a nervous breakdown at nine, it tends to stick with you for a while."[3]

Spelling also tried to express his fully justified outrage at racism in his writing—an outrage shared by many of the Jewish liberals who staffed Hollywood writers' rooms. After meeting Sammy Davis Jr., Spelling decided to write an episode starring Davis for Spelling's mentor, Dick Powell, who at that time was starring in *The Dick Powell Show*. Spelling's original script had Powell as a sheriff and Davis as his deputy and featured a climactic scene in which Davis shot a white bad guy trying to kill Powell. The sponsors rejected it outright. "I couldn't believe the sponsors would kill that concept," Spelling fumed. His replacement concept starred Davis as one of the Buffalo Soldiers. One of the key lines in the script came when an Indian asked Davis, "Why do you listen to the white man and fight his fight against us? He hates you as much as he hates us." Spelling chortled at the sponsors' idiocy: "Here I was using their forum to point out bigotry and that was okay with them."[4]

Later in his life, Spelling has written, he shifted his viewpoint toward entertainment rather than social messaging. "I believe that people are looking for a release and TV should provide it," he said. "We're in the entertainment industry. It's our job to entertain."[5] But he never let go of his tendency toward infusing his work with his politics.

Rod Serling was another one of the writers on the show who would go on to bigger and better things. Serling, like Spelling, was Jewish and grew up in a liberal home. Like Spelling, Serling experienced anti-Semitism. After serving in the Army, where he participated in the invasion of the Philippines, he went to college, then came to Hollywood. Television, he felt, presented the best opportunity for pressing his politics home. "Of all the media, TV lends itself most beautifully to presenting a controversy," he said. It allowed him to "take a part of the problem, and using a small number of people, get my point across."

That philosophy guided him in all of his writing. Of all his political causes—and they were many, ranging from the antiwar movement to opposition to Ronald Reagan's gubernatorial run—his most beloved was the fight against racism. "I happen to think that the singular evil of our time is prejudice," he said in 1967. "It is from this evil that all other evils grow and multiply. In almost everything I've written there is a thread of this: a man's seemingly palpable need to dislike someone other than himself."[6]

Serling wrote several episodes of the show. One of them, titled *A Town Has Turned to Dust* (1958), was loosely based on the killing of Emmett Till, an African-American boy murdered in Mississippi after supposedly making overtures to a white woman. (Serling had already tried to tell Till's story on *The U.S. Steel Hour* but was met with thousands of letters of protest.) The network nixed Serling's original idea, which was a direct adaptation of the Till case. Instead, Till became a Mexican and the setting changed to the 1870s Southwest.

Less righteously, Serling showed shades of the 1960s radicalism lurking beneath the fair and quiet Eisenhower-era facade. For example, he penned the first installment of *Playhouse 90*, titled *Forbidden Area*, an adaptation of the Pat Frank novel. The plot focused on a Soviet infiltration of America's Strategic Air Command; in the end, the United States decides not to start a nuclear war after finding out about the infiltration. Why didn't they launch the attack? To avoid "ecocide," the destruction of the environment.[7] Serling's Cold War semi-pacifism and indictment of anti-Red feeling began to bear its creative fruit on *Playhouse 90*.

Playhouse 90 was masterful drama often driven by the deep and abiding belief systems of its authors. Its emphasis on anti-racism was strong and morally correct. Soon, however, *Playhouse 90*'s authors would use the moral impetus they gained from that righteous stand to attack other issues far beyond racism.

THE TWILIGHT ZONE (1959–1964): SOCIAL ACTIVISM FROM ANOTHER DIMENSION

Rod Serling moved from *Playhouse 90* to a show of his own creation: *The Twilight Zone*. Serling had decided that attempting to skirt network censors on *Playhouse 90* was a losing battle. If he tried to depict real-life political situations with any accuracy, he would be shut down. On *The Twilight Zone*, on the other hand, he could do whatever he wanted, all under the guise of science fiction. "On *The Twilight Zone*, I knew that I could get away with having Martians saying things that Republicans and Democrats couldn't."[8]

Every Friday night, Serling would appear on millions of television screens. "There is a fifth dimension, beyond that which is known to man," Serling intoned. "It is a dimension as vast as space and as timeless as infinity. It is the middle ground between light and shadow, between science and superstition, and it lies between the pit of man's fears and the summit of his knowledge. This is the dimension of imagination. It is an area which we call *The Twilight Zone*." For half an hour, viewers would be transported to distant worlds, to the future or the past—and all the while, they'd never imagine that they were imbibing Serling's brand of politics.

But they were. Serling's politics were a breakthrough for liberalism, fighting in outright fashion the Cold War consensus itself. He promoted the notion that anti-Red sentiment was sinful, that the nuclear arms race was dangerous, and that détente with the Soviets was not merely desirable but imperative.

In one celebrated first-season episode, "The Monsters Are Due on

Maple Street," Serling took on general suspicions about fifth-column Communists during the Cold War. The residents of Maple Street are humming along innocuously enough when they see a flash of light in the sky—and all of their electrical machines go dead. Tommy, a boy from the neighborhood, informs members of the town that an alien invasion must be taking place . . . and that one of the members of the neighborhood has been planted by the aliens. Naturally, the neighbors tear one another apart. One of the neighbors ends up shooting another; he's then stoned by the crowd, and attempts to deflect attention to Tommy. As the lights in the town flash on and off eerily iridescent, the neighbors riot. We pan back to see that aliens have indeed landed—and they're manipulating the lights of the town, and noting that the best way to destroy humankind is to let them destroy themselves.

Serling narrates, "The tools of conquest do not necessarily come with bombs and explosions and fallout. There are weapons that are simply thoughts, attitudes, prejudices, to be found only in the minds of men. For the record, prejudices can kill, and suspicion can destroy, and the thoughtless, frightened search for a scapegoat has a fallout all of its own: for the children, and the children yet unborn. And the pity of it is that these things cannot be confined to the Twilight Zone."

Serling also tackled racism with righteous enthusiasm on *The Twilight Zone*. In one excellent season-two episode, "The Eye of the Beholder," the protagonist, Jane Tyler, has her eleventh surgery to fix her appearance to resemble everyone else. Her face is swathed in bandages throughout the episode. Eventually, the doctors remove the bandages, and we see that she is a beautiful woman. The doctors and nurses cluck their sadness—she hasn't been fixed. The audience then sees that the doctors and nurses all look like monsters, and that the woman has been trying to surgically alter her appearance to fit in. Fleeing the doctors and nurses, Jane finally finds solace in the arms of a handsome man who promises to take her to a de facto ghetto where they won't be able to bother anyone with their ugliness. The theme of the show is clear: Racism is foolish, and appearance is meaningless—focus on skin color or ethnic background is superficial, ugly, and stupid.

Later in life, even as Serling tackled themes ranging from animal rights to xenophobia and religious ignorance in movies like *Planet of the*

Apes, he became active in politics directly. In 1968, he supported Eugene McCarthy over Lyndon Johnson. In that same year, he gave a controversial speech at Moorpark College in which he called himself a "moderate liberal" who would "salute our flag and stand for our anthem and feel an affection for my native land." This, he said, "removes me from the pale of the new left." But at the same time, he embraced the violent protestors in Chicago and railed against the Vietnam War. He received no pay for the speech after refusing to sign a loyalty oath required by the university, stating that such oaths were morally repugnant and fascistic.[9]

Serling was a principled man, and his work reflects those principles. Many of the episodes seem dated today—the synopses themselves sound obvious and preachy. That's because the dramatic medium on television was just coming into its own. Its creators had not yet learned to hide their politics beneath a mask of principle-free entertainment. *The Twilight Zone* demonstrates that there is a fine line between righteous entertainment and self-righteous entertainment. That line wasn't just crossed on *The Twilight Zone*—it's been crossed on virtually every drama since.

STAR TREK (1966–1969, 1987–1994, 1993–1999, 1995–2001, 2001–2005): SECULAR HUMANISM GOES GALACTIC

If Rod Serling took secular humanism to another dimension, Gene Roddenberry took it to another universe. Roddenberry, creator of *Star Trek*, was virulently anti-religious. As a child, he said, "Every Sunday we went to church—Baptist church. . . . I listened to the sermon, and I remember complete astonishment because what they were talking about were things that were just crazy." Later, he announced, "as nearly as I can concentrate on the question today, I believe I am God; certainly you are, I think we intelligent beings on this planet are all a piece of God, are becoming God."[10]

Many episodes of the original *Star Trek*, which ran from 1966 to 1969 on NBC, are dedicated to simplistic and thinly veiled anti-religious exposition. In "The Apple," for example, a second-season episode, the *Enterprise* crew encounters a planet on which the immortal humanoids spend their time feeding Vaal, a machine they worship as a god, which forbids them sex and love. In the end, the *Enterprise* crew destroys Vaal, making the humanoids mortal but granting them freedom.

The atheism of *Star Trek* carried over through all of its incarnations. Brannon Braga, a producer and screenwriter who has been instrumental on all of the modern *Star Trek* incarnations as well as *24* and *FlashForward*, explained at the 2006 International Atheist Conference, "In Gene Roddenberry's imagining of the future (in this case the 23rd century), Earth is a paradise where we have solved all of our problems with technology, ingenuity, and compassion. There is no more hunger, war, or disease. And most importantly to the context of our meeting here today, religion is completely gone. . . . On Roddenberry's future Earth, everyone is an atheist. And that world is the better for it."[11]

As a secular humanist, Roddenberry was an ardent environmentalist. The original *Star Trek* took on issues like overpopulation. In "The Mark of Gideon," a third-season episode, Kirk beams down to a planet called Gideon, where the people have regenerative abilities and live long lives. Members of the planet also refuse to use birth control or refrain from intercourse, since they believe there is a right to life and a right to love. Kirk's blood carries a disease which can kill members of the planet, and the planet plans to use his blood to control the population explosion. In the end, Kirk ends up transmitting that disease to a member of the planet, who then uses her blood to control the population, in Paul Ehrlich fashion. (The same topic is delved into with substantially more humor in the famous "Trouble with Tribbles" episode.)

The original series' most famous step into liberal legend was the season-three episode "Plato's Stepchildren," in which Kirk and African-American Lieutenant Uhura kiss. Although the kiss has somehow become a breakthrough moment in historical retrospect, within the plot of the show, Kirk was forced to kiss Uhura via telekinesis. As conservative columnist James Lileks put it, "The clinch was forced on them by lazy immortal Grecian wannabees with telekinetic power, who amused themselves by testing the boundaries of the Network's Standards and Practices regulations. . . . Kirk understood, but he went along. You could say he did his part for God and Country, but of course Trek believed in neither."[12]

In those days, the networks were afraid that an interracial kiss would somehow provoke Southern Armageddon, so they insisted that Kirk and Uhura shoot two takes, one of which would cut out the kiss entirely. William Shatner, who played Kirk, and Nichelle Nichols, who played Uhura, purposefully sabotaged every take in which they didn't kiss. "Knowing that Gene [Roddenberry] was determined to air the real kiss," Nichols later wrote, "Bill shook me and hissed menacingly in his best ham-fisted Kirkian staccato delivery: 'I! WON'T! KISS! YOU! I! WON'T! KISS! YOU!' It was absolutely awful, and we were hysterical and ecstatic."[13] The kiss stayed.

Roddenberry was also a down-the-line leftist. As John Meredyth Lucas, a writer who worked extensively on the show, stated, "We could do anti-Vietnam stories . . . civil rights stories. . . . Set the story in outer space, in the future, and all of a sudden you can get away with just about anything. . . ."[14]

While Roddenberry was a secular humanist, he was, like Serling, a committed Kennedy liberal. But that liberalism came across not in the stalwart American exceptionalism espoused by Kennedy, but in the "Prime Directive" governing all Enterprise missions: "No identification of self or mission. No interference with the social development of said planet. No references to space or the fact that there are other worlds or civilizations." In other words, anti-imperialism.

Easier said than done. The Kirk *Enterprise* routinely violated the Prime Directive, involving itself in internecine warfare on a regular basis. Despite the fact that the Federation was supposed to look like the United Nations, it actually resembled the U.S. Congress in terms of policy. The *Enterprise* is a multicultural utopia all right, but it is peculiarly American. Kirk is infused with masculine characteristics, including the propensity toward insemination of every female alien in the galaxy. Kirk is super-American; his hero is Abraham Lincoln, a doppelgänger of whom appears in the third-season episode "The Savage Curtain," to Kirk's delight.

While the original series was jingoistic, it wasn't gung ho on the Cold War. While the Klingons are obviously supposed to be Soviet and the Romulans are obviously supposed to be Chinese and while they both oppose the Federation, which stands in for the North Atlantic Treaty Organization, Roddenberry was a peacenik when it came to the Cold War.

Rumor has it that Chekhov, the Russian member of the *Enterprise* crew, was added to the ship at the behest of *Pravda*.

Roddenberry's attitude toward the Cold War is clearly evident in the third-season episode "Day of the Dove," in which Kirk and the crew of the *Enterprise* are driven by some evil alien force to fight endlessly with Klingons who have come aboard the ship. Only when Kirk offers to make a truce with the Klingons does the brutal hand-to-hand combat end. Similarly, in the first-season episode "Errand of Mercy," the *Enterprise* crew and the Klingons fight over the supposedly primitive planet of Organia, where the population seems to simply accept the cruel tyranny of the Klingons. When the *Enterprise* crew attempts to push the Organians into action, they resist. Finally, the Organians utterly incapacitate both the Klingon ships and the *Enterprise* surrounding the planet, and reveal that they are all-powerful. Then they impose a peace treaty on both sides. Kirk ends up accepting that peace treaty and understanding that it is better for everyone. A second-season episode, "The Doomsday Machine," discusses the evils of nuclear weapons by having the crew of the *Enterprise* face down an alien machine that destroys planets and threatens to destroy its own creators (this episode is so bald-faced that Kirk actually compares the machine to twentieth-century nukes and laments the search for a weapon that could destroy everything).

Star Trek drifted further and further left in its future iterations. The original series went off the air, but popular demand brought it back again and again.

The only other iconic captain of the *Enterprise* appeared much later, in *Star Trek: The Next Generation*. His name was Jean-Luc Picard, and unlike Kirk, he was a sexless eunuch, an international bureaucrat rather than a swashbuckling hero. He didn't seek to impregnate half the alien universe, as Kirk did; instead, he was a peaceful ambassador for the Federation, almost impossible to ruffle and fully respectful of the lifestyles of virtually all civilizations. Picard would have seen Kirk's behavior as cowboyish, retrograde. Picard could only exist in the administrative, bureaucratized world of the late 1980s and 1990s—he'd have been laughed off of television in the patriotic early 1960s.

Picard is the perfection of the Roddenberry vision. As Lileks noted, "Series creator Gene Roddenberry is the Great Lawgiver; Kirk is the

Angry Prophet who prepared the way for the Most Serene Captain Jean-Luc Picard."[15] During the 2008 election cycle, the media compared then-Senator Obama to Spock. That was incorrect—he was far closer to Picard, a universalist bureaucrat convinced that non-intervention and anti-colonialism would result in a peaceful future. Obama and Roddenberry certainly shared one belief: the possibility of perfecting man via secular humanism.

THE MOD SQUAD (1968–1973): HAVE NO GUN, WILL TRAVEL

Fast forward a couple years from the original *Star Trek*. America's Cold War consensus was splintering; the burgeoning racial and sexual revolutions were in full swing. Meanwhile, ABC tried to capitalize on youth audiences in an attempt to compete with the far more powerful CBS and NBC networks. That effort bore its first fruit in *The Mod Squad*.

The first drama to capitalize on the youth movement of the 1960s was created by Aaron Spelling. *The Mod Squad* was ABC's first true urban hit, helping reshape television by directing it at young urban audiences. The show itself revolved around three hippie kids of varying races: African-American Linc (Clarence Williams III), and Caucasians Julie (Peggy Lipton) and Pete (Michael Cole). They were juvenile delinquents given a choice to help the police take down adult criminals or to go to jail.

You might think that the show was anti-crime, an ode to law enforcement in line with earlier cop shows. Not exactly. The show carried a liberal political message: Don't trust anyone over thirty and white, and don't carry a gun.

"All three were on probation and were offered a chance to redeem themselves by working on a special 'youth squad,' whose purpose was to infiltrate the counterculture and do something about the adult criminals who were always trying to take advantage of the young," Spelling wrote. " 'The Mod Squad' would never arrest kids . . . and would never carry a gun or use one."[16]

When Spelling first presented the idea of the show to Leonard Goldenson at ABC, Goldenson liked it—but folks at the network wanted a less controversial title. They suggested *The Young Detectives*. Spelling turned it down flat. "We're doing a show that has meaning," he told Goldenson. "These kids are social activists. They carry placards, but they don't carry guns. I'm trying to be different." Goldenson let him have his way. Later, Goldenson bragged, "We did the show for five years. Nobody ever fired a gun."[17] Spelling agreed, "No one ever carried a gun and no one ever fired a shot. We protested the war we were in, we made social statements about drugs, we said it was okay to have a black kid as your best buddy."[18]

Spelling had a particular fondness for the character of Linc (who had been arrested during the Watts riots) and Clarence Williams III, the actor who played him—a predictable development based on Spelling's deep hatred of racism. That hatred of racism led Spelling into the unenviable position of labeling Hollywood a racist town. "I learned from [Clarence] that even at the height of the Civil Rights movement there was still bigotry in our business, which I didn't realize until I saw things through his eyes," Spelling recalled.[19]

The Mod Squad, Spelling made clear, was not about law enforcement. It was about "honestly depict[ing] what was happening. I tried to build up the contrast between our show and the older model of a cop show, the one where I got my start, *Dragnet*. . . . They were right-wing, we were liberal. They thought everybody under 25 was a creep, we thought everybody under 25 was misunderstood. And, more importantly, *Mod Squad* had an ingredient called 'soul.'" Where did that "soul" come from? From gritty realism. "See, even the crap I came through on Browder Street was good for something," he said.[20]

The evolution of the cop show began with *The Mod Squad*. Unlike previous police shows, it didn't see law enforcement as entirely good—law enforcement was only good if used to target non-liberals. Unlike previous police shows, *The Mod Squad* wasn't interested in upholding the status quo—it was more interested in pushing the youth revolt. Aaron Spelling was the first creator to break out from the procedural nature of cop shows and move toward a more socially oriented take on the law, portraying cops as morally ambiguous and the entire law enforcement effort as inherently fraught with peril.

Spelling felt that *The Mod Squad* embodied the essence of how drama could be used politically. "It's a show of today," he explained to a reporter.

"The only way to convey ideas today is through dramatic action. . . . I think every episode should convey an idea."[21]

THE WALTONS (1972–1981): THE LIBERALISM TIME FORGOT

Most people consider *The Waltons* a conservative show. In most ways, it is. It is a wonderful family program, a clean and pure representation of honesty and decency. Many of the episodes are moving, and most of them warm the heart. It's difficult not to smile at the end of each episode, when the children throughout the house say goodnight to each other: "Good night, John Boy." "Good night, Elizabeth." In fact, growing up, my three younger sisters and I would imitate the back-and-forth each night as we fell asleep.

By the time *The Waltons* came on the air, television had transformed into a repository of urban, vulgar liberalism, with open talk of sex, drugs, and race. All the rural shows of the 1960s were gone, replaced by urban hits like *All in the Family* and *Mary Tyler Moore. The Waltons* was something different: a show that revered tradition. "*The Waltons* was so perfect," explained Lee Rich, one of the producers of the show. "People said 'That was exactly like my family,' which was generally bullshit. What that person was saying in effect is 'I *want* my family to be like that.' "[22] It was both an aspirational show and a show that described an almost mythical American past.

The series was a big hit, providing CBS with a necessary counterbalance to *All in the Family.* And Bill Paley wanted that counterbalance. "Paley loved it at the time," said Fred Silverman. "And so did I." The show was actually supposed to be a sacrificial lamb, going up against *The Mod Squad* on ABC and *The Flip Wilson Show* on NBC.[23] It broadcast for nine seasons, hitting its peak in its second season, when it reached number two in the ratings.

The key to *The Waltons* lay in its *comparative* conservatism. By today's standards, the show is almost entirely conservative, and by the standards of 1970s television, it was largely conservative. By the standards of the show's creator, though, the show was liberal.

I interviewed Earl Hamner, the creator of the show, at his offices in

Studio City, which were just what you'd expect them to be: crammed with fishing equipment, fishing paraphernalia, kites—it looked like grandpa's basement. It was a gateway to America's more rural past. And as Hamner spoke, I was transported there too. After all, I grew up on *The Waltons*, so I knew his voice as the unseen narrator.

Hamner grew up in Virginia, a Baptist and the oldest of eight kids. "We came from impoverished people," Hamner said. "I should have been in the state of Virginia and become a Baptist preacher in a small parsonage in a small town of 800 people. So I look at these things . . . from a very special place."

Hamner started off as a radio writer in Cincinnati, then moved to NBC in New York, where he did documentary stories on Thomas Wolfe and Teddy Roosevelt (for which he interviewed the First Lady, Eleanor). After writing a few television episodes, he decided to move out to Los Angeles with his family, where he wrote some scripts for *The Twilight Zone*—his big breakthrough came from Rod Serling. Then, he told me, he ran into a roadblock.

So Hamner turned to novels. One of those novels was called *Spencer's Mountain*. A decade after its publication, Hamner's agent sent it to Lorimar, where Lee Rich took a look at it. Rich and his partner sent it on to CBS, which asked Hamner to turn the book into a television movie, *The Homecoming*. When that television movie was successful, CBS asked Hamner to turn the show into a one-hour series, which he did.

When I asked Hamner why Bill Paley at CBS had picked up the show, Hamner answered straightforwardly: "I think that there was a political motivation. At that time there was a great deal of discontent with what they called the overall sexuality and violence of the medium and I believe that Mr. Paley was smart enough to see that this was [the] antidote."

Hamner's analysis is interesting in that it ignores the role of people like Paley in creating the "overall sexuality and violence of the medium." *The Waltons*, in Paley's view, was only necessary because of the nature of the medium itself—but this left unspoken the fact that Paley greenlit *All in the Family*, that other liberal executives and creators made active decisions to push television toward more graphic sex and violence. If Paley had truly been worried about the overall sex and violence of the medium, he would have greenlit ten shows like *The Waltons* and dumped those like *All in the Family* immediately. He didn't, instead pushing *The Waltons* as a silver bullet meant to respond to the new tidal wave of sex and violence (much in the same way that today's liberals point to Fox News as the balance for CNN, MSNBC, ABC, NBC, and CBS).

Although the show was a throwback, a palliative to the acidity of *All in the Family*, Hamner still saw it as teaching liberal social lessons. "To me television is the medium . . . that could elevate people, could inspire people, could instruct people; it could teach, it could lead." Yet Hamner shied away from shocking the bourgeois—he even scorned it. "If television encouraged anything, it may be the expression that I loathe . . . 'pushing the envelope,'" he said. Hamner is a Hollywood liberal in the old style—he wanted television to softly lead Americans, but he wanted television to avoid vulgarity and shock promotion, and he strongly believed in the goodness of Americans and America.

To that end, *The Waltons* consistently promoted liberal messages about tolerance of everyone (including many criminals), always through the guise of the Walton family, who together with their kindhearted neighbors composed a near-perfect society. In a first-season episode, "The Boy from the C.C.C.," for example, Gino, a city boy who has run away from FDR's Civilian Conservation Corps, is found by the Waltons hiding out in the forest. Gino stays with the family but ends up robbing them of their money, after telling John-Boy about his parents' deaths in the slums of New York. John Walton Sr. stops him, but as he considers whether to turn him over to the police, Gino undergoes a transformation, then finally rejoins the C.C.C. and helps work on a national park. The message is mild but present: Criminals are the product of bad social circumstances, proper social circumstances can cure criminality, and government can be helpful in doing so.

This is innocuous stuff next to the fire and brimstone of *All in the Family*, but it's there nonetheless. The opening episode of season nine, "The Outrage," is perhaps the clearest evidence of the show's worship for FDR. A two-parter, the episode told the story of Harley Foster, a black man who has lived on Walton's Mountain for years. It has recently been discovered that Foster escaped from prison after being convicted in a biased trial. The sheriff is forced to recapture Harley, and John Walton

Sr. works for his release. "In the closing months of World War II, the fighting, far from the serenity of Walton's Mountain, was beginning to wind down," Hamner narrates. "On the home front, however, my father found himself in the vanguard of the battle for equality and freedom that was so long overdue in America." When it becomes clear that Harley will be kept in jail without any hope of release, John Sr. appeals directly to President Roosevelt, who pardons Harley just before his death. "The train bearing the body of Franklin Delano Roosevelt moved slowly from Warm Springs, Georgia, toward the nation's capital," Hamner narrates as the show closes. "Wherever it went the people who loved him gathered to mark its passing, remembering the man who led a nation out of its most crippling depression and toward victory in its greatest war, planting seeds of brotherhood along the way." Then the show concludes with John Walton uttering the show's hallmark closing line: "Goodnight, Mr. President."

Is this liberal? Of course. But it's also classy. And Hamner dislikes what he sees on television now, because it lacks that class. "A clue to what TV has become to me," he said, "is in the fact that I watched *The Today Show* on a Friday not long ago, and they had a musical group of young kids. . . . And one of the boys . . . as he sang, kept his hands touching his penis, which I found unnecessary. I thought, 'Jesus, why do you got to do that? His singing doesn't come from his penis.' . . . The singers that I liked back in my day were like Sinatra and Rosemary Clooney. Those people sang from their hearts. These people today sing from their crotches. It seems to me that we have moved from television that was created from the heart, to television that now seems inspired from the groin."

Although Hamner's highest value was family in *The Waltons*, he told me that he disliked being seen as a totem of the right. "I wish that I could say I am not your property. You know? Because I think so much of Obama." In fact, Hamner told me that he hoped the rural liberalism of *The Waltons* helped pave the way for the election of Jimmy Carter. He also said that he was "pretty into today's liberalism. I'm for abortion. I'm for gay marriage."

While Hamner may have evolved in his liberalism, he is definitely of the old school in his style. He was cordial in his politics, and he was elegant in his attempts to infuse messages into his programming. And those messages were 1930s-brand rural liberalism—which makes *The Waltons* a uniquely balanced slice of pure Americana, when viewed in the context of its time.

CHARLIE'S ANGELS (1976–1981): BIKINI-CLAD FEMINISM

Jiggle TV in the 1970s sprang from the country's desire to escape: escape Vietnam, escape Watergate, escape OPEC. *Charlie's Angels* catered perfectly to that desire. The eye-catching program about three beautiful women—Kelly (Jaclyn Smith), Jill (Farrah Fawcett), and Sabrina (Kate Jackson)—was bashed as exploitative and sexist, but it was truly just escapist fun.

Or was it?

As we've already seen, Aaron Spelling was a master of inserting his politics into shows. He was also the first creator to transition away from cop procedurals and toward cop social dramas. *Charlie's Angels* fit well within that pedigree. While critics ripped the show as fluffy material designed to oppress women, that wasn't the intent of the show at all. Precisely the opposite: the show was meant to combine entertainment and beauty with feminism, even as it played on America's desire for escape.

By the time Spelling moved on to *Charlie's Angels*, he had already entered his "cotton candy" period—the period in which he told a reporter, "What's wrong with sheer escapism entertainment . . . cotton candy for the mind?" At the time, Spelling's programming dominated the airwaves: Aside from *Charlie's Angels*, during that decade he would launch *The Rookies*, *S.W.A.T.* (a show he would later disown for its violence), *Family*, *Vega$*, *Starsky and Hutch*, *Fantasy Island*, *Hart to Hart*, *T.J. Hooker*, *The Love Boat*, *Hotel*, and *Dynasty*, among many others.

The public never moved beyond Spelling's "cotton candy" remark. The press also dubbed him the King of Jiggle. Leonard Goldberg, who was Spelling's partner at the time, got hit with the same accusations. "I was criticized all the time," Goldberg told me. "Did it hurt? Yeah, sure it hurts. . . . To be demeaned like that was terrible."[24]

The labels were inaccurate. Not only did Spelling-Goldberg make *Family*, they also worked on television movies like *Something About*

Amelia, which tackled the taboo topic of incest, and *Little Ladies of the Night*, which dealt with child runaways and prostitution. Spelling also produced *And the Band Played On*, "where we really tried to say something about how the government mishandled the AIDS crisis," and *Day One*, in which Spelling contended that "we never should have dropped the atomic bomb."[25]

The truth is that if anything, these labels probably helped the Spelling-Goldberg public image; since their programming was considered innocuous bubblegum, guilty-pleasure material, it also drew higher ratings than it would have if the public had considered his work politically serious (*Charlie's Angels* would have outdrawn *The West Wing* any day of the week).

While the public was focusing on Spelling-Goldberg's sexy programming, though, they were utterly ignoring the underlying messages he was inserting in that programming. Even their sexiest show, *Charlie's Angels*, carried that messaging.

The show's genesis was pure Hollywood. "We went to breakfast with Michael Eisner and Barry Diller from ABC, both of them my boys, then heads of ABC programming," Goldberg related. "And we pitched them an idea for a show: 'It's going to be different from what's on, which is very realistic and ash can and gritty. It's a very high style show. It's about three girls, beautiful girls, dress beautifully, who are private detectives. It's called *Alley Cats*.' . . . And they said, 'It's the worst idea we have ever heard for a television show.' " Nonetheless, they let Spelling and Goldberg proceed.[26]

The show bombed in testing. "The average score on good pilots was 60," Spelling wrote, "and *Charlie's* was way, way below that."[27] Fred Silverman, who was in charge of ABC at the time, continues the story: "[The initial episodes] were so bad that we actually put the names of the episodes in the hat and drew straws to decide what was going to open. . . . We put them on the air and it was an instant hit."[28]

Goldberg told me that even from the show's earliest days, there was a political backdrop to the show. "When we came up with *Charlie's Angels*," Goldberg said, "we thought it would be very entertaining, but also, it was the first time that women went into what was heretofore a men's world. Women doing what men traditionally did and doing it well."[29]

Cheryl Ladd, who played Kris, the replacement for and sister of Farrah Fawcett's Jill, said at an Equal Rights Amendment fund-raiser, "I think ERA and *Charlie's Angels* do go together. . . . [The series is] not just pretty ladies. We don't act like dummies and bimbos on the show. *Angels* shows that women can function in a man's world."[30]

Of course, Farrah Fawcett thought differently: "When the show was number three, I thought it was our acting," she said just before leaving the show in 1977. "When we got to be number one, I decided it could only be because none of us wears a bra." Spelling rejected Fawcett's comments wholesale. Spelling did admit, however, that the show was "camp."[31]

It was that balance of camp and political subversion that would drive Spelling's work for the rest of his career. While Spelling revolutionized the television cop drama, his most significant genre transformation came in the form of primetime soap operas, which took the linear, serialized nature of daytime soaps and glitzed them up for a broader audience. *Dynasty*, which was the biggest hit on television for one of its nine seasons and finished in the top ten for four of those seasons, was "pure camp," said Spelling, but it was a hit "because it showed that rich people have as many problems as poor folks, and there's nothing TV viewers love more than to see rich people skewered."

Furthermore, *Dynasty* also pushed the gay rights message with Steven Carrington, one of the first openly gay characters on television. "You have to remember that when we did *Dynasty*, gays were afraid to come out of the closet in real life," Spelling reminisced. "One great line summed it all up for us. Remember, this was 1981, and Blake [Steven's father] came to see his son, who was now living with his gay lover. 'I've been wrong,' Blake said. 'I'm glad you found someone who loves you as much as I do.' That was a hell of a thing to say at the time, and we were all very proud of what we did." Spelling would also push acceptance of homosexuality in *Heartbeat* and more famously, on *Melrose Place*.[32]

Later on, of course, Spelling would dive into the teenage set with *Beverly Hills, 90210*, where he would pursue the same political agenda (on *Beverly Hills, 90210*, he brought in Darren Star, who would later create *Sex and the City*). "What set us apart from the other shows was our realistic portrayals of issues," Spelling wrote. "On *90210*, we entertained, but we also said a lot. We dealt with so many timely topics—drinking, drugs, AIDS, gun control, and even consensual teenage sex. We ended our first season with Dylan and Brenda going to a hotel on prom night, and we really dealt with the consequences of having responsible sex at their age."[33]

That's what Spelling was all about: creating massively entertaining material that seemed like fluff but had political content embedded within it. Over his career, the balance may have shifted toward fluff—but the sweeter the fluff, the easier for the audience to swallow the serious content.

GENERAL HOSPITAL (1963–PRESENT): DAYTIME TELEVISION'S BALANCE

The soap opera genre is much derided for its supposedly cardboard acting (and yes, there's a lot of cardboard acting) and ridiculous plotlines (how else are you supposed to keep a show going for *fifty* years?). But of all television's genres, the daytime soap is probably the most reflective of American society. Since soaps run on a daily basis, their fans are obsessive and deeply involved in the shaping of the show—the soap opera audience provided Internet-like response to creators long before the Internet. And creators worked the show according to the whims of the audience.

Not always, of course. Soaps are still created by liberal creators, and they still push liberal messaging. They're not merely reflective of audience trends, they're transformative of them. But soaps tend to lag behind primetime television in their radicalism. Perhaps that's why they've lasted so long.

General Hospital is, at last count, the longest-running show in the history of television. It has been on the air continuously since 1963. As you'd expect, during that time, the soap opera has undergone dramatic changes in terms of tone and content. Early on, the show actually focused on a hospital, as well as general themes of love and marriage and crime and lust. In the 1970s, as the show's ratings sank, Fred Silverman, then at ABC, told the creators that they'd better spice things up or the show would be canceled.

Spice it up they did, with one of the most famous storylines in soap opera history: the Luke and Laura love affair. Doctor's daughter Laura

(Genie Francis) fell in love with Luke (Anthony Geary), a low-level Mafioso. They began courting, and then Luke raped/seduced her (the show has always gone back and forth on whether it was rape or seduction). Later she fell in love with Luke and married him. This was an incredibly hot topic at the time—their wedding became the highest-rated episode of soap opera in TV history, with 30 million people tuning in, and the couple appearing on the covers of *People* and *Newsweek*.

The story was politically incorrect, particularly in an era when feminism suggested that there was a stark distinction between rape and seduction (in most cases, obviously, there is, but the vagaries of rape law are well-known). The story was also reflective of audience sensibilities—the audience simply liked Luke and Laura. The fallout was dramatic but it raised the ratings.

From there, the show took off in an action-adventure direction until finally rethinking itself for the last time in the 1990s as an issue-oriented potboiler, with AIDS storylines (the characters who got AIDS were straight), gay storylines, cancer stories, and abortion (on which the show takes a pro-choice stance). The show has moved progressively to the left since its inception, largely at the behest of its writers—the devotees of *General Hospital* aren't issues-oriented viewers.

"A lot of what defines this show is almost escapist fare," head writer Robert Guza told me. "[But w]e as the creative people say, 'We want to do some real stuff, we want to do a story on teen breast cancer,' which we did, or 'We want to do stories on bipolar disorders,' which we did."

Although many of the writers for *General Hospital* are liberal, it tends to be more balanced than most shows. For example, last season it featured an abortion storyline in which one of the characters, Lulu, decided in favor of terminating her pregnancy. The issue was treated with more balance than would have been contemplated on other shows; Lulu even expressed regret over the abortion afterward, though she stated that she believed she had made the right decision. "We tried to show the whole complex of social attitudes in regard to abortion at that time on the show," said Guza.

General Hospital responds to audience predilections and to both sides of the political debate better than other shows because it has to fill time and please viewers. Whereas a primetime show may produce a couple of dozen episodes a season, a typical soap produces *hundreds*. "[Our need for balance] is really clearly a reflection of the audience," Guza told me. "Basically all of daytime, we're really responsive to viewers. . . . Also, because we're so starved for material, we want to cover all of it. It's hard to do an hour every day."

The soaps may be moving to the left—see, for example, the lesbian wedding on *All My Children*—but they're generally far more reflective of the real political debate going on in the country than primetime. And that's a good thing. Even though those in Hollywood and around the country scorn soaps as minor league artistry, they could stand to learn a thing or two from the soaps in terms of politics.

LOU GRANT (1977–1982): EVEN FAKE JOURNALISTS ARE LIBERALS

When *Lou Grant* premiered in 1972, the country was reeling from Watergate, from Vietnam, from the sexual and civil rights revolutions. By the time it went off the air, the country had responded to the liberal administration of Jimmy Carter by electing Ronald Reagan, voting for smaller government and less restrictive regulation. In essence, the country had rejected the politics of *Lou Grant* by the time the show went off the air.

But it took a radical liberal to actually kill the show.

That radical liberal was Ed Asner. Born in Missouri, the Jewish Asner served in the army, then went to New York, where he joined the city's artist subculture. That subculture was reflected in Asner's political views. Asner is a member of the Democratic Socialists of America. He believes that cop killer Mumia Abu Jamal is innocent. Most disturbingly, Asner is a 9/11 truther—a nut who thinks that the American government allowed 9/11 to occur. "Could it all be accidents?" he asks in a bizarre YouTube video. "Four planes destroying four different buildings? . . . Was it Osama? We all think in the deepest recesses of our mind, I gather, could there have been great culpability and criminality within the framework of the United States?"[34] Somehow, the palpably insane Asner is considered worthy of work in Hollywood but those who believe in cutting taxes and killing terrorists are not.

Asner blew up *Lou Grant* in 1982 because of his politics. The story was national in scope, and went something like this: Asner, the actor who played the title character, was liberal. So liberal, in fact, that he held a press conference in which he announced he would be sending $25,000 in medical aid to victims of the Salvadoran regime and supporting the rebel cause (which was Communist). The blowback was immediate, with the right wing pushing advertisers to cancel their investments. That season, CBS canceled the show.

The show itself, of course, was almost entirely left. A spin-off of *The Mary Tyler Moore Show*, it carried the same creative team—Brooks, Burns, and Tinker, and added a familiar face in Gene Reynolds. All of them were still liberal, and all of them were happy to be doing a drama where they could really sink their teeth into political material. Reynolds in particular was overjoyed that he could shed the dead weight of comedy and focus on drama—he was sick of hearing from network executives that his shows didn't have enough jokes.

The show started as a comedy, since it was supposed to relate to *Mary Tyler Moore*. Burns said they had based the idea for *Lou Grant* on Woodward and Bernstein. "We were fascinated by the putting together of that story with Woodward and Bernstein. And the way the paper worked, and we were fascinated by that."

The network wasn't satisfied with the idea. "Guys," the executive told Burns, Brooks, and Tinker, "you're giving us the *New York Times* when people read the *Daily News*." Tinker, Burns related, "exploded. And he said, 'I can't ---- believe what I'm hearing. You wouldn't want the *New York Times* on your network?' And they said, 'Not if it doesn't get ratings.'" At the end of the meeting, the CBS executive informed the creators that their job was to think over his prescriptions and to make the show "a little more Kojak-ish." Tinker quickly responded, "That's not what I heard at all. I heard that these guys are going to keep doing the show that they're doing and you're going to promote it and it's going to be a hit."[35] Tinker got his way, and *Lou Grant* did become a hit.

He also got his way in terms of the politics: The show *was* a version of the *New York Times*. "Most television (and movie) writers are somewhat left-leaning, and it's probably fair to say that the *Lou Grant* group leaned a bit more than others," Tinker admitted.[36] The show's take on issues ranging from homosexuality to nuclear politics to illegal immigration was unwaveringly liberal in orientation.

In the episode dealing with illegal immigration, for example, we see the INS haul off an illegal immigrant without regard for her two children and then we learn that illegal immigrants are often victimized by the coyotes who bring them across the border. The show does not contemplate the criminality of those who cross the border illegally. In another episode, Lou Grant and company uncover safety risks at a nuclear plant, à la *Silkwood*; in yet another episode, Lou Grant has to deal with a Latin American country torturing members of its populace (a thinly veiled swipe at El Salvador).

All of this was fine and dandy. The problem for the series arose when Asner, who was also president of the Screen Actors Guild, began using his position as Lou Grant to push his politics. Anthony Hopkins took out a letter in the *Hollywood Reporter* expressing his displeasure with Asner: "I wish to state that he does *not* represent my views and I resent being spoken for by him. His barking, self-important militancy in the name of liberal causes, righteously sheltering behind the name of the Screen Actors Guild, is chillingly reminiscent of East European political debate." Charlton Heston seconded the motion: "I would suggest that the serious professionals in the Screen Actors Guild would not want the guild to take positions on El Salvador or solar energy, but on acting." Asner had already used his position as head of SAG to cancel an award to be given to Ronald Reagan, former president of SAG, since Asner and the board didn't want to reward Reagan for shutting out the air traffic controllers (besides which, Asner had called Heston a "----sucker" in public).[37]

Asner's outspokenness killed the show, since he refused to disassociate himself from his Lou Grant character. That frustrated the creators of the show no end. "After the controversy had started . . . , Allan Burns and two other producers on *Lou Grant* came into my dressing room to ask me to stop what I was doing," remembered Asner. "One of them said, 'I think there are two ways to make a point in this life; one is in the way Lou Grant was doing it and one is the way you're doing it, and I think our way is better, with Lou Grant.'" Essentially, Burns and the other producers on the show were asking Asner to embrace the "spoonful of sugar" idea that has served Hollywood liberals so long and so well—they were asking him to channel his politics through *Lou Grant*, rather than using Lou Grant's name to promote his politics off the air.

Asner turned them down. But one fact was clear: Asner's agenda and Lou Grant's agenda were the same.[38]

HILL STREET BLUES (1981–1987): LIBERALISM IN CRISIS

"Be careful out there." So warned Sergeant Phil Esterhaus every morning at the station house before sending the cops out to police the streets and break up gang activity, drug rings, and prostitution rackets. *Hill Street Blues*, which ran on NBC for seven seasons beginning in 1980, was the first criminal law show to depict cops not as defenders of the law but as flawed human beings who sometimes use the law as a weapon—and, by contrast, to depict criminals not as villains, but as complex characters. This followed in the footsteps of *The Mod Squad* and *Charlie's Angels*, which used cop shows to push political messages. Unlike those Spelling productions, however, *Hill Street Blues* embraced its politics by pitting inherently political characters against one another.

That's what made the show so good. That's also what made the show so liberal.

The show was commissioned by Fred Silverman and Brandon Tartikoff from MTM's Grant Tinker. Silverman had just seen the film *Fort Apache: The Bronx* starring Paul Newman, and he suggested to Tartikoff that they do an hour show "that's like *Fort Apache* meets *Barney Miller*." (If you haven't noticed, that's the standard Hollywood pitch: one successful movie meets another. Every television show, therefore, owes something to *Abbott and Costello Meet Frankenstein*.) *Barney Miller*, ABC's long-running cop sitcom, portrayed cops as quiet heroes going about their business but facing down societal prejudices in an utterly liberal manner—it was the transition step from *Dragnet*'s all-out cop worship.

Tartikoff, Silverman continued, "went to Steve Bochco and brought in Mike Kozoll and that ended up being *Hill Street Blues*."[39] The co-creators of the show, Bochco and Kozoll, were both liberal. Bochco, who would go on to bigger shows than *Hill Street*, grew up in Manhattan, where he attended the High School of the Performing Arts, then went to Carnegie Tech, then worked his way up at Universal Pictures. If you're looking for the perfect example of the industry baby, Bochco is it. Kozoll, by contrast, hailed from Wisconsin—but like Bochco, he had extensive experience with the cop genre. Also like Bochco, he leaned left.

Bochco stridently denied at the time of the show that he was a "cop-lover." His overall liberalism pervaded *Hill Street*. "We don't answer questions that people desperately want answered simplistically," he told author Todd Gitlin. "The appeal of a Ronald Reagan . . . to a great many people has always been solid, simple answers to very complex questions. I think what Michael means when he says that we are unfashionably liberal is in our perception that those simple, easy answers don't yield results. They never have."

Bochco also announced that he was going to make life hell for the people at the standards department, in true bobo fashion. He bugged them on everything from sex to violence. There is one particular point, however, on which he did not bug them, according to Gitlin. Jerome Stanley, the head of NBC's West Coast Standards and Practices, told Bochco and Kozoll to tone down the presence of minority criminals in the pilot. "Our quarrel with them, if you want to call it that, was that they were simply going to have to fictionalize it to the extent of saying that all criminals weren't black," he told Gitlin. Bochco and Kozoll agreed, and changed some of the criminals in the pilot into whites, resulting in an oddly multicultural gang attacking some of the cops.

The political debate on the show took place on the character level. Captain Frank Furillo is a liberal, a secular priest suffering for the flock. Detective Henry Goldblume (Joe Spano) is the in-house liberal, constantly attempting to utilize caring rather than bullets. Goldblume was Bochco's favorite character, because "he's terribly, terribly troubled all the time, about being an essentially passive man in a violent world, and yet remaining in it because of his hope that he can be a pacifying force."[40] Goldblume's foil is the insufferable Detective Howard Hunter (James Sikking), a racist moron bent on using lethal force whenever and wherever necessary—and often, even if it was unnecessary. In the opening episode, Hunter sums up his character nicely in an exchange with Furillo regarding how to deal with a hostage situation.

Furillo: "I'm sending in Goldblume, see if we can open communication, defuse the situation. It's by the book, Howard."

Howard: "Goldblume! Goldblume couldn't defuse a roll of kosher toilet paper."

Not exactly an even-handed depiction of the muscular cop.

Goldblume, by contrast, is a saint. In one episode, he sums up the liberal's despairing question about crime after watching three teenagers arrested for several brutal slayings: "Where do you put all the hate?" The conservative would answer: in prison, or better yet, in the electric chair. The liberal would answer: hate springs from social conditions, so we must change society.

There's no question where the creators of *Hill Street Blues* stood in principle. But they also recognized that liberalism had tried and failed to correct the social situation. From the very beginning, the philosophy of the show despaired of the law enforcement situation. It quickly deteriorated to outright nihilism. Esterhaus's slogan, "Let's be careful out there," eventually made way for Sergeant Stan Jablonski's far more ethically questionable "Let's do it to them before they do it to us." As Kozoll told Gitlin, "Like a lot of onetime liberals, I think we've gotten to a point where we just throw up our hands and say let's be honest. There's no visible way to change anything anymore . . . there is very little illusion about things ever getting better."[41]

The cops in *Hill Street* are like the soldiers in *M*A*S*H*: victims of a mad society surrounding them. And as in *M*A*S*H*, the unspoken assumption is that broader societal change will have to take place in order for criminality to truly be cured.

Bochco went on to produce shows with the same philosophy—breaking stylistic taboos while pushing a sophisticated post-liberalism—including *NYPD Blue*, in which he somehow finagled the network into allowing him to use the words *douchebag* and *dickhead*, as well as showing Dennis Franz's bare buttocks, and *L.A. Law*, which introduced the world to the sweeps-week lesbian kiss. All of these depictions were gratuitous and superfluous to story—even the lesbian kiss did not affect the overarching storyline—but that's Bochco's mentality. Like so many others in television, he feels that he needs to push the boundaries, shock the bourgeois.

Bochco's contention was that such groundbreaking forays into vulgarity and sexuality were necessary because television wasn't "very smart . . . not very funny . . . not very truthful, or very real . . . not very enlightening, and only occasionally thoughtful . . . it's just not very good." Newton Minow had come 180 degrees; instead of advocating higher standards of television programming, Bochco was arguing to lower the bar in the name of vulgar vanguardism. But like Minow, Bochco also argued for greater liberalism on television. "The television business, like it or not (and I don't), has become politicized," Bochco wrote in 1992, approximately thirty years after television became politicized. "Networks have become increasingly skittish about any program content that is perceived by pressure groups as objectionable. Does this mean that television shows have, by and large, become more conservative? You tell me. . . . Networks don't want controversy. They don't want bad language. They don't want sex, particularly sex between individuals of the same gender. What they do want is big ratings. . . ."[42]

Of course, like any creator, so does Bochco. And that's where the meeting of the minds came with the network, which essentially allowed Bochco to funnel his envelope-pushing politics into his shows, destroying network standards wholesale. Was that good for television? It certainly made for fascinating watching in the case of Bochco's work. But as with *All in the Family*, groundbreaking stylistic choices infused with political comment tend to fade away, and in their place, we tend to get the vulgar form rather than the politically fascinating substance.

ST. ELSEWHERE (1982–1988): THE POLITICS OF HEALTH

The medical genre has always been a staple of primetime schedules. Like most genres, it began as a semi-conservative procedural, upholding the virtue of doctors without attacking the status quo. Shows like *Ben Casey* (1961–1966) and *Dr. Kildare* (1961–1966) and even the later *Marcus Welby, M.D.* (1969–1976) dealt mainly with doctors trying to treat patients rather than doctors rebelling against society. They were Kennedy-esque in their liberalism, focused on the progress of human technology and often learning lessons about tolerance. *Marcus Welby, M.D.* was so focused on patient care that it even ignored the more radical liberal ideas of its day—one episode had the good doctor advising a patient struggling with homosexuality to resist the impulse, stating that his homosexual tendencies are driven not by actual homosexuality but by fear of homosexuality. The episode drew massive protest from the gay left.

By the 1980s, however, liberals were despairing of the medical system the same way they were despairing of the law enforcement system. Liberal angst about the inability to provide universal medical care, about the rise of new diseases and conditions, about the ability of mankind to fight health problems altogether—all of it finally took form in a show called *St. Elsewhere.*

Despite *Hill Street Blues*'s first-season troubles, NBC was looking to class up its schedule. They did so by picking up *St. Elsewhere*, also from MTM. While Grant Tinker would get the credit for *St. Elsewhere*, it was Silverman who picked up the show initially.[43] The show itself was never a major success—it barely broke the top fifty during its six seasons—but it was a *prestige* show, largely due to its intelligent writing, great acting (the show launched the career of a young man named Denzel Washington, as well as the less-prominent careers of Ed Begley Jr. and Howie Mandel, among others), and provocative storylines.

The creator of the show was a young writer named Joshua Brand; like most television writers, Brand sprang from the New York milieu. Brand majored in English at City College in New York, then went to Columbia for graduate school, where he began writing poetry and fiction. At his sister's wedding, he met a screenwriter who gave him some tips on entering the industry; after Brand had written a few spec scripts, the screenwriter suggested that he move to Los Angeles. His screenwriting didn't work out initially, but he did write a play, which ended up opening the door to television.

Brand truly got started when he broke in with *The White Shadow*, a CBS show produced by MTM and starring Ken Howard as a former NBA star now teaching at a largely minority school. The show was produced by Bruce Paltrow—father of Gwyneth, an outspoken liberal, and the same fellow who would later produce *St. Elsewhere* (and allegedly discriminate against conservative actor Dwight Schultz when he auditioned for a part in the show).

When *The White Shadow* was canceled, Brand decided to cowrite a show with another *White Shadow* staff writer named John Falsey. He based his idea for the show on his best friend, who was doing his medical residency at the Cleveland Clinic. Brand pitched the idea for a show at a teaching hospital, and Tinker and NBC bit. Brand and Falsey wrote the stories for the first season, then left after that—but the course of the series had been set by then.

The thematic of the series, Brand insisted, had to be realism. That meant, as usual in Hollywood, that social issues would be tackled from a liberal perspective. Brand said that he didn't intend to make the show about social issues, but in a hospital, they were unavoidable. "We didn't think that that was driving us. But inevitably, when you're dealing with people who don't have enough money to get good medical care and all sorts of stuff like that, how could it not be social?"

And it *was* social. More specifically, it was socially left. The first season featured an episode in which Dr. Mark Craig (William Daniels) had to confront the fact that his old college roommate was gay and seeking a sex change. Eventually, of course, Craig comes to accept his friend's decision. Where did that episode come from? I asked Brand. "To be honest with you, what has motivated myself for the most part is I try to do things that were interesting to me," Brand answered. (Brand's take on homosexuality became even more apparent later, when his *Northern Exposure*, which he described as a "non-judgmental universe," featured television's first gay wedding.)[44]

The show routinely took the socially liberal position on health issues ranging from transsexuality to abortion to AIDS to sex education. Tackling such issues was a conscious decision by creators like Tom Fontana, who wound up producing the show and writing many of its episodes before going on to produce shows like *The Bedford Diaries* and *Oz*. "There was never a moment where we ever talked about *not* bringing up issues," he told me. "We were always looking for what was out there that was going to throw doctors and nurses off their pedestals. So that's how we looked for stories—whatever was going to confuse our characters. So things like transsexuality or AIDS or testicular cancer or mastectomies or abortion—we did at least one abortion story a season, and we always tried to tell it from a different point of view."[45] Usually, a different liberal point of view. To his full credit, though Fontana is politically liberal, and though the show was politically liberal, Fontana's commitment to politically interesting television means that he actually wants more right-wing writers to enter the industry.

The watchability of *St. Elsewhere*, like that of *Hill Street Blues*, does lie in its realism. But as with most drama, the creators can stack the case against one political side or another, and they did it frequently on the show, whether by design or simply by political osmosis.

THE DAY AFTER (1983): TRYING TO RUIN REAGAN?

As Reagan's first term in office neared its end, liberal desperation reached its breaking point. How could they remove this idiotic cowboy from office, demonize his policies, and make nuclear détente a popular policy rather than a sign of weakness?

They could run a television movie.

On November 20, 1983, ABC ran *The Day After*. It chronicled the fate of Lawrence, Kansas, and the surrounding area in the aftermath of a nuclear war with the Soviet Union. *The Day After* was easily the most-watched television movie of all time, clocking in with 100 million viewers (the entire population of the United States in 1983 was approximately 234 million, which means nearly half the population watched the show).

At the time, Fred Pierce of ABC told me, the made-for-television movie was the chosen vehicle for political messaging on issues ranging from homosexuality (*That Certain Summer*) to AIDS (*An Early Frost*) to incest (*Something About Amelia*) to child prostitution (*Little Ladies of the Night*). But none of those movies could compare in impact to *The Day After*.

The movie itself was unclear on who led off the nuclear war; characters in the movie argued about it. But the point of the movie was clear: A nuclear war under any circumstances would be utterly apocalyptic. The show had an intense impact on the nuclear debate. Right-wingers denounced the basic assumptions of the program as misleading—i.e., the assumption that mutually assured destruction would ultimately fail—and left-wingers celebrating the program as a necessary step in convincing the population about the necessity of disarmament.

"*The Day After* was a very important program," wrote ABC president Leonard Goldenson, "but it would almost certainly not have made it to the network had not Brandon Stoddard several times put his job on the line to argue that we *must* broadcast it."[46]

I sat down with Stoddard on a sunny day in his Santa Monica, California, offices, just blocks from the beach. The office had a relaxed, Hawaiian decor. Stoddard, who now teaches classes at the University of Southern California, was kind enough to give me several hours of his time. We discussed *The Day After* at length. "It was my idea and I made ABC do it. . . . I was six-three when I started doing it," the diminutive Stoddard joked. "It was the most difficult and probably the most controversial [thing] ever put on TV."[47]

The lead-up to the movie was enormous. The National Education Association issued a national alert to parents warning that children under twelve should not view it. The New York City School Board was less strident: "ABC's intention in presenting [*The Day After*] is to educate the public about nuclear war. However, the scenes of terrible destruction, people being vaporized, mass graves, and death from radiation sickness may NOT be helpful or educational for children or young people. This is not just one more horror film . . . the threat of nuclear war is real."[48]

Stoddard wanted the film to transform people's lives. "That movie was not necessarily reflective," he told me. "Of course, the left thought it was about nuclear peace and thought it was the best thing in the world. People walked up to me with lit candles saying, 'Oh my God, you're the most wonderful person I've ever met.' The right wanted to kill me. . . . [*The Day After*] was transformative."

Stoddard was adamant that *The Day After* wasn't a political statement. In fact, he pointed out that, a few years after he did it, he also produced a made-for-television movie first suggested by Ben Stein in an article criticizing *The Day After*—a movie called *Amerika*, about what would happen to the country in the wake of a Soviet takeover. "And the left thought this was the most horrible idea they had ever heard," Stoddard reminisced.

"'How could you do this?' [I] literally had death threats at my office and at home." Stoddard laughed as he remembered a conversation he had with hard-left actress Shirley MacLaine, in which he complained about the scorn he was receiving from the left. "Brandon," MacLaine replied, "don't you know they'll kill anything for peace?"

Stoddard wasn't the only creator involved with *The Day After* who said that the movie was supposed to be free of political content. I met with the movie's producer, Robert Papazian (who later produced HBO's *Rome*), who told me the same thing. "What was important was this particular thing was terrible for the world. And as a result of it exploding, this is what is going to happen," Papazian said. "It was about the process of destruction, and what the nuclear arms race was about and not why it should be stopped or how it should be stopped, but if it *does* happen, here's what's going to happen to the world and humanity as we know it."[49]

Lionel Chetwynd, who was close with Reagan, ripped Stoddard's suggestion that the show was apolitical. "There was nothing to be proud of on *The Day After*," he fumed. "Nothing whatsoever. It was an attempt to undermine Ronald Reagan."[50]

The film's director, Nicholas Meyer, came down on Chetwynd's side of the argument. Meyer, who directed *Star Trek II*, *Star Trek IV*, and *Star Trek VI*, is a vocally liberal ideologue. I met him at his large house off of Sunset Boulevard, where he ushered me in after I narrowly avoided being eaten by his enormous dog. "The motives for people such as myself, such as Jason Robards . . . the motives for many of the people involved in the making of the film were certainly political, they were antinuke," he said. "But what I began to realize very early on, and where I sort of agree with Brandon [Stoddard], is that if we had proselytized, the whole thing would have backfired. . . . So it evolved in my mind into a kind of gigantic public service announcement."

Meyer told me, "My . . . grandiose notion was that this movie would unseat Ronald Reagan when he ran for reelection. In this I was hopelessly mistaken."[51]

Even if the film wasn't meant to be a political statement, it certainly achieved political ends. According to one scientific study, watching *The Day After* made subjects more likely to push for "a more conciliatory approach to U.S.-Soviet relations." The show also had an unintended impact on President Reagan—the same Reagan that Meyer derided and hoped to unseat. Reagan, a visual learner who was always disproportionately affected by what he saw on film, wrote a diary entry after watching a prescreening of the movie on October 10, 1983. "In the morning at Camp David," he penned, "I ran the tape of the movie. . . . It is powerfully done, all $7 million worth. It is very effective and left me greatly depressed. So far they haven't sold any of the 25 ads scheduled and I can see why. . . . My own reaction: we have to do all we can . . . to see that there is never a nuclear war."[52] Shortly after Reagan signed the Intermediate Range Nuclear Forces Treaty, according to Meyer, he sent Meyer a letter reading, "Don't think your movie didn't have any part of this, because it did." Meyer noted, "The making of the film was to date the most worthwhile thing I ever got to do in my life. Any movie that the president of the United States winds up saying changed his mind about the idea of a winnable nuclear war is not an insignificant achievement."[53]

It is controversial to suggest that *The Day After* was a turning point for Reagan or that he dramatically reshaped his thinking to cope with what he saw in that show. But if *The Day After* represents the truth of any proposition, it is this: Television is immensely powerful. As Stoddard told me, "If you're putting *The Day After* on . . . , you reach 120 million people in one night, [and it's] seen around the world and translated into seventeen languages and is played in Russia—the first American film ever played in Russia."[54] How can anyone argue that television doesn't change the world?

MACGYVER (1985–1992): A *MOD SQUAD* OF ONE

With the spectacular failure of the movie *MacGruber*, it's sometimes difficult to remember that its source material, *MacGyver*, was a highly successful series for ABC, wherein the main character made internal combustion engines from gum and paper clips. The creator of the show was a former *Hill Street* writer, Lee David Zlotoff. Zlotoff went to Brooklyn Technical High School, where he became an expert in pre-engineering; his dad was an engineer. Hence MacGyver's invaluable mechanical skills.[55]

But as executive producer Vin DiBona told me, there was more to the show than that. The show, he said, had a liberal sensibility to it. "Oh, absolutely. Yeah, that was the whole premise of the program, that MacGyver used his brain power and skill of stuff and science, and he solved all the difficulties through ingenuity. . . . No guns, no knives." DiBona told me that MacGyver was also active with respect to the environment and racial equality. "Absolutely," he said. "[MacGyver was a] good guy."

DiBona, who also said that he was "happy" that Hollywood was completely liberal, said that the point of television was "finding what the common man needed to know and give that information out in an entertaining fashion that makes it get the message across." Certainly *MacGyver* fit that bill.[56]

THIRTYSOMETHING (1987–1991): BABY BOOMERS' WHINY BOBO REVOLUTION

As the Baby Boomers came of age during the 1980s, their generational struggles were reflected on television. On comedies like *Family Ties*, the bobos struggled with their kids. On the hit dramatic series *thirtysomething*, they struggled with their urge to buy matching dinnerware.

When *thirtysomething* came on the air in 1987, it was an anomaly. In a world of glitzy, glamorous shows like *Dallas* and *Dynasty*, ABC and Brandon Stoddard decided to counterprogram a bunch of yuppie urban couples chatting about sex and kids. While the show never reached smash hit status (in its four-season run, it never cracked the top thirty), it had a cultural impact that stretched far beyond its actual viewership.

The show revolved around a group of friends who had grown up in the 1960s and taken part in the counterculture. Now they were grown up, married with kids, or single and looking to settle down. They were looking for an identity they had lost with the descent from the heady liberalism of their younger years. "I think *thirtysomething* was about trying to find out who and what you are," Stoddard told me. "What person? Who are you? And what do you stand for? What are your values?" The goal was to connect with this new generation of viewers, to connect with the suburban angst of the new jet set.[57]

The creators of the show, Ed Zwick and Marshall Herskovitz, were both liberals. Zwick grew up a member of the liberal suburban elite, attending Harvard and writing for the *New York Observer*, *Rolling Stone*, and the *New Republic*. He got his start in film working for Woody Allen. He then moved on to *Family* under Spelling and Goldberg. Herskovitz grew up in Philadelphia, where he attended a private school run by "public school teachers who were Communist Party members who had been thrown out of the system in the early 1950s."[58] He, too, got his television start on *Family*.

They both recognized that the yuppie lifestyle of the characters clashed with their purported liberal sensibilities—and that these yuppies weren't satisfied by the white picket fence, the house, the two kids, and the dog. They recognized the bobo conundrum long before David Brooks coined the term.

"It's very clear that the politics of the characters on *thirtysomething* are basically very liberal—we get a lot of letters complaining about that," Zwick told *Playboy*. That liberalism took shape on the show, where one married couple argued about whether or not the wife should use her diaphragm and where the network took a $1 million advertising hit to depict two gay men in bed together.

Zwick and Herskovitz admitted to being taken aback by the furor surrounding their decision to put two men in bed together. "I felt like we were in Hollywood in 1958, having a black man kiss a white woman," Herskovitz lamented. Sexuality, he continued, "is the area where it's hardest to tell the truth in television. It's a never-ending battle."

"It's the area we keep coming back to and trying to explore," Zwick agreed.

"And we've made lots of headway—whether it's Hope putting in her diaphragm or teenagers having sex," Herskovitz said. He summed up the philosophy of the series: "It's important to note that morality is not the first concern when we make the show. It's third or fourth on the list. Our prime concerns are . . . dramatic and psychological. . . . The fact that we are more concerned about showing the truth than about moralizing disturbs a lot of people. . . .

"We—this generation, that is—are attacking the basic construct of our culture: the way we raise children, the way we behave toward our parents," Herskovitz finished. "What our sexual relationships should be," Zwick added.

"Whining as revolution?" asked the editor of *Playboy*.

"Exactly," said Herskovitz.[59]

That whining *was* revolutionary: it summed up an entire generation of people who wanted to rebel against social standards while maintaining a comfortable lifestyle. In a Hegelian sense, if 1960s radical liberalism was the thesis, and if 1980s Reagan middle-class conservatism was the antithesis, then *thirtysomething*'s middle-class social rebellion constituted the synthesis. It also provided the groundwork for show after show reinforcing that perspective, from *Seinfeld* to *Friends* to *Modern Family*.

L.A. LAW AND *BOSTON LEGAL:* LIBERALISM FOR SWEEPS WEEK

The TV drama genre has four major standbys you will see every season: the cop show, the medical show, the daytime soap opera, and the law show. As in the other major genres, law programming began with the typical "lawyers as heroes" form. They praised the American legal system as a structure designed to reach just conclusions. The early legal shows, like *Perry Mason* (1957–1966), actually leaned conservative, since they were designed to convict the guilty. Shows like *The Defenders* (1961–1965) were liberal, of course—*The Defenders* focused on getting suspected criminals off—but they never questioned the merits of the legal system or the motives of the lawyers.

Over time, the image of lawyers began to shift. As liberals grew more and more disenchanted with the criminal justice system, which they saw as racist and classist, they began to portray lawyers as either heroes struggling against the system or as willing participants in the fleecing of the American public. No single figure has been as instrumental in crafting our modern view of law as David E. Kelley.

Kelley, like Zwick and Herskovitz, grew up a member of the liberal elite. He spent his childhood in Maine, then attended Princeton University and the Boston University School of Law. He used his legal background as a way to join the industry; after writing a movie script that would later turn into a Judd Hirsch movie, he was selected by Steven Bochco to become a writer and story editor on a new series called *L.A. Law* (1986–1994). Law, Kelley said, was always "a natural for me. . . . It's a franchise that causes people to unearth their ideas and beliefs, and it's such a natural spring board to tell stories about characters."[60]

Kelley's philosophy was openly liberal, and he brought his politics to bear in *L.A. Law.* The show took on the usual range of issues, from the usual limited range of viewpoints—that is, moderate left to far left. The biggest political scandal of the show was reserved for season five, though. As the ratings for the show collapsed, the writers decided to have a bisexual kiss a lesbian on national television. Naturally, this occurred during sweeps week. As Michelle Green, one of the actresses involved in the scene, later said, "On *L.A. Law* they never intended to explore the issue of a relationship between two women; it was about ratings during sweeps, so I always found it a bit cynical."[61] It was still groundbreaking, though, and it didn't undercut the general message of the series, which had always forwarded the gay rights agenda.

The lesbian kiss eventually became a staple of sweeps week, with shows ranging from *The O.C.* to *Roseanne* doing it. Sandy Grushow of Fox even admitted to me that the lesbian gambit on *The O.C.* was a ploy: "I think it's true, there's no question from an insider's perspective that sweeps created a need to tell stories that would be more likely than not to attract attention."[62] Kelley has used them repeatedly, whether it's teenage girls kissing and considering lesbianism during sweeps on *Picket Fences* or whether it's adults doing it on *Ally McBeal*. Kisses between men are far less popular, for obvious commercial reasons.

Kelley is, of course, one of the greatest success stories in the history of the industry. The husband of Michelle Pfeiffer, Kelley has created *Picket Fences* (1992–1996), *Chicago Hope* (1994–2000), *The Practice* (1997–2004), *Ally McBeal* (1997–2002), and *Boston Legal* (2004–2008). Kelley's take on law is almost always classist: The poor are virtuous and the rich are scumbags. That holds true whether we're talking about clients, criminals, or lawyers. The lawyers on *The Practice* struggle to make ends meet—and they are righteous truth-seekers flailing against the unjust system. The lawyers on *Ally McBeal* and *Boston Legal* work for huge firms that find motivation in profit—and those lawyers are largely nasty, venal, and corrupt, with a penchant for sin.

No matter which Kelley show we're talking about, however, the best lawyers all have one trait in common: they're liberal. Bobby Donnell (Dylan McDermott), Lindsay Dole (Kelli Williams), Eugene Young (Steve Harris), and Ellenor Frutt (Camryn Manheim), the partners of *The Practice*, are all outspoken liberals. Even the prosecutor, Helen Gamble (Lara Flynn Boyle), is a liberal who struggles with her conscience while going after criminals. While the partners on *The Practice* occasionally struggle with the ethics of putting criminals back out on the street (particularly white criminals—minority criminals are never portrayed as possible recidivists), those qualms are generally outweighed by their certainty that criminals are products of their social environments. Liberal legal truisms roll off their tongues. "It's better that ten guilty men go free, than one innocent man suffer," Bobby claims, paraphrasing famous jurist William Blackstone without citation, ignoring the fact that those ten guilty men will go on to hurt dozens of innocent people. "What kind of fairness is this?" Bobby protests in another episode when a judge rules against him. "You're putting the system before a person's life." And vintage Bobby on why defense attorneys should be fine with defending the O. J. Simpsons of the world: "Once in a while you get an innocent, and that's why we do this." When Bobby loses, he does so because the judge is a bigot or a racist or a fool.

On *Boston Legal*, to take another Kelley example, the lawyers routinely mock conservative viewpoints. The show's resident Republican, Denny Crane (William Shatner) is a homophobe, a charming scumbag, a greedy smooth-talker along the lines of Michael J. Fox in *Family Ties*. He's also a quasi-idiot. After finding out about a liberal attempt to ban red meat, for example, he sputters, "We're carnivores. When the pilgrims landed, first thing they did was eat a few Indians." On environmentalists: "They're evildoers. Yesterday it's a tree, today it's a salmon, tomorrow it's, 'Let's not dig up Alaska for oil because it's too pretty.' Let me tell you something. I came out here to enjoy nature, don't talk to me about the environment." His conservatism is of the most simplistic brand, summed up in one episode thusly: "It's a good feeling, you know, to shoot a bad guy. Something you Democrats would never understand. Americans . . . we're homesteaders, we want a safe home, keep the money we make, and shoot bad guys." In the show's last episode, Crane marries his liberal partner, Alan Shore, in order to protect his assets—and the man performing the wedding is a look-alike of conservative Justice Antonin Scalia.

Kelley's unique ability to stack his shows with leftist politics makes him one of the most critically popular figures in television. His peers worship his work. Larry Gelbart described Kelley as "entrepreneurial," one of the few in Hollywood willing to push his politics.[63] Allan Burns told me that Kelley's shows were "important . . . about the law, and how to use it for the good."[64] Vin DiBona said he and his wife would never miss an episode of *Boston Legal*.[65]

Kelley's style is unique—and uniquely political. His philosophy of programming has never changed: Politics had to be an inherent part of the story. "Our show," he told the *Pittsburgh Post-Gazette* about *Boston Legal*, "is about ideas and it became very organic to make politics part of this show. . . . One of our writers was an ex-journalist and he used to get calls from his colleagues in the news business and at newsmagazine shows saying they were envious. We got to tell stories they wanted to do but were not allowed to because it was not hot enough copy for the news."[66] That's why any Kelley show tackles the issues from a liberal perspective.

LAW & ORDER (1990–2010): FROM PROCEDURAL TO SMEAR JOBS

The cop genre has its ebbs and flows in terms of liberalism; it encompasses a broad variety of perspectives. Steven Bochco twisted the cop genre from outright reverence to despairing pessimism, but Don Bellisario pushed conservative messages on law enforcement in shows like *NCIS* and *Magnum, P.I.*

The latest turn of events in the law enforcement genre has been a merger of Bochco and Bellisario—maintaining reverence for cops while ripping conservatives in storylines. These shows are apparently conservative because they uphold the status quo through a somewhat wooden procedural format, but they paper over that conservative groundwork with storylines painting conservatives as criminals and crazies.

Dick Wolf started that trend. The creator of the *Law & Order* chain was born in New York, then went to the University of Pennsylvania for college, working afterward in the advertising industry. That experience no doubt gave Wolf an understanding of the commercial nature of the industry, knowledge he would put to good use after moving to Hollywood. He got his start under—who else?—Steven Bochco, writing for *Hill Street Blues*.

Wolf is himself apolitical. He reportedly supported Fred Thompson's 2008 presidential candidacy. His programming philosophy is a softer version of Kelley's: he rips from the headlines but does so without any serious political messaging. "When Brandon Tartikoff bought the show way back in the last century, he said, 'What's the Bible?' " Wolf told an interviewer. "And I said the front page of the *New York Times*. And it has not been a bad piece of source material because for better or worse we can't come up with stories better than a headless body found in topless bar."[67]

Michael Moriarty, a conservative actor who starred as D.A. Benjamin Stone on the original *Law & Order*, said that Wolf "is a careerist. 'Anything that works,' you know?" Moriarty stated that the series wasn't anything new; he compared it to *Dragnet*. He did, however, point out that the series had moved to the left since its inception.[68]

And he's right. *Law & Order has* moved substantially to the left. Wolf has never made openly political statements—although like Bochco, he has ensured that the vast majority of victims and perpetrators are non-minorities, and according to the *Wall Street Journal*, "limits the number of shows containing minority victims, including blacks and Muslims, to four or five episodes a season out of 22 to 24."[69]

But now the show has moved beyond mere racial quotas. A glimpse at the early episodes of the show, which were straight procedurals examining how cops and DAs worked to put criminals behind bars, shows the difference: today's episodes are filled with liberal calling cards. In a 2009 episode of *Law & Order: SVU*, a franchise spin-off, for example, a lawyer played by John Larroquette suggested, "Limbaugh, Beck, O'Reilly, all of 'em, they are like a cancer spreading ignorance and hate. . . . They've convinced folks that immigrants are the problem, not corporations that fail to pay a living wage or a broken health care system. . . ." That set off O'Reilly, who responded by rhetorically punching Wolf between the eyes, calling him a "despicable human being."[70] In the past few years, *Law & Order* has also run episodes prosecuting government lawyers for okaying torture (Jack McCoy, played by ultraliberal Sam Waterston, says that he would prosecute the Bush Administration for "assaulting suspected terrorists"); stumping for gay marriage; pushing for hate-crimes legislation protecting gays and lesbians; labeling the question of abortion "pro-choice or no choice"; and the list goes on and on. (It is worth noting that although *Law & Order* has moved to the left, it provides balance on occasion, as it did in 2009 in an episode on abortion.)

Moriarty and others on the right see the culprit for *Law & Order*'s leftward slide in executive producer René Balcer, a self-proclaimed liberal who says, "There's a balance, but anyone who's been watching knows our best shows make the public question what's going on."[71] Though Balcer may pretend balance, his programming strategy isn't truly balanced. "I think probably on the whole, like most writers, you're about liberty, free expression, and you generally stand up for the little guy," Balcer said in an interview with the far-left *American Prospect*. "It seems like the people defending the little guy more often than not [seem] to be progressive, liberal."[72]

Balcer is militant in his views—he stated regarding Fred Thompson, who appeared for years on *Law & Order*, "when they brought me back on the show, I said I'm not coming back as long as that guy is on the show. I didn't think much of his acting or the character." This is the essence of the blacklist—it suggests that because a creator or executive doesn't like an artist's political stance, that artist can be quickly and easily labeled untalented and then dumped.

Thompson said that when he appeared on the show, he had an agreement with Wolf that "as long as we had an exchange of ideas and it wasn't skewed to the other side, is all I wanted. To have an opportunity to make some conservative points along with the ever-present liberal points." Balcer fought for the liberal point of view as hard as possible, Thompson recalled: "[He] was fixated on Iraq and it was all about oil or it was a premeditated deal." Thompson noted that once Balcer took over, things changed.[73] Balcer, said Moriarty, "is the shamelessly far-left villain. . . . [He] became the major inspiration for Dick's consistent desires to please the Obama White House."[74]

Law & Order isn't the only crime procedural that layers its conservative foundations with liberalism. *CSI* (2000–present), created by liberal

Anthony Zuiker, targets criminals and praises law enforcement. But its story arcs often target conservatives in pathetically blatant ways. In the 2010 premiere episode, "Shock Waves," teen heartthrob Justin Bieber played an anti-government juvenile delinquent, obviously a member of the Tea Party, who helped bomb a police officer's funeral. In an interview with radio host Laura Ingraham, Zuiker admitted that his own political persuasion stood behind the ridiculous plotline. "We wanted to take, you know, a position of a faction—and, again, Tea Party, I have no idea what all that means, so, forgive me. But, in terms of talking, we call it the Church of Crazyology in the room, meaning when we were breaking the story, we just wanted to have, you know, a faction taking a position that we shouldn't have driver's licenses, and why pay taxes, and just take that position," Zuiker rambled nonsensically. After Ingraham grilled him on his ignorance—he doesn't know what the Tea Party is, but he calls those who agree with it the Church of Crazyology?—Zuiker called upon the usual Hollywood defensive playbook. "We took a position in that particular fictional faction to be anti-government, and that's about as deep as it went," Zuiker protested. "Our job is to be, just entertain people. And that's what we did."[75]

Law & Order is easily one of the most addictive shows on television, because it is plot-driven rather than character-driven. For a lawyer, it's a pleasure to watch because it is meticulous in its adherence to legal standards, and until very recently, most of the episodes have attempted to argue both sides. The writing is tight, and the stories move quickly. So quickly, in fact, that unless you're watching, you might miss what has now become the dominant politics of the show. But whether you miss it or not, it's there.

COPS (1989-PRESENT): WHITE CRIMINALS WANTED

It's not truly honest to classify *Cops* as a drama; it's really a reality show, of course, following the exploits of law enforcement officers across the United States as they chase down and capture the bad guys. Its success—2010 marks its twenty-third season on the air—stems from Americans' love of police officers and hatred for criminals.

Because *Cops* is a law-enforcement support show, it has become the target of hard-left types like Michael Moore, who interviewed producer Richard Hurlin for his hit-piece documentary *Bowling for Columbine*. Hurlin tells Moore, "If you look *liberal* up in the dictionary I think my picture will be in there somewhere." Moore then proceeds to grill Hurlin about the supposed racism of the show, saying that racism raises the ratings. "Maybe because we in the television business tend to demonize black and Hispanic people, then those watching it at home are going, 'I don't want to help those people. I'm not going to do anything to help them because I hate them now because they may hurt me.' You know what I'm saying?" Moore asked/demanded. Hurlin, who clearly did not know what Moore was saying, answered, "I know what you're saying, I don't know that's what we're doing. I'm not sure we're demonizing black and Hispanic people particularly."

Cops does have a lot of minority criminals, but that's because there *are* a lot of minority criminals. John Langley, the creator of the show, rejected Moore's argument head-on. "What irritates me sometimes is critics will watch *Cops* and say, 'They misrepresent people of color,'" Langley fumed. "That's not true. *Au contraire*. I show more white people than is statistically what the truth is in terms of street crime. If you look at the prisons, it's sixty-something percent people of color and thirty-something percent of white people. If you look at *Cops*, it's sixty percent white and forty percent people of color, it's just the reverse. And I do that intentionally, because I don't want to contribute to negative stereotypes."[76]

Even the conservative shows are liberal in Hollywood.

THE REAL WORLD (1992–PRESENT): NOT *THAT* REAL

MTV spent most of the 1980s as a music video station, providing little but cutting edge fast-cut rock and roll. It was specifically geared toward young, disenfranchised audiences—the crowd that wouldn't watch *The Cosby Show*. And despite its supposedly cutting-edge content, MTV remained relatively tame for cable.

Then came *The Real World*. Doug Herzog, who was an executive at MTV at the time, remembered the origins of the show. "We were trying to develop a soap opera, a teen soap opera, or an adult soap opera. . . . And we gave [creators Mary-Ellis Bunim and Jonathan Murray] some money to go shoot a test over a long Thanksgiving weekend in a SoHo loft with seven strangers."

The result was *The Real World: New York*, which tackled issues of sexuality, gender, race, and class. It's pure liberalism all the way around, with episodes dealing with homelessness (one of the castmates lives in a homeless shelter for a night to learn about the subject), pornography (one of the castmates has posed nude for advertisements), homosexuality (one of the castmates is gay and scores a boyfriend), among other hot topics. The voyeurism of the show was undoubtedly based on having young attractive singles living together in one house; in later seasons, that situation would devolve, predictably enough, into sexual arrangements among the housemates.

One of the most provocative storylines on the series came during the second season, *The Real World: San Francisco*, when one of the housemates, Pedro, revealed that he was HIV positive. His affliction was treated with sensitivity and acceptance by everyone, particularly a young woman named Cory and another young woman from a conservative family, Rachel. Everyone, that is, except David "Puck" Rainey, a politically incorrect dirtbag who put boogers in the peanut butter and wore a shirt with a swastika made of guns emblazoned on it. Rainey constantly irritated Pedro to the point where Pedro's health was endangered, at which point the castmates threw Rainey out of the house, in an ultimate triumph of tolerance over xenophobia. Pedro ended up taking part in a same-sex wedding ceremony with his boyfriend.

Herzog knew at the time that this was liberal politics masquerading as entertainment. "MTV was started by and continues to be run by a group of people that believe . . . that through the medium of television we try to make the world a slightly better place," he told me. "For me, one of my proudest moments was Pedro and Cory's story on *The Real World*, way back when, and bringing the issue of sexuality and AIDS to TV."

Over time, *The Real World* has only gotten more liberal, featuring threesomes with housemates, as well as other fringe behaviors. When I asked Herzog about some of the criticisms of *The Real World*—namely, that the show was at least partially staged, Herzog laughed. "We're not making documentaries, we're making TV," he said.[77]

ER (1994–2009): THE CLINTONIAN CONSENSUS

In the aftermath of the 1992 election, President Clinton attempted to ram through a health care proposal that would have dramatically reshaped the American medical system. It frightened Americans, and it made them worry about the sustainability of private-sector health care.

Television's liberal creators provided two solutions, both of which were geared toward promoting the Clintonian universal health-care agenda. First, David E. Kelley's *Chicago Hope* placed liberal doctors in a private charity hospital, a fantasy land where everyone was cared for equally, without regard to cash or status. Second, there was *ER*, a show taking place entirely within an emergency room—another area of the medical system where money is no object. "This is a place where you go and you sort of know who the people are, and you feel that they care about you," explained show creator and massive liberal John Wells. *Newsweek* magazine featured the cast of *ER* on the cover, emblazoning it with the headline, "A Health-Care Program that *Really* Works."[78]

And what a cast it was. George Clooney. Julianna Margulies. John Stamos. Shane West. William H. Macy. Maria Bello. Angela Bassett. The cast of *ER* reads like a who's who of television and film stardom. That makes sense, since the show ran a whopping fifteen seasons, finishing first in the ratings three times and within the top ten no less than ten times.

In the aftermath of *St. Elsewhere*, and going up against the David E. Kelley medical vehicle *Chicago Hope*, *ER* was expected to fall apart early. Instead, it exploded out of the gate. Chris Chulack, the longtime producer of the show and the quick-witted and down-to-earth writer of many of its finest episodes, sat down with me in his offices on the Warner Bros. lot, which were decorated with sketches from another one of Chulack's shows, the short-lived but excellent *Third Watch*.

Unlike many of those I talked to, Chulack got into the business through the technician's door. He actually split his time in college between studying and driving a moving truck. Then he realized that he had a distant uncle who worked in television as an editor on *Hawaii Five-O*. Chulack worked his way up from a low-level position in the editors' room to riding his bicycle around the Warner Bros. lot delivering dailies and movies to projection rooms. Eventually, he became an apprentice film editor, then an assistant, then an assistant picture editor, then an assistant sound effects editor, then a sound effects editor, and then a looping editor. "I kind of moved up and really kept my mouth shut and my nose to the grindstone, ears open," he said. Finally, he became a producer and a director, and signed an overall deal with Lorimar, then run by Les Moonves.

That's when Chulack met Wells, who was working on a project based on an old Michael Crichton script entitled *EW* (Emergency Ward). Wells is more of an outspoken liberal than Chulack; even as he produced *ER*, he worked with Aaron Sorkin to create *The West Wing*, which we'll discuss momentarily. Just before the 2010 election, he held a major Hollywood fundraiser for Obama.[79]

Through a series of odd circumstances, Chulack ended up as a producer, director, and sometime writer on the show. "It'll probably be nine [episodes] and out," Wells told him at the time. "But we'll have fun." Fifteen years later, the show wrapped.

ER restored the glory of drama to television. After a decade in which drama had ruled the roost—the weakness of comedy in the early 1980s has already been well-documented—sitcoms had taken over, with *Cosby*, *Roseanne*, *Family Ties*, *Cheers*, and the other big comedies of the day eating drama's lunch. "*ER* came and had this different rhythm," Chulack noted. "It wasn't just a medical show; it felt like an action show because of the nature of being in an *ER*, where time is heart muscle, as the doctors say."

Social messaging wasn't at the top of Chulack's heap when it came to priorities. "I don't think anybody set out to put any political messages." Chulack admitted that the creators of the show and the writers of certain episodes had their own "particular slant, and sure, that's going to come through, but at least for my money, being in the room, and I was in the room, the discussion was always about 'was that interesting?' . . . We tried to arm both sides, if you will, and tried to have an honest dialogue."

The characters, Chulack said, may be liberal—they "may carry a political torch"—but the creators tried to balance it "the best way we could. . . . So I don't think that we put a message out there, but I think we asked a lot of questions on a lot of levels. . . ."[80]

In the television business, political balance very often means merely giving passing attention to opposing points of view before settling on the correct, liberal position. For example, in the season-twelve episode titled "If Not Now," a pro-choice doctor who is Catholic convinces an underage teenager to allow him to induce a miscarriage after she is raped, citing the Bible. The pro-life position is presented but rejected from a religious point of view, a political oddity to say the least.

ER was clearly a show of the left, with Christian characters counseling abortion, liberal treatment of gay and lesbian issues, and even jibes about the war in Iraq. *ER* differed from some of the other dramas of its time, however, in that it presented the other side before rejecting it. *ER* countenanced the debate, at least; unlike comedies of the same time period, or other dramas of the same period, it didn't dismiss arguments out of hand, even if it finally rejected most conservative positions. *ER*'s politics were Clintonian in nature: Everyone's pain was felt, even if not everyone's position was legitimated.

THE WEST WING (1999–2006): THE LEFT WING

John Wells went from working on *ER* to working on a show called *The West Wing*, with a creator named Aaron Sorkin. Sorkin was yet another member of the new generation of liberal writers—he grew up a privileged yuppie child in New York. Sorkin spent his early career in New York, struggling to find work as an actor. Finally, he penned an antimilitary piece titled *A Few Good Men*, which made it to the screen directed by none other than hard-left Rob Reiner. The movie was well-written and respectful of the military—read Col. Jessup's famous "you need me on that wall" speech out of context, and it is Patton-esque—but it also suggested that high-ranking officers routinely sanction abuse of enlisted men in order to "toughen them up." That was his ticket; soon he was writing mainstream liberal hits.

His next movie, *The American President*, abandoned the purported balance of *A Few Good Men* and skewed wholly liberal. In that propaganda piece, a nefarious conservative senator, Bob Rumson, exposes the president's lover when he discovers that she burned a flag in college. That leads to this long-winded speech by the liberal president (Michael Douglas): "For the record: yes, I am a card-carrying member of the ACLU. But the more important question is why aren't you, Bob? Now, this is an organization whose sole purpose is to defend the Bill of Rights, so it naturally begs the question: Why would a senator, his party's most powerful spokesman and a candidate for President, choose to reject upholding the Constitution? . . . You want to claim this land as the land of the free? Then the symbol of your country can't just be a flag; the symbol also has to be one of its citizens exercising his right to burn that flag in protest." And so Sorkin turns flag burning into a vindication of American freedom.

Not long after Sorkin wrote *The American President*, he was scheduled to have lunch with Wells. He didn't expect to be pitching an idea but quickly realized that Wells was looking for a pitch. "And so, on the spot," Sorkin recalled, "I started saying, 'What about the White House . . . ?' "[81] Out of such meetings are legends made.

And *The West Wing* was a legendary show: legendary for its liberalism, legendary for its insane amounts of dialogue, legendary for its preachiness. It lasted for seven seasons, reaching a high in the ratings of number seven during its third season, before experiencing gradual decline to number seventy-two in its seventh season. Sorkin's main character, President Josiah "Jed" Bartlet, was a saintly liberal hero who supports the leftist agenda on every point. Bartlet's point of view invariably won, and Bartlet was invariably the good guy in all of his arguments. The show pursued the same "ripped from the headlines" strategy as David E. Kelley and *ER*; it was designed to respond to current events. In one episode, the show commented on Dr. Laura Schlessinger's famously controversial comments on homosexuality by having Bartlet lecture "Dr. Jenna Jacobs" about gay rights, citing supposedly obsolete proscriptions from the Bible—a strategy Sorkin allegedly cribbed from an anonymous online letter to Dr. Laura. That was rather typical of the show, which made Republicanism look ignorant and foolish on a weekly basis.

The West Wing wasn't quite as bad as *The American President*—the occasional conservative was portrayed in a mildly sympathetic light, though always as a dissenter from his/her own party or as a potential convert. Annabeth Schott (Kristin Chenoweth) started off as an assistant to the Bill O'Reilly knock-off Taylor Reid; she ended up joining the Bartlet Administration in the press department. Bruno Gianelli (Ron Silver) was a political strategist based on Dick Morris; after working for Bartlet, he ended up campaigning for a moderate Republican, Arnold Vinick (Alan Alda), whom he routinely directed to ignore his more conservative base (Silver, who became a Republican in 2004, was routinely mocked around the set as "Ron, Ron, the Neo-Con"). Vinick himself was so liberal that he ranted at his conservative base when they simply asked him to attend church.

Overall, however, *The West Wing* brutalized right-wingers. The premiere episode of the show had Bartlet ejecting conservative ministers from the White House; the ministers were ignorant (they didn't know the First Commandment), stupid, and loathsome. The episode ended with Bartlet preaching to *them* about religion: "Now, I love my family, and I've read my Bible from cover to cover so I want you to tell me from what part of Holy Scripture do you suppose the Lambs of God drew their divine inspiration when they sent my twelve-year-old granddaughter a Raggedy Ann doll with a knife stuck through its throat? You'll denounce these people Al, you'll do it publicly, and until you do you can all get your fat asses out of my White House."

Demonstrating his complete lack of political understanding outside the cloister of New York and Los Angeles, Sorkin stated, "I would disagree this is a liberal show." Wells agreed, stating, "Nothing goes into the show without a full pro and con." Well, almost nothing—when it came to gun control, Wells said, "I don't think any of us really believes in the other side of the argument very much."[82] No wonder—the staff was stacked. On it sat Patrick Caddell, Jimmy Carter's former pollster; Lawrence O'Donnell, who worked for Democrat Daniel Patrick Moynihan (and now has his own hard-left show on MSNBC); Dee Dee Myers, former Clinton White House press secretary. Every one of the show's political consultants was a Democrat.[83] Yet Sorkin averred, "I don't think that television shows, or, for that matter, movies or plays or paintings or songs can be liberal or conservative. I think they can only be good or bad."[84] This is patent nonsense.

Sorkin sums up the goal of *The West Wing* well: He wants to entertain with liberal politics. If a by-product is mass political conversion, so much the better. "I think we're all very flattered when we hear that the show illuminates certain things. . . . We're delighted when we hear that, but that's not our goal. Our goal is the same as David Kelley's goal on *The Practice* and *Ally McBeal* and John [Wells's] on *ER*, and Steven Bochco and David Milch's on *NYPD Blue*. It's simply to captivate you for an hour. . . ."[85] Sorkin's right, of course—entertainment obviously has to come first for everyone, including liberal ideologues. It's just that Sorkin's politics are so ubiquitous in the milieu he inhabits that he doesn't bother acknowledging that by entertaining, he's foisting his politics on millions, just as Kelley, Bochco, and Wells do.

DESPERATE HOUSEWIVES (2004–PRESENT): PARADOXICAL LIBERALISM

On October 3, 2004, America met the women of Wisteria Lane. And they loved them. They adored Teri Hatcher's Susan Mayer, a divorced mother with a penchant for clumsiness; Felicity Huffman's Lynette Scavo, a saintly suffering wife taking care of her four children despite an absentee husband; Marcia Cross's Bree Van de Kamp, an uptight conservative whose addiction to perfection utterly destroys her family; and Eva Longoria's Gabrielle Solis, a former fashion model who spends time shagging the gardener. The banter was witty, the plotting intricate, and the show was always pretty to look at. It was, in short, one of the most entertaining things ever put on television.

The show was also controversially liberal. Susan Mayer talks about her sex life openly with her daughter; Lynette, the only one of the four with a lasting marriage, has to suffer through her husband's wandering eyes and idiotic career moves; Bree, the Republican, has to deal with a gay son, Andrew, whom she predictably attempts to "convert" back to heterosexuality, with disastrous consequences; and Gaby's cheating is looked upon as a natural consequence of her husband's neglect. The show's frankness regarding sexuality and casual approach to serious moral issues deeply bothered those on the right.

However, the show never treated the lives of the housewives themselves with the scorn so often heaped on suburbia. It wasn't *thirtysomething*, with trite people complaining about trite problems. It was a dramedy, but it took its characters seriously and didn't dismiss them for staying home and attempting to bring up their children (however badly).

This seeming philosophical split comes directly from the incisive mind of Marc Cherry, creator of the show. When I met Cherry at his home in the San Fernando Valley, his street looked suspiciously like Wisteria Lane itself. His home was perfectly painted and manicured, and spotlessly clean.

Cherry is gay, and he is also a Republican, which makes him a rarity both in the general population and in Hollywood (where it is more common to be gay than conservative, and certainly uncommon to be both). Cherry went to Cal State Fullerton, where he got his degree in theater. He soon decided, however, that there wasn't much he could do in the acting field—Cherry isn't a leading man type, he's got more of a character-actor look—and so he started writing spec scripts for television. In the spring of 1989, Cherry and his writing partner got into the prestigious Warner Bros. Writers' Workshop, and parlayed that into a job on a show called *Homeroom*, which then translated into another job working for Susan Harris on *Golden Girls*.

Cherry loved working on *Golden Girls*. "Very few writers ever get to work on their favorite TV show, and I was lucky enough to have that opportunity," Cherry told me. After *Golden Girls*, Cherry went through a dry spell in which he was unemployed. Then he wrote the spec pilot for *Desperate Housewives*.

The story of how the show got on the air has become famous in the industry. It was viewed and rejected by virtually every network, including cables HBO and Lifetime. Finally ABC bit, and it became one of television's longest-lasting major hits. It is now in its seventh season, and it has spent every season in the top ten except season six.

Cherry drew the inspiration for *Desperate Housewives* from his mother, who once told him that during his childhood, she felt desperate. But his artistic influences are wholly of the left: "I would read Aaron Sorkin and David Kelley, because they were two television writers who I admired tremendously . . . probably the primary influence was Alan Ball, who had created *Six Feet Under* and who had done *American Beauty*." But Ball had something Cherry never had: a hatred of suburbia. "The thing is that I love suburbia. I grew up there. I was raised in Orange County," he continued. "While I was certainly up to writing about the problems of women in suburbia, housewives going slightly crazy, I didn't approach it with any kind of disdain. . . . I actually think that these are good people, and the backbone of the country, if you will."

Cherry told me he didn't really understand the conservative hubbub over *Desperate Housewives*. "I knew in my heart I'm not doing anything particularly groundbreaking here in terms of the sexuality or the depiction of it."[86] Cherry had one particularly big supporter on this topic: Laura Bush. "I am married to the president of the United States, and here's our typical evening: Nine o'clock, Mr. Excitement here is sound asleep, and I'm watching *Desperate Housewives*—with Lynne Cheney," the First Lady joked at the 2005 White House Correspondents' Association Dinner. "Ladies and gentlemen, I am a desperate housewife. I mean, if those women on that show think they're desperate, they oughta be with George."[87]

As Cherry mentioned, he's conservative fiscally and on foreign policy, but he's certainly not socially conservative, which means he was happy to promote gay rights on Wisteria Lane. "One of the things I'm proudest about is the addition of the neighbors, the gay neighbors on Wisteria Lane, because they're there, they're part of the neighborhood, no one seems to notice it." That style of political persuasion, Cherry said, is "the most effective political message . . . it's not particularly aggressive. It's just there and it's slowly changing a perception."

It's that stylistic approach that makes Cherry's work so popular. In the 1970s, Cherry explained, "I think they hit people over the head with the messages, and I think we've gotten a little more subtle about it. . . . I think we're a little bit more sophisticated than to do the preachifying that was going on back then." Don't be fooled by messaging subtlety, Cherry said. "There's all sorts of different messages that can be implanted into entertainment and just because a lot of the people doing television today don't feel like doing political messages doesn't mean that they're still not getting out what they want to say."

Even though Cherry recognizes that television is often used as a vehicle for message promotion, Cherry told me he doesn't believe that America has a lot of values left that need transformation outside of gay rights. "I'll tell you something," he said. "Because I'm fairly conservative,

I feel that most of the social issues that needed to be talked about have already been talked about, and they won. Does society need to be more permissive? I don't think so." Here, Cherry puts his finger on the liberal conundrum—where can they channel their outrage against society if they've won all the battles?

Cherry is not interested in shocking the bourgeois. Cherry actually takes a rather objective view of his own show—he objects to its being watched by children. "I have to admit, I'm constantly horrified when women with twelve-year-old children come up and meet me in malls and stuff and they say, 'Oh, my daughter and I love to watch your show together.'"

It seems to be an internal contradiction for Cherry; he doesn't embrace the sexualization of children—that's something he "heartily disapprove[s] of," he said—but at the same time, he doesn't want to restrict his own creative output too much, since "one salacious image in one man's eyes is a necessary storytelling tool about an important social issue in another's." Cherry doesn't pretend to have the answer to that internal contradiction. Instead, he says that he can only be "responsible for the images I put out on a television show."

Cherry's willingness to take responsibility for his work, like his open embrace of his political positions both in his shows and nationally, is a refreshing rarity in Hollywood. So is the complexity of his politics, which allows him to somehow stand on the razor's edge between promotion of certain social messages and an innate conservative sense that the job of television is to entertain, and that the never-ending social revolution has to end sometime. In a certain way, *Desperate Housewives* may be the culmination of the political debate over the last forty years: acceptance of more liberal social standards, simultaneous recognition of the role of women as mothers and wives, and celebration of the continued presence of the American dream—even if *Desperate Housewives* exaggerates that dream's dark side. *Desperate Housewives* is a ringing endorsement of the bohemian side of the bobo experience.

HOUSE (2004–PRESENT): THE BALANCED EXCEPTION TO THE LIBERAL RULE

Gregory House is easily the most sadistic, meanest, cruelest bastard ever to be made the hero of a television show. He's a pill-popping, unrepentant narcissist and reprobate, uncompassionate and brutal. He's also tremendously fun to watch because he's politically incorrect, quick on his feet, and smarter than everyone else in the room.

His main political characteristic is his atheism—House is militant in the Bill Maher mold. "I choose to believe that the white light people sometimes see . . . they're all just chemical reactions that take place when the brain shuts down," he says in one episode. "There's no conclusive science. My choice has no practical relevance to my life, I choose the outcome I find more comforting . . . I find it more comforting to believe that this isn't simply a test." More to the point: "You can have all the faith you want in spirits, and the afterlife, and heaven and hell, but when it comes to this world, don't be an idiot. Cause you can tell me you put your faith in God to put you through the day, but when it comes time to cross the road, I know you look both ways." Upon doing a brain scan of a religious character: "Isn't it interesting . . . religious behavior is so close to being crazy that we can't tell them apart." Getting the message yet?

The beauty of the show lies in House's interplay with the nice people who surround him. House's theory of life strips bare all pretensions—he doesn't care about playing nice, about social standards, about bedside manner, about comforting people. All of his colleagues do, and they're constantly trying to convince him to be decent to other people. House's view is that other people *aren't* decent and therefore don't deserve decent treatment.

Because House is a liberal anti-hero rather than a liberal hero, his liberalism is vulnerable to attack. He's often confronted by his insensitivity and his moral apathy. The show, while leaning liberal, therefore often tends toward balance on particular issues. For example, in season three's "Fetal Position," House is forced to save a twenty-one-week-old baby in the womb of a mother who refuses to abort; we see a 4D ultrasound of the baby, and the show even reenacts the famous picture in which an unborn child caresses a surgeon's hand. House is obviously moved as the baby's hand touches his, before he covers it over with his usual cynicism: "It's all right—I just realized I forgot to TiVo *Alien*." It's one of the strongest pro-life messages ever placed on television. That same season, *House* ran an episode titled "One Day, One Room," in which *House* convinced an STD-ridden patient who was raped to abort the baby. Both episodes were done with sensitivity and richness of character. *House* handles such hot-button issues routinely in the same way, from euthanasia to abuse to promiscuity (although, as always in Hollywood, when it comes to gay rights, there's no doubt where *House* stands—just ask Olivia Wilde, who plays television's most notorious bisexual).

If *House* is more balanced than other shows, the credit should go to the show's creator, David Shore. Shore was a lawyer before deciding to move to Los Angeles and try to write. "I packed up my stuff and hit the road and then I started writing," he said. "It was a really stupid decision that worked out very well."

He got his first break writing for David E. Kelley's *The Practice*. He interpreted Kelley's style as even-handed, although Shore's work is far more even-handed than Kelley's. "I've aspired throughout my career to do a good job of not just creating straw men, [but] creating a situation that people of good will and intelligence can take contrary positions on," Shore said.

House started as a "hot procedural show, and basically a medical procedural show," Shore told me. "A whatdunit instead of a whodunit, a cop show in which the germs are the suspects. And it evolved from there, obviously, because it became much less of a procedural and much more of a character study." Shore came up with House's atheism because he thought it would be interesting—and because he saw a vacuum of atheism on television (although in truth, organized religion on television has been watered down to the point of nonexistence and replaced instead with new-age-y references to the power of the universe). "Probably in the back of my mind, certainly, I saw the vacuum on TV, if you will, of true rationality," Shore said.

Rationality is the hallmark of Shore's work—the theme of the show, which is why he takes debate so seriously. "I lean over backwards not to take any specific political stances. I think what's interesting about stuff—frankly, preaching is boring on TV." Shore's goal is Socratic in its essence: "What I do try and do is to try and present both sides of an argument, and . . . [to get people] to just frankly think a little more. Not for people just to blindly follow the rules that are placed before them, but to think about it." Which rules did he think people ought to challenge, I asked. "It's about the stuff that you believed since you're six years old," he answered. "Why do you believe it? It makes [the rules] ultimately valid [if you consider them]."

Because *House* so often challenges both sides of the political debate—and because the left is not used to being challenged seriously in any way by television's product—*House* received an inordinate amount of flak for "Fetal Position." "As you can imagine, we're in Hollywood, we've got our share of rabid left-wing Democrats here," Shore said. "I remember when we were doing 'Fetal Position,' there is that image of that little finger of the fetus clasping Dr. House's hand. And it was a powerful image. And we recognized at the time that's going to go up on billboards and websites for pro-life organizations. But it was true, and it was accurate, and it was real." This may be one of the only times in television history that anyone in the industry has called the pro-life message "real."

Shore's commitment to balance is what makes *House* such a unique property on television—and what makes it television's best water-cooler show. No other show can spark debate—real debate—because no other shows take the issues so seriously, refraining from taking the easy way out.

GREY'S ANATOMY (2005–PRESENT): HOT AND HEAVY AT THE HOSPITAL

Nobody had ever heard of Shonda Rhimes until she burst onto the scene in 2005 with *Grey's Anatomy*. She'd never written on another major show. She'd never had a successful movie, other than *Princess Diaries 2*, which was bound to do decently (she also penned the Britney Spears starrer *Crossroads*, which was a box office disaster). She's the perfect example of the obscurity-to-riches fame that television can bring when it finds a talented creator.

Rhimes grew up in University Park, Illinois, then attended

Dartmouth. Finally she headed to USC to study screenwriting. She began writing television pitches; her first was about "four women who covered war and drank a lot and had a lot of sex and on a bad day, people died." The networks rejected it because war television doesn't get ratings. Then she wrote another pilot, about a hospital in Seattle. It was picked up by ABC.[88]

Rhimes believes that it is her moral duty to infuse politics into her shows. It's clear that she does it on a regular basis—for a while, *Grey's Anatomy* was the only show to feature an ongoing lesbian relationship (with open conversation about the procedures of lesbian sex), and it has taken liberal stands on abortion, teen sex, and euthanasia, among other issues. When the show first began, Rhimes, who is African American, set down a "mandate" to the cast and crew. "I remember everybody in the room looking at me like I was crazy," she told *Ebony* magazine. "But I was like, 'There will never be any Black drug addicts on our show. There will never be any Black hookers on our show. There will never be Black pimps on our show.' A lot of shows feel the need and enjoy stereotyping, and we're going the other way." Of course, it's not stereotyping for *some* drug addicts or hookers or pimps to be black—it's reverse stereotyping, in fact, to suggest that there's no such thing as a black drug addict or hooker or pimp. (At least she's racially blind when it comes to casting, where Rhimes says she has never cast by looking at race, with the excellent result that a massively diverse cast now stars on one of television's biggest hits.)

In similar fashion, Rhimes has stated that she wants women to know that they don't need men. "It's fabulous to have a partner," she said. "But if you don't, you're going to be fine."[89]

Grey's Anatomy is, according to Rhimes, "chick" television—that is, television designed for women. In Hollywood, "for women" is synonymous with "pushing the 1960s feminist agenda."

GLEE (2009–PRESENT): SUBVERSIVE LIBERALISM

High schoolers singing in choir club. That's the premise of *Glee*, a Fox show that has received enormous critical attention, including nineteen

Primetime Emmy nominations after its debut season. How could writers draw so much attention to a show about a high school glee club? By making it subversively liberal, of course.

Glee isn't *High School Musical*. It's more like *Gossip Girl* meets Disney Channel. While the show's candy coating lies in its rehashes of hit pop tunes, its colorful cast, and its well-choreographed routines, the show's core is pure sexualization, anti-Christian bias, and pro-gay-rights messaging. One of the main characters is a teenager who gets pregnant; one of the main female characters has two dads; another is a flamboyantly gay high school kid; two others are cheerleaders with lesbian tendencies (in one episode, the two make out, with one remarking that it's "a nice break from all that scissoring"—scissoring, by the way, is a lesbian sexual practice). A teacher on the show suggests that Lincoln was gay. One episode features four teenagers fantasizing about having sex while singing Madonna's "Like a Virgin." Another mocks abstinence education, with one of the main teenage characters telling the other teens, "Did you know that most studies have demonstrated that celibacy doesn't work in high schools? . . . The only way to deal with teen sexuality is to be prepared. That's what contraception is for."

The show constantly throws unnecessary darts at the right wing. In one episode, the guidance counselor laments the female role models present in the world today: "You've got Britney Spears and her shaved head. Lindsey Lohan looks like something out of *Lord of the Rings*. Ann Coulter." In that same episode, the caustic female gym coach rips two girls, stating, "You must be two of the stupidest teens I have ever encountered, and that's saying something . . . I once taught a cheerleading seminar to a young Sarah Palin." In another episode, when the pregnant teenager tells her dad that she's been knocked up, he responds by throwing her out of the house. By the way, he's Christian and a fan of Glenn Beck.

All this makes sense when we consider the creators of *Glee*: Ryan Murphy, Brad Falchuk, and Ian Brennan. Murphy is the creator of the most sexualized television show in basic cable history, *Nip/Tuck*, which has graphically depicted virtually every possible incarnation of sexuality. Falchuk worked on *Nip/Tuck* with Murphy; though he grew up in Newton, Massachusetts, as a young Republican, he left that behind when he moved to Hollywood. So far behind, in fact, that after he and Murphy collaborated on *Nip/Tuck*, they pitched a series to FX revolving around a transsexual gynecologist. As for Brennan, he was the newcomer to the group and based the show on his own experiences in glee club in high school. Brennan says the show was designed for everyone: "We were writing a show that kids and their parents *and* their college-age siblings would want to watch. . . . I would die a happy man if our show resulted in better communication between parents and children about difficult issues, though that wasn't our intent."[90]

Murphy, who is openly gay and quite militant about gay rights, makes no bones about the fact that he's seeking to proselytize with the show. After *Newsweek* columnist Ramin Setoodeh, who is gay, wrote a column suggesting that Sean Hayes's performance as a straight man in a Broadway revival of *Promises, Promises* wasn't believable, Murphy responded by seeking a boycott of *Newsweek*. He then issued an invitation to Setoodeh to visit the set of *Glee*: "Hopefully then he can see how we take care to do a show about inclusiveness . . . a show that encourages all viewers no matter what their sexual orientation to go after their hopes and dreams. . . ."[91]

When asked whether he would tackle gay marriage in the show, he said, "That's a great idea. I think I would love to tackle that in the future but I haven't thought how." Murphy plotted out in detail how he wanted to inoculate the public gradually over having the two quasi-lesbian cheerleaders kiss: "I think the key is to do it a couple times so that it doesn't seem forced." He also rips shows like *Modern Family* that don't show gays kissing. Yet Murphy still feels that he's censoring himself for the sake of the kids who watch *Glee*, which demonstrates how cloistered he is in his social politics. "I'm the one who censors that because I have a very young niece who wants to watch the show and I don't want her to see things that her stepmother has to say, 'Wait, what?' I feel a responsibility because young kids watch the show so I had wanted to do the opposite of *Nip/Tuck*."[92] Unfortunately, the show is hardly the opposite of *Nip/Tuck*—it's more like a watered-down, musicalized, high school version of *Nip/Tuck*.

Is *Glee* a good show? Certainly it's a clever and well-made show. But unlike *Desperate Housewives* or even *Nip/Tuck*, which are clearly targeted at adults, *Glee* is targeted at teens and preteens, which means that its insertion of political messages is more cynical and dangerous than most.

STACKING THE DECK

The power of scripted television lies in its ability to twist our emotions. The best dramatists can pull our heartstrings or break tension with a laugh; they can tell us what we feel. That power can easily be used to create and twist situations to the full advantage of particular political agendas. And artists in television do it all the time, whether consciously or unconsciously.

It's not hard to do. For example, consider the situation of a young woman who gets pregnant accidentally. Her boyfriend originally decides to stick with her, but he can't take the heat and begins drinking. In a violent quarrel one night, he hits her, then runs out, abandoning her. She is three months pregnant with the child by now. She visits an abortion clinic, where she is counseled that to have his baby is her choice. She proceeds with the abortion.

Now consider a second young woman. She is promiscuous and has had a prior abortion. One night she goes to a bar, where she has a quickie in the bathroom with a total stranger. She realizes she's pregnant, but instead of seeking an immediate abortion, she waits three months simply because she's been planning a trip to Europe. When she comes back, she gets an abortion.

The moral equation here hasn't changed for either side of the abortion debate; in both cases, the pro-choice side would say that abortion is a proper choice, and in both cases, the pro-life side would say that abortion is an improper choice. But in the world of drama, we're looking solely for *sympathy*. If you're going to paint the pro-choice picture in a positive light, therefore, you'd use the first scenario; if you're going to paint pro-life as the right choice, you'd use the second. It's no coincidence that we've seen variation after variation of the first choice on television, and not a single prominent instance of the latter case on TV.

The solution, of course, is balance in the writing constituency. A few rare authors have the ability to step outside themselves and write the opposing political viewpoint with accuracy and dignity, but many television creators are not even aware of the world outside the big cities (these are the people who think that simply invoking Rush Limbaugh, Ann Coulter, Glenn Beck, Bill O'Reilly, or Sean Hannity can stand in for a laugh line). More than that, many creators don't feel the necessity to present both sides of a particular debate—and since so few shows *do* present both sides, these creators face little market pressure to do so. When television drama is a virtual liberal monopoly, why should liberal television creators try to move outside that safe space?

They should move out of that safe space because open debate makes for better television. There's a reason nobody buys season tickets to the Harlem Globetrotters—the winner is a foregone conclusion. The same holds true when we watch drama: We want to see the interplay between the forces, and we want the unpredictable. The market is looking for balance, or at least diverging viewpoints.

But that's not how liberals in Hollywood see it. Where they come from, the market requests—no, demands—that programming skew wildly liberal. Liberals use the success of liberal shows as a way to shut up conservatives, ignoring the countervailing evidence. The market is the liberals' most powerful argument. That argument, however, is foolish, ignorant, and cynical in the extreme. It is precisely that market argument we will now debunk.

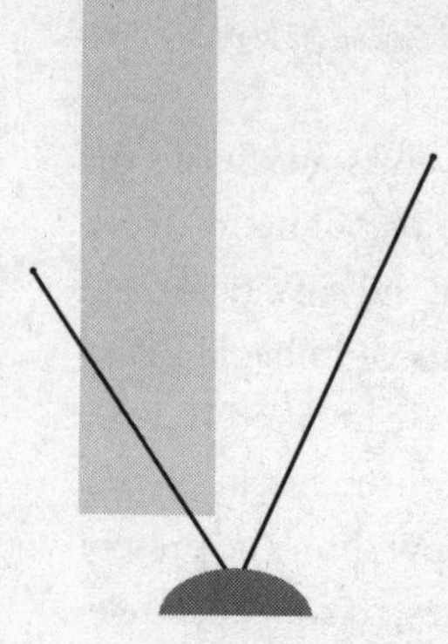

"SHUT UP AND CHANGE THE CHANNEL"

How the Left Uses the Market Myth to Silence Its Critics

We've seen how Hollywood became leftist; we've exposed Hollywood's discrimination against conservatives; we've surveyed the most popular comedies and dramas in television history, spoken with their creators, and decoded their hidden political messages.

Now we must answer the biggest question of all: how does Hollywood justify its continued ideological tilt? How can the industry that attacked McCarthyism and excoriated racism excuse itself for continuing to exclude those who don't share its ideological viewpoint?

Their typical initial response to this charge is that such discrimination simply doesn't exist. Leftists dominate the medium solely due to luck or talent. And if television's creators and executives happen to be liberal, they say, there's nothing wrong with infusing politics into their work. After all, they contend, the infusion of politics makes their work more interesting and trenchant.

"I felt the obligation to be funny," George Schlatter of *Laugh-In* and *Real People* fame explained to me. "Promoting social justice and equity was just one of the ways that we were funny."[1] The late Larry Gelbart, the moving force behind *M*A*S*H*, told me that his goal was "to use whatever craft I had learned, to marry that with issues which concerned me."[2] Susan Harris, creator of *Soap* and *The Golden Girls*, said to me that while her goal was to entertain, "If while entertaining, we could inject some social reality, and make some points, that was terrific."[3] Gary David Goldberg, creator of *Family Ties* and *Spin City*, stated that the tension between entertainment and messaging was a "tension we welcomed. It's good to have it. I always thought the higher the stakes, the deeper the laughs, if you can accomplish it."[4]

Executives, too, feel the need to message their programming. Fred Pierce, president of ABC-TV during the 1970s, stated, "We never thought that you could do something that wasn't commercially appealing that didn't have a message."[5] Brandon Stoddard, head of programming for ABC during the late 1980s, said that his career was a constant adventure in drawing the balance between "being able to say something but also putting something on the air that was entertaining."[6]

How could it be otherwise? Creative people *always* infuse their worldviews into their work. Tolstoy wouldn't be Tolstoy if he wrote simplistic adventure stories; Aaron Sorkin wouldn't be Aaron Sorkin if he wrote evenhanded scripts about tax policy.

More than that, though, creative people generally want to feel that their work has meaning beyond the transient value of ratings points. They want to be able to look back at their work at the end of a long career and say that their work deepened human understanding, touched people's minds and hearts. As Gelbart told me about four months before he passed away, "William S. Paley said television was the best cigarette vending machine that anybody ever thought of, and that's still pretty much what it is. I'd just like to see it grow up, and really be the best thing it can be."[7] Perhaps Josh Brand, creator of *St. Elsewhere* and *Northern Exposure*, put it best: "I suppose each of us has our own conscience."[8]

The "luck" argument requires creators and executives to disown any purposeful political agenda on television. That's why so many creators and executives shy away from taking credit for their programming progressivism when asked about it directly. When asked about whether their work is designed to proselytize, most claim innocence, perhaps fearing that if the business labels them ideologues of any stripe, they'll lose work. Gelbart, the king of inserting politics into his shows, told me with a straight face, "We're worker ants . . . largely we do what we're told, and so we don't dictate the liberal or permissive or progressive line in anything."[9] As Gelbart's own statements about his work show, this is plainly untrue. The "luck" argument simply doesn't fly.

Which is why the left comes up with a different, far more insidious argument. The Hollywood left insists that the market demands liberal material on television. Creators and executives down the line state that their moral guide is the Nielsen Ratings, but that the ratings demand odes to gay rights and statements about universal health care. Lee Rich, who headed Lorimar Productions and produced *Dallas*, *Eight Is Enough*, and *The Waltons*, among others, put the argument well: "I'm not out to change their views about politics or religion or anything. I'm there to entertain them. And as long as they like what I give them, they'll view my product. If they don't, they won't."[10]

This makes no intuitive sense. Conservatives know that they watch television, and they know they aren't demanding the latest exploration into teenage pansexual Wiccan experimentation. How can Hollywood leftists cite the market as the reason for such storylines with credibility? If Hollywood is interested first and foremost in drawing viewers, why does its work take political positions that alienate vast swaths of the American public?

Up until now, conservatives have utterly ignored this argument. Perhaps conservatives are simply happy to have the left finally agreeing that the free market is a positive good. Perhaps they're scared off by the left's free market rhetoric—how can conservatives *attack* the free market? Perhaps they simply don't want to engage in the seeming dirtiness of looking inside Hollywood's business workings, at television's dirty laundry.

For whatever reason, the market argument has allowed liberals to dominate television for decades. The question is: Are they right? Does the market truly desire a one-sided political product so strongly that a blacklist in Hollywood can be justified on laissez-faire grounds?

Of course not. The market in television isn't free—it's been corrupted, over and over and over again. Now we'll explore that corruption.

THE MARKET MYTH

Leftists are rarely interested in crediting the free market with anything. The free market, they usually argue, is exploitative, cruel, and inhumane. Yet ironically enough, Hollywoodites are lightning-quick to cite the power of the free market while justifying the monochrome nature of Hollywood politics. The creators of television use the same logic Red Skelton used at movie mogul Harry Cohn's funeral, when asked why so many people had shown up to watch the tyrant's burial: "It just goes to show you . . . if you give the people what they want, they'll come out."

The creators' apparent reverence for the free market is wondrous to behold. When defending their politically oriented creative decisions, writers, producers, and executives constantly cite the power of the free market. Their guiding principle seems to be, "If they don't like it, they can turn it off." Success somehow justifies political content on television—the people are the true creators of television, in this view, and television's moving forces can't be held accountable for providing what the audience wants.

Marta Kaufman, co-creator of *Friends*, told me that while she did push the gay and lesbian rights agenda during the first season of the show, "We never felt we wanted to preach. You know our feeling was always, if you don't like what you're watching, forget the V-chip, just turn it off."[11] Billie Piper, star of HBO's pornographic *Secret Diary of a Call Girl*, says the same thing: "I think if you don't like it, don't watch it."[12] In 1972, Norman Lear summed up the feelings of creators across Hollywood when he told a Senate subcommittee, "The American public is the final arbiter anyway, and it tells us very quickly what it likes and does not like . . . the writer deserves the right to express life as he sees it."[13]

Executives, with slightly more credibility, make the same argument. Tom Freston, former chairman and CEO of MTV Networks, said, "If we programmed to our personal taste, we'd be out of business."[14] "The audience decides [what they want to watch]. And in that sense, it's a pretty clean business," Sandy Grushow of Fox told me.[15]

This is all nonsense, of course. Creators and executives don't kowtow to the wishes of the audience (if they did, *M*A*S*H*, *All in the Family*, *Hill Street Blues*, *Family Ties*, and *Seinfeld* all would have been gone after one season). Creators and executives see the audience as a vast swath of rubes waiting to be manipulated. If audiences boycott a show or decide not to watch it because of its politics, these supposedly free-marketeering creators savage the benighted audience at the drop of a hat. Then they continue to program how they want to program.

Television creators have a love/hate relationship with the audience. They love the audience when they watch—they hate them when they don't, since every viewer who doesn't watch their show is effectively voting for cancelation. In short, TV's creators only like the market argument when it cuts in their favor. When it doesn't, they're critical of it to the extreme.

Executives are more answerable to the audience than creators. If executives cite the market argument to turn down creators' shows, creators rip into the executives (and by extension, the audience) with unmitigated righteous ire. The most common word you hear in this context is *gutless*. Schlatter said, "Business has taken over now . . . there's so much timidity there."[16] Gelbart railed against what he called the "praetorian guard of corporate types which so profess to care about our morality—these are the people who are on the road probably a good deal of the year staying in hotels, which perhaps their corporations own, which are filled with X-rated stuff, just for the nice anonymous charge to your hotel bill."[17] Gene Reynolds, producer of *M*A*S*H*, *Room 222*, and *Lou Grant*, all groundbreaking political shows, criticized the networks' "ridiculous formula: keep it light, keep it simple."[18] Susan Harris commented, "Television is run like a business, and as long as it's run like a business and run by huge corporations, they don't care about the entertainment end of it at all."[19] What happened to the creators' reliance on the market to justify their politics? Suddenly, the free market is the enemy, and the executives are fifth columnists sent to turn television into a bourgeois instrument of capitalist commerce.

Peter Mehlman, one of the writers on *Seinfeld*, colorfully and insistently characterized the networks as content-free zones. "Content is the tenth priority. . . . Content is the last thing they think of."[20] Josh Brand said that for the most part, the networks were playing it "very safe."[21] Gary David Goldberg said the networks are "Detroit. They talk to each other, they have no actual sense of what people are interested in, they have no respect, and they have gotten what they have deserved. Unfortunately they've screwed up the whole business."[22]

Chris Chulack, whose excellent drama *Southland* was picked up for renewal after a few episodes, then canceled when NBC decided it would be cheaper to broadcast Jay Leno during the 10 P.M. hour, had reason to be upset at the networks: "Their bottom line is money money money, every penny, and they're trying to appeal to the lowest common denominator. And there is no artistic stand. . . . There's no opportunity."[23]

Sometimes executives, too, use the market argument as convenient cover for their own political or cultural sensibilities. While executives often invoke the market argument to turn down politically oriented shows, many of them don't apply the market argument consistently. Executives are just as much in the dark as anyone else when it comes to what gets the numbers. Scott Siegler, former CBS vice president for drama and comedy development, summed up the problem well: "Because it's a mass audience—it's an unimaginably large audience—the audience tastes are so diffused and so general that you've got to be guessing."[24] For every Mike Dann who based his decision-making on numbers, there is a Fred Silverman, who based his decision-making on his gut response; a Bob Wood, who relied on his instinct; and a Doug Herzog, who uses a combination of all those factors.

Executives, like creators, want it both ways. They want to be seen as champions of art, and yet they want to justify their anti-conservative discrimination by citing the power of the marketplace. The most eloquent example of this phenomenon was Grant Tinker, former head of NBC. In his autobiography, *Tinker in Television*, he mused, "I have considerable impatience with the maximum profit fixation of the current network owners."[25]

It was the same Grant Tinker, though, who continued to push the myth that executives are interested in catering to the largest audience for the greatest profit, without regard to their own politics or personal biases. In his speech to NBC's affiliates in 1983, he averred, "Instead of running a boutique which attracts only people with the same taste as ours, we're running a giant department store, which has everyone in the country as a potential customer. If we're doing our job well, we're appealing to a great diversity of tastes—not just our own. . . . Our job is to get all of America into our tent, and we're going to be doing that with programs that have great popular appeal."[26]

This is simply untrue. Executives and creators have little interest in great general appeal. They're far more interested in programs with specific appeal—and with specific viewpoints.

Both creators and executives conveniently cite the market argument when it suits them, and discard it when it doesn't. It's a convenient scapegoat for abdication of broadcast responsibility. Boiled down to two words, the market argument in the television world is the Nuremberg Defense—creators claim they are not to blame for any political or social content in their programming, since they're ultimately taking orders from the audience. Of course, ask those same creators if they'd be willing to write a sequel to a racist film like *Birth of a Nation* if they knew it would get a guaranteed thirty share, and they'd turn you down flat (and rightly so).

In the end, politics on television isn't driven solely by the market. It's the politics of those who write, create, produce, and distribute television that shapes the political content on television. The market argument, in a nutshell, is post facto justification by those who desperately want to maintain the industry's cliquish status quo. The market doesn't want liberal shows any more than it wants conservative shows. It wants *entertaining* shows. But the creators and executives want only *liberal* entertaining shows.

HOLES IN THE MARKET MYTH

Nonetheless, the market argument continues to carry weight, because television is clearly a hugely successful industry. It's difficult to contend that liberal programming has brought television to some sort of market impasse when the networks and cable channels continue to rake in billions of dollars.

So where's the hole in the market argument?

Actually, there are four major holes.

First and foremost, television isn't a traditional free market. At least not where the audience is concerned. The proof is in the pudding. How many shows have audiences loved, only to see them canceled? And how many have audiences hated, only to see them run forever? There's a reason for that: television's businessmen don't really care about the viewers. They care about whether they can use the viewers to make money from advertisers. Even the advertisers, though, aren't fully informed consumers in the traditional model. Advertisers have to gauge where to spend their advertising dollars by measuring audience numbers, but the numbers are often skewed. And those numbers are then funneled not to the advertisers directly, but to advertising agencies, which help allocate ad dollars—and in which corruption runs rampant. The bottom line: there are several layers of disconnect between those who spend the money (advertisers), those they are seeking to reach (audiences), and those who actually rake in the dough (television creators and executives).

Second, television producers and distributors are not traditional free market actors—they collude with each other. With the help of governmental regulation and an unspoken agreement not to target each others' narrow-casted audiences, television's powers-that-be create a diversity of programming without real competition. If you want to watch a home improvement show, you'll probably have to do it through the Scripps Network (Home and Garden Television, Do It Yourself Network). If you want to watch sports, you'll do it through ESPN and its myriad spinoff channels. There's generally nowhere else to turn.

Third, the market argument assumes that the producers involved are attempting to cater to the broadest possible market in their search for profits. This is pure bunk. Broadcasting is out. Narrowcasting is in. Rather than producers catering to vast swaths of consumers, producers have attempted to shape a hierarchy of consumers to whom they wish to cater. In other words, television's creators and executives have spent the last fifty years defining for themselves what their audience is, rather than their audience defining for the creators and executives precisely what they want to watch. That allows television honchos to program politically, get low ratings, and claim audience victory while doing so. It also leads to the liberalization of television content in general.

Finally, there is an unspoken assumption that viewers will turn the channel if they don't like what they're watching. That assumes that viewers have something to turn *to*. They don't. Programming is largely homogeneous when it comes to politics. Incredibly enough, the evidence suggests that when viewers are given the choice to pick more conservative product, they do so—believe it or not, conservatives' viewing patterns are far more predictive of television success than liberals' viewing patterns. If the television creators had any brains, they'd be looking to please Joe Sixpack rather than Joe Biden.

HOLE NUMBER ONE: TV DOESN'T MEET THE CONSUMER MODEL

When creators and executives tell us that they are merely catering to the market, we assume they're talking about us, the watching audience.

They're not. They couldn't care less about us.

The true television audience is advertisers. They're the ones who pay the bills. Audiences don't pay programmers directly—only advertisers do that. Audiences only matter in an indirect way; since advertisers are interested in getting as many eyeballs on their commercials as possible, programmers target audiences, then sell those audience numbers to advertisers.

This can still work under ideal market conditions. In a dream scenario, advertisers are concerned only with reaching the highest number of viewers, and television provides them a direct outlet for doing so. In that case, everyone's interests would coincide, since advertisers would only buy advertising on shows that garnered the most viewers. Think about the Super Bowl: advertisers are willing to pay millions of dollars to networks because the Super Bowl draws tens of millions of viewers at one time. Audiences aren't important because they're interested in watching the Super Bowl—they're important because they watch the commercials during the time-outs.

The dream scenario would depend on two basic assumptions. First, it would require perfect information—audiences would have to be effectively measured and their viewing habits efficiently calculated. Second, the dream scenario would require that audience information be conveyed in a timely manner to potential advertisers, who make rational cost-benefit analyses.

In reality, such informational flow is hampered by a couple of barriers: the ratings system itself, and the advertising agencies.

Television ratings are handled by the Nielsen Company. The Nielsen Company has two ways it measures ratings: the normal ratings, and the "sweeps." Normal ratings are taken in top markets on a regular basis. During sweeps, samples are taken in the 210 viewing markets. The purpose of sweeps week is to provide ratings for local advertisers, who must know how many people in their city or area are watching a given program. National advertisers can base their advertising rates on the general ratings, since they're aiming at the broader market.

In local markets, Nielsen employs the archaic "diary system." The diary system works like this: Nielsen's sample viewers receive a piece of paper on which they are asked to write down what they're watching as they watch it. "Keeping your diary is very easy," read one 2009 Nielsen letter to a Nielsen participant. "When your TV is on, please enter programs as you watch them. . . . This will only take a few minutes a day."[27] The problems with the diary system are obvious: People forget to fill in the diary, people purposefully misreport what they watch (who wants to admit to watching *Secret Diary of a Call Girl*?), and people misremember what they did watch. People can also be paid to write down shows they don't actually watch. While major markets now employ more accurate and automated ratings systems, small towns still use the diaries.[28]

The diaries have historically had a massive impact when it comes to sweeps week. Networks program their big new programs so that their ratings will jump during sweeps week; meanwhile, local markets have a huge say as to which shows stay on the air based on their ratings during sweeps week. Since the local markets all use diaries (or at least did up until 2009), the numbers are deeply questionable at best. Les Moonves questioned the diaries/sweeps dominance back in 2000: "It is such an antiquated way of doing business. On the edge of a technical revolution, we're using a system that belongs to the dinosaurs. It's ludicrous."[29] In late November 2010, the Media Rating Council, an independent organization maintaining ratings standards, revoked its accreditation of Nielsen in the 154 remaining diary-only markets. According to *Broadcasting & Cable*, the problem sprang from Nielsen's decision to stop sampling people via traditional phone lines, which have become obsolete, and to start sampling people based on address. Resultant sample sizes were too small to be representative.[30]

Nielsen has historically been slow to adapt to changing technology, as the continued use of diaries suggests; it took them years to catch on to the effect of TiVo, which time-shifted viewing of certain programs; it took them years to catch on to the fact that college students away from home watch television (they used to measure only home television viewership); and now they have been slow to adapt to the rise of Internet viewing.

There are other flaws in the system, too. Even Nielsen's electronic monitoring devices require users to hit an individual button on their remotes that show Nielsen who is watching the television. If a family of four is watching a show, for example, Dad, Mom, Billy, and Jane all have to hit their individual buttons to show Nielsen that they're watching. This adds back in the element of self-reporting that makes the diary system so flawed. Furthermore, Nielsen doesn't measure how many commercials are actually being watched during a particular program—it measures how many people are watching a particular program. As everybody knows, you wait until the commercials come on before grabbing a beer from the fridge or hitting the john. Nielsen doesn't measure that.

A huge problem with the Nielsen ratings is the problem with every survey: self-selection. Nielsen creates a statistically valid sample and then solicits involvement by those chosen—but many people who are selected simply refuse to participate. The "response rate" to solicitation is egregiously low in many cases. The diary response rate can run south of 30 percent in some cities during sweeps. "It's become a big problem," Jack Loftus, chief communications officer of Nielsen communications, said in 2000.[31] Local people meters (LPMs), essentially small monitoring boxes which require viewers to type in their identity while viewing, only get a slightly higher cooperation rate; in Miami's roll-out in October 2008, for example, there was just a 45.4 percent response rate, which was a massive increase over their previous set meter/diary response rate of 24.5 percent.[32] When it comes to consistent ratings using people meters, the response rate as of 2003 had risen to 40.6 percent.[33] Such percentages do not provide fully representative samples.

Even more problematic is who self-selects. Historically, those who have complied with Nielsen's requests have been "younger, better educated . . . cooperators were disproportionately inclined toward the . . .

most irreverent, politically liberal, and convention-subverting programs on the air. . . ."[34] The same may hold true today, particularly since conservatives tend to populate rural and non-major urban areas that use the diary system, meaning their response rate is even lower than normal. In other words, it is more than possible that Nielsen statistically oversamples political liberals.

Even if the information gathered by Nielsen were perfect (and we *can* assume that they are always trying to improve their product), there is no guarantee that the information provided by Nielsen is taken at face value by advertisers. Television advertising buyers are the middlemen between television networks and advertisers, and they have a cozy relationship with the network executives. They have an interest in overbuying television time, and on occasion, they even receive kickbacks from particular networks. Their clients—advertisers—know little about the business of advertising and trust them implicitly, which is why they hire them. The Nielsen statistics are highly fungible, being susceptible to manipulation by media buyers—a media buyer may suggest that an advertiser look at a subset of viewers rather than the entire viewing audience, for example, if a show has poor ratings but the media buyer has a stake in the network running the show. There is a good deal of leeway for misbehavior here, all of which distorts the supposedly perfect market.[35]

In fact, the history of television demonstrates that the cloudy nature of the numbers, disguised by their supposed exactitude, has been used consistently by the television industry in its never-ending quest for both cash and liberal programming. That history is an amazing tale of PR genius, informational manipulation, and outright snake oil salesmanship. It has shaped our entertainment and our culture in ways we can only begin to comprehend.

HOW TELEVISION TWISTED AUDIENCE NUMBERS

Audience numbers didn't start as an excuse for leftism. Early on, executives were chiefly concerned with grabbing the most eyeballs. David Sarnoff, founder of NBC, quickly discovered what was later termed Sarnoff's law: The value of any radio or television network lay in the number of consumers it reached. Radio was only valuable if it got listeners; TV was only valuable if it got viewers. Executives aimed at the audience more broadly, avoiding narrowcasting at all costs. Pat Weaver of NBC said that television's greatest challenge would be to stay away from the precedent set by the movie industry: "We must beware of the terrible example of the movies, who went for a regular part of the whole audience and tailored a product for them so completely that motion picture going became a minority experience in American life." The goal, said Weaver, was "to *reach everyone*."[36]

Programming reflected the attempt of the networks to touch as many viewers as possible. Popular shows included rural-slanted shows like Westerns, which were cheap to produce and immensely popular (in 1959, there were twenty-eight Westerns on the air, about a quarter of all primetime programming),[37] and quiz shows. Successful shows ranged from *The Beverly Hillbillies* to *Gunsmoke* to *I Love Lucy*—all of them geared toward family audiences. Anybody—mom, pop, son, or daughter—could plop down in front of the tube and know that the programming would likely appeal to them.

While Sarnoff at NBC was pushing the notion that viewers were the target audience, Bill Paley at CBS had hit upon a different, more sophisticated idea: target the sponsors, not the audience. Whereas Sarnoff focused largely on garnering the largest number of listeners and viewers, Paley focused on grabbing affiliates and advertisers. That's where the money was. Paley forged brilliant business strategies based on Paley's law, and CBS began to grow rapidly.[38]

In the beginning, Paley's law and Sarnoff's law yielded the same results: advertiser dollars were directed toward the shows with the most viewers. But at ABC, the executives took notice of Paley's law and realized one crucial fact that had escaped both Paley and Sarnoff: even if you didn't have viewers, if you could snooker the advertisers into *thinking* you had viewers, you could make a bundle. Advertisers could be separated from audience numbers so long as advertisers believed that smaller, more targeted viewer groups were better than large, dispersed viewer groups. This made sense for ABC, which lacked big stations and big numbers. ABC would have to con advertisers.

But first, they needed the data with which to con those advertisers. In the 1950s, they got it. In that decade, ABC head of programming Ollie Treyz commissioned Dr. Paul Lazarsfeld of Columbia University to analyze television audiences. The goal: come up with a new way of capitalizing on ABC's weak, mostly urban station roster. Lazarsfeld returned with his analysis. And ABC President Leonard Goldenson ate it up, because it provided him a selling point for advertisers.

"The top programs at CBS and NBC, built around stars that came out of radio, appealed mostly to older audiences," Goldenson later explained. "But this was not the audience most sought by advertisers, said Lazarsfeld. Older persons are more set in their ways and less likely, for example, to switch brands of toothpaste or laundry detergent. They are also less likely to change their television viewing habits. . . . *Younger audiences, those between eighteen and forty-nine years old, are more open to change.* They are more willing to turn the dial looking for something new and different." It was too good to be true. But the good news kept on coming: "Even better, suggested Lazarsfeld, younger audiences spend more money per capita than older ones. These are the people with growing families, those who buy most of the household products which are the staples of mass-marketing. . . . Lazarsfeld recommended we go after the young audiences. We should build programs around the casts of young, virile people, he said."[39] Goldenson couldn't have been happier.

Lazarsfeld's concept was simple and brilliant. It was also weak. The social science data to support these assertions were tenuous at best. The 1950 census shows men aged 14–24 had a median income of approximately $1,054 for veterans of World War II, $2,185 for non-veterans. Men aged 25–44 had a median income of $2,904. Men aged 45–64 had a median income of $2,644. Taken together, men under 45 actually had a lower median income than those over 45 according to these statistics. Lazarsfeld was correct that urban families earned significantly more than rural families—$3,429 for urban families versus $2,552 for nonfarming rural families and substantially less for farming rural families.[40] But there was a tremendous income gap in urban areas that only escalated over time; by the end of the decade, almost half of poor Americans lived in metropolitan areas.[41] This meant that while there were many middle-class families living in the cities and the suburbs, there were also large numbers of people who had no money. Targeting young urban audiences meant targeting poor people, at least a large portion of the time.

It is also worth noting that Lazarsfeld's analysis focused on income, as opposed to savings. Americans who are older often have more disposable income than those who are younger, particularly in a day and age when older people receive government benefits while younger people pay for those benefits. Even in 1950, homeowners were disproportionately older—67.9 percent of homeowners were at least 65 years old.[42] Those were the people who didn't have to pay for rent and could afford to spend money on other products. Today, U.S. citizens over age 65 now comprise a higher percentage of the population than teenagers; over-55 households have double the assets of 45- to 55-year-old households. Households led by those aged 45–55 spend 17 percent more money than the average American household; 55–64-year-olds rank second best, spending 15 percent more than the average household.[43]

As for Lazarsfeld's contention that the elderly were less prone to switch their viewing and purchasing habits, social science data is mixed at best. Some studies suggest that there is "no evidence to suggest that older consumers were likely to be less innovative in their consumptive behavior."[44] Others state that "older adults have been shown to be among the last to adopt a product, service, or idea innovation."[45] However, many of those studies about the difficulty of persuading older people to buy products note that older consumers are *more* likely to buy when prodded by mass media, as opposed to younger consumers, who rely on friends and family.[46] One national telephone survey of 1,000 Americans suggested that while those aged 55–64 were more skeptical of advertisements than other age groups, they also believed more strongly than any other age group that most advertising is informative, that advertised brands worked better than unadvertised brands, and that the government should not regulate advertising.[47]

Lazarsfeld's endorsement of younger audiences was unequivocal, however. ABC swallowed it hook, line, and sinker.

This suggests an obvious question: Just who in the hell was Paul Lazarsfeld? According to Lazarsfeld biographer Michael Pollak, Lazarsfeld grew up in the house of a militant Social Democrat in Austria; his father, a lawyer, gave free legal services to those charged with political crimes, and his mother used to give tea parties for socialist pseudointellectuals. When Lazarsfeld became a researcher, "he made an effort to coordinate his research with the political priorities of the [Social Democrat] Party."[48] Two of his closest clients were Max Horkheimer, famously of the Frankfurt School, and the Socialist Party. Lazarsfeld's relationships with members of the Frankfurt School lasted throughout his life; he helped members of the Frankfurt School immigrate to the United States.

What was the Frankfurt School? It was a group of philosophers dedicated to "cultural Marxism," the implementation of Marxism in capitalist countries through cultural means—in other words, they wanted to take over countries by taking over American institutions like campuses, the media, and Hollywood. The Frankfurt School saw that traditional Marxism had been unable to penetrate capitalist society in pure economic terms, and they decided to direct their efforts toward a cultural takeover.

While his biographer argues that Lazarsfeld's emigration to America "marked the end of Lazarsfeld's political involvement," Lazarsfeld's political agenda came across in his actions. Lazarsfeld got Frankfurt School member and socialist Theodor Adorno a job with the Princeton Radio Research Project, despite the fact that Adorno was not a researcher. During World War II, he worked alongside Frankfurt School members like Herbert Marcuse at the Office of Strategic Studies in the War Department (the OSS was the predecessor to the CIA—a bizarre place to store Marxist intellectuals).

He finally landed at the Columbia Sociology Department, a far-left department dedicated to remaking "social science, if not the world," according to student Seymour Martin Lipset. His biographer admits that "Where possible, [Lazarsfeld] accepted research projects that corresponded to his earlier political commitment. . . . His writings in media sociology and his Austro-Marxist traditions suggest that he firmly believed that administrative and marketing research would help the elites manage society more enlightenedly in accordance with 'what the people really want.' "[49]

Lazarsfeld was a through-and-through top-down elitist when it came to television. In testimony before the FCC in December 1959, Lazarsfeld stated that he believed television standards should be set by "a group of competent and detached people . . . a standards committee composed of artists, psychologists, and research technicians." He also suggested that networks be allowed to collude openly with one another to prevent competition for ratings—such competition, he felt, could only lead to an attempt to garner the most viewers. In short, he said, "In a democracy, the basic decisions are made by the public. And yet, we do not determine the programs of our schools or of our health services by referenda. On certain cultural and scientific issues we accept the guidance of experts. Television should be one of those issues."[50]

Lazarsfeld felt that mass media presented the very significant danger of reinforcing the capitalist status quo. "These media have taken on the job of rendering mass publics conformative to the social and economic *status quo*." The American people, he said, were suffering from "narcotizing dysfunction."[51]

What does any of this have to do with Lazarsfeld's dubious findings on the merits of marketing to younger viewers? A lot. By directing programming at younger viewers, Lazarsfeld had to recognize that programming itself would become more liberal—it would attack antiquated notions about sexuality and family life that the Frankfurt School despised. Younger viewers are always more likely to be critical of social mores and standards, more open to government redistributionism, less likely to be offended by the imposition of foreign morality on American shores—or on American television. Lazarsfeld must have known this—his mother, Sofie, wrote tracts explaining that "Generally, there is a tendency on the part of young people to 'chase after' sexual pleasure, almost to the exclusion of everything."[52]

This isn't to say that Lazarsfeld purposefully biased his research due to his political persuasion. There's little evidence for that proposition. But like artists, scientists generally allow their political viewpoints to bleed into their research, creating conclusions and then directing their research toward those preconceived conclusions. Lazarsfeld was strongly political all of his life, and his conclusions just happened to support his liberal ideals. Perhaps that was coincidence. More likely, it was not.

What *certainly* wasn't coincidence was ABC's decision to take Lazarsfeld's results at face value. It would be one thing if the people at ABC thought Lazarsfeld was right when he argued for the value of the younger viewer. But they had good reason to doubt his conclusions. After all, ABC was getting its posterior handed to it both in terms of revenue and in terms of ratings. From 1950 to 1970, ABC had a grand total of twenty shows that hit the top ten. That's one per year. And there were only three networks.

All ABC had to sell was their flimsy numbers based on Lazarsfeld's research and their rural weakness. Leonard Goldberg, head of programming at ABC during the mid to late 1960s, told me as much: "We used to sell those [specialized] ratings because once you got out [of those statistics], you died. . . . We used to sell the 18 to 49, the 18 to 34 ratings. This was back in the early 1970s. And people would say, 'Who cares?' We had presentations . . . about the value of those people who hadn't set their patterns. . . . We did it out of self-preservation, it's all we had."[53]

Advertisers bought into the ABC cooked-book concept. Perhaps it was because most advertising executives are younger than fifty.[54] Perhaps it was because advertising executives were more interested in pushing dollars toward more liberal, sexier programming—after all, advertising agencies are nearly as liberal as Hollywood. But in any case, advertiser comfort with what ABC was selling translated into bucks for networks willing to skew young and liberal.

ABC's new strategy frightened the more straight-laced, affiliate-wealthy folks at CBS and NBC. They were bamboozled by ABC's marketing efforts and the burgeoning advertiser frenzy for youth audiences. Mike Dann, the senior vice president of CBS from 1966 to 1970, bought into the ABC marketing effort. "We were the hillbilly network," he said to me. This despite the fact that as of 1968, CBS featured six of the top ten shows on television, while ABC featured zero.[55]

But now, the numbers weren't good enough. Now they had to be the *right kind* of numbers. "ABC definitely had the young people's crowd, because they had all these Warner Bros. hours that were scheduled from eight to nine o'clock, a *Sunset Strip* kind of thing," Dann averred. "Their early hours were so geared to a pack of young men and women, and they just knocked us out, you see."[56] By any objective measure, ABC was still getting crushed at the time. But that didn't stop the movement at CBS.

One day, Dann got called into the Big Boss's office. "I got called in by Bill Paley," Dann remembered. Paley grilled him about ABC's programming. "[ABC was] very able to dance us off our feet, because our programs were entrenched and their programs were new. Now that's a big difference," Dann remembered. He sighed. "They were very, very good. They were so good that they frightened us at CBS."[57]

Scared of the ABC strategy (and no doubt by the harsh criticism of Bill Paley), Dann told me he was instrumental in picking up *All in the Family*, which was "so dramatically *not* the hillbilly network." He wanted instead to focus on the urban audiences. "Big cities and boroughs became seventy percent, seventy-five percent of our audience" during this period, Dann said. When I pressed Dann on the statistics, he admitted, "We weren't even sure of that. Those estimates were always made up and argued with Nielsen, where our audiences were, because many advertisers did not like the rural audience. They were interested in seeds and hay and that kind of crap and they stopped viewing at ten o'clock. They were asleep. It was the urban centers that became predominant."[58]

In other words, the numbers relied upon by the advertisers were just as flukey and phony as anything else in the TV industry. Leonard Stern, who produced *Get Smart* and *He & She*, among others, told me that he actually fought this battle with the executives at CBS. "I remember speaking out against it," he said. "I spoke at CBS on this . . . I was always looking for evidence to prove that the networks were lying on statistics." In fact, Stern went so far as to commission research on the Nielsens, which he says showed that their information was deeply flawed.

"We did battle the best we could, and we proved to our satisfaction that the Nielsen's were consistently off the mark," Stern explained. Stern's research featured viewers using—you guessed it—Lazarsfeld's viewer tests. And surprise, surprise: Stern discovered that the results of those tests were flexible. "I remember one of the scientists saying that the results were malleable but they could be interpreted as being 100 percent correct four percent of the time," Stern laughed. "You could introduce bias subtly into the questioning process, and the result could reflect what you wanted."[59]

The burgeoning urban movement was tinsel, but it was effective in changing the entire face of the industry. That's because motivated advertisers and executives and creators wanted that change. They'd had enough of catering to the "hillbillies"—that word came up frequently in conversation with the former executives. Now they wanted to cater to their neighbors and friends.

In all likelihood, it wasn't Dann who bought into the ABC youth-first version of reality—it was Bob Wood. Wood, whom Paley promoted over Dann to head CBS in toto, took credit for the movement away from rural programming. When he was made president of the network, Wood's first priority was asking, "What can we do to maintain the leadership of our network while at the same time putting it through a test—of changing the character of the network from more bucolic material to more fresh or updated, contemporary, whatever you want to call it."[60]

Fred Silverman, then working under Wood and Dann, backed up Wood's gambit.

"What was behind the programming shift?" I asked him.

"Money," he answered. "Simple economics. We were a rural network . . . from a demographic point of view, an age point of view, the audience was ancient. . . . And ABC was making a lot of money with a lesser schedule by appealing to the eighteen-to-forty-nine audience. . . . So here we were with this old hillbilly audience. And it was a matter of survival."[61]

It wasn't quite simple economics, though. "To me," said Silverman, "I said it's great. . . . We in one year cancelled ten shows with a collective share of audience of a 36. These were shows that were top-ten shows." Why would Silverman be happy about this? Only for ideological reasons, not fiscal ones.

The substitutes? In Silverman's words, they were "initially, really terrible shows. There wasn't a show that was a keeper in the whole group."[62]

The man most hosed by the industry's sea change was Marty Ransohoff, the profit-first programmer who saw his babies—*The Beverly Hillbillies, Green Acres, Petticoat Junction*—canceled in one fell swoop. "In the early 1970s, these shows all went off the air," Ransohoff said as he sipped wine at a trendy Los Angeles restaurant. Ransohoff's shows were pure entertainment. "We weren't concerned with politics when we made these shows. We were making shows for an audience. That was the only way to stay on the air."[63]

Not after the programming shift. Now, targeting a specific audience was the best way to stay on the air. Preferably, programming liberal to target a specific audience. It didn't matter if *All in the Family* started rough out of the gate—it was pulling that young, urban audience in a hip, liberal manner. Said Silverman, "*All in the Family* just singularly made the CBS television network. It gave us that one hit, that one defining show. Not only was it an enormous audience hit, but it just was kind of a model for what Bob Wood and I wanted that network to look like: being very, very progressive . . . being very, very urban . . . being very cutting edge."[64] *Broad*-casting was entering its final death throes. The time of the handpicked audience had begun.

To this day, targeting young audiences remains the advertisers' goal. In the United States as of 1998, advertising agencies paid $24 per 1,000 audience members to reach people 18–35, as opposed to $10 per 1,000 for older audiences.[65] Because of CBS's high numbers among older viewers for the past few decades, *M*A*S*H* writer Burt Prelutsky told me, they commissioned a study asking about the consumption habits of older viewers. "They wanted to prove that this whole concentration on youth was nonsense," he said. "They were already the old *kocker* network. They found, first, that old people were just as likely as young people to try a new product [and] even though the young people had more discretionary income because their folks were paying their bills, the older people were making so much more money, that even though it was a smaller percentage, it was still more.

"As an example of the stupidity that was rampant in ad agencies and with sponsors, there was a show called *Tour of Duty*, which was in the 60s in the ratings rankings, but it skewed young . . . and at the same time, *Murder, She Wrote* was on the air, which was either first or second each week," Prelutsky related. "*Tour of Duty* was charging $165,000 a commercial minute; *Murder, She Wrote* was $95,000. And yet there were more people in the target group watching *Murder, She Wrote* than all of them watching *Tour of Duty*. What are they thinking?!"[66]

What are they thinking, indeed. Goldberg, who pushed the 18-to-49 concept, believed the theory back in the 1960s and 1970s—but now, on the board of the highly successful and older-skewing CBS, he thinks it's outdated. "I don't think it's still true to the same extent, although now that's all everyone talks about, the 18-to-49 crowd. Also, if you look at what age people lived to back in the late 1960s, early 1970s versus today, sixty is the new forty. So I think it's exactly the reverse. . . . Now when they're pitching it, they say, . . . 'Oh, CBS is an old network. Yeah, they're number one, but not in the 18-to-49, they're just number two there.' I say, 'So what? Who do you think is going to buy anything of value? Who has the damn money?' "

When I mentioned to Goldberg that targeting the young audience skewed liberal and lost the viewers in Birmingham, Alabama, he nodded vigorously. "You're absolutely right," he said. "And that is why CBS under Les Moonves is number one by a wide margin every year. He puts on shows for the *television audience*. . . . All the media darlings [compete with each other] every week, but who comes out number one every week? CBS."[67] Goldberg's right. CBS does it with older viewers. And the younger viewers make for bankrupt networks. This year, CBS live primetime viewers' median age was fifty-six. The youngest median viewers visit the CW network. Who's first? CBS. Who's last? CW.[68]

Despite the play in the numbers, the vagaries in determining the "value" viewer, the pure guesswork that is television programming, networks continue to rely almost exclusively on the numbers—and they use them as a cover to justify their programming decisions.

Ratings supposedly trump everything. But in reality, executives aren't all about the ratings, as we'll discuss shortly—they were fine with *All in the Family*, *M*A*S*H*, and *The Smothers Brothers* for political as well as financial reasons, as shown by the fact that each of those programs started off with low ratings. But the numbers continue to provide a convenient, if flawed, cover for the market argument. And it's all due to that true Hollywood story, the con job that took over the entire advertising industry.

HOLE NUMBER TWO: TELEVISION'S BUSINESSMEN COLLUDE

I own a fruit stand. You own a fruit stand. Our fruit stands are across the street from each other. And in the center of the street stands a hungry kid.

If I want that hungry kid to buy from my fruit stand, I lower my prices and raise my quality. I undercut you. You try to do the same. That's how competition in the free market is supposed to work.

Now suppose that there are two people in the center of the street: a hungry kid and a hungry adult. Suppose also that the hungry kid wants an orange and the hungry adult wants an apple. As the fruit stand owner, I have two choices. First, I can try to undercut your fruit stand by selling both cheap apples and cheap oranges. That would create competition, just as in the first scenario.

Second, I can walk across the street and make a deal with you: You'll sell apples and I'll sell oranges. We'll fix the prices on each so that we can each make a decent profit. Instead of competing and lowering our own profit margins in order to draw customers, we'll instead have higher prices and distinct goods that we sell.

The television industry embraces this second idea with fervor. Television channels do not compete with each other; they involve themselves in a soft form of collusion. That's why we've got Lifetime, which boasts the slogan "Television for Women," and Spike, previously known as the "First Network for Men." That's why we've got TNT, which specializes in drama, and Comedy Central, which specializes in raunchy riotousness. That's why there's Logo, catering to gay audiences, and ESPN, which caters mainly to straight male sports fans.

The television executives call this diversity of programming. They say that narrowcasting on cable has created a plethora of viewing options for the public. But how many times have you sat down on your couch, flipped through your 350-plus channels, and asked yourself, "How the hell is there nothing to watch?"

Very often, there's nothing to watch because there's no variety *within genres*. If you're a young male, you're basically herded towards one of a few channels. You're not going to be visiting Oxygen, nor are you going to be checking out E! Your choices are quite limited, due to both government regulations that make competition in the television sphere virtually impossible, and vertical integration, which has put several major studios in charge of all programming.

Governmental regulations have restricted the number of networks available—ABC, NBC, CBS, and Fox all had to go through extensive legal hoops in order to build their businesses. Such barriers to entry make free and open competition virtually impossible. Not only that—the vast amount of cash required to buy up the affiliates necessary to broadcast original programming on a national scale is prohibitive.

Such monopoly becomes even more obvious when we look to the cable television industry, which is largely owned by the same players. Originally, as Clint Bolick of the Hoover Institution and the Goldwater Institute writes, the FCC heavily regulated the nascent cable industry, hoping to alleviate "unfair competition" complaints from rival media services. When the FCC finally backed off, the local governments picked up the regulatory slack. "Nearly every community in the United States allows only a single cable company to operate within its borders," wrote Bolick in 1984.[69] As of 1998, almost 100 percent of cable markets in the country had only one cable company active in them. Meanwhile, customers paid the price: "An FCC survey found that cable systems with monopolies charged an average of 65 cents a channel per month while those that faced competition charged only 48 cents per month."[70] Satellite TV has alleviated this situation somewhat, but continued federal and local regulations make it nearly impossible for any competition to exist among cable companies—a situation that pleases current cable companies and their corporate owners no end.

Vertical integration has also crowded out competition in the marketplace. There are currently six companies that own virtually all of the major television channels in existence, as well as the distribution systems. All six have heavy relations with the government due to their size, contributing to their tendency toward programming liberalism.

General Electric. GE owns NBC and all of its spinoffs (MSNBC, CNBC, etc.), the History Channel and its spinoffs, A&E, the Biography Channel, Bravo, USA Network, SyFy, Oxygen, Chiller, Hallmark channel, Sundance channel, and Telemundo, among others. It also owns television production giant Universal Television and movie production giant Universal Studios and its subsidiaries. (More consolidation is on the horizon: Comcast, the cable operator, is looking to buy most of these holdings—and Comcast already owns E!, Versus, the Golf Channel, etc.)

Time Warner. The company that bought up Ted Turner's outfit owns CNN and its spinoffs, HBO and its spinoffs, Cinemax, Cartoon Network, TNT, TBS, Turner Classic Movies, and CW. Like GE, it also owns several major production companies, including all of Warner Bros. (which in turn owns New Line Cinema, Castle Rock Entertainment, Hanna Barbera, and WB). Time Warner also owns Time Warner Cable.

The Walt Disney Company. The great American success story that is the Mouse House now owns ABC and its spinoffs, including ABC Family, ESPN and its spinoffs, and Disney Channel. It also owns equity in Lifetime, A&E, the History channel, the Biography channel, and several other channels. It is an equity partner in Hulu, the online source for television content, along with GE and NewsCorp. Its production companies include Touchstone, Miramax, and Marvel Studios.

News Corporation. News Corp., Rupert Murdoch's outfit, is smaller in television than most of the other groups. It owns Fox, of course, as well as Fox News, the Fox Movie Channel, FX, National Geographic, and Fox Sports, among others. It, too, has its own set of production companies, as well as all the subsidiaries of 20th Century Fox. News Corp. also owns a large chunk of DirecTV.

CBS Corporation. The only major television corporation that began in the industry, CBS owns half of CW, as well as Showtime, and the Movie Channel. CBS Television Studios are highly successful.

Viacom. Short for Video and Audio Communications, Viacom was spun off by CBS in 2005. Although Viacom is headed by the estimable Les Moonves, 80 percent of the voting stock is owned by Sumner Redstone, who also owns 80 percent of the voting stock of CBS. Viacom owns Paramount Pictures, as well as MTV, Nickelodeon, and United International Pictures (a joint venture with NBC's Universal). It also owns Spike, VH1, BET, CMT, Comedy Central, Logo, and Viva.

These six competitors do substantial business with one another. Not only do their channels carry programs produced by other corporations' production companies, their channels are in many cases joint ventures between corporations. While there are certainly rivalries among them (Les Moonves and Jeff Zucker of NBC have famously gone at it for years), there is also shared interest in maintaining an oligopoly that has only become more obvious with centralization of cable networks under the banner of major corporations.

The best evidence of oligopoly here isn't merely the lack of competition in programming, which is at least arguable. It's the industry's attempt to shut down online television, which threatens the entire cable/programming order. According to Free Press, "giant cable, satellite and phone companies and many leading programming networks, led by Comcast and Time Warner, are colluding on an industry-wide initiative called 'TV Everywhere.' . . . TV Everywhere is designed to eliminate the threat of online competition, limit consumer choice, and build on the cable TV model that gouges consumers."[71]

Here's how it works: TV Everywhere wants to prevent online users from accessing current cable channels unless they also pay subscription fees to a cable, satellite, or phone company. This plan obviously only works if the channels collude with one another—if one of the channels decides to make its content available online without subscription while the others abide by the plan, that free-riding channel will benefit from increased viewership. Hence, as the *Wall Street Journal* reported, "The satellite television, telecommunications and cable industries—longtime rivals—agree on one issue: The need to put TV shows that are available online, most of which are now free, behind a pay wall." The *Wall Street Journal* even noted that the major communications executives were wary of crossing legal lines: "The electronic media chiefs, including [Time Warner CEO Jeffrey] Bewkes, Jeff Zucker of NBC Universal and Philippe P. Dauman of Viacom, among others, have been more careful, so as to avoid being accused of collusion."[72]

The issue is one of control. The corporations have it. The American people don't. And that has an impact on what is being watched all over the globe.

HOLE NUMBER THREE: PROGRAMMERS AREN'T INTERESTED IN PROFIT ALONE

The market argument assumes that the executives involved are attempting to cater to the broadest possible market in their search for profits. They aren't. They need to get numbers, of course. But they often keep shows on the air that don't get numbers simply because they like them.

When shows are successful, it's difficult to tell when executives are fibbing about political motivation. After all, their job is to put hit programs on the air—if they're performing that job, then how can they be faulted for infusion of their political beliefs?

But this investigation becomes far easier when we take a look at the unsuccessful shows that executives keep on the air. There, it's clear that liberal shows almost universally get more of a chance than conservative shows. Executives will cite everything from positive reviews to personal faith in a show to keep it alive. Often, it boils down to politics.

Grant Tinker, head of NBC during the early 1980s, was the king of this domain. He famously kept shows alive simply because he liked them. "Too often, network programmers, with their jobs on the line, look at dismal early ratings, decide they were wrong about a show's potential, and yank it off the air," Tinker wrote. "But if you believe that the show the producers are delivering is as good as you hoped it would be, you must have some confidence that the audience will eventually think so, too." Tinker actually went further—he said that low ratings could be an indicator that you had something unique.[73] He acted that faith out by keeping two horrific failures alive: *Hill Street Blues* and *St. Elsewhere*. Later, that faith would be justified. (Conversely, the argument can easily be made that if you keep something in a decent time slot long enough, it will likely find an audience.)

Hill Street had been a Fred Silverman greenlight before Silverman's exit. And Silverman had shown similar faith in the show. Before its launch, *Hill Street* produced, in Silverman deputy Brandon Tartikoff's words, "some of the worst numbers Fred or I had ever seen. To his credit, though, Fred never wavered in his loyalty to the show. . . . 'This is something completely different,' he said. 'And completely different always tests badly.' "[74]

It didn't just test badly. It bombed like the *Enola Gay*. It ranked eighty-third in popularity, close to the bottom of all primetime programming.[75]

Why did Silverman renew it? Because it had cachet. Like Al Gore, it had gravitas. As Tartikoff stated, "The television critics would, quite simply, have had us for a barbecue if we took the show off the air."[76]

There is another reason. To put it in the words of Michael Kozoll, co-creator of the show, *Hill Street Blues* was liberal. "I guess you'd say we're liberal," Kozoll said of himself and partner Steven Bochco. "I guess we all feel that the government could be doing more to help ameliorate some terrible situations." Bochco said that he thought the liberalism of the show was actually the reason the show wasn't drawing ratings. "That could be a source of some of our ratings problems. Because there's no other explanation for why people aren't watching us in droves," Bochco told Gitlin.[77]

Silverman was gone after that season, but in his place came Tinker. Tinker had a connection with *Hill Street*—he'd produced it. That basically guaranteed that he'd stick with it. And his Silverman holdover number two, Tartikoff, backed him up. Why? "In keeping with the gambling spirit, we renewed *Hill Street* simply because we liked it—at first simply for what it was. . . ."[78]

If Tinker and company kept *Hill Street* alive because they had faith in it, they kept *St. Elsewhere* alive because it was their baby. Predictably pitched as *Hill Street in a Hospital*, *St. Elsewhere* was similar to *Hill Street* stylistically, politically, and in terms of initial ratings. "The first season of *St. Elsewhere*," he later wrote, "was brilliant creatively, but almost no one watched . . . most of our NBC decision-makers wanted to dump it. . . . 'It's a good show,' I said. 'Let's pick it up.'" It didn't hurt that Tinker's son Mark was a writer on the show and that during the second season, Tinker's youngest son, John, would also join the writers' room.[79]

It wasn't just Tinker, Silverman, and Tartikoff who monkeyed around with scheduling based on personal predilection despite low ratings. Bob Wood stuck with *All in the Family* even though it drew terrible ratings at the beginning. Similarly, *M*A*S*H* stayed on the air despite initial ratings that made CBS executives nauseous—largely because the executives at CBS were liberal and *M*A*S*H* was a militantly liberal show. *Soap* lost money for ABC year after year, but the network kept airing it because the executives liked it; Marcy Carsey, who initially greenlit *Soap*, told me she thought it was "fabulous," an opinion shared by ABC's executive team.[80] The executives at NBC aired the 1989 made-for-television movie *Roe v. Wade* despite twenty-three of twenty-four advertisers dropping out.[81] Brandon Stoddard, who headed all of ABC's programming during the late 1980s, explained to me, "It depends how much passion the networks have for a show, if they hang in there."[82]

The converse is also true. Successful shows get yanked off the air or censored if the executives don't like them. *Unsolved Mysteries* was a highly successful series of specials for NBC, but Tartikoff refused to greenlight *Unsolved Mysteries* as a full series until nine individually ordered specials had rated well. Similarly, Tartikoff treated one of NBC's few hit shows, *The A-Team*, with utter scorn, according to series star Dwight Schultz, because it wasn't "quality TV."

For the latest example, take a look at the treatment of *South Park*. The executives who greenlit *South Park* clearly loved it. But when *South Park* veers into territory that makes them nervous—i.e., conservative territory—they censor it with impunity.

Doug Herzog, president of MTV Networks Entertainment Group, which oversees Comedy Central, admits that his programming strategy begins with his personal opinion—"We start with, do we think it's funny? Is it funny to us? . . . Generally, if we think something's funny, we'll find a way to put it on television."[83] That opinion-based reasoning forced him into political territory when *South Park* decided to target the Islamic prophet Muhammad in April 2006. It was one thing for *South Park* to make fun of Jesus (in fact, it was Matt Stone's and Trey Parker's targeting of Jesus in their short Christmas video, *Jesus vs. Santa Claus*, that got them their gig on Comedy Central originally). It was something else entirely for the *South Park* creators to try to depict Muhammad, particularly in the aftermath of the Muslim world's rioting over cartoons of Muhammad in Denmark. Comedy Central prohibited that depiction, releasing a statement: "In light of recent world events, we feel we made the right decision."[84]

When I asked Herzog about that censorship in July 2009, he replied, "I think if we had to do it all over again we would do it differently. . . . You know, there was concern that it might not be the most prudent thing to do at that time, and people were kind of losing their heads over it, I think wrongly so." I asked Herzog whether allowing the Muhammad image would have been imprudent commercially or politically. "I think combination," Herzog replied.[85]

Herzog's liberal sensitivity clearly affected his judgment over Muhammad depictions in *South Park*. Despite his statement to me that he would do it differently if it ever came up again, when it did come up again, he proceeded along precisely the same lines. He censored it, provoking the ire of the *South Park* creators, who released a statement on their website complaining, "We do not have network approval to stream our original version of the show."[86]

Compare the treatment of *South Park* to the treatment of *All in the Family*. When network executives challenged Norman Lear on *All in the Family*, Lear told them to shove it. He knew he had power, and he was willing to use it. He reached a sort of détente with the network censor, William Tankersley. But that wasn't much of a surprise—Tankersley and Lear thought alike. Later in life, Tankersley reports, Lear called him up on the telephone. " 'I'm just calling you to tell you about the great respect I've had for you over the years. That's all I want to say.' . . . [I] told him what I thought of him as a patriot who would spend eight million dollars on one of the copies of the Declaration of Independence. And I said, 'I hope that you're still a good Democrat.' He assured me that he was. So am I."[87] You can bet that same conversation wouldn't take place between Stone and Parker and Herzog.

If political concerns drive censoring decisions, they also drive broader programming decisions. Television's executives almost universally admit that factors other than pure profit motive drive their decision making. "Through the medium of television we try to make the world a slightly better place," Herzog told me.[88]

Fred Silverman, who at one time or another ran all three major television networks and was criticized for being a proponent of "jiggle TV," said, "I would hope in some ways that we kind of led the audience, that we didn't follow the audience, but that on some of the shows we were at the forefront of movements."[89]

Brandon Stoddard explained that his goal was to find material that was able to both "say something but also putting something on the air that was entertaining."[90] Marcy Carsey agreed, telling me that social messaging and marketing were not in competition.[91] Barbara Fisher of Hallmark Channel (and formerly of Lifetime) said, "I'm not paid to do the Barbara Fisher initiative or my pet projects. I'm not. That doesn't mean I don't bring some of my personality—I do."[92] Even Mike Dann—the same Dann who told me that the ratio of social responsibility to entertainment in his mind when it came to greenlighting was "About five to one"—said that he hoped his legacy in television would be "shows . . . like *East Side/West Side*," a commercial flop and a commonly cited masterpiece among liberals.[93]

Still, executives say that their programming choices are market-based.

The myth survives because it is only half-myth. The executives *do* want to make money—otherwise they'd be fired forthwith. The networks aren't PBS. But that doesn't mean that executives are worried exclusively about the buck in Ayn Rand style. They're concerned with their messaging—a praiseworthy concern, but one that becomes troubling if the executives are universally liberal.

And essentially, they are. By now, it's become a self-perpetuating system. Today's television executives grew up on television, mainly in urban areas, attained high levels of education, and know the ins-and-outs of typical Hollywood fare. They're young because everyone is seeking the "young" audience. Larry Gelbart describes network executives in typically colorful style: "Why do our TV sets seem like copy machines with moving pictures? Everything we see on the box represents choices made by network executives, who tend to be young."[94] Hollywood's executives tend to think alike, vote alike, and program alike. And when they're seeking to "do good," they push the same political messages.

HOLE NUMBER FOUR: AUDIENCES DON'T CHANGE THE CHANNEL

Television creators and executives claim that the market bears out their artistic choices because, after all, viewers can change the channel if they don't like what they're watching. For example, I quizzed Michelle Ganeless on how Comedy Central can call itself an "adult" channel while catering largely to kids. (Ganeless admitted to me that at least 20 to 30 percent of the Comedy Central audience is below eighteen years of age.) She answered, "We have standards, obviously, standards and practices the network lives by, but if a parent doesn't want their ten-year-old watching a show, the parent needs to be responsible for that at any network, not just ours."[95]

There are a couple of problems with the assumption that people will simply switch the channel if they don't like what they're watching. The first is the most obvious: Many people simply don't. Whether the remote has died and they're glued to the couch or they're taking in whatever content the television spits out, viewers aren't quite the perfect consumers the television honchos would have us believe. Scientists say that television is addictive. You wouldn't hear liberals making the argument that smokers can always throw out their packs of Marlboros. Instead, they call for regulation of the tobacco industry.

The second problem with the "turn the channel" argument is that it assumes there's something to turn the channel *to*. If you don't like the political take on *Friends*, you can always find something more conservative; if you don't like *All in the Family*, you can always find a *Waltons*. Again, that's false. Viewers have a limited selection of politically motivated programming from which to choose. Aside from *24*, it is difficult to think of a single conservative-oriented entertainment show on television over the last decade. The best conservatives can do is innocuous fare like *Everybody Loves Raymond* or *Extreme Makeover: Home Edition*, which aren't conservative so much as apolitical. Liberals, on the other hand, can pick from several shows every night of the week.

Actually, conservative viewers *do* turn the channel when they don't like what they're watching—but they turn the channel to less liberal shows, since conservative shows aren't available. Ironically enough, their viewing choices are far more predictive of a show's success than liberals' viewing choices. In November 2010, the *Hollywood Reporter* ran an astonishing story about a study by leading media-research company Experian Simmons. The study looked at the viewing habits of self-identified conservatives and Republicans, and compared those viewing habits to the viewing habits of self-identified liberals and Democrats. Here are Republicans' favorite shows, in order of preference: (1) *Glenn Beck*, (2) *The Amazing Race*, (3) *Modern Family*, (4) *American Idol* and *V* (tie), (6) *The Big Bang Theory* and *The Mentalist* (tie), (8) *Survivor*, (9) *Dancing with the Stars*, (10) *Desperate Housewives*, (11) *NCIS*, (12) *The Bachelor* and *Lie to Me* (tie), (14) *How I Met Your Mother*, and (15) *Two and a Half Men*. These shows are all hits, and are all immensely popular. None except *Beck*, *V*, and *NCIS* could be described as remotely right-wing (and even *V* is a stretch), but Republicans choose these shows because they come closest to being apolitical or at least not openly insulting to conservatives.

Democrats' top shows, by contrast, draw far smaller audiences: (1) *Countdown with Keith Olbermann*, (2) *Mad Men*, (3) *Dexter*, (4) *Kourtney & Khloe Take Miami*, (5) *90210*, (6) *Private Practice* and *Brothers & Sisters* (tie), (8) *30 Rock*, (9) *The Good Wife*, (10) *Damages*, (11) *Community* and *Law &*

Order: SVU (tie), (13) *Friday Night Lights*, (14) *Parks and Recreation*, and (15) *Breaking Bad*. As reporter James Hibberd noted, "if you look at the list of broadcast shows that are Republican favorites, it closely mirrors the Nielsen top 10 list, whereas Democrats tend to gravitate toward titles likely to have narrower audiences. To Hollywood, the data suggest a potentially disquieting idea: The TV industry is populated by liberals, but big-league success may require pleasing conservatives."[96]

Disquieting? This should be breathtakingly exciting to folks in Hollywood, who are supposedly interested only in reaching the broadest audience and raking in the dough. Imagine you're a car manufacturer, and you suddenly discover a new country full of people dying to buy cars. Wouldn't you be excited? The same should hold true for the television creators and executives. It means that they've been ignoring an enormous chunk of the market that they can exploit.

But they're not excited. They're frightened. If, in fact, the market for their shows demands *conservative* content, they can't keep their market myth alive. They'll have to—horror of horrors!—open up the industry to conservatives.

For now, at least, the industry remains one-sided, with creators and executives ignoring the market data. Flipping the channel has become like voting in Cuba. You can do it, but your preference isn't going to make much of a difference when the choices are all the same. And as the television industry has discovered, it isn't who votes or watches—it's who counts the votes and the watchers. They measure the audience. They slice and dice up those measurements and then market them to the advertisers. And the advertisers decide whom they want to target based on that faulty information. But leaving aside the internal politics of the industry and the business demands of the networks, there are two external forces that also drive the television industry to the left. These forces have far more sway over what you see on your television than you and a hundred million of your friends. These partners in crime control the means of production, the means of distribution, and the public debate.

They are, of course, liberal interest groups and the government. Together with the television industry, they form a Celluloid Triangle. And that Celluloid Triangle is far more powerful than the military-industrial complex ever was.

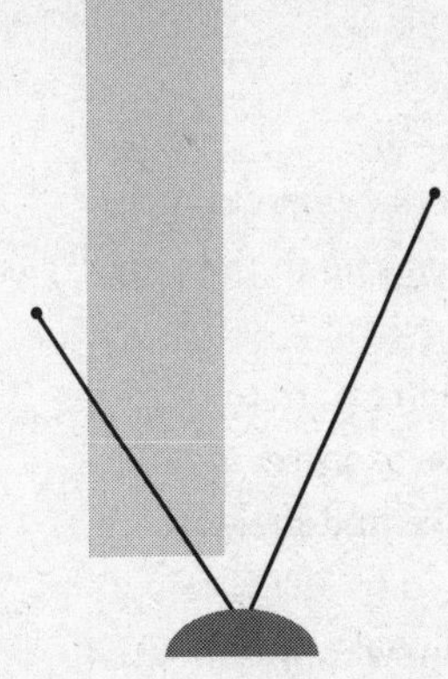

THE CELLULOID TRIANGLE

How Interest Groups, Government, and Hollywood Conspire to Keep TV Left

The markets may not dictate programming. The audience may not dictate programming. But two outside forces do combine to dictate programming: liberal interest groups and the government. Both of them want conservative programming shut down and conservatives shut out of the business altogether.

Television has a broad and deep impact on American hearts and minds. The government therefore has an interest in regulating the television industry—and in particular, the government has an interest in promoting pro-government politics. To that end, the government intervenes in the television market on a regular basis.

But because the government helps control the television airwaves, constituents contact the government when they see something that upsets them. When interest groups decide to make a fuss, they often call in their government representatives to do their dirty work. Legislators fear vocal pressure groups and respond to them, knowing that when mobilized, such groups can sink reelection campaigns. So legislators often take constituent views on television programming seriously—far more seriously than the networks themselves. A few dozen letters may get a Congressman mobilized to pick on a network, whereas a few dozen letters directly to the network would likely end up in the paper shredder.

At the same time, members of the government don't want to tick off the television industry by consistently cracking down on them—they know full well that the television industry can make and break them. They remember Richard Nixon, relentlessly skewered by television anchormen and comedians. They remember Sarah Palin, who was mocked and savaged by the television community, turning her from a mainstream heroine into a representative of the "fringe" right wing. And they certainly know about Barack Obama, who was the first media-created president in American history.

The government therefore engages in a corrupt ménage à trois with liberal interest groups and the television industry. Here's how it works: liberal interest groups and their media allies require that television include certain messages, messages that television executives are all too happy to insert; government enforces those requirements by threatening troublesome interference with the television honchos; television bows to both the other players and in return receives accolades and government goodies.

Why does this work only with liberal interest groups? Actually, for a change, it doesn't. On the rare occasions when conservative interest groups mobilize and protest what they see on the tube, and when they find receptive ears in government, television responds accordingly. The difference is that while television's powers-that-be respond to liberal interest group criticism with sensitivity, understanding, and the shocked expression of the backstabbed fellow traveler, television's liberals respond to such conservative crusading with anger. Television fights conservative groups and legislators with righteous fury; it responds to liberal groups and legislators with conciliatory humility.

"THE PUBLIC INTEREST"

To understand how the Celluloid Triangle works, we must first examine government's power to control the industry. It is only because government has the power to control the television business that government can parlay with creators and executives and liberal interest groups to help create a coherent leftist agenda on your television screens.

The main body tasked with regulating the television industry is the Federal Communications Commission (FCC). It is governed by two groups of constituents: Congress, which can override the FCC's regulations at any time, and the interest groups, which often control Congress.

The FCC and the television industry have a love-hate relationship. The television industry loves the FCC when it's controlled by liberals and hates it when it's controlled by conservatives. Fortunately for the television industry, the FCC has almost universally abdicated its role as policeman of the airwaves in favor of an anything-goes attitude—at least when it comes to sex.

The television industry works well with the FCC when the FCC promotes the liberal agenda. The FCC has historically intruded into the television business when it wants to "elevate" the public—in other words, when liberals at the FCC, in Congress, and in lobbying organizations want to use the airwaves to promote their political agenda. The television industry rarely says "boo" to such intrusions. Their ire is reserved for the legislators and regulators who don't want to promote the liberal social agenda or hear the F word emanating from their television screens.

The FCC's power springs from the 1934 Communications Act, which states that only those radio and (later) television stations that best serve the "public interest, convenience, and necessity" would be granted licenses. The notion here was that the airwaves were a public good and had to be used to everyone's benefit. To that end, regulators required that licensees direct some programming toward "minority interests." Minority interests were those interests understood to be underrepresented in the public debate, such as rural communities. "In building programs for the majority of listeners," wrote NBC executive Judith Waller in 1944, "no radio station can wholly forget that there are minority groups which must be considered. They have a place in our democracy; they must also have a place in radio." Bill Paley said, "We have a responsibility to minority tastes, minority groups."[1]

Moral standards, too, were governed by the "public interest." "The Columbia Broadcasting System has no thought of setting itself up as an arbiter of what is proper for children to hear; but it does have an editorial responsibility to the community," CBS told the public in 1935. This meant that "deviant behavior must never go unpunished." NBC felt the same way, stating in its 1948 program policies manual, "The sanctity of marriage and the home must be maintained."[2] The standards, obviously, were very conservative in nature.

The original television executives hated these standards. These were sophisticated New York and Los Angeles folks, after all, and they weren't interested in gauche notions of traditional morality. "On matters pertaining to sex, America as a whole proclaims itself to be one way and acts another," spat one network executive.[3] But they knew where their bread was buttered—both government and advertisers supported the law. Those advertisers, who had to deal with the public at large and couldn't afford to tick them off, actually set the networks' early broadcast standards and practices.

At Young & Rubicam, for example, David Levy helped develop *Father Knows Best*, *Maverick*, and *The Life of Riley*, among other shows (he went on to become vice president of development at NBC). He knew that his sponsors would not tolerate controversial material that generated boycotts. He wrote letters to producers across town, explaining, "We will not have any profanity. We will never take the Lord's name in vain. There will be no exceptions. None, because if you do that, you start a hole in the dike."[4] Levy's words were prophetic—as soon as the television creators and executives found the leeway to push the envelope, to begin the ball rolling down the slippery slope, there was no way to stop them from encroaching more and more into radically leftist moral territory.

Young & Rubicam wasn't the only advertising agency seeking to control content. Procter & Gamble was the industry's largest advertiser, and it required that "The moral code of the characters in our dramas . . . be synonymous with the moral code of the bulk of the American people." Stockton Helffrich of the National Association of Broadcasters (NAB) explained, "We don't dictate to the audience. The audience dictates to us from the sanctity of its living room." That meant, in practical terms, more traditional and patriotic fare.[5]

Conservative sponsor control of content didn't make creators happy. Some of that unhappiness was justified; sponsors sometimes shut down episodes because of fears about anti-racist messages.

But most of the unrest among the creators was simple liberal angst. The host of CBS's *Seven Lively Arts* complained, "On television, what love there is, is always terribly connubial. Everyone is married. The suspicion exists that animal passion is frowned on because the advertiser doesn't want to distract attention from the toothpaste."[6]

THE NETWORKS TAKE CONTROL

The networks responded to advertiser concerns about serving the traditional audience in two ways. First, they created a new business model, allowing advertisers to disperse their ads over several programs rather than sponsoring single programs. This allowed more creative freedom to the writers and producers, who no longer had to listen to one advertiser. At the same time, it allowed sponsors to hedge their bets—if one program drew large numbers but was controversial, the advertiser, as one among many, wouldn't be boycotted. Even better, advertisers wouldn't have to spend inordinate bundles of cash to fund an entire program.

Second, the networks installed their own standards-and-practices departments—as Frank Stanton of CBS put it, the networks became "masters of our house."[7] The networks instituted an industrywide set of self-regulations to be enforced by the in-house standards-and-practices departments. In 1952, the NAB, the chief lobbying group for the radio and television industries, set the Television Code. The Code stated that programs had to avoid trampling on the sensibilities of the American people. That meant that programming had to avoid presenting "cruelty, greed and selfishness as worthy motivations"; criminality had to be "presented as undesirable and unsympathetic"; the "use of horror for its own sake" had to be banned; law enforcement had to be "upheld," and officers had to be "portrayed with respect and dignity." In other words, no vanguardism.

The Television Code was an attempt by the industry to make an end run around "the shadow of incipient censorship by Government regulation," as Thad H. Brown, director of television for the NAB, put it before a subcommittee of the Committee on Interstate and Foreign Commerce in the House in 1952.[8] It worked. The FCC largely went along with the networks' end-around.

Standards and practices took control of the industry. At the beginning, they stalwartly ensured that the Television Code was maintained. Sometimes this took the form of absurd notes from network executives, as Leonard Stern has documented in his hilarious booklet, *A Martian Wouldn't Say That!* For example, CBS executives asked that Norton from *The Honeymooners* be made something other than a janitor, since "you can't expect people to watch a sewer worker while they're having dinner."[9] Overall, though, there wasn't much for standards and practices to do—it was a different time, a cleaner time.

When the transition toward more liberal standards came, it came not from the industry itself, but from the government. The newly enshrined JFK administration decided that it wasn't enough for television to uphold traditional moral standards—television had to push the liberal social agenda. To that end, the FCC reinterpreted the "public interest" requirement. "Minority interests" that required representation on television were reinvented; no longer were "minority interests" the interests of underrepresented economic or religious communities with clear political agendas—now they were the interests of ethnic and racial minorities who were simply assumed to be liberal. Government, given the power to target the television industry, decided to put that power to use.

In 1961, Newton Minow, JFK's chairman of the FCC, gave the most famous speech in television history before the NAB. Minow's views of television's failures mirrored the concerns of socialists like Paul Lazarsfeld and Theodor Adorno, who both worried that television laminated the status quo rather than forwarding social change.[10]

In the speech, Minow spent the vast majority of his time warning the television industry that if they didn't up their lowbrow standards—if they didn't stop catering to the masses and instead try to educate them—they'd be doing a disservice to the industry and would bring the heavy hand of government down upon them.

He opened by noting the industry's debt to government. "You earn your bread by using public property," he intoned. "When you work in broadcasting you volunteer for public service, public pressure, and public regulation. You must compete with other attractions and other investments, and the only way you can do it is to prove to us every three years that you should have been in business in the first place."

This was not an auspicious opening—it boded ill for a laissez-faire approach to oversight. It quickly got worse. "I admire your courage," he averred, "but that doesn't mean that I would make life any easier for you. Your license lets you use the public's airwaves as trustees for 180 million Americans. The public is your beneficiary. If you want to stay on as trustees, you must deliver a decent return to the public—not only to your stockholders." Minow placed in stark opposition profit and public interest, as if income were a sin, a shameful Cain-like mark on the forehead of the industry. Then he laid down the bottom line: "Clean up your own house or the government will do it for you."

His job, Minow said, was to "uphold and protect the public interest." But he was not going to interpret that rather vague phrase as it had been previously interpreted—he wasn't going to enforce traditional morality via regulation. And he forcefully rejected Frank Stanton's definition of the public interest as "what interests the public." Instead, he defined the public interest as the JFK Administration agenda. "In today's world . . . with social and economic problems at home of the gravest nature, yes, and with the technological knowledge that makes it possible, as our President has said, not only to destroy our world but *to destroy poverty around the world*—in a time of peril and opportunity, the old complacent, unbalanced fare of action-adventure and situation comedies is simply not good enough."

Television, Minow assured the NAB, was not doing that. No, it was a "vast wasteland . . . a procession of game shows, formula comedies about totally unbelievable families, blood and thunder, mayhem, violence, sadism, murder, western bad men, western good men, private eyes, gangsters, more violence, and cartoons. . . . True, you'll see a few things you will enjoy. But they will be very, very few." This, of course, was false. People did enjoy those shows. During the 1960–61 season, the top ten shows in terms of ratings were *Gunsmoke, Wagon Train, Have Gun Will Travel, The Danny Thomas Show, The Red Skelton Show, Father Knows Best, 77 Sunset Strip, The Price Is Right, Wanted: Dead or Alive*, and *Perry Mason*—exactly the collection of westerns, adventurers, cops, and game shows Minow said nobody enjoyed.

But Minow wasn't truly worried about whether people enjoyed the programming. He was worried about what *he* enjoyed. And what *he* enjoyed was liberal television. He would use his position, he threatened, to enforce the presence of such liberal television. After all, Minow said, "I happen to believe in the gravity of my own particular sector of the New Frontier." This was code. The New Frontier was a shorthand term used by JFK throughout the 1960 presidential campaign to signify the entirety of his agenda—and Minow was signaling that he took his job as a JFK lackey seriously enough to restrict television's role to that of quasi-propaganda arm for the JFK agenda.[11]

Not much came of the Minow speech in the end. Many of the network heads publicly dismissed Minow, and one—Jim Aubrey of CBS—went so far as to make fun of Minow by naming the S.S. *Minnow* on *Gilligan's Island* after him. But where the networks *did* become more sensitive to FCC concerns, they did so in a largely liberal direction, in keeping with the goals of Minow's speech. That meant increased funding for liberal news departments, as well as standards-and-practices focus on those "minority interests" that Minow cited—liberal interest groups being the most vocal advocates for "minority interests."

THE MINORITY TAILS WAG THE NATIONAL TELEVISION DOG

Minow frightened the television industry. That, of course, was his goal. Minow wanted to make the industry feel that it was under a microscope, that every episode of every show would be watched for the correct and "enlightening" agenda he sought.

But Minow knew that he couldn't watch every episode of every show. Therefore, as Minow made clear in his speech, he would rely on the public to act as a watchdog for him.[12] That put a good deal of power in the hands of small but active minorities, who quickly made their presence in the industry felt. That wasn't unexpected, considering that Minow's boss, JFK, was elected largely because of the support of such minority interest groups. Broadly speaking, there is almost always a tacit agreement in politics between candidates for office and such groups: The groups help get candidates elected, and candidates then turn around and act on behalf of those groups.

If that's true for most politicians, it's especially true for liberal politicians, who believe in the tenets of multiculturalism—fragmentation of American society into constituent groups identifiable by ethnic, racial, religious, or sexual status. To liberal politicians, interest groups aren't merely tools to be used in election battles. They are fundamental goods in and of themselves, representatives of true democracy at work, since true democracy can only be enjoyed by collectives of Americans rather than melting-pot individuals.

While the elder generation of Hollywood creators and executives viewed Minow's words with fear, the younger generation embraced his mantra: interest groups were representatives of a "tolerant" and "diverse" America, and keeping them happy was one of television's chief obligations. Because Hollywood's executives and creators are and were generally liberal, they believed in the tenets of political correctness long before such political correctness went mainstream. All interest groups were to be taken seriously—at least at the beginning. Later on, only liberal interest groups would be considered legitimate. But even in the beginning, minority blocs were changing the face of television for the vast and silent majorities watching at home. Multiculturalism was taking root on television screens across the nation.

For example, in 1959, ABC premiered an action show about Eliot Ness and his band of Prohibition-era agents titled *The Untouchables*. It was one of the network's first big hits, rocketing in the ratings from forty-third in its first season to eighth in its second season.[13] During that second season, though, ABC head of programming Ollie Treyz was confronted by an Italian-American interest group. He capitulated. "We take out all the Italians and make them Greeks," he later wrote. "Then the Greeks get mad, so we change the Greeks into Anglo-Saxons, and all the bad guys were named Smith."[14] Viewers weren't stupid, even if the network was. As Treyz explains, the predictable result was that "the show died. Everyone knows very well that Al Capone was Italian. So we take the show off the air."[15]

Later, when *Soap* became the first network television show to feature an open homosexual (Billy Crystal's Jodie), the creators of the show met with gay advocacy groups to vet their characterization. "Y'know," Paul Junger Witt, the show's producer, told interviewer Allan Neuwirth, "we did meet with gay groups who were concerned that the first openly gay character on television would be seen as wildly effeminate . . . we also explained that, you know, there *was* going to be an evolution."[16]

ABC's chief censor for thirty years, Alfred Schneider, dedicates an entire section of his book, *The Gatekeeper*, to dealing with interest groups. Despite his eventual suggestion that "Special-interest groups cannot be allowed to superimpose their wills, their standards, their special objectives and goals . . . on television programming,"[17] Schneider tells several stories in which interest groups—almost always liberal interest groups—changed actual programming content. In 1973, for example, long before the gay rights movement gained mainstream credibility and just four years after the Stonewall riots in New York, the Gay Activist Alliance protested ABC for an episode of *Marcus Welby, M.D.* in which a schoolteacher molested one of his male students. Somehow the GAA received entrance to the ABC office building and sat in outside ABC head Leonard Goldenson's office. ABC decided to allow the GAA to control the debate, striking all references to homosexuality in the episode and contacting affiliates and advertisers to let them know that the episode was not intended to insult gays.[18]

Something similar happened in 1981, when a TV-movie script began circulating about a woman who left her husband to begin a temporary lesbian love affair, only to return to her husband. Standards and Practices nixed the last scene, which implied that lesbian discovery was not in fact permanent in all cases. "Don't you realize that will offend every lesbian in America?" they asked. As Ernest Kinoy, writer of *Roots*, *Roots II*, and *Skokie* noted, it would be near-impossible to make a show or a movie involving "a hero who is a homosexual and is distressed about it and goes to an analyst and they decide that this is not a good way to be, and so he works on it, and because the analyst says yes, this is a character disorder, and he becomes much improved. You can handle homosexuality—as long as you handle it in a lovely, tolerant fashion that will not upset the gay-liberation lobby." Similarly, Nigel McKeand, one of the producers on *Family*, told author Todd Gitlin, "no one can (whether you believe this or not) say that, for instance, homosexuality is infantile, and it is an absurd way to lead your life, and it's an arrested development. You can say two lesbians should be allowed to live in peace."[19]

Eventually, checking with left-leaning interest groups became common practice before airing even mildly controversial episodes. In 1986, NBC invited a select set of public interest lobbying organizations to Florida to take part in a conference in which the interest groups (largely liberal groups like the National Gay and Lesbian Task Force and the American-Arab Anti-Discrimination Committee) were asked to develop a relationship with the network and provide input on programming.[20] This wasn't out of the ordinary. Jerome Stanley, head of West Coast Broadcast Standards for NBC in the late 1970s, explained the process to Gitlin: "Where we see a property that deals with a special-interest group, and if we feel that there is any potential problem, a derogation, or misrepresentation, we will then get in touch with them, and either send them the script, or we will oftentimes ask the production company to invite them in as technical consultants." Wary of sounding too self-censoring, Stanley added, "Under no circumstances [though] do they have the right of approval."[21]

But there *are* some cases when networks *do* give interest groups rights of approval. In 2010, CBS announced that it would add three gay characters to its primetime shows after receiving a flunking grade from the Gay and Lesbian Alliance Against Defamation (GLAAD) for diversity. "We're disappointed in our track record so far," lamented CBS entertainment president Nina Tassler. "We're going to do it. We're not happy with ourselves."[22] So much for the idea that profits are the first priority—CBS won the 2009–2010 ratings season without the gay characters.[23]

In the movie business, the same thing takes place with regularity; in the most recent example, GLAAD forced the Vince Vaughn starrer *The Dilemma* to cut a joke calling electric cars "gay" from the trailer for the film. Vince Vaughn, no flaming right winger he, objected to the censorship, explaining, "Comedy and joking about our differences breaks tension and brings us together. Drawing dividing lines over what we can and cannot joke about does exactly that; it divides us. Most importantly, where does it stop?" The joke stayed on the cutting room floor.

GLAAD followed that victory up by complaining that the leading gay agenda show on television, *Glee*, used the word *tranny* in one of its episodes. Even Susan Sarandon, a woman so liberal that she celebrated being hit with tranny projectile vomiting at an avant-garde New York stage show, thought this was ridiculous: GLAAD, she said, was "getting like PETA—way out of control." That doesn't stop Hollywood from screening its films and shows for GLAAD, however.

Perhaps the most infamous case of a network bowing low before an interest group surrounded one of the only conservative-leaning major television shows in history, *24*.

The show's popularity was based on its uncompromising view of terrorists and how they should be treated; the show made no bones about the fact that the hero, Jack Bauer, was perfectly fine with torturing terrorists if they could help him stop attacks. Bauer knew that he was "running out of time!" and that he couldn't worry about the ACLU's niceties. And he also knew that those who declared war on the United States, whether they were Serbian ex-dictators (season one), German terrorists using Arab terrorists as a front (season two), or ex-British spies and Mexican narcoterrorists (season three), needed to feel the swift hand of justice.

Well, almost everyone who declared war on the United States. During season four of *24*, in 2005, the show ran into an interest group buzz saw in the form of the litigious Saudi-funded terrorist-supporting front group, the Council on American-Islamic Relations (CAIR). Season four was the first season of the show to actually suggest that Muslims might indeed be terrorists (as opposed to dupes of evil white folks in season two), and CAIR mobilized immediately. They met with agents of Fox and producers on *24* to try to blackmail them into a more friendly portrayal of a Muslim "sleeper cell" family on the show. The spokesperson for CAIR said that *24*'s portrayal of Muslims was "very dangerous and very disturbing." Eventually, CAIR pressured Fox to run a free advertising campaign for CAIR, as well as having Jack Bauer—Kiefer Sutherland—preface episodes of the show with a politically correct disclaimer.

Thanks to CAIR, viewers of the show during season four were treated to a stone-faced Sutherland explaining, "While terrorism is obviously one of the most critical challenges facing our nation and the world, it is important to recognize that the American Muslim community stands firmly beside their fellow Americans in denouncing and resisting all forms of terrorism. So in watching *24*, please, bear that in mind."[24]

Leave aside for a moment the fact that this disclaimer was

inaccurate—high-ranking members of CAIR have provided material aid to terrorism supporters, and the longtime CAIR communications director Ibrahim Hooper believes that Islamic law should be instituted as the governing vision of the United States.[25] Focus instead on the fact that a minority group was able to shape the programming policy of a major network's hit show. Focus on the fact that a group with almost no sway in the American commercial market—a CAIR-initiated boycott of talk show host Michael Savage in 2007 was utterly unsuccessful, for instance—somehow finagled what it wanted out of Fox. There's something more than merely responding to the danger of an advertiser boycott here. There's a pernicious tendency in the television industry to kowtow to any minority group that raises an alarm, no matter how foolish or weak the claim or how peripheral the interest group.

Unsurprisingly, vetting programming by catering to interest groups makes television less controversial—and less fun. Even liberals are beginning to recognize the danger. George Schlatter, who created *Laugh-In*, suggested that the presence of such political correctness destroys comedy, relegating it to simple fart and sex jokes: "Everything's about sex, and I think that's unfortunate, because there are other things that are funny. But that's easy, see, because there's no groups fighting. You do a joke about an Italian, and you get in trouble. You do a joke about an orgasm . . . and there's no group writing in to say 'You're making fun of my people.' "[26] He's quite correct. It was fear of ethnic interest groups that caused ABC to pass on *All in the Family*, for example.[27] If anything, the pressure is far more severe now—there is no chance a show like *All in the Family* would ever be aired today.

The Hollywood contingent has gone even further than mere approval for interest groups—it has formed its own interest groups *within the industry*. These are often cause-driven groups dedicated to pushing liberal messages in programming. Historically such groups have taken on issues ranging from drinking and driving to Earth Day to antidrug messages.[28] Today, one of the most active industry insider interest groups is the Entertainment Industry Foundation (EIF). The EIF suggests that its mission is to harness "the collective power of the entire industry to raise awareness and funds for critical health, educational and social issues in order to make a positive impact in our community and throughout the nation."[29] Its real mission is to promote *liberalism* on health, education, and social issues.

One of the EIF's latest initiatives was the "Play Your Part America" movement, designed to activate people on behalf of President Obama. According to an industry-exclusive press release, the EIF stated, "President Obama has called for a new era of responsibility." Based on their allegiance to Obama, the EIF called for the television business to "*turn up the volume* for service and volunteerism, engage more people, make it part of who we are and what we do to bring our country together."

How did the EIF propose to "turn up the volume"? By infusing messages of "service and volunteerism" into programming. They secured an "unprecedented week-long of television programming on all four leading broadcast networks . . . and other networks, beginning October 19." Such programming would " 'organically' create and produce as many stories as possible about service and volunteerism and connect them in the plots of network dramas, comedies and reality shows." Notice the EIF's own scare quotes around the word "organically." They knew that messaging wouldn't be "organic"—they just wanted programming to seem authentically integrated.

Messages to be focused on by the industry included: "Education and children; Health and well being; Environmental conservation and reduced energy consumption; Economic development and financial security; Support for military families." Some of these messages—"reduced energy consumption"—are clearly concerns of the left. Others are nonpartisan, such as supporting military families.

But the true leftism of this proposal lay in its attempt to use television entertainment programming as a Trojan horse to drive Americans to Democratic Party–approved sites and events. "We will ask the public," EIF announced, "to take action through the campaigns resources, namely via an online destination currently in development with the leading web companies."[30]

The website to which the campaign directed its viewers was a leftist tool called iparticipate.org, as well as a website called createthegood.com. As Big Hollywood columnist Larry O'Connor documented, when visitors to the website attempted to get information about "volunteering and service" regarding health care, they were directed to events sponsored by Planned Parenthood, as well as a video entitled "How to Spread the Truth About Health Care Reform." At IParticipate, the "volunteering" efforts were no less partisan, including an opportunity as "Global Warming Ambassador" and one as a member of the Crane Project, an anti-war outfit.[31] Shows participating in the IParticipate campaign included *Cold Case, Criminal Minds, CSI: Miami, CSI: New York, America's Most Wanted, Bones, So You Think You Can Dance, 30 Rock, Community, The Biggest Loser, The Office, Cougar Town, Desperate Housewives, Grey's Anatomy, Modern Family, Private Practice,* and *Ugly Betty*, among many others.[32]

Despite the mildly troubling leftism of the overall IParticipate campaign, the real problem here is the potential for collusion among networks to push a certain set of values. This isn't an exception—it happens repeatedly. Each year, NBC spends an entire week coordinating its programs to fit the "green" message. In 2007, this meant that Al Gore appeared on *30 Rock*, that the title character in *Chuck* visited a Stanford University "green" festival, that *ER* concerned itself with the dangers of a "rolling brownout." As the *Los Angeles Times* reported, "almost every prime-time show was mandated by Chief Executive Jeff Zucker to include some sort of environmental theme."[33] And 2007 provided merely the third of the network's Green Weeks; 2010 marked the sixth Green Week, which was designed to "drive consumer awareness around the environment," according to Beth Colleton, vice president of Green Is Universal.[34] This isn't entertainment—it's propaganda.

CENSORING VIOLENCE, SANCTIONING SEX

Despite the obviously leftist tilt of Hollywood's pandering to interest groups, the television community likes to appear evenhanded. They don't want to be obvious about their liberal agenda. Their solution is elegant and simple: Focus on violence on television rather than sex. Liberals claim that they are conservative by opposing superfluous blood and gore on TV, even as they greenlight every creepy and degraded form of sex for broadcast.

This supposed attempt at upholding traditional standards by targeting violence and ignoring sex is a fraud, of course. There is nothing inherently conservative about opposing television violence. Violence is neither liberal nor conservative. When Jack Bauer tortures terrorists on *24*, he uses violence in a conservative way; when Captain Planet uses violence against polluters, he uses violence in a liberal way.

In fact, cracking down on television violence across the board, it can be argued, fits with the liberal agenda more broadly. Violence on television is almost exclusively the domain of men. Men with testosterone. Not metrosexuals who read *Twilight* books. Cracking down on television violence is yet another way to teach young boys who watch television that violence is always wrong—a pacifist line, not a conservative one. Liberals think that violence on television leads to violence in real life; conservatives acknowledge the possibility, but also acknowledge that sometimes violence is necessary. Conservatives believe that violence should be used when required to defend family, to preserve country, to destroy evil. Liberals tend to believe that violence is almost never necessary, and that violence is in and of itself an evil to be defanged. Conservatives don't talk about "cycles of violence" because conservatives recognize that not all violence is the same—liberals do, because they believe all violence is wrong (which leaves them in the unenviable position of explaining what we should have done to stop Hitler).

Minimizing sexual content on television, however, is a uniquely conservative position. Conservatives believe that sex on television teaches kids to engage in sex, that children and teenagers are incapable of fully anticipating and understanding the consequences of sex, and that the most fulfilling sex comes in the context of a marital relationship. Liberals believe that sex is a purely physical act, that sexual experimentation is part of finding out "who you are," and that hemming teenagers in with traditional moral standards is brutal, unfeeling, and unrealistic.

If the conservative censor got hold of television, he'd leave much of the violence and do away with much of the sex. If the liberal censor got hold of television, he'd get rid of much of the violence and keep virtually all of the sex. It's obvious which censor controls the small screen.

The left's focus on television violence traces its lineage to the earliest days of the sexual revolution. During the 1960s, the FCC and the Democrats in the federal government paid very little attention to the burgeoning sexual revolution brought on by the teenage Baby Boomers. Instead, they held hearing after hearing examining the effects of violent television on juveniles, despite little or no evidence showing that moderate television violence has any effect at all on kids. This provided Congressmen the ability to posture without ticking off those who were buying into the newly forming socially liberal Zeitgeist. (This is also, by the way, a typical liberal tactic: By playing up the relatively minor threat of television violence, liberals shifted attention from the very real effects of television sexual depictions, which affect children far more deeply than car chases and gunfights.)

In 1962, Senator Thomas Dodd (D-Connecticut), the father of Senator Chris Dodd, focused his laser eye on the television industry's program schedule, which he said was "overloaded with 'crime and violence.'" In 1964, he held more hearings, this time for the purposes of determining the impact of television violence on juvenile delinquency—as though watching a few episodes of *The Untouchables* was likely to turn teens into budding Al Capones rather than incipient Eliot Nesses. As ABC censor Alfred Schneider noted, "it became increasingly politically correct for government officials, supported by academic encouragement, to indict television programming. . . . What was lacking was some substantial evidence—research that could prove television 'caused' violent behavior."[35]

But lack of evidence has never stopped Congress from posturing. In 1969, despite the relatively low levels of television violence and the increasing uptick of sexual envelope pushing, the Senate Subcommittee on Communications held yet another set of hearings on television's brutality. These hearings were led by Senator John O. Pastore (D-Rhode Island), who forced through a pseudoscientific report on television violence, which he released on March 23, 1972. "If the mass media seduce only one child each year to unfeeling, violent attitudes," he blathered, "and this child influences yearly only one other child, who in turn affects only one other, there would be in 20 years, 1,048,575 violence prone people." This was idiotic, of course; this sort of pyramid scheme of violence doesn't work any better than the Social Security pyramid scheme. But Pastore enlisted Nixon's surgeon general, Jesse L. Steinfeld, who warned, "The broadcasters should be put on notice. The . . . report indicates that television violence, indeed, does have an adverse effect on *certain* members of our society."[36] This argument does not persuade, it cudgels. Everything on television undoubtedly affects *somebody* negatively. Television's depiction of women no doubt has some adverse effects on potential rapists. That doesn't mean the government should ban women from television. But logic has never been government's strong suit.

Even as the government focused on violence on television, it ignored sex on television almost completely. Throughout the 1960s—with a few well-publicized exceptions—increasing sexuality on television went largely unchallenged. The government *did* challenge open pornography on television—in 1969, Nixon appointed Dean Burch to chair the FCC, and Burch quickly stated that the FCC and Department of Justice would prosecute broadcasters for putting obscenity on the airwaves. But such governmental strictures were directed solely at the most egregious cases, not at the loosening of standards more generally.[37]

The government's laxity allowed the networks to pursue their political leftism when it came to sex. The NAB changed its moral guidelines to reflect increasing sexual permissiveness. By 1972, the NAB had revised its code to provide encouragement to "programs that are innovative . . . that deal with significant moral and social issues, that present challenging concepts that relate to the world in which the viewer lives." More specifically, the NAB changed Code Section 7. Previously, it read, "sex perversion as a theme or dialogue implying it may not be used." In 1972, the NAB decided that instead, "special sensitivity is necessary in the use of material relating to sex."[38] That, of course, opened the doors to a more liberal version of sexual politics, of which the networks took full advantage.

Those at the networks celebrated this new opportunity. Instead of acting as ABC's censor, Alfred Schneider became, in his own words, "the censor turned advocate." "While you have to reflect society," censor Schneider wrote in defending *Soap*, "you have to inch ahead, too. This is your responsibility." Later on in life, Schneider could look back with pride, celebrating "how quickly the daring and dangerous taboos disappear."[39]

The predictable effect of focusing on violence rather than sex was that sexual activity on television increased dramatically while violent content was heavily curtailed. In practical terms, this meant more raunchy comedies in the mold of *All in the Family*, more sexy dramas like *Dallas*, and fewer Westerns and action-adventure shows. In 1960, 58 percent of ABC affiliate schedules were packed with action-adventure, Westerns, and detective shows; by 1972, the percentage dropped to 32 percent. The networks knew this at the time, and they were largely fine with it. While ABC hired Dr. Melvin Heller, director of the Division of Forensic Psychiatry at Temple University, to help come up with a set of standards to manage violence on television in the 1960s, they largely ignored him when he stated in 1972, "to the extent that you're successful in curing, limiting in some way, toning down violence, to that extent you will be inviting to fill that vacuum with increased emphasis on sex."[40]

Of course, the networks couldn't afford to go whole hog and embrace the cable mind-set. In the early 1970s, most Americans were still quite conservative on matters sexual, even if the counterculture was growing in influence thanks to television's new urban programming strategy. That meant that the networks constantly fought it out with creators on minor matters while leaving major issues unscathed. Larry Gelbart of *M*A*S*H* stated, "They did let us talk about the futility of war and they did allow us to be highly political. On lesser, sillier matters, we negotiated, script by script, on a daily basis."[41]

Other creators were less blasé about even minor censorship by the networks. Those creators enjoy a self-perception of heroism that far overstates the nature of most of their battle wounds. They're a lot like Richard Dreyfuss in *Jaws*—a few scratches and bite marks, but no gunshot wounds. Carl Reiner, for example, *did* walk away from a show, *The New Dick Van Dyke Show*, when the network nixed an episode in which Dick Van Dyke's screen daughter walked in on him having sex. Reiner put his money where his mouth was in defense of his bobo ideals. But that doesn't mean he was standing up to ruthless McCarthyism. He was standing up to some poor network *shlub* who didn't want kids to see Bert from *Mary Poppins* shtupping on network television.

THE "FAMILY HOUR" FIASCO

The television industry isn't interested in taking on sex. They're interested in promoting sexual content. In fact, they're so uninterested in taking on sex that they can't even agree to cut it out to shield children. The best example of the industry's reliance on sex: the death of the so-called Family Hour.

Ironically enough, the attempt to create a Family Hour free of sex started because of fears about television violence. In 1974, based on the furor surrounding NBC's made-for-television movie *Born Innocent*, which featured a young girl (*The Exorcist*'s Linda Blair) being raped with a broomstick by several other females in a juvenile facility, the government began investigating violence on television once more.

In an attempt to head off the government at the pass once again, CBS President Arthur Taylor took the lead in condemning television violence. This was no surprise, since CBS's main programs were sexual rather than violent in nature; industry self-regulation of violence would chiefly affect CBS's rivals. Taylor proposed, quite reasonably, that television add a three-pronged standard to its programming: first, programming in the 8 to 9 P.M. hour should be family-appropriate; second, when non-family-friendly specials were broadcast during that timeslot, they should be preceded by a notice to parents; third, in the other primetime hours, notices should be provided to adults when material offensive to a large portion of adults was broadcast.[42]

ABC, unsurprisingly, took the lead in opposing CBS. More of ABC's programming was based on violence, which meant they had to oppose CBS's measures in order to maintain share. NBC, too, didn't like CBS's proposal, which felt too much like a competitor dictating terms to the entire industry.

This all came to a head at the NAB Code Review Board meeting on January 7, 1975. CBS insisted on a family viewing policy before 9 P.M. ABC, led by Schneider, opposed it—or at least wanted it extended to cover sexual situations, not out of principle, but out of desire to ensure that CBS would feel the burdens of its proposals. "Well," said Schneider, according to transcripts, "if you are not going to move the goddamn program 'All in the Family,' we are not going to move the goddamn 'Rookies.'"[43]

In the end, CBS got its industrywide standard regarding violence, and ABC got to tie down CBS on matters of sex. In April, the NAB passed a proposal stating, "Entertainment programming inappropriate for viewing by a general family audience should not be broadcast during the first hour of network entertainment programming in prime time and in the immediately preceding hour." The NAB Code Authority would be designated as the appeals authority if anyone believed a particular network program was unsuitable for the so-called Family Viewing Hour.[44]

It was one thing for the networks to come together to restrict violence on television, according to the creators. It was quite another for them to agree to hold back the rising tide of the collective libido. Norman Lear, who wanted *All in the Family* to continue in its massively successful Saturday 8 P.M. slot, was particularly fearful of the new policy.[45]

Seeing no other choice, Lear joined with Danny Arnold (*Barney Miller*), Larry Gelbart (*M*A*S*H*), and the Writers Guild to file a lawsuit against the networks.[46] Luckily for them, they were assigned a liberal judge, Warren J. Ferguson. Ferguson issued a ruling striking down the Family Viewing Policy on the grounds that the NAB had colluded to restrict First Amendment rights and that the FCC's informal imprimatur of approval made the Family Viewing Policy unconstitutional. The decision is utterly legally fallacious, absurd. Ferguson makes several unsupportable claims, including the incredible announcement that "neither the FCC nor the NAB has the right to compromise the independent judgments of individual station owner licensees."[47] As a broad matter, this is obviously untrue. The NAB is an independent private organization; whatever influence it wields is legitimate so long as it violates no antitrust law. The FCC routinely weighs in on local station issues. It constantly wields the threat of license withdrawal in order to maintain certain standards—just ask Newton Minow.

But the Family Viewing Hour was effectively killed, to the delight of the creators and many of the executives in Hollywood. It is worth noting once again that it was killed because the creators insisted on their sexual content, not their violence. For years they'd dealt with censorship of violent programming, but it was only when sexual content came under close formal scrutiny that they rebelled in toto.

It is also worth noting that sexual mores came into play only due to competitive rivalries between the networks—not because anyone at any of the networks was interested in actually upholding traditional standards of American sexual propriety. The same folks at ABC who pushed for a Family Viewing Hour ban on *All in the Family* later pushed for cultural acceptance of *Soap*.

The Family Viewing Hour debacle, then, is not a story of conservatives in the industry attempting to curb television's wayward tendencies. It is a story of the industry attempting to prevent governmental censorship at all costs in order to preserve popular left-leaning programming, and a concomitant story of business rivals attempting to gain competitive advantage. Those two competing forces are, in a nutshell, the story of Hollywood overall.

FIGHTING THE RIGHT-WING INTEREST GROUPS

The Family Viewing Hour frightened creators within the television industry and bothered many executives. But it did not release their full fury.

That fury was reserved for the Religious Right. By the late 1970s, it was becoming clear that television was awash in sex. One study showed that a single week in primetime television in 1979 depicted 806 sex incidents. That included four depictions of implied intercourse, 208 incidents of sexual language, and 331 instances of innuendo.[48]

The Religious Right mobilized. Led by Rev. Donald Wildmon's National Federation for Decency and Rev. Jerry Falwell's Moral Majority, religious Americans began protesting the vast quantities of sex and liberalism they were receiving via their television sets. Soon, Wildmon and Falwell joined forces under the rubric of the Coalition for Better Television (CBTV). Their protests had an effect on advertisers, who responded to the market. In 1978, after being labeled as the nation's third-largest advertiser on sex-soaked programs by Wildmon, Sears pulled its sponsorship from *Three's Company*. Overall, by mid-1981, advertisers were withdrawing 5 to 8 percent of their commercials from controversial programs.[49]

This freaked out the powers-that-be in television, who see any conservative boycott as a repeat of the Salem witch trials. In May 1981, television's creators and executives got together in scenic Ojai, California, to batten down the hatches against the conservative onslaught. Grant Tinker of NBC trembled over the "galvanizing specter" of the religious right, which he labeled, "the first group to attack the entire medium." (This was an inaccurate label—the religious right would have had nothing to complain about if television had been a steady diet of *Gunsmoke* reruns and episodes of *The Waltons*.) "We will not change or remove any of our programs. Although TV is today's target, movies, books, magazines, and newspapers will not be far behind," CBS senior vice president Gene Mater said.

Thomas Wyman of CBS was most vehement, slandering the CBTV and the Moral Majority as "a constitutionally immoral minority" trying to "disenfranchise the real majority of viewers from making their own decisions about what to watch." He said that Wildmon and Falwell "strike at the heart of the American ideal of a free marketplace. We must make it clear that what is at stake is not the propriety of the networks but the freedom of the airwaves."[50]

This was just plain dumb. The freedom of the airwaves includes the freedom of people to vote with their remotes, and with the dollars they spend on products—in fact, it's those freedoms that make the freedom of the airwaves possible in the first place. Falwell and Wildmon were simply participating in the market of television, and the television executives and creators didn't like it. The utter scorn in which Hollywood holds the Religious Right is incredible. Susan Harris, whose *Soap* became, according to her, "the first fatality of the Moral Majority," sums up the Hollywood feeling about the Religious Right well: "Idiots talking. . . . There are a lot of people who really have medieval minds in all sorts of ways. Who aren't open to anything new. Aren't open to anything reasonable. Think science is a matter of belief. And that's who you're dealing with. People ran out and bought guns because they thought Obama was going to take their guns away. This is what you have out there. It's not an audience, I think, I could ever speak to."[51] Falwell and Wildmon represented the vast unwashed; television wouldn't stand for any attempt by those rubes to recapture control of the airwaves.

For a while, that didn't stop Falwell and Wildmon. They were able to wield enough power to cut down shows like *Love, Sidney*, a relatively innocuous series about a gay man played by Tony Randall.[52] They also brought economic pressure to bear on shows like *thirtysomething*, which lost $1 million in advertising by broadcasting two men together in bed. Objectively speaking, this was no different from gay groups threatening boycotts of *Soap*. But for the Hollywood left, this was an outrage.[53]

It was almost impossible for targeted boycotting to work against an entire industry determined to promote particular messages and values. Despite Wildmon's and Falwell's efforts, the industry continued to promulgate the material with which it agreed—and because the industry was virtually homogeneous, it was almost impossible for Wildmon and Falwell to succeed. By 1991, according to Wildmon's American Family Association, NBC, CBS, and ABC primetime television broadcast more than ten thousand sexual "incidents" annually; the ratio of single people having sex to married people having sex was fourteen to one. These incredible statistics were confirmed in part by a survey carried out by a Florida State University professor, who found that between 1979 and 1989, sex talk and sex acts rose dramatically on television. The FCC, following television's lead, actually loosened restrictions on the network affiliates in 1987, allowing "indecent" programming to dominate television between midnight and 6 A.M. Just three years later, the FCC went even further, allowing affiliates to run "indecent" material anytime from eight P.M. to six A.M.[54] So much for the Family Viewing Hour!

In order for the Religious Right to have had any lasting overall impact, conservatives would have had to boycott not just one or two target sponsors, but a vast array of sponsors advertising on a vast array of shows. The television industry is a hydra—no matter how many advertisers are cut off, others will surely rise to take their place. And the television industry has demonstrated that it is unwilling to come to the table with conservative interest groups in the same way it routinely comes to the table with liberal interest groups. That left the Religious Right with one real alternative: Turn off the television. That's what the Religious Right did in some measure. And the predictable result was the conservative movement's self-excision from the television community, aiding and abetting the discrimination that goes on daily in Tinseltown.

WHY HOLLYWOOD NEEDS THE TRIANGLE

So why does the Hollywood community take liberal interest groups so seriously, while ignoring conservative interest groups? It's not just because liberals dominate the television industry. It's because members of the television industry have an interest in bigger government generally:

They recognize that if they push leftist programs and leftist politicians and work with leftist interest groups to do so, they'll help convert the American voter to put their buddies in power.

And it is bigger government that has given Hollywood oligopoly. In the same way that welfare recipients vote Democrat to ensure the continuation of their welfare checks, Hollywood pushes liberal messages at least in part to ensure the free flow of laws that help them out. If there were open competition in the television world, no doubt rates would drop for advertising, payment would drop for writers, actors, and producers, and networks would have to compete on an even footing with entrants into the market. Right now, it's an extremely lucrative industry for everyone inside the industry—and everyone else is a waiter. That's the way the industry likes it.

In the beginning, members of the television industry had a thoroughly contrarian view toward government. They wanted as little of it as possible. They wanted to be left alone to pursue their profit making. They objected to governmental regulation. But as the industry matured—as the honchos began to protect their territory—they began to realize that governmental relations could benefit them. The networks, the creators, the producers all began to work hand in glove with the government and government officials. Instead of the industry being purely capitalist, it became corporatist.

Today, you will never see a tax-cutting argument in a scripted television show, even though you'll see hundreds of arguments about the merits of climate-change legislation or antismoking regulations. You'll see rips about Dick Cheney but never a word about Joe Biden. You'll hear about the merits of gay marriage and abortion, but you'll never hear about the human rights case for the war in Iraq. The Democratic Party agenda, combined with the interests of the liberal interest groups, predominates.

Liberals in Hollywood support liberal interest groups who support liberals in government. That's because Hollywood is being paid off by the government on a regular basis, as we'll explore next.

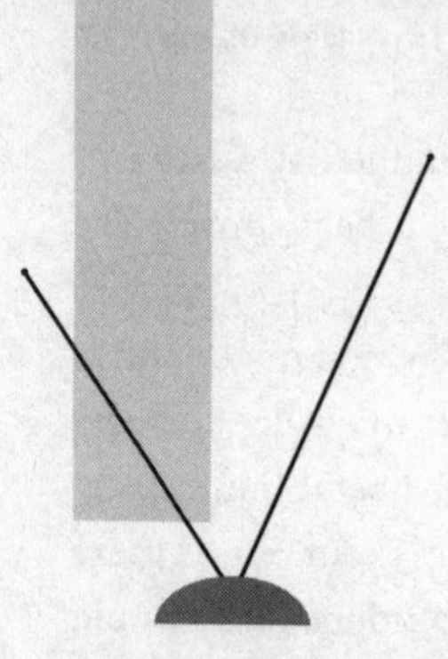

THE GOVERNMENT-HOLLYWOOD COMPLEX

How Hollywood Became the Federal Government's PR Firm

We've already heard liberals in television talk up the merits of the free market in defending their liberal programming. If they took their own rhetoric seriously, they'd realize that government usually serves only to quash business's profit-making capacity—in other words, they'd be conservatives.

Yet they still program in favor of big government.

Why? Because government *doesn't* quash profit making in Hollywood. To the contrary, with the help of the government, TV's powers-that-be are able to retain and maximize their oligopoly, crowding out competition. Executives and creators in television aren't interested in the free market—they're too busy swallowing subsidies from the government at the expense of the taxpayer and their potential competitors.

It's not that the executives in Hollywood need an unfair advantage because they're untalented. In fact, it is their *immense* talent in business that drives them toward manipulation of the market by working with government. The problem isn't truly Hollywood—it's the vast growth of government unforeseen by the Founding Fathers. Once government became a grab bag of cash and favorable regulation, it was only a matter of time before Hollywood, like all other businesses, took advantage. Hollywood works just like GM: It's bloated, unwieldy, and unionized. When its product is good, it does well. When its product declines, it goes to the government for a handout.

Liberals in government are only too happy to help out Hollywood. Unlike GM, however, Hollywood doesn't help out its friends by throwing around cash. Instead, Hollywood goes directly to the public, teaching audiences why they should vote liberal. While other businesses simply make campaign payoffs to get what they want from legislators, Hollywood is an opinion-making and opinion-shaping business.

Hollywood is the most powerful actor in the hierarchy of free speech. It uses that free speech to put money in its own pocket by aiding its political allies in government, destroying its political enemies, and then hiding behind the First Amendment when people complain. In return, it only asks a little help from its governmental friends.

"I'LL BE THERE FOR YOU"

The buddy-buddy relationship between television's power brokers and government actors is well-documented—executives and creators in the industry work together.

That's been true since the beginning. Because television has historically been intertwined with government, television honchos have cultivated close relationships with those who regulate them. David Sarnoff of NBC, despite his economically conservative leanings, quickly learned that connections with the government could be most useful. He cultivated a friendship with FDR; during the FDR administration, Sarnoff even helped the president install a recording system in the Oval Office.[1] During World War II, FDR often used Sarnoff, skillfully deploying him all over the globe. During that time, Sarnoff found himself in direct communication with FDR on a consistent basis.[2] Such kindnesses did not go unrewarded: When FDR appointed commissioners to the newly formed FCC in 1934, he appointed "friends of the industry." He even took part in NBC's Washington headquarters grand opening, and on RCA's 25th birthday in 1944, he penned a celebratory letter to Sarnoff.[3]

Sarnoff didn't get along as well with President Truman (Truman actually thought Sarnoff hated him),[4] but he loved Eisenhower, particularly because he had served directly under him during World War II. He supported Nixon and became part of his inner circle during the 1960 election cycle—in fact, Nixon's supporters later blamed Sarnoff personally for convincing Nixon to appear in the famous Kennedy-Nixon debate in which he blew the election (though Sarnoff claimed they never discussed the matter).[5] He had a wary but respectful relationship with LBJ—then-Senator Johnson once referred to RCA as "a key element in our defense structure."[6] In return for Sarnoff's support of major politicians, NBC was granted regulatory largesse, particularly with regard to experimentation on color television.

The same held true at ABC, where Leonard Goldenson cultivated government figures on a regular basis. Goldenson received business advice from Senator John Pastore (D-Rhode Island), despite the fact that ABC was television's most prominent purveyor of television violence, and Pastore was Congress's most ardent foe of television violence. Suspiciously enough, Pastore advised Goldenson how to build his news department (a Senator advising a major network on its news coverage tactics certainly isn't altruistic). Pastore informed Goldenson that ABC would be wise to "build a more competitive news and public affairs operation in order to enhance its public image." Goldenson, recognizing an offer he couldn't refuse, acted quickly, snapping up Dwight Eisenhower's press secretary, James Hagerty, to act as president of ABC's news division. Hagerty would end up playing a role in the denouement of the Cuban Missile Crisis, acting as go-between for the Russians and the Kennedy Administration.[7]

Goldenson also had an exceedingly warm relationship with the Kennedy clan. Because of that closeness, he forced Mike Wallace to back down from allegations made by columnist Drew Pearson (whose philosophy Goldenson wrongly described as "right-wing, conspiratorial") that JFK's *Profiles In Courage* had been ghostwritten by JFK speechwriter Theodore Sorenson.[8] Of course, as subsequent history has shown, Sorenson did indeed write the book. There can be little doubt that Goldenson's personal predilection for JFK, whom he called "energetic, witty, warm, courageous" and credited with lighting "the spirited flame of hope . . . in our national consciousness," contributed to his actions.[9]

Goldenson's fondness for Democratic politicians never waned. Goldenson thought that LBJ was rude, crude, and dictatorial, which he was. Nonetheless, Goldenson was so close with President Lyndon Johnson that he went skinny dipping in the White House pool with him (Eric Massa would have been LBJ's ideal staffer). Goldenson even allowed LBJ to illegally run a blind trust without reporting him.[10]

Bill Paley, a nominal Republican, reached out to the FDR White House in an attempt to warm up Roosevelt. In 1935, Stephen Early, FDR's press secretary, told FDR, "He is friendly. So is Columbia. Confidentially, I understand that he desires to tell the president something of Columbia's political policy, plus a willingness to be of service during the campaign."[11] Paley often lunched with FDR at the White House, and in fact, FDR attempted to throw business Paley's way; according to historian Robert J. Brown, "Paley and the president worked out a plan to expand the scope of [CBS radio's] shortwave activities to include much of South America."[12]

During the 1930s, even as he tête-à-têted with Roosevelt liberals, Paley allowed anti-FDR sponsors to dominate the airwaves with pro-business messages. When profits were threatened by political partisanship on the airwaves, however, he suddenly swung CBS's position—CBS, he now said, had to be "wholly, honestly and militantly nonpartisan. . . . We must never have an editorial page." Then, when it became clear that Eisenhower would become president in 1952, Paley offered Eisenhower a regular slot on CBS, stating, "I feel strongly that you should have a regular platform for the discussion of some of the serious issues confronting the country. . . ." Eisenhower reciprocated by offering Paley a spot in his cabinet, writing, "You'll be the one man around here who can come into my office at any time without knocking." Paley turned him down. It was a pattern that would continue the rest of Paley's life—bowing to governmental actors in order to ensure profit margin, no matter who the politicians were.[13]

It was a wonderful time for the networks. The government stood strongly in their corner—government regulation essentially restricted other networks from starting up by limiting the number of "very high frequency" (VHF) channels available, as well as limiting the number of stations that networks could own. This created a situation in which the major cities generally had only three available signals, one owned by each network.[14] At the same time, networks couldn't own more than five VHF stations at a time.[15] Following the logic through, this meant that CBS, NBC, and ABC could make profits from the biggest markets and shut out any potential competitors; potential competitors would be relegated to the boonies, where they couldn't rake in the cash. It was extraordinarily convenient all the way around.

PANDERING GOES PARTISAN

The early television honchos connected with every power broker they could find in Washington. That mercenary state of affairs began to break down with the advent of the Vietnam War. The executives continued to try to placate government officials, particularly LBJ; some government officials, like Robert Kintner, were former television executives. But the creators in Hollywood were increasingly upset with the war and with LBJ. For the first time, space emerged between the creators in Hollywood and the executives with regard to the television-government nexus. The liberal consensus that governed everyone in Hollywood was straining.

The first show to expose that gap between executives and creators was *The Smothers Brothers Comedy Hour.* Tommy Smothers, you'll remember, was a politically active comedian who identified with the pacifistic hippie movement and consistently ripped LBJ. This irked both LBJ, and by extension, the network; eventually, the show was cancelled.

The election of Richard Nixon in 1968, however, allowed the executives and creators to come together once more. No longer was Vietnam a liberal war; now it was a conservative war. And the executives didn't have to worry about cultivating Nixon and his allies in order to maintain market share—they knew Nixon didn't like them, and the feeling was mutual.

Nixon's hatred for the media began with the news media, which he felt had always unfairly targeted him, a perception that was true to some extent, particularly in reference to the 1960 election, when he was raked over the coals while the sycophantic media played up to JFK. Later, Nixon's hatred for the media would lead him to cover up Watergate, the move that would shatter his presidency. William Safire, a Nixon speechwriter who would later become a media member, summed up Nixon's attitude: "When Nixon said, 'The press is the enemy,' . . . he was saying exactly what he meant: 'The press is the enemy, to be hated and beaten.'" Safire saw this perspective as Nixon's "greatest personal and political weakness and the cause of his downfall."[16]

Nixon's hatred for the press extended to a deep-seated hatred for the television industry. It was a hatred no amount of Hollywood kowtowing could have appeased even had they tried (which, of course, they didn't). Nixon tried to force the FCC to deny license renewals to particular stations he thought were unfairly critical of his presidency. Spiro Agnew, his vice president, castigated the "small band of network commentators and self-appointed analysts who provided only instant analysis."[17] Nixon called television reporting "outrageous, vicious, distorted."[18] Agnew actually went even further, insulting the heads of the networks themselves: "Is it not fair and relevant to question [television's] concentration in the hands of a tiny, enclosed fraternity of privileged men elected by no one and enjoying a monopoly sanctioned and licensed by government?"[19]

Nixon wasn't unhappy just with network news—he was unhappy with the urban programming shift that resulted in shows like *All in the Family*. On May 13, 1971, Nixon went off on *All in the Family* in the White House, as can be heard on the Nixon tapes. Nixon laments the fact that he was watching a baseball game on CBS when *All in the Family* came on the air. It was, says Nixon, "the damndest thing I ever heard, two magnificent, handsome guys and a stupid old fellow [Archie Bunker] and a nice girl—they were glorifying homosexuality . . ." Nixon goes on to describe the episode—"Judging Books by Covers"—in colorful language, and concludes, "I turned the goddamned thing off. I couldn't listen to any more. . . . I do not think that you glorify on public television homosexuality." Finally, Nixon avers that homosexuality and "dope" destroy societies, which is why "the Communists and the left-wingers are pushing the stuff: they're trying to destroy us."[20]

It was no wonder that in 1971, Nixon attempted to break apart the networks by threatening them with continuing antitrust lawsuits. "If the threat of screwing them is going to help us more with their programming than doing it, then keep the threat," said Nixon. "As far as screwing them is concerned, I'm very glad to do it."[21]

Nixon's negativity toward Hollywood was the first step in the total disintegration of the right-wing presence in Hollywood. Already the left dominated the industry. But with Nixon's visceral hatred for the media and for the television industry, he made it possible for Hollywood to root out anybody remotely conservative. Despite the fact that Nixon helped pave the way for Hollywood's beloved investment tax credit,[22] the television industry's new principle was simple: If you were a friend of Nixon, you simply couldn't be a friend to Hollywood. When Taft Schreiber, an executive at Music Corporation of America (MCA), tried to hold a fundraiser in Los Angeles for Nixon, he was rebuffed over and over, despite the fact that he told Hollywoodites that Nixon would help the television industry with an investment tax credit.[23] After talking to dozens of members of the television industry who were active during the Nixon era, it is clear that Hollywood hated Nixon the way they later hated George W. Bush.

Once Nixon took office, the quid pro quos between government and the television industry began to shift almost solely toward the Democratic Party. Now television executives and creators engaged in open back-scratching with liberal politicians while concentrating their fire on Republican politicians. Gerald Ford, as innocuous a Republican as has ever walked beneath the sun, was attacked savagely, particularly after he allowed the Justice Department to sue the networks for violation of antitrust laws.[24] Jimmy Carter, by contrast, received tremendous backing from Hollywood superagent Lew Wasserman, who recruited his friends and supporters to sign checks for the diminutive man from Plains, Georgia.[25]

Hollywood despised and ignored Reagan, despite the fact that he was a lifelong friend of Hollywood and a former president of the Screen Actors Guild, because he was a conservative like Nixon (in actuality, Reagan was far more conservative than the economically liberal Nixon). Reagan, unlike Ford or Nixon, attempted to help the television creative community by pushing to keep the so-called Fin-Syn rules that prevented networks from owning large chunks of programming outright. In fact, Reagan's action on Fin-Syn cut directly against his laissez-faire economic approach.[26] Still, the Hollywood creative community did not give him credit for his generosity. Gene Reynolds, producer of *M*A*S*H*, *Lou Grant*, and *Room 222*, for example, told me the consolidation of the industry "definitely started with Reagan."[27] Michael Brandman, formerly of HBO, credited Reagan with "singlehandedly destroy[ing] the relationship between the artist and the museum that presumably hung their art."[28]

Bill Clinton, by contrast, benefited from the total weight and force of the Hollywood creative and executive community. Lew Wasserman raised $1.7 million for the Arkansas governor in a single $10,000 per plate dinner in his home—what he termed "the most successful dinner in a private home in American political history." Wasserman was worshipful of Clinton, just like the rest of Hollywood: "I am crazy about him. If you got me going on the subject of Bill Clinton, I'll sound like a love-struck teenager."[29] Clinton was similarly worshipful of Wasserman: "He helped me become president. He helped me stay president. He helped me be a better president."[30] David Geffen personally signed Clinton a check for $120,000.[31]

During the 1990s, the Democratic Party raised $8 million per campaign cycle from the Hollywood contingent. Remember, that's three campaign cycles *every year.* Some of the biggest donors: Geffen, at $200,000 per year; Jeffrey Katzenberg, then at Disney, who clocked in at $125,000 per year; ABC Family network head Haim Saban, $250,000 per year; Disney as a whole, $1 million per year; AOL Time Warner, $500,000 per year.[32] One estimate stated, "Hollywood had given the Democratic Party contributions roughly equivalent to what Republicans received from their friends in the oil and gas industries."[33]

Clinton was Hollywood-produced all the way, from playing the sax on Arsenio Hall to talking about pot smoking and boxers on MTV. MTV held a "Rock n' Roll Inaugural Ball" for Clinton, featuring the Eagles, Don Henley, and U2.[34] During his first 125 days in office, he entertained stars at the White House, including Billy Crystal, Barbra Streisand, Christopher Reeve, John Ritter, Joanne Woodward and Paul Newman, Liza Minnelli, Richard Dreyfuss, Richard Gere, and Sharon Stone, among others.[35]

Once again, Clinton engaged in that typical left-wing misdirectional tactic when it came to legislation—focusing on violence on television.

Through Attorney General Janet Reno, he pushed mandatory inclusion of the V-chip in television manufacture, as well as a bill that would allow Congress to regulate violent programming.[36] Clinton also appointed FCC regulators who did their best Newton Minow imitations. Kids, said Reed Hunt, chairman of the FCC under Clinton, live in a "wasteland of crime . . . scenes of violence fill television."[37]

What came of Clinton's supposed "hard hand of regulation"? Nothing. Rather, Clinton gave Hollywood what it was looking for: favors. That meant consolidation of the cable industry through deregulation, as well as tax cuts for the Hollywood upper crust. The 1996 Telecommunications Act eliminated restrictions on cable pricing without doing anything about local government-created monopolies, leading to skyrocketing cable prices and profits. Meanwhile, Clinton instituted a "research and development tax credit," according to film scholar Ben Dickenson, worth $1.7 billion to the industry. By acts of deregulation, Clinton even helped the television industry move to Canada to take advantage of tax subsidies (talk about shipping jobs to foreigners!).[38]

It was no wonder that the television industry supported Al Gore in 2000. When Gore was on the verge of becoming president in 2000, he asked NBC president Jeff Zucker whether he'd join the Gore administration as press secretary. Zucker turned him down, but that didn't stop Zucker from heading NBC's coverage of the Gore-Bush election. Zucker's bias bugged GE chairman Jack Welch so much that he accused Zucker of turning the *Today Show* into *Pravda* (Welch is close friends with Zucker and was a key mover and shaker behind Zucker's career trajectory, which shows just how much Zucker's bias bothered him).[39]

Despite Gore's ties to Hollywood, the television industry became less than enamored of him when he selected cultural moderate Senator Joe Lieberman (then D-CT) as his running mate. Lieberman had spent a good deal of time bashing the entertainment industry for both violence and, more important, sexual content. And the industry didn't like it, not one little bit. Gore's campaign suffered from lukewarm Hollywood industry support. It wasn't until later, when Hollywood regretted the election of George W. Bush, that they finally rewarded Gore with an Oscar for his soporific and faulty documentary, *An Inconvenient Truth*.

Once Gore was history, George W. Bush became the chief target of the television industry, which saw him as an enemy despite the fact that his tax cuts benefited the television industry honchos at a disproportionate level. And as Nixon did, the Republicans saw Hollywood and the television industry as enemies. They acted accordingly. In 2004, for example, Democrats included $1 billion in tax credits in an international tax bill. Republicans sliced it out. The media speculated that those tax credits ended up on the scrap heap because the Motion Picture Association of America had hired Democrat Dan Glickman, secretary of agriculture under President Clinton, to head the organization. One Republican lobbyist summed up the situation: "They were not overly helpful to Republicans, so Republicans don't want to be overly helpful to them."[40]

Similarly, Bush's FCC regulators were far more conservative in their interpretations of applicable laws. Originally, like their more liberal predecessors, they ignored the ire of groups like L. Brent Bozell's Parents Television Council (PTC), a secular moral descendant of the Wildmon/Falwell conservative lobbying groups of the 1970s and 1980s—the FCC called letters about sex and profanity from the PTC "spam."[41] But things really heated up when Justin Timberlake pulled down Janet Jackson's bustier during the 2004 Super Bowl halftime show in a staged act of gratuitous quasi-nudity. The FCC cracked down, issuing a ruling for a $550,000 fine against CBS.[42] That year, the FCC under Michael Powell levied $3.7 million worth of fines, doubling the aggregate proposed fines in the prior decade.[43] Frightened, Fox put all of its live shows on a five-minute tape delay, ABC put the Oscars on tape delay, and CBS canceled its *Victoria's Secret Fashion Show*.[44]

FCC commissioner Kevin J. Martin (later FCC chairman) soon threatened, "If cable and satellite operators continue to refuse to offer parents more tools, basic indecency and profanity restrictions may be a viable opportunity."[45] "Certainly," wrote Martin in a letter to the PTC in 2003, "broadcasters and cable operators have significant First Amendment rights, but these rights are not without boundaries. They are limited by law. They also should be limited by good taste."[46] Republican Senator Ted Stevens (AK) suggested that broadcast indecency rules be applied to cable channels. He focused particularly on sex: "We wonder why our children are sexually active at a young age. . . . The public airwaves are increasingly promoting sex. . . . Cable is often worse."[47]

This sort of censorship drove members of the industry up the wall. "The FCC is loaded with conservatives, it's three to two conservatives," lamented Gene Reynolds. "When I was producing shows through a variety of administrations, I saw the Democrats, I saw Reagan in there, I saw Clinton, I didn't see Bush. But I could feel a different breath coming from the networks depending on the administration."[48] During the Bush years, the networks got together and founded the TV Watch, a front organization designed to fight off groups like the PTC. "Everybody should be frightened by the notion that this process could be hijacked by a very few people," spokesman Jim Dyke said. "They are trying to make decisions about what our children can see."[49] "It's scary," one cable executive said of Stevens's proposal. "It's raised everyone's antenna," said another. "You used to be able to get away with a lot more butt crack than you can now," observed Mark Cronin, president of Mindless Entertainment and the man responsible for VH1's *The Surreal Life*. "We're in the eye of the storm of moral America," explained yet another cable executive. "That's just the climate of the country right now."[50]

There's a reason the television industry hated Bush: the Bush Administration represented the first true attempt by any Republican since Nixon to fight back against the irreversible liberal slide of the culture. It didn't work, for a variety of reasons.

And the result was President Barack Obama. Obama, as we'll see shortly, was the most slickly produced, widely backed television candidate in the history of the medium. If Clinton was worshipped in Hollywood, Obama is the object of Aztec-type figurative human sacrifice. The cult-like obedience with which the faithful imbibe his words is truly Biblical in nature.

That's just on the surface. Behind the scenes, Obama is subject to the same back-scratching quid pro quos as every Democratic president since FDR.

The patented Hollywood-D.C. back-scratch became an intensely common phenomenon during the Obama Administration. After greasing Obama's path to victory in the 2008 election, Hollywood quickly received benefits from its new friend in the White House. In June 2009, the Department of Homeland Security announced that it would be focusing on Internet piracy of Hollywood's copyrighted wares. New FCC

Chairman Julius Genachowski, who was a former counsel for industry honcho Barry Diller, began to ignore all of the indecency regulations and the investigations of rising cable TV prices. "We feel like we've got the wind at our back," said Warner Bros. chairman and Obama donor Barry Meyer. "We're getting a good hearing on the issues that matter to us."[51]

A couple of extreme examples stand out. In November 2009, NBC's Green Week included concerted storyline changes designed to focus on environmental issues. Historically, NBC's Green Week has been a way to promote GE's products—NBC premiered its Green Week efforts in 2007, two years after the May 2005 launch of their "Ecomagination" advertising campaign geared toward demonstrating "GE's commitment to address challenges such as the need for cleaner, more efficient sources of energy, reduced emissions and abundant sources of clean water."

But now, Green Week was being expanded. The reason? GE was using its programming as a payoff to the Obama Administration and Democrats in Congress, attempting to gin up public support for GE's legislative agenda. General Electric, which owns NBC, spent 2008 and 2009 focusing its lobbying efforts on creating "green jobs" via governmental stimulus. According to the 2008 GE Annual Report Letter to investors, "In the US, stimulus will target clean energy and smart grid technology. GE is well positioned to capitalize on these investments." GE's Green Week was simply another way to promote such legislation.

The logic was simple. GE took a major hit in 2008, but the company's energy sector grew by 19 percent—and GE expected that sector to grow even more in 2009 if it could win some of the government's stimulus contracts. Jeff Immelt, the head of GE, was an ardent supporter of the ineffective Obama stimulus package and Obama's healthcare agenda, stating, "We at GE will continue to support and advocate swift passage of legislation that is acceptable to the Senate, the House, and the Administration, and that can be promptly signed into law by the President."

Immelt, like his corporate counterparts, is close with President Obama (though he seems to waver depending on the day). What's more important, his lobbyists are close with President Obama. According to Timothy Carney of the *Washington Examiner*, during the fourth quarter of 2008, even as GE's stock fell 30 percent, GE used $4.26 million to lobby Congress for legislation like the Climate Stewardship Act, the

Electric Utility Cap and Trade Act, the Global Warming Reduction Act, the Federal Government Greenhouse Gas Registry Act, the Low Carbon Economy Act, and the Lieberman-Warner Climate Security Act. Over the course of 2008, GE spent $18.66 million on lobbying for such causes. Could that be the reason that when GE was investigated for massive financial fraud in August 2009—an investigation resulting in a $50 million fine from the SEC—Immelt kept his job? "GE bent the accounting rules beyond the breaking point," explained Robert Khuzami, director of the SEC's Division of Enforcement. In Obama's America, such malfeasance usually results in the decapitation of high-ranking executives. At GE, it resulted in Immelt keeping his job with no questions asked. No wonder Immelt labels the Obama Administration a "financier" and a "key partner."[52]

Perhaps the most egregious example of Obama-television back-scratching came on July 22, 2009. On that date, President Obama held one of the most boring news conferences in the history of televised presidential events. This one was an attempt to restart his stalled healthcare agenda. For nearly fifty minutes, Obama talked about private and public health care plans, red pills and blue pills, costs and benefits. During the last five minutes of the conference, Obama finally awoke slumbering viewers with some controversial comments about the Cambridge Police Department and Harvard Professor Henry Louis Gates. But the press conference, which was broadcast on ABC, NBC, and CBS, received atrocious ratings—among the coveted 18-to-49 crowd, a 1.8 for ABC, a 1.7 for NBC, and a 1.2 for CBS. Fox actually won the night with *So You Think You Can Dance*.

In the aggregate, the networks received a household rating of 16.3. It was a dramatic ratings drop for Obama, who had held a press conference February 9, 2009, that received a combined household rating of 30.8, one in March that scored 25.9, and one in April that hit 18.8.[53]

The networks had been unhappy about broadcasting Obama's fourth primetime news conference altogether. "It's an enormous financial cost when the president replaces one of those prime-time hours," said Paul Friedman, CBS's senior vice president. "The news divisions also have mixed feelings about whether they are being used." Nonetheless, the networks complied. Howard Kurtz suggested that they did so because they "have deemed Obama a box-office draw, featuring him on everything from '60 Minutes' to 'The Tonight Show' to a 90-minute ABC town meeting on health care."[54] That clearly wasn't the case, as the numbers showed. The real reason they did it was for the payoff from the Obama administration.

Rahm Emanuel, Obama's hatchet man, began calling the networks shortly before Obama spoke. He didn't call the program chiefs at the various networks, however—he called their bosses at the corporate level. Normally, such requests should have been channeled through Nancy Tellem at CBS, Jeff Zucker at NBC, and Anne Sweeney at ABC. Tellem and Zucker both donated to the Obama campaign. But instead of going to the television executives, Emanuel went over their heads. According to Kurtz of the *Washington Post*, Emanuel called up Les Moonves, chief executive of CBS, Jeff Immelt of GE, and Bob Iger, chief executive of Disney, which owns ABC.[55] Soon Obama was booked on all three networks (though not on Fox).

So what was the payoff? There were two. First, the Obama Administration has made it crystal clear that Obama will only reach out to networks that treat him well. He has largely frozen Fox's access to administration officials because he dislikes the Beck-O'Reilly-Hannity lineup.

The second reason is less direct—and more troubling. It involves the pharmaceutical companies. On August 8, 2009, just days after Kurtz revealed the pressure the White House levied against the networks to put his health care primetime talk show on the air, the *New York Times* revealed another Obama White House shakedown. This time, the subject of the shakedown was the drug companies, who feared the consequences of Obama's health care overhaul. In return for the Obama administration's commitment that the drug industry's costs would be capped at $80 billion over ten years under the health care bill, Obama extracted a key concession: The drug companies would underwrite a $150 million television commercial campaign in favor of Obama's health care overhaul. By way of comparison, the Obama campaign spent a grand total of $236 million on television ads during the 2008 cycle; John McCain spent $126 million.[56]

Could the networks' willingness to run Obama's infomercial for healthcare have had anything to do with the fact that Obama was pushing the drug companies to spend $150 million on television advertising? Of course not.

The relationship between the television industry and the Democratic Party grows ever stronger. As of June 2010, 73 percent of entertainment industry donations during the 2010 election cycle had gone to Democrats. Comcast had given approximately $1.3 million to Democrats and $756,000 to Republicans, a 64-to-35 percent advantage to the Democrats. Senator Chuck Schumer (D-NY) grabbed $329,800 in Hollywood donations. Not surprisingly, Representative Henry Waxman (D-CA), who chairs the House Commerce and Energy Committee, which has jurisdiction over communications issues, gathered $82,500 from the industry.[57]

And so the circle of cash and favors continues.

THE CABLE OLIGARCHY

One of the biggest cash cows for the television industry is cable. And cable continues to benefit from the government's helping hand.

Today, the FCC allows television companies to vertically integrate, resulting in the total dominance of the corporate Six Pack (GE, Time Warner, Disney, NewsCorp, CBS, and Viacom). Worst of all, the FCC and local government allowed a few market players to monopolize the cable industry. This doesn't just mean that a few players make the programming some of us watch—it means that in a given area, one or two players may be deciding what *everyone* watches.

The cable system is currently run by the same players who participate in the programming arena. The two biggest players in the cable industry are Time Warner Cable and Comcast (which is currently seeking to buy GE, leading to even further vertical integration). Consumers pay the cable companies to provide channels hand-picked by the cable companies—that's why you can't choose not to take TBS or Comedy Central. Programmers provide the cable companies with their programming and in return receive a chunk of revenue. Becoming a cable programming provider is expensive and difficult—second-tier programmers generally have to pay cash to the cable companies or take a far smaller chunk of revenue.[58]

So why isn't there competition among cable companies? In a normal market system, outside cable companies would be able to compete with larger cable companies by offering channel selection, faster service, etc. But local governments have worked with the cable companies to create carve-outs that guarantee certain areas to certain cable companies. As Congress recognized in 1992, "For a variety of reasons, including *local franchising requirements* . . . most cable television subscribers have no opportunity to select between cable systems."[59] The franchise requirements mentioned by Congress are largely a local regulatory invention. In essence, local regulators, very often subject to the lobbying of particular cable companies, hand out monopolistic exclusive franchises to certain cable operators. The U.S. Public Interest Research Group explained, "Cable operators have successfully used regulatory lobbying and a variety of pricing and other tactics to deter competitive entry and maintain their monopolies."[60] One of the most effective tactics has been cable operators' insistence that new cable operators be required to invest enough money to cover entire markets. This requirement obviously raises the bar on entry costs, making competition prohibitive.[61]

Just like the federal government with the network conglomerates, local governments work with cable operators because they expect kickbacks. "Local politicians have cut deals, written and unwritten, with their chosen cable operator to keep out competition," wrote former FCC official Sol Schildhause. Local communities extract concessions from high-bidder cable operators seeking to enter particular markets.[62]

Attorney David Saylor states that cable operators have been gouged by the government in order to receive their monopoly: "Cable operators have had to participate in auctions to balance local budgets. They have been forced to disgorge five percent (and sometimes more) of their gross revenues in the form of 'franchise fees.' . . . Cable operators have even given city councils absolute programming control over certain cable channels."[63]

These are prices cable companies are willing to pay. Because cable operators are able to foreclose all competition in local marketplaces, they are also able to decide which programming to carry for entire swaths of the country. "The cable marketplace is choked to death because would-be competitors are prevented from being in the game," observed then-Senator Al Gore (D-Tennessee) in 1992. "Any new programmer who comes into the cable business is going to be coughing up a share of his company [to a cable operator] as the price of showing his wares to the public."[64]

Yet Gore's tough talk died once he became vice president. In 1996, he spoke to the cable industry's national conference. His speech praised the cable companies to high heaven; Gore told them that they had shown "good judgment, vision and a willingness to compromise." "The cable television industry is picking up some friends in high places, just when it needs them most," the *New York Times* gushed. "Mr. Gore's speech amounted to a pep rally for the cable industry."[65]

The industry became centralized in the first place not merely because local governments restricted entry, but because Congress and the FCC prevented telephone companies and satellite companies from becoming cable companies. In 1956, the government entered into a consent decree with AT&T whereby the nation's largest telephone company was forced to demolish any cable efforts.[66] In 1968, the FCC ruled that FCC permission was required in order for any telephone company to engage in cable television operation. In 1970, the FCC declared that telephone companies could not provide "cable television service to the viewing public in its telephone area, either directly, or indirectly through an affiliate." The idea behind that decision was that telephone companies would attempt to create their own monopoly by preventing aspiring cable operators from using their telephone poles. As with most antitrust measures, the result was counterproductive—now there was no competition among cable companies.[67]

Congress has ostensibly attempted to end such coordination between government actors and cable companies, but their action has been utterly feckless, leaving in place the regulatory regimes they so love. The 1992 Cable Act passed by Congress over President George H. W. Bush's veto, for example, increased FCC control over cable companies, placing tremendous regulatory burdens on those cable companies in order to cure monopoly—all while leaving the monopolies in place. One of those regulations required the cable companies to pay for and carry local broadcast station signals. That regulation forced the FCC to decide which local broadcast station signals served the "public interest." This led to ridiculous results—one 1993 FCC ruling decided that home-shopping programs served the public interest and had to be carried by the cable companies.[68]

In 1994, the Supreme Court upheld the 1992 Cable Act based on the liberal desire to "ensure that private interests not restrict, through physical control of a critical pathway of communication, the free flow of information and ideas." Justice Sandra Day O'Connor dissented convincingly, but not convincingly enough: "The First Amendment as we understand it today rests on the premise that it is government power, rather than private power, that is the main threat to free expression."[69] Liberals on the court overruled her, stating that the government could effectively restrict free speech so long as it had good intentions.

The effect of monopolistic dealings between cable operators and government is devastating. Local cable operators remain dominant, with 68 percent of local consumers controlled by single local cable operators as of 2007.[70] As of 2003, according to the U.S. Public Interest Research Group, vertically integrated programmers owned just "40 percent of the most popular programming," but owned twenty-five of the top twenty-six channels in terms of subscribership and prime-time ratings (the lone exception was the Weather Channel). Eighty-six percent of regional sports fell under the ownership of the major cable companies, too. Just 2 percent of cable households have access to cable competition.[71]

Consumers are the ones who lose when cable companies hold monopolies. Last year, for example, Cablevision, the cable operator for New York City, engaged in a knock-down drag-out battle with Fox because Fox wanted Cablevision to pay fees to carry its programming. Fox was blacked out for two weeks on Cablevision, preventing New York viewers from watching the live broadcast of the World Series. A few months earlier, Cablevision had blacked out ABC during contract negotiations, preventing the live broadcast of the Academy Awards. Cablevision, predictably enough, pushed for government intervention, hoping that the feds would force Fox to kowtow. Due in all likelihood to the nearing 2010 Congressional elections, the feds didn't intervene. Cablevision was forced to pay Fox's asking price, whining all the while. Fox pointed out that "this entire dispute was solely about Cablevision's misguided efforts to effect regulatory change to their benefit."[72] Fox was absolutely right—Cablevision and other cable providers rely inordinately on government regulation to maintain their market share and profit margin.

In fact, total deregulation of the system would serve everyone better. Government creates monopolies in order to control them; corporations are happy to go along for the ride, since they are guaranteed market share. This is corporatism at its finest, and the end result is that the American consumer pays the price, in terms of freedom of selection, higher pricing, and freedom from government-controlled messages on television.

"SHOW ME THE MONEY"

Beyond monopoly and restriction of competition, there's another benefit that government hands over to Hollywood's executive establishment—a benefit that Hollywood liberals are loath to admit they enjoy. That benefit is tax cuts.

In 2009, Ohio's Democratic Governor Ted Strickland offered a $10 million tax incentive for Hollywood moviemakers and television creators to film in the state. In 2004, Maryland and Pennsylvania (both blue states) waged an ongoing tax break race in an attempt to woo filming of the James Franco dud *Annapolis*. Wisconsin and New Mexico offer incentives to film- and television-makers to bring their cameras. During 2009, Texas considered tax rebates of up to $60 million to those filming in the state; in Michigan, such tax breaks cost the state $48 million in 2008.

California, of course, is attempting to keep the film industry at home, carving out an enormous $500 million tax credit for Hollywood filmmakers. Los Angeles sought out a full-time film czar dedicated to keeping filmmakers in the city—and dedicated to lobbying Sacramento for more cash.

At least when it comes to states, there's an honest attempt to woo business. The federal government has no such excuse. Nonetheless, in the October 3, 2008, spending bill passed by a Democratic Congress and signed into law by President Bush, Hollywood received a $470 million tax break. President Obama's stimulus package had a $246 million tax break for Hollywood in the first draft; only Republican blowback prevented it from becoming law.

What ever happened to Hollywood's complaints about George W. Bush's tax cuts for the rich? "The rich," apparently, is a label to be applied to a select group of Republican fat cats. It is never to be applied to Hollywood's jet-set crowd. At least that's the impression you'd get by looking at George Lucas, one of President Obama's biggest financial supporters. He personally donated $50,000 to the Obama Inauguration Fund, as well as another $4,600 to Obama's presidential campaign and another $28,600 to the Democratic National Committee—a whopping total of $83,200 during the 2008 election cycle. Obama campaigned on the promise not to raise taxes for those making under $250,000 per year; obviously implicit in that promise was the caveat that he would likely raise taxes on those making more than $250,000 per year.

But that didn't stop Lucas from complaining in the media when Obama actually pursued such taxes. He also suggested that it would be unfair for Obama to cap executive salaries in Hollywood, even as Obama capped executive salaries in other industries. "Hollywood isn't asking for a bailout," said Lucas. "So, you know, they are not using taxpayer money, and obviously the cornerstone of American capitalism is that you can make as much money as you want when you work for a company."

A praiseworthy sentiment, to be sure. Except that Hollywood has received government largesse, from tax cuts to beneficial regulation, at every turn. They just don't want to be held accountable for it, even though they complain incessantly about the benefits "the rich" receive in America. Score another one for Hollywood's limousine liberals.

THE TELEVISION CANDIDATE

If the relationship between the Obama administration and the television industry is hot and heavy, there's a reason for that: The television industry made Obama. Never before has there been a candidate fêted, celebrated, and coddled like Senator Barack Obama (D-IL). Simply put, the television community loves him with the unmitigated ardor of a teenage boy watching his first episode of *Baywatch*.

Even with President Obama's approval ratings dipping precipitously, members of the Hollywood contingent stand by Obama with a fervid loyalty that can be described only as religious. When I visited the writers' office of *Lost*, at ABC's studio in Burbank, I walked in to find Carlton Cuse's assistant wearing a T-shirt that mashed together the show's imagery with Obama's cult of personality. For those who aren't *Lost* devotees, one of the key organizations in the *Lost* universe was the Dharma Initiative. This was its symbol:

Cuse's assistant was wearing a shirt that had this insignia instead:

When I asked Cuse's assistant where he'd gotten the shirt, he replied, "Damon [Lindelof, co-creator of the show] handed them out to everybody on the staff right before the election." The shirt wasn't the only contribution Lindelof made to the Obama run—he also donated $5,600 over the course of two years to the Obama campaign, as well as another $8,700 to the DNC Services Corporation during the 2008 election cycle.

I didn't bother asking whether anyone in the *Lost* office had been a McCain supporter. The fact is, as Barbara Fisher, vice president of original programming for Hallmark Channel, told me, if anybody wore a McCain T-shirt on the set of a show, they'd be treated far worse than if they wore an Obama shirt. "I'm sure that's true," she said. "You know what, that's a real example. It's a real example. There would be an uproar if it had been McCain. You're right. I can't deny it."[73] Here was a real-life example in action, although we can certainly hope that Mr. Lindelof would be tolerant of opposing viewpoints (I didn't have the opportunity to speak with him).

The Hollywood assumption couldn't be clearer—if you're working in this town, you must be an Obama supporter.

And the assumption is almost universally correct. Of the dozens of people I interviewed, only a handful did not vote for Obama during the 2008 election cycle. Earl Hamner, creator of the family-friendly show *The Waltons,* had a JFK-like picture of Obama staring into the distance hanging from his wall. Hamner pointed at it and said, smiling, "My hero." Nicholas Meyer, director of *Star Trek II, Star Trek IV,* and *Star Trek VI,* as well as the made-for-television blockbuster *The Day After,* had framed front pages from the Obama election day coverage lining the walls of his sizeable Sunset Boulevard estate. Gary David Goldberg, the man responsible for *Family Ties* and *Spin City,* was kind enough to meet me for coffee in Santa Monica, where he regaled me with Obama campaign stories. "I was deeply involved for Obama, went to work for him in Florida," he gushed. "[My daughter] Cailin was in Nebraska in the one district that he won. We were in Florida, Cailin was in Pennsylvania. She started out as a Hillary supporter, a big feminist, but she made the turn, she really made the turn. And I love Obama—we met him here, big dinner, and I thought he's the most gracious politician I've ever met."[74] I didn't have the heart to suggest that Obama's graciousness springs from the fact that he was *at a fundraiser.*

Michael Brandman, a former HBO executive and now a producer of the *Jesse Stone* made-for-television movies for CBS, described the Obama Administration in demigodlike terms. "Ironically, in the days of the Obama administration, the most important messages of our time are being delivered as part of an ongoing drama and television is allowed into this drama more than it has been allowed into anything of this kind in my lifetime," Brandman stated.[75]

It's not just that the television community loves Obama. It's that they actively utilized their power to push his candidacy. Leave aside the press's nonfeasance when it came to reporting on Obama's views and background—it was the entertainment industry that made Obama what he became.

According to the UK's *Daily Mail,* during the campaign, Obama received advice from former *ER* star George Clooney "on things such as presentation, public speaking and body language." Apparently, the granite-jawed actor was also sending Obama texts and e-mails "about policy, especially the Middle East."[76] Actor Edward Norton followed Obama around with a film crew during the campaign.[77] When Obama spent his campaign cash on a half-hour infomercial airing on CBS, NBC, Fox, Univision, and some cable networks in October 2008, he got help from *Deadwood* producer and director Davis Guggenheim to put it together.[78]

Comedienne Sarah Silverman tried to convince Jews to vote for Obama by posting an inane YouTube video accusing older Jews of being racists. "If Barack Obama doesn't become the next president of the United States, I'm going to blame the Jews," Silverman nasally intoned. "You know why your grandparents don't like Barack Obama? Because his name sounds scary, his name sounds Muslim, which he's obviously not." Then, with her trademark cutesy smile and cognitively dissonant potty mouth, she said, "Vote for McCain, to me you're a shit stain. I just made that up off the top of my head!"[79] Kal Penn, one of the actors from *House*, phone-banked for Obama—and was later appointed to the Obama administration, which necessitated an awkward suicide on the show. Edie Falco, star of *The Sopranos*, also spent her time ginning up support for Obama.[80] Hill Harper, an actor who stars on *CSI: NY*, served as a member of Obama's national campaign finance committee and helped produce the "Yes, We Can" YouTube video.[81]

The list goes on and on. It is fair to say that the Hollywood community mobilized behind President Obama with force and verve unsurpassed since their anti-Nazi mobilization in World War II. With this much backing from Hollywood, it was no wonder that in July 2008, Obama granted his first whole-family interview to none other than *Access Hollywood*.[82]

And when it comes to Hollywood fund-raising, Obama made Clinton's Wasserman dinner look like a tea party. As early as January 2007, Obama was receiving help from his friends in Los Angeles; at the beginning of the year, DreamWorks heads David Geffen, Steven Spielberg, and Jeffrey Katzenberg teamed up to send a letter to seven hundred Hollywood figures asking them to show up at a $2,300-per-person event at the posh Beverly Hilton Hotel.[83] At one fundraiser in September 2008 sponsored by Barbra Streisand, he raised $9 million. Each seat cost $28,500.[84] Hollywood raised almost $12.7 million for Democrats during the 2008 cycle.[85] Then Hollywood provided Obama the cash for his unprecedented inauguration celebration. Samuel L. Jackson, Sharon

Stone, Halle Berry, Jamie Foxx, producer James Lassiter, MTV president Christina Norman—all handed over $50,000 apiece to help Obama pay for his anointment. Overall, the entertainment industry forked over $2.3 million for the big day.[86]

HOLLYWOOD'S HOPE-AND-CHANGE MACHINE

It wasn't just money. The television industry should have received an executive producer credit on the Obama campaign. Obama's biggest Hollywood supporter was, of course, television mogul Oprah Winfrey. She announced on May 1, 2007, on *Larry King Live* that she would support Obama's campaign for president—and she announced precisely how she would support him: "I think that my value to him, my support of him, is probably worth more than any check."[87] Oprah turned her show into a yearlong infomercial for the Illinois senator; she appeared alongside Obama at his campaign rallies in South Carolina and Iowa. Campaign estimates stated that Oprah put ten thousand new volunteers into action for Obama per rally. Oprah paid a price for her support of Obama—her favorability ratings, and her actual ratings, dropped dramatically and have never recovered.[88] But her support was so invaluable to the Obama team that when Obama left his Senate seat to take his Oval Office seat, opportunistic and corrupt Illinois Governor Rod Blagojevich considered appointing Oprah to the vacated Senate slot.[89]

The daytime hosts universally rallied to Obama's side. Ellen DeGeneres also supported Obama, dancing with him on her show in October 2008 and testing him on such topics as Halloween costumes and George Clooney.[90] Meanwhile, when Ellen interviewed McCain in May 2008, DeGeneres grilled him on gay marriage: "Women just got the right to vote in 1920, blacks didn't have the right to vote until 1870, and it just feels like there's this old way of thinking that we're not all the same. We are all the same people. All of us. You're no different than I am. Our love is the same."[91] Never mentioned by Ellen was the fact that Obama's position on gay marriage was identical to McCain's: Obama opposed it. Incredibly, Ellen even released a statement after the election that simultaneously celebrated Obama's election—"Change is here. . . . We were watching history"—and derided California's Proposition 8, maintaining the traditional man-woman definition of marriage—"I was saddened beyond belief. Here we just had a giant step toward equality and then on the very next day, we took a giant step away."[92] Again, it went unmentioned that in California, the high black turnout for Obama's presidential election likely won passage for Proposition 8.

The women's vote was key to Obama during the 2008 election cycle—so important that when his approval ratings slid to crisis levels in 2010, Obama quickly booked an appearance on *The View*—the first presidential appearance on a daytime talk show since the advent of television.[93] Fortunately for Obama, the daytime hosts universally worship him.

Daytime talk show hosts helped Obama. But when it came to the campaign, comedy was key, as it always has been. Saul Alinsky was completely on the mark when he wrote, "Humor is essential to a successful tactician, for the most potent weapons known to mankind are satire and ridicule."[94] The entertainment community has acted on that principle for decades, from their relentless Nixon-bashing on *Laugh-In* to Dana Carvey's George H. W. Bush impersonation (Hollywood's takes on Clinton and Carter have been downright respectful).

The most successful take-down of all time—at least up to the 2008 cycle—was probably Chevy Chase's devastating Gerald Ford impression during the 1976 election cycle, when he played Ford, the former All-American athlete, as a bumbling clown. Ford did his best to cope by laughing at himself—he appeared on *Saturday Night Live* from the Oval Office and did a political dinner alongside Chase—but Ford was never able to overcome the perception that he was a klutz. Chase knew what he was doing was unfair, but he did it because he despised Ford. "Ford is so inept that the quickest laugh is the cheapest laugh, and the cheapest is the physical joke," Chase said in 1976.[95]

In 2008, Obama escaped all scrutiny from comics entirely. "We're doing jokes about people in his orbit, not really about him," explained Mike Sweeney, head writer for Conan O'Brien. "The thing is, he's not buffoonish in any way. He's not a comical figure," agreed Mike Barry, comic writer for David Letterman. Then there was the race question. "Anything that has even a whiff of being racist, no one is going to laugh," Letterman's executive producer, Rob Burnett, opined.[96] Chris Rock said that Obama was a "comedian's worst nightmare," because "He's just one of those guys, you know, like Will Smith. There's no Will Smith jokes. There's no Brad Pitt jokes. . . . [With Obama] it's like, 'Ooh, you're young and virile and you've got a beautiful wife and kids. You're the first African-American president.' You know, what do you say?"[97]

This was all cover, of course. These comedians were simply holding up their end of the bargain; by playing nice with Obama, they hoped to get him elected. D.L. Hughley admitted as much: "I think before [the election], there was so much trepidation, that everybody wanted this to happen so bad that nobody wanted to upset the apple cart. Nobody wanted to do anything that made the proposition less likely."[98]

The bias was so egregious that one study of late-night political jokes found that comedians were obviously avoiding humor about Obama, even as they savaged outgoing President Bush, Senator McCain, and Senator Hillary Clinton. Between January 1, 2008, and July 31, 2008, the study by the Center for Media and Public Affairs found Jay Leno, Conan O'Brien, and David Letterman only made 169 jokes about Obama, compared with 428 about Bush and 328 about McCain. Hillary Clinton drew almost as many as Bush, 382.[99]

Comedy Central comedians supposedly were more even in their treatment of Obama and McCain/Palin, according to the study. Stephen Colbert made 129 jokes about McCain during the study period, to just 91 for Obama. Jon Stewart, by contrast, made more jokes about Obama than McCain.[100]

That study, though, is misleading. It doesn't suggest what *kind* of jokes were being made about McCain or Palin versus Obama. And the simple fact is that while Palin and McCain were being destroyed by the media, most of the jokes about Obama played on his brilliance, his eloquence, his aura.

Chief practitioner of this subtle art of titular balance, substantive bias were Stewart and Colbert. Together, they were perhaps the biggest factors in Obama's winning campaign. Gary David Goldberg summed up the impact of Stewart and Colbert well: "I don't think you could get Barack Obama elected without [Stewart and Colbert], I think. And they just make the other side look stupid."[101]

They both played at balance. "We're carrion birds," said Stewart. "We're sitting up there saying 'Does he seem weak? Is he dehydrated yet? Let's attack.'" But Stewart didn't attack Obama. He jibed him softly. That's because Stewart was an Obama partisan—when he announced Obama's election, he actually teared up on camera. "How we gonna make this shit funny?" Stewart asked in the aftermath of Obama's election, while the media fêted Obama with laurels.[102] There's no question that Stewart is a liberal; in an interview with *Entertainment Weekly* from September 2008, Stewart claimed, "You 'good values people' have had the country for eight years, and done an unbelievably s----ty job. Let's find some bad values people and give them a shot, maybe they'll have a better take on it."[103]

Colbert is similarly left-leaning. "Any change is as good as a vacation at this point," Colbert said during election 2008. "I don't know if you've paid much attention to the past eight years, but it has been a s----burger supreme. If somebody gives me an empty burger, it's better than eating s----."[104] Colbert is, of course, the same man who used his opportunity as host of the 2006 White House Correspondents Dinner to level his guns directly at George W. Bush and ridicule him as an ignoramus and a fool.

Both of their routines were biased toward Obama. When *Entertainment Weekly* asked them what the "prevalent comedic take" was on Obama, Colbert quickly responded, "He's a hope-ronaut. He's in a rarefied level of hope where the rest of us have to take tanks up with us." This paean prompted even the interviewer to ask, "Is that really a comedic take? Seems more like a compliment."[105]

Stewart's interview with John McCain was extraordinarily contentious. Stewart asked McCain whether he should be nicknamed "Grumple Stiltskin." By contrast, all of his interviews with Obama were odes to civility in which the famed comic asked questions like "How are things going?" And "Tell me about this half-hour special that aired earlier tonight." Stewart's audience was so well-trained that on the rare occasions when Stewart did poke at Obama, his audience of hardened liberals actually stood up to him, prompting Stewart to grumpily respond, "You know, you're allowed to laugh at him."[106] But how could Stewart possibly expect them to know that? After all, he hadn't been laughing at Obama. It should be no surprise to learn that after Obama's election, *The Daily Show*'s writing staff provided him material for the 2010 White House Correspondents Dinner.[107]

Doug Herzog, president of MTV Networks Entertainment Group and one of the people responsible for putting Stewart on the air, acknowledged that Stewart was biased in his coverage of the election. "I think there is no discussion where Jon's heart lies," he responded when I asked him why Stewart treated Obama with kid gloves. "I think he wears it on his sleeve to a certain degree. . . . It's hard for me to separate my own personal politics from that discussion, but I think George Bush was an easier target."[108] Michelle Ganeless, president of Comedy Central, was more defensive about Stewart's bias. In fact, she claimed he had no bias. "If any of those people watch the show on a regular basis, they'd know that Jon takes on every political figure, every public figure. . . . I think [conservative critics] are people who don't watch the show on a regular basis."[109] Stewart can be mildly even-handed; he does attack people on both sides. But during election 2008, that simply wasn't the case.

The biggest problem with Stewart and Colbert during the 2008 election cycle is that when it came to liberals, they just *weren't funny*. That should be a cardinal sin when you're broadcasting on Comedy Central. "Job one for Jon Stewart and Stephen Colbert . . . is to make you laugh," said Herzog. "Now if they can make you think while doing it, if they can make you laugh at something and bring to life social issues, that's great too, but their first job is to make you laugh."[110] But laughter is only possible when it's relatively nonpartisan. Stewart's famous interview with CNBC's *Mad Money* host Jim Cramer, in which he raked Cramer over the coals for half an hour, did not even attempt comedy. Stewart often wants to play the Edward R. Murrow journalist when he interviews right-wingers but pass himself off as a comedian when he interviews left-wingers. The result, at least in 2008, was tremendous bias. (That bias didn't stop in 2008. Stewart's anti–Glenn Beck, anti-Tea-Party rally in Washington, D.C.—which he called the Rally for Sanity, implying that anyone who opposed the Obama agenda was psychologically disturbed—wasn't just unfunny, it was insulting.)

Meanwhile, John McCain and Sarah Palin were pilloried by comics. Palin, in particular, became the entertainment industry's chief enemy. They didn't like McCain, but the sheer hatred they held for Palin was shocking to behold. You couldn't mention her name in public in Hollywood without someone jumping down your throat. Stewart was particularly vicious: "[Palin] is like Jodie Foster in the movie *Nell*. They just found her, and she was speaking her own special language," Stewart said, guffawing, on October 9, 2008. "Have you noticed how [Palin's] rallies have begun to take on the characteristics of the last days of the Weimar Republic?"

"You know, I just want to say to her, just very quickly: F--- you," he growled on October 17, 2008. In case she didn't get the message, a couple of days later he reiterated: "What I meant to say is, 'F--- all y'all.' "

Colbert was just as vitriolic. Right after her selection, Colbert joked, "We're still waiting with bated breath for the big news: Who will John McCain pick as his running mate. . . . Is it Romney? Is it Pawlenty? Wait, . . . she is?! Are you serious?! Who the f--- is Sarah Palin? What? The sexy librarian?!"

Stewart and Colbert weren't alone in going after Palin. The most effective attack against her came from comedienne Tina Fey, who did a brilliantly spot-on impersonation of Palin for *Saturday Night Live*. Of course, it didn't help the McCain-Palin cause that *Saturday Night Live*'s most brutal sniping at Obama consisted of pieces such as a sheepishly awful faux musical number entitled "Solid as Barack," praising Obama's virility.

Much of the Hollywood entertainment establishment mobilized to destroy McCain and Palin. In a particularly awful example, an October 2008 episode of *Family Guy* featured Stewie Griffin and Brian (his talking dog) stealing the uniforms of a couple Nazis. Stewie looks down at his uniform. "Hey, there's something on here," he intones. Then we get a close-up of a McCain-Palin button. "Huh, that's weird," Stewie says. The obvious implication: only Nazis vote McCain-Palin.

After the election, the triumphalism began. *Boston Legal* had James Spader's character, Alan Shore, castigate the half of America that didn't vote for Obama: "Almost 47% of this country didn't vote for Obama, perhaps because they disagreed with him on the issues, which is fine. But some, no doubt, because they thought he was Muslim with terrorists on his speed dial, and others because they were convinced he was not only socialist, but even worse, a bad bowler, and others still because they simply loved those cream-colored jackets Sarah may have to give back. But there's one thing all those idiots have in common. . . . They still get to vote."[111] *Law & Order*'s post-election episode had a reporter asking

Sam Waterston's character, "Mr. McCoy, is it true you've been asked to join the Obama Administration?" René Balcer, producer of *Law & Order*, joked that if Obama had lost, they would have had to use computer-generated imagery to place black armbands on the cast.[112]

No doubt Balcer is correct. Hollywood staple-gunned itself to Obama's coattails. Obama was only too happy to staple himself to Hollywood's coattails in return.

The television contingent gleefully takes credit for Obama's victory. Michael Nankin, who wrote for and produced *Life Goes On*, *Chicago Hope*, and *Picket Fences*, told me, "I think that creators of television reach out into the world for inspiration and then manipulate it into a world that they want to live in. I mean, I think that the country was ready for Obama, but I think ten years of seeing black presidents on TV and in movies helps."[113]

THE PERFECT SYMBIOSIS

Normally, industries hedge their bets when it comes to politics. The communications/electronics industry has spent a grand total of $809.6 million on elections over the last twenty years: $475.9 million went to Democrats, and $328.5 million went to Republicans—a 59 percent to 41 percent split. The defense sector has spent $154.3 million over that same period; the donations split in favor of Republicans, 57 to 43 percent. The healthcare sector has spent $904.9 million on politics; the split favors Republicans 56 to 44. Most industry splits are relatively even.

Except for the labor industry and the legal sector—which, as you'd expect, split 92 to 8 and 71 to 29 Democrat, respectively—the biggest split of all comes in the entertainment industry. Over the past twenty years, Hollywood has given almost $271 million to political organizations and candidates—and 70 percent of it has gone to Democrats.[114] Unlike organized labor, which is a traditional and key Democratic constituency, and unlike the legal sector, which has always been at odds with the Republican establishment, Hollywood's one-sided politics makes little business sense. Where other industries may have business reasons for skewing their donations (is a trial lawyer really going to donate to the tort reform party?), Hollywood has virtually none.

But Hollywood's allegiance to the Democratic Party—and the totally ineffective response of the Republican establishment—has resulted in the most powerful medium in human history acting in symbiosis with the party of government. Republicans could have touted their tax cutting to Hollywood; they could have touted their historic ties to the industry. They could have engaged. Instead, they've stood aside, glaring at the industry in anger, blaming it for all of society's ills.

Yes, liberals in the industry are largely to blame for the industry's lopsidedness when it comes to monetary, philosophic, and influential support for the Democratic Party. But Republicans are just as responsible for forfeiting their position and allowing the continued dominance of the Government-Hollywood Complex.

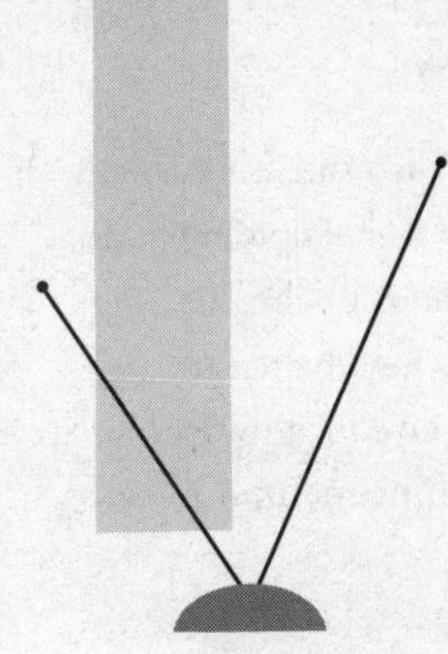

ROBBING THE CRADLE

How Television Liberals Recruit Kids

It may be tolerable to insert political messages into shows geared toward adults: At least they have the capacity to analyze what they are watching. Children's television should be nonpartisan. It should teach basic values—values like care for one's fellow citizens, patriotism, and hard work—while entertaining kids in innocent fashion.

But it doesn't. Today's children's television very often inserts liberal messages, generally quite broad and almost invariably connected with self-esteem and tolerance of all behaviors. That's because children's television carries an inherent danger that other television programming does not: In order for it to be effective as an educational tool for poorer children, it must be publicly funded. And in order to remain publicly funded, it must make everyone feel good.

Less economically fortunate parents are a poor target for advertisers because they have no money. That means that for better or for worse, middle-class–to–wealthy families become the catered-to audience. The responsibility for private-sector children's programming lies with them.

The left argues that it's dangerous to leave children's television in the hands of the wealthy parents and by extension, the private sector—and in today's day and age, they're right, thanks to the laxity of parents. More and more, advertisers look to promote their products to children, and what better way to reach children than to program cartoonish violence (*Power Rangers*) or cute pop stars with a laugh track (*Hannah Montana*)? And as long as wealthier parents don't turn off the television, and as long as they keep buying their kids advertised products, the advertisers and show creators get away with noneducational children's programming. That's not educational television—it's watered-down primetime television for kiddies.

Which means that true educational television is largely relegated to public television. The problem there is that the same folks who staff public television also staff the halls of our federal government. As you can guess, they skew liberal.

The Corporation for Public Broadcasting (CPB) was created by LBJ in the Public Broadcasting Act of 1967, with the express purpose of providing "strict adherence to objectivity and balance in all programs or series of programs of a controversial nature." The Public Broadcasting Service (PBS) was created by the CPB, as was National Public Radio. Both are quite liberal.

Supposedly, the CPB is geared toward balance: the composition of the CPB changes on a rotating basis, with nine board members who serve six-year terms. They are selected by the president and confirmed by the Senate, and no more than five of the members may come from any one political party. During the Bush years, therefore, there were five Republicans; the current president of the CPB is Patricia Harrison, a former co-chair of the Republican National Committee.

So why is CPB tilted to the left? For the same reason that Republicans in government have failed to cut spending: Members of the federal government bureaucracy need to continually justify increasing government in order to justify their own existence, and few Republicans are willing to stand up to them. As one conservative former member of the CPB board told me, "Just because the board is conservative doesn't mean the programming on PBS will be."

During the Bush years, an open fight broke out between the board of CPB and the president of PBS (who is an employee). Kenneth Tomlinson, the Republican chairman of the CPB board, began investigating PBS's political bias; Pat Mitchell, the liberal president of PBS, denied any bias whatsoever. "PBS does not belong to any single constituency, no one political party, no activist group, no foundation, no funder, no agenda of any kind," Mitchell said. "Our editorial standards ensure this, and public opinion polls verify it."[1] Tomlinson went so far as to hire conservative consultant Frederick W. Mann to screen PBS's news shows for bias. "I hope we never have a situation where journalists perceive intimidation in all this," Tomlinson explained.[2] Tomlinson ended up leaving in disgrace after being investigated for conservative political bias, even though the left objected to any investigation of liberal bias in PBS programming.

But PBS is just the beginning of the story. Other channels geared toward kids, including Nickelodeon and Disney Channel, have moved substantially to the left over the past two decades, to the point where political liberalism is almost as common on those channels as it is on the main networks or the adult cables. This liberalism isn't nearly as militant—that would be counterproductive and silly—but it is more insidious because of the nature of the target.

THE EARLY DAYS

Originally, children's television was designed to entertain and inculcate traditional values. *Howdy Doody* (NBC), the most popular children's show of the 1950s, starred a marionette voiced by Buffalo Bob Smith, the show's producer. Howdy had forty-eight freckles, one for each state of the union at the time. One episode featured footage from Independence Hall. The show patterned its look on the popular Westerns of the time, which added yet another patriotic layer. *The Mickey Mouse Club* (ABC) was similarly innocent. The lead Mouseketeer on the show, selected by Walt Disney himself, was a religious Christian singer named Jimmie Dodd. In each episode, Dodd would tell children his "Mousekethoughts," which were invariably traditional in orientation. One of Dodd's favorites was this anonymous advice: "I expect to pass through life but once. If therefore there be any kindness I can show, or any good thing I can do, to any fellow being, let me do it now and not defer or neglect it, as I shall not pass this way again."[3] At the same time, local television often broadcast a fifteen-minute religious show produced by the Lutheran Church entitled *Davey and Goliath*, which was an educational tool for Christianity. The show also broke ground by introducing many African-American kids to children's television. (To show just how far children's television has come, *The Simpsons*—which, pathetically enough, is considered children's television—has parodied *Davey and Goliath* at least four times for its open advocacy of religion.)

The traditional perspective on children's television began to evolve when one star of the original *Howdy Doody*, Bob Keeshan, went out on his own and with the help of CBS created *Captain Kangaroo.*

Keeshan was politically liberal, although that didn't come out clearly in the show most of the time. His philosophy of children's television was directly at odds with that of Buffalo Bob Smith, he later said. Smith's idea of educational television was "Shouting, loud, fast-moving, very little reference to the education of the child. . . . I felt education and entertainment combined could be of a greater service to young people."

To that end, Keeshan revolutionized the business of children's television by bringing in experts to help tell him what children needed in order to develop emotionally. Keeshan asked the experts to tell him "what the needs of the child are, what's important in the life of a typical four-year-old, what's typical in the life of an atypical four-year-old, a child who has this problem or that problem or doesn't have the kind of home setting that would be ideal in raising a child." The experts were happy to do so.

Whereas *Howdy Doody*'s philosophy was that kids were kids and adults were adults and kids needed to listen to adults, *Captain Kangeroo*'s Keeshan subscribed to the Benjamin Spock view that children needed their self-esteem padded. He described the theme of the show: "Giving you that sense of well-being, giving you that confidence, that good feeling that you were able to do anything, that you were able to accomplish some things." Parents, said Keeshan, too often "hear about beat the devil out of the kid and you'll achieve your purpose. This is the way you destroy a child."[4]

In the 1960s, during a time of great political turmoil, this philosophy wasn't all bad; by focusing on the welfare of children and their need to feel secure, Keeshan provided kids with a security blanket. And victimized children *do* need a sense of self-esteem. When Keeshan's self-esteem thematic is combined with Keeshan's suggestion that self-esteem comes not from television or educators but from *parental involvement*, it's mostly correct. Unfortunately, the same generation that granted unearned self-esteem to children also spent little time with their children, so a generation of thirtysomethings resulted. Furthermore, the reliance on "experts" to insert appropriate messaging for children provided the basis for kids' TV's long descent into liberal politics; many of today's experts are nothing of the sort.

SESAME STREET: "DIVERSITY," THE NEXT STEP IN SELF-ESTEEM

The first shift in children's television happened in 1969, two years after the launch of the CPB and PBS. The game-changer was a show called *Sesame Street*, produced by the Children's Television Workshop and funded by the CPB, the Office of Economic Opportunity, and the Office of Child Development (the same people responsible for administering one of the great education failures of all time, Head Start).[5]

The show was staffed largely by members of *Captain Kangaroo*'s old crew. "Most of the people who created *Sesame Street* came from my organization," bragged Keeshan.[6] The show also picked up on *Kangaroo*'s legacy of research. "They actually measured what [material provided] improvement . . . in a child," Mike Dann, former vice president of CTW, told me. "They had . . . psychiatrists and doctors who would know whether a red E was better than a green E, or whether the word *money* was a certain way. . . . If you watch Sesame Street carefully, there isn't a thing on that show that hasn't been cleared by a board of very creative people, lovely people." "Experts," it should be noted, are usually among the most unreliable sources when it comes to teaching values; they are almost invariably leftist academics.

The goal of the show was simple, Dann told me. "It was underwritten and created primarily for black children, Spanish-speaking children. It was not made for the sophisticated or the middle class," Dann said. "And they had a department at Children's Workshop run by Evelyn Davis, a black lady, who dealt with all sorts of civic activities for black people. And that took a foothold. As a matter of fact, there's no written material in a black household. But there is television."[7]

Davis was actually a foot soldier, an inner-city Paul Revere designated to inform minority areas about the importance of watching *Sesame*

Street.[8] "The task of reaching and teaching preschoolers of poor families of all races can only be accomplished," Davis said, "by the active interest and participation of all parts of the community."[9]

Because the show was designed to target inner-city children in particular, it swung liberal in its politics. It wasn't merely about teaching ABCs and counting with the Count; it was about legitimizing urban liberal lifestyles—after all, the goal of children's television had swung toward the enhancement of self-esteem, and how could urban children gain self-esteem if children's television didn't totally embrace the urban liberal lifestyle?

Unlike other children's shows, *Sesame Street* took place in a dingy setting—an urban neighborhood street. One of the characters, Oscar the Grouch, lived in a garbage can. Oscar the Grouch's presence on *Sesame Street* was designed to address "conflicts arising from racial and ethnic diversity," according to *Sesame Street* historian Robert Morrow.[10] The first season of *Sesame Street* launched an entirely new politics into the world of children's television. One 1969 episode had Grover parleying with a hippie and learning subtle lessons about civil disobedience.[11]

The politics of *Sesame Street* would become more overt over time. Joan Ganz Cooney, creator of the show, said that she wanted to reflect reality as much as possible, although she did draw a line at teenage pregnancy: "I am not about to put a fifteen-year-old girl with a baby on *Sesame Street*," she told *New York* magazine in 1987.[12]

In 1989, though, writer/director Jon Stone (the former *Kangaroo* staffer) explained that he intended to tackle other big issues. "My two projects for this year," he said, "are drugs and divorce."[13] They never tackled drugs. The creators struggled with the divorce issue, then finally decided that Snuffleupagus's parents would get a divorce. The episode showed an inconsolable Snuffy, with one of the hosts explaining to Big Bird why divorce is an affirmative good: "Well, they loved each other when they got married . . . uh . . . and I'm sure they tried very hard to keep loving each other . . . but they probably . . . they just couldn't love each other anymore." The creators decided not to air the episode after testing it on an unlucky group of preschoolers, who reacted by believing that fights led to divorce, that divorced fathers abandoned their kids, and that divorced parents don't love their kids. In other words, the kids ended up learning from *Sesame Street* precisely what most kids learn from divorce. "This is clearly not what we wanted," said Ellen Morganstern, director of media relations for the show. She pledged to simplify the messages, and said that "It is very likely that a preschooler will hear the word *divorce*. We want them to understand what that is."[14] It never happened; *Sesame Street* shelved the issue.

The liberalism of the show is overarching. In the aftermath of the 2001 terrorist attacks, the research group for the show, led by Dr. Lewis Bernstein, approached co-executive producer Arlene Sherman and told her, "We have four more shows to write. We have to do something." The creators settled on a segment about peaceful conflict resolution—an odd message in the aftermath of a devastating terrorist attack on American soil. In the end, the *Sesame Street* creators shelved that one, too, after one showing.[15]

The animating philosophy of the show is "diversity," which means politically correct multiculturalism. The *Sesame Street* website lectures parents to examine "your own cultural assumptions and biases" as a "good place to begin your anti-bias work. For example, do you respond differently with your child when a person of another race is coming toward you, such as clutching his hand tightly or locking your car doors?" *Sesame Street* should start by talking to Jesse Jackson, who once explained, "I hate to admit it, but I have reached a stage in my life that if I am walking down a dark street late at night and I see that the person behind me is white, I subconsciously feel relieved."[16]

Speaking of challenging cultural assumptions, the website also urges parents to "Try to use gender-neutral language. Use plural pronouns such as 'they' and 'them,' instead of masculine pronouns such as 'he' and 'him.' Use words such as firefighter, flight attendant, garbage collector, and humankind to replace the use of 'man' as a generic noun or ending."[17] The website even encourages parents to find toys and books with characters "that break stereotypes about men and women, for example, dolls for boys and building toys and puzzles for girls."[18] This is disgracefully idiotic—even Larry Summers, former president of Harvard University and Clinton and Obama official, no ardent right-winger, has explained that such tactics are outmoded by current scientific knowledge.[19] Is it any wonder that in a rather obvious inside joke, the show invited gay television star Neil Patrick Harris to appear on the show—as a character called "The Fairy Shoeperson"?[20]

Multiculturalism has become another touchstone for the show. Rather than teaching kids patriotism or traditional values, the show encourages educators to "Explore the differences and similarities among the children in your classroom. Together, notice the physical aspects, such as hair and skin color, size, etc., as well as personality traits and such unique qualities as family traditions and languages spoken. Point out how all the differences and similarities make your classroom extraordinary and special."[21] In and of itself, there's nothing harmful about this—except that it implicitly endorses the values of all of the children and their families, no matter how skewed those values may be. It also separates people into specific ethnic and racial subgroups—which is historically what *Sesame Street* has done by catering to specific racial minorities and reacting to criticism from their interest groups.[22]

To that end, the show now has versions of itself in countries all over the world, all of which lean left. *Sesame Street* is now viewed by 75 million people globally. "We definitely have a social agenda," explained Shari Rosenfeld, vice president of developing and emerging markets. "In Israel, we focus on mutual respect and understanding and child empowerment. In Palestine, on boys' education and positive role models. . . . But we don't dictate that agenda."[23] In case you missed it, this is negative multiculturalism at work—preaching tolerance to Israelis while preaching boys' education in the Palestinian territories isn't exactly evenhanded, particularly when the Palestinian population's normal children's television teaches children about terrorism and murder. Just to ram the point home, Gary Knell, president and CEO of the Sesame Workshop, says that he's proud to point out to Israelis that "the Arab child in the village near your home in Haifa has aspirations to be a doctor, just like you" (which, of course, the Israelis already know, since they are the only country in the Middle East that allows Arabs to vote); he says nothing whatsoever about what Palestinian children are to be taught, though the lesson not to murder seems much simpler.[24]

The bias at *Sesame Street* really broke out into the open in 2009, when

Oscar the Grouch trashed Fox News on his Grouchy News Network. "From now on I am watching Pox News," a caller to the show stated. "Now there is a trashy news show." The PBS ombudsman suggested that the parody was "too good to resist."[25] It wasn't an idle pun—in the same program, CNN's Anderson Cooper showed up to chat with the children.

"EVERYONE IS SPECIAL"

It wasn't a long way from *Captain Kangaroo*'s self-esteem philosophy to *Mr. Rogers' Neighborhood. Mister Rogers' Neighborhood* was based on the same premises of diversity and tolerance as *Captain Kangaroo*, which was no surprise, since Rogers had been trained at the Arsenal Family and Children Center, founded by Dr. Benjamin Spock (a socialist and the founder of the modern children's self-esteem movement) and Margaret McFarland, who would become chief advisor to the show.

Fred Rogers was a Presbyterian minister who believed that poor children in particular needed self-esteem. "We don't need a lot of loud, fast-paced, violent images to fill the minds of children," Rogers once said, no doubt with *Sesame Street* at least partially in mind. "I think it's easy to make that kind of thing attractive. I think it's difficult to make goodness attractive."[26] His slow-paced program was an antidote to the frenetic *Sesame Street*, which some educators argued made it a better choice (certain psychologists suggest that *Sesame Street*'s *Laugh-In*-esque quick-cutting promotes ADD in children).

Rogers was apolitical, but he combined a conservative view of the world with a liberal view of humanity. "The world is not always a kind place," he said once. To teach children that lesson, he took on issues like divorce, telling kids that it wasn't their fault; war, assuring children that they would be safe; and even death. Morality still played a role in his show, whereas it didn't in later children's productions. In one song, he sang, "It's great to be able to stop / When you've planned a thing that's wrong."[27] During another episode of the show, he encouraged kids to turn off the television when they saw something violent or scary. On a specific level, Mr. Rogers drew distinctions between right and wrong behavior.

But at the same time, Rogers believed that everyone needed to be accepted for "who they are," no matter what their behavior. "You make each day a special day," he'd say on his program. "You know how, by just being you. There's only one person in this whole world like you. And people can like you exactly as you are."

That second message became the basis of later children's television, while the first message—traditional morality—faded away. The apotheosis of the self-esteem movement hit the airwaves in 1992. It centered on a make-believe big purple dinosaur who annoyed millions of teens and adults, but enthralled millions of children. The show, of course, was *Barney & Friends.*

Whereas *Mister Rogers* dealt with tough issues and attempted to cope with children's feelings, Barney had one message and one message only: Everyone is special. In fact, it was a message the dinosaur often sang. "I love you, you love me, we're a happy family!" Barney sang in his clumsy, good-natured voice. "With a great big hug and a kiss from me to you / Won't you say you love me too?" This was innocuous. But another song was not. "Oh, you are special! Special! Everybody's special!" went another ditty. "Everyone in his or her own way." This is strict liberal thought down to the correct usage of alternative gender pronouns.

In one sense, *Barney* was a step up from *Sesame Street*: Its milieu was strictly middle class, a clean preschool playground where you'd be astonished to find a monster that lived in a garbage can. And *Barney* was unsparingly saccharine, with no bad guys in sight. Critics preferred the occasional grumpiness and wink-wink urban nature of *Sesame Street.* "Barney is molding the future of our nation," complained James Gorman in the *New York Times,* "and he's a bad influence. . . . It's as if the National Association for the Promotion of Blandness had created its dream show."[28] In a certain sense, then, *Barney* was a reversion to historic children's shows, which sought mostly to entertain rather than to address controversy.

PBS's response was the creation of another puppet show, *The Puzzle Place.* This show was unabashedly political, far more so than even *Sesame Street.* One third-season episode of the show, "Family Fun," for example, featured discussion of same-sex parents. Cartoon shows from PBS became more and more openly liberal over time: In 2005, *Postcards from Buster,* an animated show about a traveling rabbit, courted controversy when it showed Buster traveling to Vermont and meeting gay parents. Brigid Sullivan, producer of the show, said that the show was designed to incorporate diversity into "the fabric of the series to help children understand and respect differences and learn to live in a multicultural society." Sullivan added, "we are trying to do a broad reach and we are trying to do it without judgment."[29] *Arthur*, a well-made and tremendously popular PBS series produced by the same people as *Buster*, says that its purpose is to "chronicle the adventures of Arthur (an eight-year-old aardvark) through engaging, emotional stories that explore issues faced by real kids. It is a comedy that tells these stories from a kid's point of view without moralizing. . . ."[30] What, exactly, is the problem of "moralizing" to children? Isn't that the point of parenting and/or educational television?

Tolerance and diversity geared toward fostering often unearned self-esteem is now the order of the day on children's television. No longer are children even given the guidance they received from Mr. Rogers; now they're told that they are special, that accepting everyone no matter their behavior is the epitome of goodness, and that all cultures are equal.

Children's television programs universally embrace these messages. For example, in 2005, the good-hearted We Are Family Foundation (WAFF), created by Nile Rodgers, the legendary guitarist, organized a program spanning most children's television shows, including *Barney*, *Arthur*, *Sesame Street*, *Bob the Builder*, *Clifford the Big Red Dog*, *Jimmy Neutron*, *The Magic School Bus*, *Rugrats*, and *SpongeBob SquarePants*, among dozens of others.[31] The goal: the creation of a video "celebrat[ing] . . . the vision of a global family by creating and supporting programs that inspire and educate people about mutual respect, understanding, and appreciation of cultural diversity."[32]

This is all well and good, except that appreciation for cultural diversity often means accepting lifestyles that are problematic (the treatment of women in Saudi Arabia would be an excellent example) or at the very least controversial (the Tolerance Pledge posted on the WAFF website included a request for respect for homosexuality, and the website itself also included lesson topics ripping "the concepts of homophobia and compulsory heterosexuality").[33] The more controversial material wasn't included in the video, so the kids weren't exposed to it. Nonetheless, Rodgers defended it, stating, "The fact that some people may be upset with other peoples' lifestyles, that is O.K. We are just talking about respect."[34] That, of course, is the point—many parents don't want their children exposed to these issues at an early age and taught values that jeopardize their innocence.

Did the video itself damage kids? Of course not. But as standards are lowered with regard to material appropriate for children—a process that occurs continuously—it may not be long before seemingly apolitical messages graduate into fully political ones.

NICKELODEON: MTV FOR KIDS

On PBS, political messages are sometimes concealed. Not at Nickelodeon. Nickelodeon is owned by MTV, which should say something right off the bat as to what they believe children should be seeing. Robert Pittman, a vocal liberal whom you may remember from our earlier discussion of MTV's rise, ran the children's network. Early on, it struggled. Then, in the mid-1980s, Pittman elevated Geraldine Laybourne to head Nick. Laybourne would later go on to found and head the Oxygen Network alongside Oprah and the Marcy Carsey/Tom Werner team. Her philosophy sounds eerily like that of the *Sesame Street* folks. "We are here to accept kids, to help them feel good about themselves," she explained. Her mission was "to connect with kids, and to connect kids with their world through entertainment."[35]

In true MTV style, Nick's goal of catering to kids wasn't in conflict with Nick's attempts to achieve ratings in any way possible. That marriage of convenience and liberal sensibility cleared the way for the most vulgar cartoon ever aired on television up to that time: *The Ren & Stimpy Show*. Ren was a Chihuahua; Stimpy was a cat. The show gloried in snot, farts, and excrement, as well as sexual innuendo. It was hardly educational, unless you call a trip to the public park urinal educational.

The creator of the show was John Kricfalusi, a wild man by all accounts. Vanessa Coffey, vice president of animation production at Nickelodeon, recalled Kricfalusi's pitch for *Ren & Stimpy* to the Nickelodeon leadership: "I thought he was out of his f--- mind—but I was interested in his stuff." Kricfalusi's philosophy was simple: Outgross the competitors.

"We're making this for kids," he told Allan Neuwirth. "They *love* gross stuff. So let's give 'em boogers and farts!"[36] Terry Thoren of animation company Klasky Csupo (responsible for *Rugrats* and *Aaahh!!! Real Monsters*), said the show "tapped into an audience that was a lot hipper than anybody thought. [Kricfalusi] went where no man wanted to go before—the caca, booger humor."[37] *Ren & Stimpy* eventually vulgarized its way off Nickelodeon entirely and onto MTV, then onto Spike TV, where new episodes featured a gay relationship between Ren and Stimpy.

Ren & Stimpy was indicative of the politics of the network, which quickly became the number-one cable channel in the country; Kricfalusi, who would leave the show after a couple of years, ended up changing the direction of Cartoon Network, as well. Nickelodeon was constantly pushing the envelope. They created a Saturday night block of programming complete with a *Saturday Night Live* for kids entitled *All That*, as well as a horror show, *Are You Afraid of the Dark?* This clearly wasn't *Sesame Street*.

Every so often, the politics of the network would break through. The main vehicle for open politics was Linda Ellerbee's *Nick News*, a show that featured kids talking about hot topics ranging from war to homelessness, and invariably taking the leftist position. The episode that drew the most ire came in 2002, when Ellerbee ran a special that clearly stumped for acceptance of gay rights. Titled "My Family's Different," it featured militant gay activist Rosie O'Donnell as co-host. The episode featured children talking about hate crimes, the comments of a gay school principal, and a profile of a gay firefighter with three adopted kids.

Ellerbee, who formerly worked at CNN and NBC, is a liberal. She framed the show as "about tolerance. . . . It is not about sex. It does not tell you what to think." But naturally, it did, as most "tolerance of all behavior" messaging does. The section of the show about hate crimes was particularly effective. "It is never wrong to talk about hate," said Ellerbee. "That's all our show is about. It is not in any way about the homosexual lifestyle."[38]

Another controversial episode of *Nick News* featured Ellerbee praising World Can't Wait, a communist front group, protesting prisoner treatment at Guantánamo Bay, wearing orange jumpsuits and shouting "We are not okay with people being tortured by American soldiers!" That installment also followed a teenager who created an anti-Iraq War video depicting wounded Iraqi kids.[39]

Nickelodeon also takes a blasé view about teen sex. After Jamie Lynn Spears, star of the hit series *Zoey 101*, got pregnant at age sixteen, the network considered running a special—hosted by Ellerbee, of course—regarding sex and love, despite the fact that the chief audience for Spears's show was aged nine to fourteen.[40] Nickelodeon even puts sex talk tips on its website for parents, as well as the usual patter about "respect": "6 to 10 million children have lesbian, gay, and bisexual parents. Everybody—kids, teachers and parents—should avoid generalizations about people based on their sexual orientation, or any other characteristic."[41]

When it comes to President Obama, Nickelodeon is on the same page as MSNBC: It's entirely fine with being utilized as a propaganda tool. In March 2009, shortly after Obama took office, Nick Jr., the portion of Nick's programming aimed at the youngest audiences, broadcast a cartoon homage to Obama. "Nickelodeon celebrates President Barack Obama and some of his favorite things," the cartoon proclaimed. "Barack Obama is the first African-American to be President. That is what's called a historic event. . . . For more about President Barack Obama, go to parents.nickjr.com." Needless to say, Nick did nothing of the sort about President Bush.[42]

Lately, Nickelodeon has been programming more explicitly toward older audiences. *Glenn Martin, DDS* is often rated TV-14 (i.e., appropriate only for audiences aged fourteen-plus), an odd designation on a channel that targets children aged six to twelve. The show is not for kids—it's full of double entendres and features controversial characters and subject matter. One recent episode featured a female character taking off her shirt, a male character lying on top of her, and the female character casually stating, "Makeup sex is the best." The show has also joked about a pornographic car GPS system that directs drivers to "Moorehead, Minnesota" and "Climax, Florida." Characters have also watched pornography while babysitting. Cyra Zarghami, president of the network, admitted that the line between younger Nick audiences and older ones would "start to be a little blurrier."[43] "It is really an adult show," Michael Eisner, creator of the show, admitted. "Children may be naturally attracted to animation . . . , but it is not a children's show any more than any prime time comedy is aimed at children."[44]

More and more, it's becoming clear that Nickelodeon is aimed at feeding its viewers to MTV. Visitors to the Nickelodeon website can visit AddictingGames.com (owned by parent company Viacom), which is linked directly from Nick and which carries the Nick imprimatur, where they can play games like Naughty Park, in which players attempt to get joggers naked, or Perry the Perv, in which players help Perry get glimpses of big-bosomed women without getting caught.[45] Nick frequently shows commercials for MTV products. The symbiosis between the two channels is obvious. "We are managing this company for one thing and one thing only," said an unapologetic Sumner Redstone, chairman and CEO of Viacom, which owns both MTV and Nick. "To build shareholder wealth. You can count on us to exploit every opportunity to grow revenues."[46] Zarghami was clearer: "MTV Networks goes from cradle to grave."[47]

DISNEY CHANNEL: MANUFACTURING STARS

Disney children's television has always been at least partially about the creation of stars. The original *Mickey Mouse Club* featured future movie personalities like Annette Funicello, who would go on to star in all of the Beach Party movies with Frankie Avalon. *The Mickey Mouse Club* remained a font for future stars until its cancellation in 1996—Christina Aguilera, Britney Spears, and Justin Timberlake were among the most famous.

The success of *The Mickey Mouse Club* in creating future mainstream crossover stars eventually took over the channel. No longer would Disney Channel be the repository of clean and innocent children's television; now it would appeal to "tweens"—preteens who were to be treated as teenagers. That transformation truly began to accelerate after Anne Sweeney, a former executive at Nickelodeon and the former CEO of the adults-only FX Network, took the helm. "We found there was this huge demo that was too old for Nickelodeon and too young for MTV," she said.

"We realized this was an opportunity for Disney to establish itself in the lives of these kids." With Sweeney's marketing genius, Disney quickly became one of the biggest profit makers in the Disney pantheon. Disney started programming specials starring Aguilera, the Backstreet Boys, 'N Sync, and Spears. When those acts went too raunchy, Disney began creating fresh ones. "We're not naïve or coy about saying that we knew if we could do it for others, we could do it for ourselves," said Rich Ross, president of Disney Channels Worldwide at the time. That meant creating teen sensations like Hilary Duff and Miley Cyrus/Hannah Montana, as well as franchises like *High School Musical*.

This is all relatively mild stuff, of course. Until, that is, the teen stars of these programs go adult. "It keeps me up at night," Gary Marsh, then Disney Channel's president of entertainment, told Portfolio.com. "Our job is to make sure none of this stuff gets out of control."[48] And yet Disney Channel seems utterly unconcerned about its stars' consistent attempts to sex things up. Miley Cyrus, Disney's most successful star, is only the latest to follow this path. After pole-dancing at the 2009 Teen Choice Awards, then touring the world while simulating lesbian kisses, Cyrus is due to star in *LOL: Laughing Out Loud*, a movie in which she will reportedly smoke pot, get drunk, lose her virginity, display her waxed vagina, and make out with two other girls.[49] Disney Channel isn't responsible for its stars after they leave, of course, but it's worth noting that Hilary Duff has now appeared in *Gossip Girl*, where she participated in a threesome; Spears's and Aguilera's controversial hijinks are well known; Vanessa Hudgens has posed nude; Lindsay Lohan, another Disney kid (*The Parent Trap*), is the poster child for tween queen to quasi porn star.

Perhaps Disney Channel isn't concerned about what these stars do because Disney Channel's older sister, ABC Family, openly promotes such behavior. That channel started off as a mild network featuring old family sitcoms like *Boy Meets World* and *Sister, Sister.* Then it transitioned, like Disney Channel, into a vehicle for older viewers. That meant more sex, drugs, and drinking on the network. Sweeney, now the president of Disney-ABC Television Group, defended the decision using the old tried-and-true "realism" argument. "The best way to resonate with your audience is to be authentic," she said. "You're only authentic if you are holding up a mirror to your audience and saying, 'I see you.'"

Sweeney disowned the traditional family values of *The Adventures of Ozzie and Harriet* and *The Mickey Mouse Club*, explaining, "We've continued to evolve our [stories] because we want to maintain a strong connection with our audience." The programming shift drew audiences and advertisers. "I'd love for these shows to be 'Little House on the Prairie,'" said Pat Gentile, Procter & Gamble buyer and chairman of the Alliance for Family Entertainment. "But that isn't going to happen. Family programming is all about bringing families together to watch shows so that they can dialogue about these sensitive topics."[50]

Some of the ways in which ABC Family has addressed those "sensitive topics": teenage lesbians making out on *Pretty Little Liars*, pregnant teenagers considering abortion on *The Secret Life of the American Teenager*, college students getting drunk and having sex while parroting leftist anti-Christian rhetoric on *Greek*, and straight girls kissing each other in a bid to forward gay rights on *Kyle XY*.

To place these programs on a channel called ABC Family is an exercise in cognitive dissonance. To reconcile the world of antitraditional primetime television with the label "family programming" requires a change in the definition of *family*. And that's precisely what the creators and executives do. Paul Lee, president of ABC Family, was crystal clear on this: "When we came in, one of the key things we wanted to achieve [was] to reclaim that word 'family' for what it really means in real families across America. And when you talk to 14–28-year-olds," he told gay men's website AfterElton.com, "one of my shocking realizations early on—unlike my generation, who were not talking to their parents at all—this is a generation that is really interested in and passionate about families. But they define families in a very, very different way. It is not *Ozzie and Harriet*, 'two parents, two and a half kids living in a farmhouse' family. . . . [Teenagers define family as] you know, 'it's my stepmom, and it's my friend Julie and it's my dog, and it's my best friend.' The modern American family is a very fluid, very important, very passionate unit, defined in a very different way."[51]

MYTHICAL GAY CHARACTERS

The most controversial topic that could be tackled on children's television is gay rights. Because there are gay parents, and because parenting plays a large role in the thematics of most children's television, there's certainly a temptation to take on the issue in many corners—and it's been tackled from time to time. Nonetheless, this is such a hot-button issue that even the liberals who control children's television don't want to touch it for fear of blowback.

That's why it's generally ridiculous for those on the right to find gay rights messaging where none exists in children's television. Very often, the right is responding not to the shows themselves, but to the gay reaction to the shows.

The most famous example of such misdirection came in 1999, when Jerry Falwell went after the Teletubbies. *Teletubbies* was a BBC children's production imported in 1998 by PBS. It featured four characters in bizarre outfits of various colors. One of those characters was the notorious Tinky-Winky, a purple character who carried a handbag and had an inverted triangle on the top of his head. "He is purple—the gay-pride color; and his antenna is shaped like a triangle—the gay-pride symbol," wrote Falwell.

The press, naturally, thought he was nuts and lambasted him. Steven Rice, a spokesman for Itsy Bitsy Entertainment, the U.S. licensing company for the *Teletubbies*, guffawed, "It's a children's show, folks. To think we would be putting sexual innuendo in a children's show is kind of outlandish. To out a Teletubby in a preschool show is kind of sad on his part. I really find it absurd and kind of offensive."[52] Using Falwell's ill-advised and rather silly critique as a club to wield against the cultural right, the media concurred.

There was a reason Falwell made the comments, though: he was responding in knee-jerk fashion to the gay left's usurpation of Tinky Winky as an icon. Hijacking pop culture icons is something the gay left does frequently—just ask Judy Garland or Marilyn Monroe. Two years before Falwell's comments, CNN reported, "Tinky Winky . . . has become something of a gay icon."[53] Similarly, Joyce Millman of Salon .com reported a year before Falwell's statements, "to the BBC's dismay, gay groups in Britain hailed Tinky Winky (the purple one with the coat hanger coming out of his head) as the first queer hero of children's TV because he often carries around a big red purse."[54] Michael Colton followed that up with a piece in the *Washington Post* in which he jokingly declared Tinky Winky "in" as a gay icon, while declaring Ellen DeGeneres "out."[55] Falwell made the mistake of conflating the gay community's embrace of Tinky Winky as actual evidence that Tinky Winky was gay and dangerous for kids.

Unfortunately, this is a mistake those on the right seem to make with some frequency. Some on the right have taken on SpongeBob SquarePants of Nickelodeon, stating that he and Patrick, a starfish who is SpongeBob's best friend, represent a homosexual couple. Like the fallacious Tinky Winky criticism, this perspective is misinformed and bizarre. Creator of the show Stephen Hillenberg told the *Wall Street Journal* that SpongeBob wasn't gay: "I always think of them as being somewhat asexual," he said. That's backed up by the fact that SpongeBob reproduces as a sea sponge would. At the same time, Hillenberg acknowledged SpongeBob's popularity with the gay population, explaining, "Everybody is different, and the show embraces that. The character SpongeBob is an oddball. He's kind of weird, but he's kind of special."[56] Hillenberg added, "It doesn't have anything to do with what we're trying to do."[57]

Similar hubbub has surrounded Bert and Ernie of *Sesame Street*, for similar reasons; the gay left has embraced Bert and Ernie as gay icons, and misguided members of the right have taken the bait. *Saturday Night Live*, *Glee*, *Friends*, *American Dad!*, *The Mentalist*, and *Family Guy*, among others, have all joked about the possibility that Bert and Ernie are gay. And certain conservatives, in response, have commented about Bert and Ernie's supposed sexuality. When the right legitimates the left's hijacking of characters as "gay icons," it makes the right appear ignorant and bigoted, as though they're looking for homosexuality in every nook and cranny.

YES, VIRGINIA, THERE'S POLITICS IN CHILDREN'S TELEVISION

Whenever conservatives talk about political messaging on children's television, the media pooh-poohs it. Even the most obvious attempts at infusing liberal messages into kids' TV—incidents like the *Buster* episode in Vermont or the *Nick News* installment on gay parents—are considered completely legitimate by the leftists who cover television. Those leftists gain credibility every time the right launches a misguided attack on SpongeBob or the *Teletubbies*.

But children's television, as we've seen, is hardly immune to the siren's call of liberal messaging. Even the most innocent programs are often chock-full of leftism.

Take, for example, *Captain Planet and the Planeteers. Captain Planet* was a cartoon show created by Ted Turner for TBS and produced by Andy Heyward, creator of *Inspector Gadget, The Adventures of Teddy Ruxpin, Sonic the Hedgehog, Sabrina: The Animated Series*, and *Speed Racer X*, among others. On the surface, it was a simple adventure tale. Slightly below the surface—but only very, very slightly—it was a tale of environmentalist triumph. "Captain Planet was an idea that Ted Turner had to create a super hero that would be an environmentally based show," Heyward told me. They tackled "the ozone layer . . . global warming . . . the idea was to educate a generation of kids who would later become adults regarding issues surrounding the environment. There is no doubt in my mind that much of the awareness today about the environment and the issues surrounding it are a result of what people saw in *Captain Planet*."

Heyward told me that the messages he tried to get across to children didn't have much to do with "the classical reading and writing and stuff you would see in a lot of shows on PBS." Instead, "they could be social lessons that had to do with ethical values," presumably liberal values. The point of the entertainment, Heyward said, was to "have educational themes embedded in the entertainment. It's very important that it's embedded in there, because if it's just educational and tutorial, the kids aren't interested in that stuff. You have to have something they would actually want to watch—the stories."

When I asked Heyward whether *Captain Planet* promoted a politicized point of view, a leftist point of view, he responded, "Well, what would the other point of view be?"[58]

Unfortunately, that's the state of the debate in children's television. There is no true right-wing perspective. Whether it's environmentalism or the extreme diversity and tolerance movement, whether it's self-esteem or sexuality, children's television is a one-sided political machine in the same way the rest of television is. Unlike the rest of television, though, children's television does have the obligation to respect parental authority; the market should *not* be the decider, even if the market argument worked perfectly.

From cradle to grave, then, television promotes liberal values.

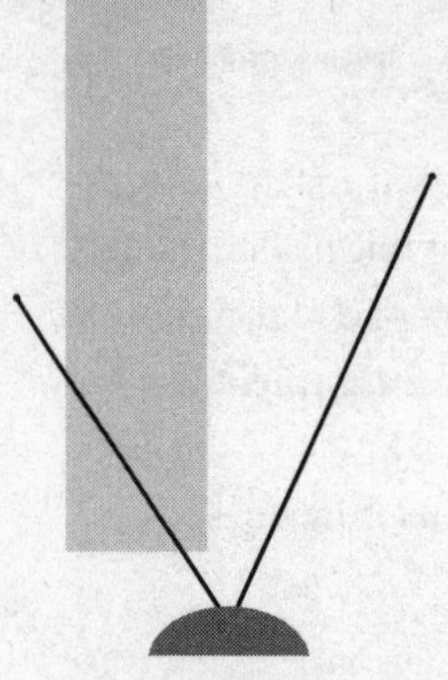

THE END OF TELEVISION?

How to Fix TV

The gods of television have controlled our minds and hearts for too long.

We might be able to accept their reign if they were benevolent, impartial gods. But in many cases, as we've seen, they're politically motivated gods who worship idols of their own: big government, multiculturalism, moral relativism. They live in a wealthy and privileged bubble, believing that their politics reflect America, when in fact they mainly reflect their own parochial beliefs. They hide behind the mask of "social realism" when they're truly shaping social attitudes and mores. And they discriminate, often proudly, against those who disagree.

We might be able to kowtow to the gods of television if they were merely catering to our whims. But as we've seen, they aren't. They've created a fantasy market that allows them to cater to liberal viewers and ignore others who are conservative, to cater to the young while neglecting the old. They've bamboozled advertisers into believing that twenty-one-year-olds with $100,000 in college debt are more valuable as consumers than fifty-five-year-olds who own their houses and are on the verge of retirement. They've manipulated the market to fit their own creative ends rather than adjusting their programming to fit the wants and needs of the actual market.

It would be one thing if the gods of television didn't rely on government to maintain their ideological monopoly. It would be different if they could compete in an open market free of government sponsorship. But they can't. Without government's thumb on the scale, buttressing their profit margins, the television industry can't sustain its current levels.

The gods still rule our airwaves. But they have one problem government can't help them with. Olympus is crumbling.

For the first time since Sarnoff, Paley, and Goldenson stepped into the field of television, the industry itself is on the verge of total transformation. Satellite technology has exponentially increased our ability to choose our own programming. The Internet, as it has already done to the old broadcast news media, is in the process of destroying television's central value proposition; we can now watch television whenever we want to, and only the copyright lawyers are preventing the Internet from simply ripping the commercials out of programming altogether. TiVo has overridden the notion of television as a time-bound medium—no longer do millions watch television shows simultaneously. Now they watch it on demand.

It's terrific for the television consumer. It's the death of the television industry as we know it. Every single person I talked to, without variation, recognized that the traditional television model had one foot in the grave.

"The networks are struggling to find an identity," said Carlton Cuse, co-creator of *Lost*. "The audience has been provided with technological tools that makes the traditional network model obsolete. . . . I don't think the network business will exist in its current form for much longer."[1]

"I have no idea where [television] will be in twenty years," said Susan Harris, creator of *Soap*. "With cable, who knows if there will even be TV as we know it. I have no idea."[2] "I believe that network television will be also paid subscriber fees," said Mark Burnett, creator of *Survivor*. "Because clearly nobody watches television except on cable."[3]

Some were excited about television's potential metamorphosis. "We're in the twenty-first century; it's not the century of *M*A*S*H*," explained John Langley, creator of *Cops*. "It's probably not the century of *Cops*, either. We're going to see hybrid shows, all forms of new admixtures of the

Internet and television."[4] Gene Reynolds of *Room 222*, *M*A*S*H*, and *Lou Grant* agreed. "There's going to be such enormous changes. The variety will be very great, the different platforms will be amazing."[5]

"It makes for an exciting and interesting period of time," Carlton Cuse said.[6] That sentiment was seconded by Michael Nankin of *Chicago Hope* and *Picket Fences*: "I think [television] will be unrecognizable in ten years. . . . Internet and television and movies are going to merge; there's not going to be such a delineation between them."[7] Don Bellisario, creator of *NCIS* and *JAG*, suggested that television would press the bounds of our imaginations. "It's developing technically so rapidly, you know, it wouldn't surprise me if we had holographic television, you sat in your living room and the whole thing was there as a hologram."[8]

Others were downbeat in the extreme, suggesting that the future of television was grim. "I don't think we'll recognize TV in twenty years," said George Schlatter of *Laugh-In* in his inimitable, colorfully vulgar style. "I think that the inmates will definitely be in charge of the asylum. Today, the Writers Guild, the necessity for skilled, honed, articulate writers, has been replaced by a thing called Twitter. The only [reason] Twitter is amusing is because it's so close to twat."[9]

"It's still there for the snake oil and next year's model car," Larry Gelbart poignantly observed. Then he stopped himself: "But that's not a certainty anymore, is it. I don't know, but thankfully I won't be around to see it."[10]

Fred Silverman said he was already seeing the effects of the transformation. "I think you're seeing television change dramatically . . . I question whether in five years the networks [will exist]."[11] Allan Burns echoed Silverman's suggestion: "I don't think there are going to be any networks left in twenty years. It will all be cable stuff," he said.[12]

Michael Brandman, formerly of HBO, thought that the new television model would lead to increasing fractionalization of the viewing audience. "Lee [Rich, former head of Lorimar] says, his belief, and I tend to agree with it, is you see the structure changing and collapsing in front of us. There won't be any more network television. . . . No one growing up today understands the difference between NBC and TNT. So there's this great smorgasbord of specialty networks, all of them sort of fighting for a niche." Even that smorgasbord, though, will eventually come up short, Brandman said. Television will continue to splinter.[13]

Technology is one reason the industry is fragmenting. Then there's the fragmentation of the television business overall, a result of collusion and governmental intervention preventing competition. Now if you want drama, you visit TNT ("We Know Drama"). If you want comedy, hit TBS ("Very Funny"). For edgy content, FX is your channel ("There Is No Box"). Showtime is where you go for sexy, racy, and dirty pay cable content you can't get anywhere else ("The Best Shit on Television"). The list goes on and on.

The networks have fragmented as well. CBS has done the best job of programming mainstream, which is why they have routinely led the ratings for the last decade or so, but even CBS skews old. NBC is stuck in 1998, and they can't get out; their audiences are urban elites under the age of fifty. ABC is all over the map. And Fox imitates cable by gobbling up racy fare that the other networks won't, a model copied by CW.

There's not a single influential entertainment network that can be said to provide consistently family-friendly programming. There's not a single entertainment network that can be said to appeal apolitically or even-handedly to viewers on a regular basis. Even the networks that want to *broad*cast are narrowcasting.

That's largely due to the historic bias that exists in the television industry. It's a bias that springs from business manipulation, personal predilections, conservative apathy, and liberal activism. The left embraced narrowcasting because it pushed America to the left. Whereas Dad used to identify with TV fathers like Bill Cosby, narrowcasting programs shows for Dad that cater to his teenage frat boy tendencies, promoting an endless adolescence; whereas Mom used to identify with Donna Reed, she now identifies with Samantha from *Sex and the City*. The problem is that when we all watch individually, it's difficult to create television hits that we all want to watch together. Television's liberalism is killing television.

Family-friendly fare is often rejected by television's liberals because it isn't groundbreaking enough—it's too conservative, too boring—but when it's tried, it's a winner (see *The Cosby Show*, *The Waltons*, or *Everybody*

Loves Raymond). Evenhanded dramas are often eschewed, but they, too, dominate the ratings (see *House*, *NCIS*, and *CSI*). The least political, most family-friendly show of the year comes in first every year. It's called the Super Bowl. Television needs more Super Bowls and fewer insider shows that make for titillating conversation on the Sunset Strip.

The television industry needs a new business model—one that allows them to target the most viewers. That starts by ceasing to ignore families and conservatives across the country, and instead truly embracing the market model to which they disingenuously appeal.

LIBERALS: STOP DISCRIMINATING

Tapping new markets—or rather, tapping old markets that have been forgotten—means that the liberal clique in television must open its mind to those outside Los Angeles, New York, Chicago, and San Francisco. Those in the red states are not stupid rubes whose politics can be easily dismissed, their children converted, their values left for dead. They deserve respect and tolerance, too. After all, they're the ones who push ratings success.

Unfortunately, as we've seen, too many conservatives are shut out of the industry. Too many of them lose jobs. Too many are forced to hide their politics in order to get work. What should be a medium for open debate and discussion therefore turns into a one-sided medium for political messaging. The left is so afraid of the right-wing slippery slope of censorship that they engage in precisely that sort of censorship against the right.

It's not fair, and it's not good business. It is utterly unjustified.

The Hollywood left must learn that American conservatism is not fascism and that those who differ on issues ranging from tax cuts to same-sex marriage are not Nazis. Allowing them to work is not an act of charity—it is an act of moral and economic common sense. The same Hollywood that excoriated Joseph McCarthy and his allies for blacklisting Communists now does the same to conservatives.

This sort of discrimination is largely accepted in Hollywood. And that is unacceptable. The market does not demand that conservatives be kept away from the levers of television creativity. Just because a creator or executive in Hollywood is conservative does not mean that he or she is untalented, and to suggest as much betrays deep and troubling discriminatory prejudices. Conservatives do empathize—it's just that the objects of their empathy may be slightly different than those of liberals. Conservatives do care, which is why they give far more charity per capita than liberals. And conservatives *can* write. Talent comes in all political packages—Ray Bradbury is talented, and so is Norman Mailer. Talent should be judged on its merits, not on the perceived political beliefs of the creator.

Unfortunately, far too often, the creator is judged on his/her level of political correctness rather than his/her ability to create entertaining content. There are more closeted conservatives in Hollywood than closeted gays; there is an entire underground in Hollywood that, for fear of firing, hides its politics when it comes to something as simple as open discussion.

It is nothing short of despicable for members of the liberal media to write off such complaints as unfounded. They wouldn't dare to do the same with blacks or gays who suggest discrimination in Hollywood, even though the evidence of such discrimination today is far scantier. There is institutional bias against right-wingers in Tinseltown, and if the media had any guts at all, they would ferret it out and expose it.

I am not calling for Hollywood creators to disown their political biases in producing their material. They are artists, and they should be free to insert their politics wherever they feel it is appropriate and warranted (although one-sided writing is inherently boring, no matter from what political perspective it springs). Artists by their very nature channel their belief systems into their work. More power to them.

All I am arguing is that conservatives should be free to do the same. Honest and open conversations in writers' rooms about social and political issues that sometimes divide Americans would not be the end of the world. Hollywood believes that we, as a society, are too easily offended by attacks on our sensibilities, which is why Hollywood has embraced offensive and cutting-edge content ranging from *All in the Family* to *Family Guy*. Is it too much to ask that Hollywood extend its own love of controversy to its writers' rooms so long as such conversations help the product rather than holding up the process?

It would also be far better for the television industry to provide a semblance of ideological balance in a country that is split down the middle on politics than to continue catering exclusively to one side of the aisle. Many shows already try to do this. They could do even better by having actual conservatives join their writing teams in order to provide credible spokesmen for conservative views on television, as opposed to the laughable straw men we so often see. The best comedies on television attack both sides of the political debate on a routine basis—and if leftists truly want to make Americans laugh, all they have to do is attack the sanctimony and political correctness of the left (there's nothing funnier in recent memory than Ben Affleck channeling Keith Olbermann on *Saturday Night Live*).

There is no market reason why Hollywood purposefully ignores at least one-half of the American audience and caters to the other when it comes to politics. It's a *political decision* for Hollywood to do so. And no industry can survive making decisions politically rather than fiscally.

But I have faith in Hollywood. Despite the rash of discrimination that seems to have infected the industry over the past few decades, I believe that television is filled with good people, open-minded people, reasonable and rational and talented people. These are the same people who tackled racism when it was truly courageous to do so. I believe that they will rise to the challenge of examining their own belief systems and realize that those who disagree with them still have a place in their industry.

That underlying faith has only been strengthened by the writing of this book. In meeting hundreds of people who have shaped the television industry, I'm more optimistic than ever about the possibility of renewed political diversification in Hollywood. I hope that the liberal power brokers read this book not as a personal criticism, but as a call to action: a call to extend their tolerant, diverse attitudes to politics.

CONSERVATIVES: ENGAGE

Conservatives in Hollywood have reason to complain. Many have faced discrimination. Many have lost jobs, friends, and careers based on a single vote for Ronald Reagan or a refusal to donate thousands of dollars to Senator Barbara Boxer.

But many conservatives have also been unwise in how they've approached their politics on the set. It's not too much to ask that liberals tolerate conservatives by engaging in conversation, but many conservatives are excessively militant about their approach to politics. That's at least partially due to their long enforced silence—at a certain point, the dam bursts. But conservatives on the set must realize—as most do—that liberals remain in control, and that those liberals have a creative vision that may not work in concert with conservative thought. Taking a conservative position on gay rights, for example, wouldn't work out well in the writers' room at *Will & Grace*. If a conservative wants to write for *Will & Grace*, it would make sense to keep their position on California's traditional marriage constitutional amendment to themselves. This isn't meant to excuse liberal discrimination—liberals should be more open to criticisms and political disagreements, as stated above. Nor is it a call for continued self-censorship. It's just a practical consideration that conservatives must take under advisement.

The real problem with conservatives in television *isn't* the conservatives who are already in television, though. It's the more general conservative solution, which has been utterly disastrous: withdrawal.

When faced with an overwhelmingly liberal industry bent on purveying its politics, conservatives have taken precisely the wrong approach: they have decided to make war on the medium itself. That means taking every opportunity to cut off corporate tax breaks for Hollywood, when they would normally approve them in the interest of creating jobs. That means urging boycotts of television generally, as opposed to certain shows in particular. Most important, that means instructing their children not to get involved with the industry in any way.

It would be difficult to devise a more foolhardy strategy. The entertainment business isn't going anywhere. Millions—including millions of conservatives—will continue to watch television and imbibe the messages that pour through the screen. That isn't to say that the interest groups on the right-wing side of the aisle aren't effective—they are a necessary counterbalance to the interest groups of the left. But that can't be the entirety of the conservative strategy.

A far wiser strategy would be to take a cue from liberals themselves—join the industry and change it from within.

Integrating the industry requires two tactics. The first is by infiltrating the creative community. More conservatives need to hone their creative skills. We need fewer conservative lawyers and more conservative writers, directors, and producers. More conservatives need to dedicate their lives to entertaining others. That doesn't mean conservatives have to force their politics into their work—there's nothing clunkier than a conservative biopic about Ronald Reagan, just as there's nothing more boring than a liberal biopic about Robert F. Kennedy. Conservatives need merely enter the realm of television creation, and their values will almost always come out naturally in their work. There are already right-wing networks opening their doors at the Internet level; there are hundreds of conservatives in hiding in Hollywood. They need to combine their efforts, not just to create new competitors for the liberal powers-that-be, but to infiltrate those creative liberal bastions.

Because conservatives need to recognize the realities on the ground, they also need to recognize that writing a series that is 100 percent openly conservative and getting it produced is unrealistic. Better to go for 50 percent—write an evenhanded pilot that takes liberalism seriously. At the very least, that will move the political gauge significantly, since right now virtually all programming is 100 percent liberal.

The second tactic in a prospective conservative infiltration is to enter the executive suites. Even the most militant liberals will acknowledge that conservatives are often excellent businesspeople. What better way to channel that entrepreneurial energy than into the most powerful mass medium in history? Television is an industry in crisis, and conservative know-how can bring a good deal to the table. Moreover, conservative businesspeople can bring one solution that liberal businesspeople very often don't: an insight into the need for balanced content in order to attract broader audiences.

Never has the industry been more wide open to conservative talent. The plethora of cable channels and the rise of the Internet mean that the industry needs exponentially more and more content. Which means that they'll even look at conservatives some of the time.

This is a mission for the best and the brightest. Loudmouths who want to invade writers' rooms or executive suites and bash away at

President Obama won't make headway here. In fact, they'll be counterproductive. The television business is inherently social, and that means that the conservatives who come here have to be social, too. They have to get along with everyone, even if they disagree. They have to make friends and influence people without compromising their values. It's not an easy task. But it's a vital one for conservatives—and for the country as a whole. If conservatives don't engage, they're putting themselves at a massive disadvantage—not only in the industry but in American politics more broadly—by foregoing access to the most effective message machine ever made.

EXECUTIVES: EMBRACE FREEDOM

The takeover of the executive hallways by liberals of all stripes is somewhat puzzling when we consider that conservatives are often the most successful businesspeople in other industries. As we've seen, that liberal takeover is due to a variety of factors: a history of urban connection, the fusion of the creative and corporate sides of the business, and most important, the industry's desire to funnel cash and beneficial legislation to itself from the government.

Television executives need to realize that none of these rationales is sufficient to justify the continued ideological imbalance. The history of the industry can be set aside in favor of a new, more ideologically diverse approach. The creative and executive sides need not be dominated by liberals; conservative talent is plentiful on both sides of the business.

As for its desire to get cozy with the government, the television industry above all others should know the dangers in this strategy. Censorship has long been the chief fear of those in Tinseltown, and with good reason—motivated government has more power over this industry than any other. Not only does television have to face the same business risks as other industries—higher taxes, more regulations, securities requirements—but television also has to face the constant scrutiny of a government that licenses it.

In the past, this has meant that television needed to parley with government in order to maintain its good standing. By catering to liberal politicians, not only have networks and stations received regulatory benefits, they've also been able to keep market share.

The future of television, though, is extraterritorial—which means that government licensing regulations no longer apply. All networks will essentially become cable networks or pay-per-view networks or Internet networks. Laissez-faire regulatory schemes will redound to the industry's benefit—as long as the industry recognizes that smaller government means more freedom for the industry.

The industry doesn't need subsidies, either. Television has always been able to flourish while adapting to technological change. It is not the newspaper industry, stuck in one mode of production. Moving images work across different distribution mechanisms, and the public will always crave entertaining content. The best strategy for network executives is to foster friendly but wary relations with the government and urge it to stay as far away from the business of television as possible.

One real problem with which the industry will have to cope, however, is the problem of the shrinking market. Yes, America's population is rising. But the number of outlets catering to that population is growing far faster than the population. In other words, more players are fighting over the same pie. In the past, the networks' response has been narrowcasting: allowing advertisers to target specific segments of the marketplace by catering to a select few.

But that select few is becoming even fewer. Soon it will disappear altogether. Either the players must collude to divvy up the market, or they will eat each other alive, and the profit margin will disappear. The answer isn't in further narrowcasting. It's in *broad*casting—just look at the dramatic success of *American Idol*. The industry needs to go back to the future. That means programming not merely to urban professionals eighteen to forty-nine who happen to be liberal, but to viewers of all ages and politics. Niche shows are the wave of the past. Viewers can already get their niche shows by searching YouTube. Broader shows are the wave of the future. We need more "event" shows—shows that everyone simply has to see. We need more shows we can all watch.

ADVERTISERS: WAKE UP

Advertisers, meanwhile, need to stop being bamboozled by their agencies and by the television industry. Younger viewers are not necessarily more profitable. Edgy shows are not necessarily the best way to draw consumers.

The 18-to-49 crowd is no better—and now, it is significantly worse—than the 50-plus crowd, since the 18-to-49s have less disposable income and represent a shrinking percentage of the population as a whole. Those 18-to-49s demand more liberal programming, but they shouldn't be in the driver's seat anymore (in fact, they never should have been in the first place). Those in the driver's seat should be those who have money—who, by the way, also happen to be the same folks who pay taxes and skew conservative. The *New York Times* recently reported, "One-third of people in their 20s move to a new residence every year. Forty percent move back home with their parents at least once. They go through an average of seven jobs in their 20s, more job changes than in any other stretch. Two-thirds spend at least some time living with a romantic partner without being married. And marriage occurs later than ever."[14] These aren't ideal consumers. Many of them still need help from their parents to buy a house. So why are advertisers targeting them?

Family programming should once again become a standard for advertisers. First off, family programming is boycott-proof—nobody is going to boycott pure comedies or dramas. And though creators and executives complain about the "blanding" of television, television is, first and foremost, a business. Besides, blandness isn't always a terrible thing—the urge to push the envelope evidences a constant dissatisfaction with the status quo, which is precisely the opposite of what advertisers generally want.

Advertisers already know this. That's why in 1998, two of the biggest advertisers in television, Procter & Gamble and Johnson & Johnson, got together to form the Family Friendly Programming Forum, bringing together forty national advertisers who control "one out of every three advertising dollars spent on network television." The forum has now changed its name to the Association of National Advertisers' Alliance for

Family Entertainment, and its stated mission is to bring "smart, sophisticated, responsible stories about and for everyone in the American family . . . that's always good for business."[15]

In June 2010, the Alliance announced that it raised $10 million to spend on family-friendly entertainment. "We're putting our money where our mouths are," explained Marc Goldstein, chief content officer for the alliance. "We want to support this kind of programming in a tangible manner." The alliance has done research showing that purchase intent—consumers' intent to purchase a product—rises 12 percent when consumers see commercials during family-friendly television.

The industry has already responded, pledging its support to the alliance's efforts. But as usual, that support comes with a proviso—that liberal values continue to dominate even family-friendly television. "Values alone will not lead people to watch a show," said Kevin Reilly of Fox. "It has to work creatively."[16] Of course, he's right. But values *help*. Entertainment and solid family values aren't mutually exclusive. And advertisers can ensure that programming that finds the common ground between entertainment and traditional values gets a hearing in the public square. They'll make money, the industry will make money, and the audience will finally get what it wants: Entertainment that doesn't scorn their values.

When it comes to advertising, conservatives can have a disproportionate effect immediately. Right now, conservative advertisers seem to target conservative audiences alone, which makes them an easy target for liberal government actors (just ask the gold industry). Furthermore, many conservative advertisers refuse to use the television medium altogether because they object to the politics of the shows. That's the wrong strategy. The better strategy—both from a business standpoint and a political standpoint—would be to target the most successful shows and those that are least militant in their politics (very often these coincide), and place advertiser dollars with them. Sure, that means the advertiser may be supporting a show that doesn't back its agenda 100 percent of the time. But that also means that the advertiser is reaching out to new consumers and that it's pushing television away from the more extreme shows. While some executives will stick with advertiser failures simply based on principle, this is still a business, and money talks.

If the industry refuses to abide by advertiser dictates, advertisers can simply produce their own programming, in the fashion of old-style program sponsorships. That's already happening. Procter & Gamble and Wal-Mart coordinated to produce an NBC family movie titled *Secrets of the Mountain.* They've also gotten together to make three more television pictures. "This has been a petri dish to prove out the case we're making about advertising in the right context," Ben Simon, director of Wal-Mart's brand marketing and co-chair of the Alliance for Family Entertainment, explained. "There was a significant boost to our brand equity and purchase intent, and we saw that translate to sales increases."[17]

Advertisers *will* see greater programming diversity redound to their benefit. All they have to do is demand it.

THE STORY GOES ON

Television will continue to flourish, in whatever form it takes, because people need storytelling. "People still fundamentally want storytelling. Storytelling is the most powerful way that we have of conveying the essence of the human experience to one another," Carlton Cuse told me.[18] That sentiment was seconded by Michael Nankin of *Chicago Hope* and *Picket Fences*: "I think that sitting in front of a screen and having a story told to you is something that we need and that we'll continue to need."[19] Don Bellisario, creator of *NCIS* and *JAG*, agreed: "It's still going to be the same basic stories that have to be told. It's still human beings. It's still stories of love and hope and sorrow and loss, recovery, moving on. The stories will still have to be about people. It's the one thing that hasn't changed since the Greeks, and it won't change."[20]

They're right. Storytelling is a deep human need, not a frivolity. It's how we learn to connect with one another; it's how we create shared experiences even if we're total strangers. The need for human connection is why lonely people keep the television on at night for company, and it's why we spend time at the water cooler asking each other what the hell happened on last night's *Lost.* Television is our chief storytelling mechanism. We need it as much as it needs us.

If television helps us connect with each other, it is a grave disservice to excise one-half of American political philosophy from the medium. That excision means *less* understanding of one another, *less* tolerance, *less* respect for the honest political debate that goes on every day in this country. It means a more vitriolic country where liberals don't understand conservatives, and conservatives feel victimized by liberals. If television has the capacity to bring us together, it also has the capacity to tear us apart. And for the last few decades, television has done exactly that.

Television's quality has never been in dispute; it is only its exclusive political angle that makes it divisive. It is time for television to bring us together again. For too long, the gods have controlled television from on high, telling us what to think, when to think, and how to think. It is time to bring that power down from the mountaintop and give it back to the American people. It's time for primetime propaganda to become primetime entertainment again.

Appendix: The Best Conservative Shows in Television History

Not all shows are liberal. Some are, in fact, conservative—even if they don't know it. It's time to give credit where credit is due. Here's a list of my top dozen conservative series in television history. These are not the most conservative shows in television history—they are the best shows that happen to carry conservative messages. My criteria, in order of importance: (1) portraying traditional American values in a positive light—values points; (2) taking on liberal sacred cows with total abandon—skewering points; (3) creating memorable conservative characters—we'll call these sympathy points. They had to be good, too (sorry, *Hogan's Heroes*). And no reality shows. I've tried to span the history of television (if we really did the top twelve conservative shows, the list would skew heavily to the 1950s). Also, I decided no creator could make two shows on the list. As you'll see, many of the shows here are described in chapters above, and are actually liberal. The fact that the top conservative shows in TV history lean left merely demonstrates the total domination of the television left for the last five decades. You'll see that many of these shows were also created by outspoken liberals—this is a tribute to those gutsy liberals who didn't toe the party line.

TOP TWELVE CONSERVATIVE SHOWS OF ALL TIME

12. *Lost* (2004–2010): I may be the only person on earth who believes that Lost skews conservative on political matters, but I'll stick to my guns. First off, I had to put the show on the list because it is, in my humble opinion, the best show in the history of television. More than that, however, *Lost* had the temerity to avoid leftist political tropes. It spoke early and often about God and religion. (Spoiler alert: The show's ending posited an afterlife in which we reflect on our earthly existence and come to terms with it.) It presented the notion of evil embodied. It believed deeply in repentance. And it presented several of the best conservative characters in TV history. Eko (Adewale Akinnuoye-Agbaje) was a drug dealer turned priest who used his "Jesus stick" (a stick marked with scripture) to bring justice to the sinister Others. Sawyer (Josh Holloway) was a Republican who kicked ass and took names (in season-one's "Outlaws," Sawyer says he's never voted Democrat). He toted guns with authority, bought and sold goods like Warren Buffett at a flea market, and mocked communism. He's pure tough—he rips a bullet out of his shoulder with his bare hands in season two. Locke (the magnificent Terry O'Quinn) is the most mystical character in TV history, a "Man of Faith." He teaches ten-year-olds how to throw knives. His motto: "Don't Tell Me What I Can't Do." Damon Lindelof, J. J. Abrams, and Carlton Cuse (sorry, *Walker, Texas Ranger* fans) are all liberal, but they're insanely talented and clearly willing to leave their politics out of the script. The show wins big sympathy points for its characters and a few values points for its focus on religion.

11. ***Walker, Texas Ranger*** (1993–2001): Superman wears Chuck Norris pajamas. Period. Plus, the show contained frequent Christian imagery and upheld traditional family values, all while punishing bad guys and upholding law enforcement. Big values points and sympathy points for the ninja cowboy.

10. ***South Park*** (1997–present): This show is really libertarian. It makes fun of conservatives for their social values, but it mocks liberals mercilessly for their social values, their foreign policy beliefs, their economic foolishness. Matt Stone and Trey Parker aren't conservative or liberal—they are adamant that no one can label them or their show. "I look at it like this," Parker told the Huffington Post. "I have a cat, I love my cat and it's like someone coming in and saying, 'Hey, is that cat a Republican or a Democrat?' He's my f---ing cat, leave him alone."[1] Nonetheless, liberals piss them off more than conservatives, and it shows. *Team America* is vicious in its assault on liberal sacred cows, from Michael Moore to the

Screen Actors Guild. *South Park* is even more brutal. They'll even take on Muhammad and Comedy Central. (In Hollywood, it's a fair question whether it's more dangerous to take on Muhammad or Comedy Central.) My personal favorite is the tenth-season episode "ManBearPig," in which Al Gore comes to South Park, declaring, "I am here to educate you about the single biggest threat to our planet. You see, there is something out there which threatens our very existence and may be the end to the human race as we know it. I'm talking, of course, about 'ManBearPig.' . . . It is a creature which roams the Earth alone. It is half man, half bear, and half pig. Some people say that ManBearPig isn't real. Well, I'm here to tell you now, ManBearPig is very real, and he most certainly exists—I'm cereal. ManBearPig doesn't care what you've done. ManBearPig just wants to get you. I'm super cereal. But have no fear, because I am here to save you. And someday, when the world is rid of ManBearPig, everyone will say, 'Thank you Al Gore—you're super awesome!' The end." That speech is super awesome. Huge skewering points overcome the show's total lack of values points.

9. *Everybody Loves Raymond* (1996–2005): This underappreciated comedy didn't say anything important about gay marriage, taxes, global warming, abortion, or any other hot-button political issue. That's what made it so important. In an age when politics infected virtually every comedy on television, *Everybody Loves Raymond* was the happy exception. It featured a stable heterosexual two-parent home—actually, it featured two stable heterosexual two-parent homes. It wasn't *Father Knows Best*; Raymond (Ray Romano) was a weakling bullied by his mother. Deborah (Patricia Heaton) could be a harridan, Marie (Doris Roberts) was an overbearing horror, and Frank (Peter Boyle) could be mean to his wife. But the love between the couples was obvious, the love for their children was even more obvious, and they never devolved into liberal talking points, the hallmark of a show jumping the shark. It is certainly indicative of how far television has come that a well-written, funny show about a traditional family was revolutionary. High on sympathy points, high on tacit values points.

8. *King of the Hill* (1997–2009): Who would have thought the creator of *Beavis and Butt-Head*, the asinine and vulgar MTV show that perfectly

captured the nihilism of the Cobain Generation, would be responsible for the most conservative animated show in the history of television? Incredible, but true. Mike Judge, creator of *King of the Hill*, is rumored to be a conservative, a charge he evades when asked. "I try to not let the show get too political," he told the entertainment website IGN. "To me, it's more social than political I guess you'd say, because that's funnier. I don't really like political reference humor that much. Although I liked the episode where Hank's talking to the mailman and he says, 'Why would anyone want to lick a stamp that has Bill Clinton on it?' " The politics of the show comes through in clear and unmitigated fashion, particularly in the person of main character Hank Hill, a local sales manager from Arlen, Texas. Hank is an ardent conservative, a fan of Reagan, as well as JFK; in one episode, he excoriates his kid, Bobby, because Bobby is doing a report on his "favorite president," Josiah Bartlet of *The West Wing*. He's a gun owner and NASCAR fan. Families are generally happy to shop at Mega Lo Mart (a Wal-Mart takeoff) and drive pickup trucks. The show routinely makes fun of liberal policies, even as it pokes soft fun at conservatism. The show's not quite at *South Park* level in terms of skewering points, but it gets a few points for values and a few for sympathy to joust it into eighth place.

7. ***The Waltons*** (1972–1981): Easily the sweetest show ever made. There is no better depiction of family values on television. This show wasn't as conservative as people think, but it's still a beautiful illustration of just why the traditional family structure is so necessary. Values points and sympathy points push *The Waltons* high on the list.

6. *Gunsmoke* (1955–1975): This was the archetypal American Western television show, iconic for its quality and its longevity. It was the biggest hit on television for four straight years, and finished in the top ten an incredible thirteen times. John Wayne introduced the first episode. James Arness played Marshal Matt Dillon, the upright sheriff standing up for law and order, unafraid to use a gun to get the black hats. Yes, Arness was a Republican (Lady Bird Johnson was a fan of the show and was disappointed to hear about Arness's political affiliation). High on values, high on sympathy. High on traditional American grit, toughness, and independence. You can't beat Westerns for conservatism.

5. *Dragnet* (1951–1959, 1967–1970): *Dragnet* was based on a simple, conservative premise: Cops are good, criminals are bad, and crime must be punished. Los Angeles Detective Sergeant Joe Friday (Jack Webb) was the hard-nosed and efficient policeman tracking down the bad guys. The show never got its due for its realistic portrayals of crime and detective work. Every show ended with the perpetrator caught and sentenced. The remake of the show from 1967–1970 was decidedly conservative as well, standing up against the hippie idiocy of the period. In one special episode, "The Big High," Friday tracks down two hippie pot smokers, Jean and Paul Shipley, at their home. Friday's partner notices that the Shipleys' child, Robin, isn't in her playpen. They find her floating in the bathtub, drowned. That was *Dragnet* in a nutshell. The show was a reflection of Webb's politics—Webb never bought into the notion that social circumstances and poverty caused crime. The show was uncompromising in its principles—aside from *24*, it's the most conservative depiction of law enforcement ever filmed. Extra points for targeting the counterculture.

4. *Leave It to Beaver* (1957–1963): There's a reason this show is seen as the apotheosis of conservative values on television. Ward and June Cleaver are the near-perfect couple, dispensing wisdom and advice to Beaver and Wally. The boys are innocent, the parents love each other and worry about their children, and everyone is basically happy. The real question isn't why Americans loved this show—the question is why liberals hate this show. The answer: It's wholesome, clean fun and doesn't see suburbia as a prison. It doesn't try to paint the American dream as a nightmare. For the typical Hollywood leftist view of *Leave It to Beaver*, watch *Pleasantville*, which tries to infest the 1950s-era ethos with overt and promiscuous sexuality, injecting color into the black-and-white conservative world. The very top on values and sympathy, *Leave It to Beaver* loses points only because it was one of many conservative shows on television at the time.

3. *Magnum, P.I.* (1980–1988): Don Bellisario is responsible for many of the best conservative shows in television history—*NCIS* and *JAG* among them. The former Marine's biggest accomplishment, however, was the depiction of Thomas Magnum (Tom Selleck), a private investigator and Vietnam veteran. This was the first depiction of a normal Vietnam veteran in years—television had already turned every vet into a PTSD-suffering Rambo type. Selleck was cool and collected. As Bellisario told me, "When I created Magnum, I made them Vietnam vets, and when I wrote them, I decided I'm going to write them as if they had fought in World War II and came home, not Vietnam. Now they had their Vietnam memories, they had their Vietnam flashbacks, they had their delayed stress. But they also were functioning. Functioning normally. And I began to get hundreds and hundreds of letters from Vietnam vets who said, 'Thank God somebody's finally portraying us that we're not all alcoholics, druggies, murderers.' You know, the country blamed the warriors for the war. Big, big mistake. Big mistake. Never blame the warriors for the war."[2] Bellisario helped rectify that mistake. Big values and sympathy Points for *Magnum, P.I.*, and even bigger points for standing up to the strongest meme in TV military history: the meme of the crazy Vietnam vet.

2. *The Cosby Show* (1984–1992): A show about a black middle-class family that doesn't rip the American government, doesn't fall into the self-victimization of the "racist society," doesn't portray whites as either idiots or bigots, and encourages black children to get an education, get married, and have a family. Revolutionary, even if its creators merely meant it to be a statement on racial tolerance.

1. *24* (2001–2009): You knew this would be number one. It is, with one caveat: After season four, the show began to die. The first few seasons, the show was pure conservative adrenaline: Bad guys had to be stopped, and if Jack Bauer had to torture terrorists to do it, he would, no questions asked. "We're running out of time!" was the battle cry—and it was an accurate battle cry. The show embodied the ethic of the War on Terror—we were in a battle for survival, and we didn't always have time for the Marquis of Queensberry rules. "People in the [Bush] administration

love the series," Surnow noted. "It's a patriotic show. They should love it." Then CAIR got involved. The next thing we knew, Janeane Garofalo was on the show and Jack was suffering pangs of conscience over actions he wouldn't have blinked at the year before. It was all downhill from there. But for three and a half glorious seasons, *24* took no prisoners, drew immense ratings, and created groundbreaking television with its stylized cutting and real-time storytelling. Fantastic quality, fantastic conservatism. Too bad the liberals killed it.

RESTORING HOLLYWOOD

One of my goals in this book was to help television save itself. That's a pretty big job for anyone. In truth, only Hollywood can save television. And Hollywood can only save television if they give up their liberal agenda and focus on what they should have been focusing on all along: pleasing the American people, regardless of political viewpoint.

We're the market. All we demand is the drama, the comedy, the pure joy of watching great stories told before our eyes.

Hollywood can do it. I believe in them. But they can only do it with conservative help. They can only do it if they open their minds and their doors. They can only do it if they remember what the founders of television knew in their bones: in the entertainment kingdom, the viewer is king.

Acknowledgments

If *Primetime Propaganda* was a long and enjoyable process, it was only because the gracious, kind, and intelligent people who granted me interviews in Hollywood made it so. Many of them were a window into the history of the industry, and so are not only important for their own career achievements, but as witnesses to a cultural transformation. This is hardly a full list of those with whom I spoke: some wished to remain anonymous, and others provided useful background not directly related to the book itself. Nonetheless, here is a selected list of those who granted full on-the-record interviews.

Thanks to Abby Singer (*Columbo, Remington Steele, Hill Street Blues, Gunsmoke,* among many others); Adam Baldwin (*Chuck*); Allan Burns (*Get Smart, Mary Tyler Moore Show, Room 222, Lou Grant*); Andy Hayward (*Captain Planet, Inspector Gadget*); Barbara Fisher (Lifetime Channel executive, Hallmark Channel Sr. VP of Programming); Bert Prelutsky (*M*A*S*H, Diagnosis Murder*); Bill Bickley (*Family Matters, Perfect Strangers, Happy Days*); Bob Papazian (*The Day After, Rome*); Brandon Stoddard (former president of ABC); Carlton Cuse (*LOST, Nash Bridges*); Chris Chulack (*ER, Southland*); David Shore (*House, Law & Order, Family Law*); Don Bellisario (*NCIS, JAG*); Doug Herzog (President of MTV Networks); Dwight Schulz (*The A-Team*); Earl Hamner (*The Waltons*); Fred Pierce (former president of ABC); Fred Silverman (former VP of programs at CBS, president of ABC and NBC); Gary David Goldberg (*Family Ties, Spin City*); Gene Reynolds (*M*A*S*H, Room 222, Lou Grant*); George Schlatter (*Laugh-In*); Herman Rush (*The Montel Williams Show*); John Langley (*COPS*); Josh Brand (*St. Elsewhere, Northern Exposure*); Lionel Chetwynd (*The Apprenticeship of Duddy Kravitz, The Hanoi Hilton*); Marc Cherry (*Desperate Housewives*); Marcy Carsey (*The Cosby Show, Roseanne, Third Rock from the Sun, That '70s*

Show); Mark Burnett (*Survivor, The Apprentice*); Marta Kauffman (*Friends*); Martin Ransohoff (*The Beverly Hillbillies, Green Acres, Petticoat Junction, The Addams Family*); Michael Brandman (*Jesse Stone*); Michael Moriarty (*Law & Order*); Michele Ganeless (president of Comedy Central); Mike Dann (former president of programming at CBS); Nicholas Meyer (*Star Trek II, Star Trek IV, Star Trek VI, The Day After*); Paul Bogart (*All in the Family*); Peter Mehlman (*Seinfeld*); Robert Davi (*Profiler*); Robert Guza (*General Hospital*); Sandy Grushow (former chairman, Fox Entertainment Group); Susan Harris (*Soap, Golden Girls*); Tom Fontana (*Oz, You Don't Know Jack, St. Elsewhere*); Shelley Reid (Fox Television Studios); Dave Bell (*Unsolved Mysteries*); and Vin DiBona (*America's Funniest Home Videos, MacGyver*). Special thanks to the late Larry Gelbart (*M*A*S*H*), an icon who will be sorely missed, and who was generous enough to grant me not only my first interview for the book, but as far as I know, the last interview before his death. Special thanks as well to Leonard Goldberg (*Charlie's Angels, Blue Bloods*), a class act who took the time to teach TV writing to a nonfiction author with a list of dramatic credits restricted to one play penned during high school. Thanks to the assistants for all these folks, who are generally underpaid, overworked, and incredibly kind.

Thanks to Adam Bellow, an editor par excellence whose guidance throughout this process has deepened and broadened the book significantly. Plus, we always have a fantastic time talking about the global political ramifications of *Star Trek*. Thanks as well to the marketing folks at HarperCollins, whose collaborative efforts make the process pleasurable and blessedly comfortable.

Thanks to Andrew Breitbart, whose contacts in Hollywood would shock Hollywood—if they knew about them. Without his help and guidance, I might still be writing for the UCLA *Daily Bruin*. Thanks to David Limbaugh, one of the few true *mensches* left on planet Earth. And thanks to the Newcombes and Creators Syndicate, who gave an unknown columnist a shot.

Thanks to all the Hollywood conservatives I've met who labor underground to provide us great entertainment, biting their tongues all the while to maintain their employment. Thanks to my liberal Hollywood friends, who shall remain unnamed to protect their careers. Thanks to my parents, who brought me up to recognize the value of both great entertainment and moral righteousness—and who would walk on burning coals to help any of their children chase their dreams—and to my sisters, whose warmth and hilarity are a constant source of fun.

A special thank-you to Abe Greenwald, who came up with a better title for this book in five minutes than I could in almost two years.

Thanks above all to my wife, who pushes me to follow my dreams, even though she's the true dream I've already achieved.

Notes

PROLOGUE

1. James Hibberd, "The Reign of Right-Wing Primetime," *Hollywood Reporter*, Nov. 10, 2010, www.hollywoodreporter.com/blogs/live-feed/right-wing-tv-43558.

INTRODUCTION

1. Robert Kubey and Mihaly Csikszentmihalyi, "Television Addiction Is No Mere Metaphor," ScientificAmerican.com, Feb. 23, 2002.
2. David Brooks, *Bobos in Paradise* (New York: Simon & Schuster, 2000), 67.
3. Ibid., 10–11.
4. Theodor W. Adorno, "How to Look at Television," *Quarterly of Film, Radio and Television* 8, no. 3 (Spring 1954): 213–35.
5. Paul F. Lazarsfeld, "A Researcher Looks at Television," *Public Opinion Quarterly* 24, no. 1 (Spring 1960): 24–31.
6. Newton N. Minow, "Television and the Public Interest," National Association of Broadcasters, May 9, 1961.
7. Interview with Sandy Grushow, Dec. 9, 2009.
8. Interview with Marta Kauffman, June 23, 2009.
9. Interview with Michelle Ganeless, July 6, 2009.
10. Robert B. Putnam, *Bowling Alone: The Collapse and Revival of American Community* (New York: Simon & Schuster, 2000), 231.
11. Interview with Barbara Fisher, July 6, 2009.

THE SECRET POLITICAL HISTORY OF TELEVISION

1. "David Sarnoff: US Media Executive," Museum of Broadcast Communications, www.museum.tv/eotvsection.php?entrycode=sarnoffdavi (accessed Feb. 7, 2010).
2. David Sarnoff, "Turn the Cold War Tide in America's Favor," *Life*, June 6, 1960, 108–18.
3. David Sarnoff, *The Fabulous Future: America in 1980* (New York: Dutton, 1971), 23–25.
4. Mike Brewster, "Bill Paley: Molder of Modern Media," BusinessWeek.com, June 1, 2004.
5. Jeremy Gerard, "William S. Paley, Builder of CBS, Dies at 89," *New York Times*, October 27, 1990.
6. Sally Bedell Smith, *In All His Glory* (New York: Simon & Schuster, 1990).

7. Lee Eisenberg, *Fifty Who Made the Difference* (New York: Esquire, 1984), 222.
8. Smith, *In All His Glory.*
9. Leonard H. Goldenson, *Beating the Odds* (New York: Scribner's, 1991), 177.
10. Ibid., 272–73.
11. Ibid., 398.
12. Ibid., 165–66.
13. James L. Baughman, *Same Time, Same Station* (Baltimore: Johns Hopkins University Press, 2007), 106.
14. Sylvester L. (Pat) Weaver, "Minute Inspection of Our World Via Science Wonders Lies Ahead for TV," *Billboard*, Dec. 1, 1951.
15. Ibid., 85, 87, 98.
16. Holcomb B. Noble, "Frank Stanton, Broadcasting Pioneer, Dies at 98," *New York Times*, Dec. 25, 2006.
17. Noralee Frankel, *Stripping Gypsy: The Life of Gypsy Rose Lee* (New York: Oxford University Press, 2009), 176.
18. "Television: The Many-Splendored Thing," *Time*, May 25, 1962.
19. Goldenson, *Beating the Odds*, 149.
20. Baughman, *Same Time, Same Station*, 52.
21. Ibid., 1.
22. Ibid., 2.
23. Larry Gelbart, *Laughing Matters* (New York: Random House, 1998), 182–83.
24. "Ollie Treyz Due for ABC's Presidency," *Billboard*, Oct. 28, 1957.
25. Tim Brooks and Earle Marsh, *The Complete Directory to Prime Time Network and Cable TV Shows* (New York: Ballantine, 2007), 1458.
26. Huntington Williams, *Beyond Control: ABC and the Fate of the Networks* (New York: Atheneum, 1989), 48.
27. Allan Neuwirth, *They'll Never Put That on the Air* (New York: Allworth Press, 2006), 128.
28. Interview with Leonard Goldberg, May 20, 2009.
29. Richard Oulahan and William Lambert, "The Tyrant's Fall That Rocked the TV World," *Life*, Sept. 10, 1965.
30. "*The Defenders*," Museum of Broadcast Communications, www.museum.tv/eotvsection.php?entrycode=defendersth.
31. Oulahan and Lambert, "Tyrant's Fall."
32. Interview with Martin Ransohoff, May 19, 2009.
33. Ibid.
34. Interview with Mike Dann, May 21, 2009.
35. Michael Dann, *As I Saw It: The Inside Story of the Golden Years of Television* (El Prado, NM: Levine Mesa Press, 2009), 77.
36. Larry Gelbart, *Laughing Matters* (New York: Random House, 1998), 114, 119.
37. David Halberstam, *The Powers That Be* (New York: Knopf, 1975), 252.
38. Grant Tinker, *Tinker in Television* (New York: Simon & Schuster, 1994), 71–72.
39. "Robert Kintner," Museum of Broadcast Communications, www.museum.tv/eotvsection.php?entrycode=kintnerrobe.
40. Jack Gould, "Robert Edmonds Kintner: The Man From NBC," *New York Times*, Oct 24, 1965.
41. "Robert Kintner," Museum of Broadcast Communications.
42. "Iraq Versus Vietnam: A Comparison of Public Opinion," Gallup.com, Aug. 24, 2005, www.gallup.com/poll/18097/Iraq-Versus-Vietnam-Comparison-Public-Opinion.aspx.

43. Interview with Fred Pierce, May 11, 2009.
44. Goldenson, *Beating the Odds*, 330.
45. Interview with Leonard Goldberg, May 20, 2009.
46. Charles Isherwood, "Changing Channels," *Advocate*, Feb. 18, 1997.
47. Todd Gitlin, *Inside Prime Time* (New York: Pantheon, 1983), 43–44.
48. Dann, *As I Saw It*, 148.
49. Ibid., 149.
50. Smith, *In All His Glory*, 494.
51. Ibid.
52. Interview with Fred Silverman, May 11, 2009.
53. Neuwirth, *They'll Never Put That On The Air*, 133–34.
54. Herbert S. Schlosser, "Speech: Responsibility and Freedom in Television," speech to the Association of National Advertisers, Oct. 29, 1974.
55. Interview with Allan Burns, May 26, 2009.
56. Ibid.
57. Interview with Gene Reynolds, May 7, 2009.
58. Interview with Fred Silverman, May 11, 2009.
59. Elana Levine, *Wallowing in Sex* (Durham, NC: Duke University Press, 2007), 54.
60. Interview with Marcy Carsey, July 1, 2009.
61. "Behind the Purge at CBS," *Time*, Oct. 25, 1976.
62. "Television: NBC: Headdie for Freddie," *Time*, Jan. 30, 1978.
63. Ibid.
64. Interview with Fred Silverman, May 11, 2009.
65. Interview with Michael Brandman, June 8, 2009.
66. Ibid.
67. Alan Axelrod, *Profiles in Audacity: Great Decisions and How They Were Made* (New York: Sterling, 2006), 120–24.
68. Robert Pittman, "The Man Behind the Monster," *Los Angeles Times*, July 28, 1991.
69. Ibid.
70. Ibid., 51.
71. Interview with Doug Herzog, June 22, 2009.
72. Ibid.
73. Interview with Don Bellisario, June 10, 2009.
74. Interview with Brandon Stoddard, May 28, 2009.
75. Interview with Joshua Brand, May 11, 2009.
76. Grant Tinker, *Tinker in Television* (New York: Simon & Schuster, 1994).
77. Robert Kubey, *Television and the Quality of Life* (Mahwah, NJ: Lawrence Erlbaum, 1990), 187.
78. Ibid., 103.
79. Brandon Tartikoff with Charles Leerhsen, *The Last Great Ride* (New York: Turtle Bay Books, 1992), 164–65, 170.
80. Ibid., 183.
81. Andrew Walker, "Rupert Murdoch: Bigger Than Kane," BBC News, July 31, 2001, http://news.bbc.co.uk/2/hi/uk_news/2162658.stm.
82. "Fox Broadcasting Company," Museum of Broadcast Communications, www.museum.tv/eotvsection.php?entrycode=foxbroadcast.
83. Interview with Sandy Grushow, Dec. 9, 2009.
84. "Storm on Temptation Island," BBC.co.uk, Jan. 10, 2001.
85. "The Financial Interest and Syndication Rules," Museum of Broadcast

Communications, www.museum.tv/eotvsection.php?entrycode=financialint.

86. Michael Moore and Kathleen Glynn, *Adventures in a TV Nation* (New York: HarperCollins, 1998), 4–5.
87. http://thomas.loc.gov/cgi-bin/query/z?c103:H.J.RES.365.
88. Edwin Diamond, "The Tisch Touch," *New York*, May 26, 1986.
89. Edwin Diamond, "Television's New Fall Lineup," *New York*, Aug. 22, 1988.
90. Thomas C. Reeves, *The Empty Church: Does Organized Religion Matter Anymore* (New York: Simon & Schuster, 1996), 48.
91. Richard Zoglin, Jordan Bonfante, and Martha Smilgis, "Sitcom Politics," *Time*, Sept. 21, 1992.
92. James P. Steyer, *The Other Parent: The Inside Story of the Media's Effect on Our Children* (New York: Atria Books, 2002), 80.
93. Mark Hertsgaard, *The Eagle's Shadow: Why America Fascinates and Infuriates the World* (New York: St. Martin's, 2002), 93.
94. "ABC says *Ellen* Cancelled Because Weekly Focus on Homosexuality Led to 'Sameness,'" *Seattle Post-Intelligencer*, May 6, 1998.
95. Statement of Robert A. Iger, *In the Matter of the Evaluation of the Syndication and Financial Interest Rules*, MM Docket No. 90-162, En Banc Hearing, Dec. 14, 1990, 3–4.
96. Horace Newcomb, ed., *Encyclopedia of Television* (New York: Taylor & Francis, 2004), 1166.
97. "The Ratings Game," *NewsHour with Jim Lehrer* transcript, July 29, 1999, www.pbs.org/newshour/bb/media/july-dec99/ratings_7-29.html.
98. Interview with Mark Burnett, May 11, 2009.
99. Interview with Marc Cherry, August 9, 2009.
100. Bill Carter, *Desperate Networks* (New York: Doubleday, 2006), 145, 150.

THE CLIQUE

1. Anna Deavere Smith, *Twilight: Los Angeles, 1992* (New York: Dramatists Play Service, 2003), 78–79.
2. Todd Gitlin, *Inside Prime Time* (New York: Pantheon, 1983), 115.
3. Interview with Larry Gelbart, Apr. 20, 2009.
4. Interview with Susan Harris, May 4, 2009.
5. Interview with Abby Singer, Apr. 28, 2009.
6. Interview with Andy Heyward, June 12, 2009.
7. Interview with Chris Chulack, May 21, 2009.
8. Interview with Michael Brandman, June 8, 2009.
9. Interview with Carlton Cuse, May 12, 2009.
10. Interview with Michael Nankin, June 3, 2009.
11. Gitlin, *Inside Prime Time*, 135.
12. "Writers Guild of America," *New York Times*, Nov. 5, 2007, http://topics.nytimes.com/topics/reference/timestopics/organizations/w/writers_guild_of_america/index.html.
13. Shirley Brady, "How Ben Silverman Got Started," Cable360.net, May 30, 2007.
14. Ibid.
15. Nikki Finke, "Ben Silverman Is Breaking All the Rules," DeadlineHollywood.com, June 15, 2007.
16. "NBC's 2007–2008 Primetime Schedule Heavy on Sci-Fi," TVJots.com, May 14, 2007, http://tvjots.com/nbcs-2007-2008-primetime-schedule-heavy.

17. Josef Adalian, "Full NBC Schedule Takes Shape," Variety.com, Apr. 2, 2008.
18. Erica Orden, "Just Hired!" *New York*, Aug 23, 2009.
19. Interview with Peter Mehlman, May 12, 2009.
20. Belinda Luscombe, "Ben Silverman Leaves NBC: Exit the No-Hit Hitmaker," Time.com, July 28, 2009.
21. Tanny Stransky, "Ben Silverman Exit: New NBC Honcho Jeff Gaspin Says No Big Changes Afoot," EW.com, July 28, 2009.
22. Bill Carter, *Desperate Networks* (New York: Doubleday, 2006), 260–61, 324.
23. Nellie Andreeva, "ABC Greenlights *Family, Freshman*," HollywoodReporter.com, Jan. 25, 2010.
24. Interview with Fred Silverman, May 11, 2009.
25. Interview with Vin DiBona, June 11, 2009.
26. Interview with Nicholas Meyer, June 17, 2010.
27. Paul Bond, "Republicans in Biz Feel Stifled, Bullied," HollywoodReporter.com, Oct. 20, 2008.
28. Interview with Fred Pierce, May 11, 2009.
29. Interview with Leonard Goldberg, May 20, 2009.
30. Interview with David Shore, June 24, 2009.
31. Interview with Barbara Fisher, July 6, 2009.
32. Interview with Tom Fontana, Aug. 6, 2009.
33. Interview with Marcy Carsey, July 1, 2009.
34. Interview with Michelle Ganeless, July 6, 2009.
35. Interview with Michael Brandman, June 8, 2009.
36. Interview with Herman Rush, June 22, 2009.
37. Mark Harris, "Mark Harris on TV Comedy," EW.com, Apr. 2, 2010.
38. Rick Egusquiza, "Kathy Griffin 'Gay Bashes' Patricia Heaton," NationalEnquirer.com, Dec. 26, 2006.
39. Paul Bond, "Republicans in Biz Feel Stifled, Bullied," HollywoodReporter.com, Oct. 20, 2008.
40. John Nolte, "How the Blacklist Works: Nikki Finke Twists Andrew Klavan's Words," BigHollywood.breitbart.com, Apr. 29, 2010.
41. Gary Graham, "Is There a Hollywood Blacklist?" BigHollywood.breitbart.com, May 3, 2010.
42. Dan Gifford, "Yes, There Is a Hollywood Blacklist," BigHollywood.breitbart.com, May 17, 2010.
43. Interview with Burt Prelutsky, Jan. 26, 2010.
44. Michael Moriarty, *The Gift of Stern Angels* (Toronto: Evergrowth Publishing, 1996), 258.
45. Shauna Snow, "Morning Report," *Los Angeles Times*, May 4, 1995.
46. Interview with Michael Moriarty, May 6, 2010.
47. Interview with Dwight Schultz, Apr. 6, 2009.
48. Dwight Schultz, "The Liberal Bastille," BigHollywood.breitbart.com, Mar. 16, 2009.
49. Interview with Dwight Schultz, Apr. 6, 2009.
50. Interview with Michael Nankin, June 3, 2009.
51. Interview with Allan Burns, May 26, 2009.
52. Interview with Barbara Fisher, July 6, 2009.
53. Interview with Robert Davi, Apr. 3, 2009.
54. Ibid.
55. Interview with Adam Baldwin, Jan. 26, 2010.

56. Interview with Don Bellisario, June 10, 2009.
57. Interview with Marc Cherry, Aug. 9, 2009.
58. Patrick Goldstein, "'Tea Party' Troubadour Says: 'In Hollywood, Being a Conservative Is the Kiss of Death," LATimes.com, May 18, 2010.
59. Patrick Goldstein, "Will Barack Obama Make Hollywood More Colorblind?" LA Times.com, Jan. 19, 2009.
60. Patrick Goldstein, "Universal's New Black Eye: African American Actors Disappear from 'Couples Retreat' Poster," LATimes.com, Nov. 17, 2009.
61. Richard Verrier, "Hollywood Writers' Age-Discrimination Case Settled," LATimes.com, Jan. 23, 2010.
62. Burt Prelutsky, "Book Excerpt: Hollywood's Age Discrimination," BigHollywood.breitbart.com, Mar. 2, 2010.
63. Interview with Tom Fontana, Aug. 6, 2009.
64. Interview with Susan Harris, May 4, 2009.
65. Interview with Chris Chulack, May 21, 2009.
66. Interview with Gene Reynolds, May 7, 2009.
67. Interview with Fred Silverman, May 11, 2009.
68. Interview with Gary David Goldberg, May 19, 2009.
69. Interview with Barbara Fisher, July 6, 2009.
70. Interview with Marc Cherry, Aug. 9, 2009.
71. Interview with Leonard Stern, May 26, 2009.
72. Interview with Michael Brandman, June 8, 2009.
73. Interview with Herman Rush, June 22, 2009.
74. Brandon Tartikoff with Charles Leerhsen, *The Last Great Ride* (New York: Turtle Bay Books, 1992), 24–25.
75. Amelia Atlas, "Teen Sex on ABC Family Sparks Debate," Newser.com, Feb. 1, 2009.
76. Interview with Susan Harris, May 4, 2009.
77. Interview with Fred Silverman, May 11, 2009.
78. Interview with Josh Brand, May 11, 2009.
79. Interview with Robert Guza, June 18, 2009.
80. Interview with Marcy Carsey, July 1, 2009.
81. Interview with Michelle Ganeless, July 6, 2009.
82. Interview with Marc Cherry, Aug. 9, 2009.
83. Interview with David Shore, June 24, 2009.
84. Interview with Barbara Fisher, July 6, 2009.

A SPOONFUL OF SUGAR

1. Allan Neuwirth, *They'll Never Put That on the Air* (New York: Allworth Press, 2006), 5.
2. Stephen E. Kercher, *Revel with a Cause: Liberal Satire in Postwar America* (Chicago: U. of Chicago Press, 2006), 94.
3. Larry Gelbart, *Laughing Matters* (New York: Random House, 1998), 113.
4. Ibid., 21.
5. Sid Caesar, *Where Have I Been?* (New York: Crown, 1982), 39–40.
6. Ibid., 88.
7. Gelbart, *Laughing Matters*, 23–24.
8. Interview with Leonard Stern, May 26, 2009.
9. James L. Baughman, *Same Time, Same Station* (Baltimore: Johns Hopkins University Press, 2007), 136.

10. "Carl Reiner—Archive Interview Part 1," Archive of American Television, http://www.emmytvlegends.org/interviews/people/carl-reiner.
11. Carl Reiner, *My Anecdotal Life: A Memoir* (New York: St. Martin's Griffin, 2004), 230–31.
12. Ginny Weissman and Coyne Steven Sanders, *The Dick Van Dyke Show* (New York: Macmillan, 1993), 63–65.
13. Mary Tyler Moore, *After All* (New York: Putnam's, 1995), 86.
14. Neuwirth, *They'll Never Put That on the Air*, 14.
15. Ibid., 17.
16. Caesar, *Where Have I Been?*, 92–93.
17. Patrick Kevin Day, "Q&A with Mel Brooks," LATimes.com, May 19, 2008.
18. Wesley Alan Britton, *Beyond Bond: Spies in Fiction and Film* (Westport, CT: Greenwood, 2005), 118.
19. Michael Kackman, *Citizen Spy: Television, Espionage, and Cold War Culture* (Minneapolis: University of Minnesota Press, 2005), 99.
20. Interview with Leonard Stern, May 26, 2009.
21. Interview with Allan Burns, May 26, 2009.
22. Interview with Leonard Stern, May 26, 2009.
23. Ibid.
24. Ibid.
25. Interview with Allan Burns, May 26, 2009.
26. Neuwirth, *They'll Never Put That on the Air*, 33–35.
27. Ibid., 33–46.
28. Lynn Spigel and Michael Curtin, *The Revolution Wasn't Televised* (New York: Routledge, 1997), 205.
29. Ibid., 52.
30. Gerald C. Gardner, *Campaign Comedy: Political Humor from Clinton to Kennedy* (Detroit: Wayne State University Press, 1989), 221.
31. Interview with Mike Dann, May 21, 2009.
32. Interview with George Schlatter, Apr. 21, 2009.
33. Interview with Gene Reynolds, May 7, 2009.
34. "James L. Brooks—Archive Interview Part 2," Archive of American Television, www.emmytvlegends.org/interviews/people/james-l-brooks.
35. Interview with Gene Reynolds, May 7, 2009.
36. Interview with Allan Burns, May 26, 2009.
37. Interview with Gene Reynolds, May 7, 2009.
38. Ken Bloom and Frank Vlastnik, *Sitcoms: The 101 Greatest TV Comedies of All Time* (London: Black Dog Publishing, 2007), 19.
39. Gelbart, *Laughing Matters*, 117.
40. "Norman Lear—Archive Interview Part 7 of 10," Archive of American Television, Feb. 26, 1998, www.emmytvlegends.org/interviews/people/norman-lear.
41. Carroll O'Connor, *I Think I'm Outta Here* (New York: Pocket Books, 1998), 75–76.
42. Ann Coulter, "Working Families from Malibu to East Hampton," Townhall.com, Aug. 2, 2002.
43. *Real Time with Bill Maher*, HBO, Oct. 22, 2010.
44. Interview with Paul Bogart, May 21, 2009.
45. Neuwirth, *They'll Never Put That on the Air* (New York: Allworth Press, 2006), 154.
46. "About Norman Lear," LearCenter.org, www.learcenter.org/html/about/?cm=lear.
47. Interview with Allan Burns, May 26, 2009.
48. Ben Stein, *The View from Sunset Boulevard* (New York: Basic Books, 1979).

49. "James L. Brooks," Archive of American Television, Jan. 17, 2003, www.emmytv legends.org/interviews/people/james-l-brooks.
50. David Manning White, *Popular Culture* (New York: New York Times, 1975), 311.
51. Grant Tinker, *Tinker in Television* (New York: Simon & Schuster, 1994), 94–95.
52. Interview with Allan Burns, May 26, 2009.
53. Neuwirth, *They'll Never Put That on the Air*, 114–15.
54. Moore, *After All*, 69–70.
55. Joe Flint, "Super Bowl XLIV Game a Ratings Winner," *Los Angeles Times*, Feb. 9, 2010.
56. Gelbart, *Laughing Matters*, 31.
57. Interview with Gene Reynolds, May 7, 2009.
58. Ibid.
59. "Alda, Alan," Museum of Broadcast Communications, www.museum.tv/eotv section.php?entrycode=aldaalan.
60. Interview with Gene Reynolds, May 7, 2009.
61. Interview with Larry Gelbart, Apr. 20, 2009.
62. Gelbart, *Laughing Matters*, 31–32.
63. Ibid., 36.
64. Interview with Gene Reynolds, May 7, 2009.
65. Gelbart, *Laughing Matters*, 55–57.
66. Interview with Larry Gelbart, Apr. 20, 2009.
67. Stein, *View from Sunset Boulevard*, 19, 24, 70, 119.
68. "Hollywood Comedy Stars Release Four Pro-Obama Videos," JewishJournal.com, Oct. 22, 2008, www.jewishjournal.com/bloggish/item/hollywood_comedy_stars_release_four_pro_obama_videos_20081022.
69. "Proust Questionnaire: Penny Marshall," *Vanity Fair*, May 2007. http://www.vanity fair.com/culture/features/2007/05/proust_marshall200705
70. Elana Levine, *Wallowing in Sex* (Durham, NC: Duke University Press, 2007), 179.
71. Interview with Bill Bickley, June 11, 2009.
72. Levine, *Wallowing in Sex*, 197.
73. Interview with Fred Silverman, May 11, 2009.
74. Kirsten Fermaglich, "Bea Arthur," *Jewish Women: A Comprehensive Historical Encyclopedia*, JWA.org, http://jwa.org/encyclopedia/article/arthur-bea.
75. Interview with Susan Harris, May 4, 2009.
76. Dennis Ayers, "Billy Crystal's Place in Gay Pop Culture History," AfterElton.com, Oct. 12, 2007, www.afterelton.com/blog/dennis/Billy-Crystals-place-in-gay-pop-culture-history.
77. Leonard H. Goldenson, *Beating the Odds* (New York: Scribner's, 1991), 367–68.
78. Interview with Marcy Carsey, July 1, 2009.
79. Interview with Fred Silverman, May 11, 2009.
80. Interview with Susan Harris, May 4, 2009.
81. David Bianculli, *Teleliteracy: Taking Television Seriously* (New York: Continuum, 2000), 283.
82. Susan Faludi, *Backlash: The Undeclared War Against American Women* (New York: Three Rivers Press, 1991), 157.
83. Ken Levine, "The *Cheers* Episode I'm Still Writing in My Head," KenLevine.blogspot.com, July 21, 2008, http://kenlevine.blogspot.com/2008/07/cheers-episode-im-still-writing-in-my.html.
84. Bianculli, *Teleliteracy*, 266.
85. Interview with Gary David Goldberg, May 19, 2009.

86. Interview with Marcy Carsey, July 1, 2009.
87. Brandon Tartikoff with Charles Leerhsen, *The Last Great Ride* (New York: Turtle Bay Books, 1992), 17–18.
88. Darrell Y. Hamamoto, *Nervous Laughter* (New York: Praeger, 1989), 136.
89. Tartikoff with Leerhsen, *Last Great Ride*, 16–17.
90. Michael Eric Dyson, *Is Bill Cosby Right?* (New York: Basic Civitas Books, 2005), 2–3.
91. Interview with Marcy Carsey, July 1, 2009.
92. Ibid.
93. Ibid.
94. Interview with Brandon Stoddard, May 28, 2009.
95. Louis Chunovic, *One Foot on the Floor* (New York: TV Books, 2000), 111.
96. Robert Kubey, *Creating Television* (Mahwah, NJ: Lawrence Erlbaum, 2004), 139, 146.
97. Brian Doherty, "Matt Groening," *Mother Jones*, Mar.–Apr. 1999.
98. Mark I. Pinsky, *The Gospel According to the Simpsons* (Louisville, KY: Westminster John Knox Press, 2007), 6.
99. Chris Turner, *Planet Simpson: How a Cartoon Masterpiece Defined a Generation* (New York: Da Capo Press, 2005), 223.
100. Interview with Sandy Grushow, Dec. 9, 2009.
101. Kubey, *Creating Television*, 147.
102. Bonnie J. Dow, *Prime-Time Feminism* (Philadelphia: University of Pennsylvania Press, 1996), 154.
103. Dan Quayle, "Address to the Commonwealth Club of California," May 19, 1992, www.vicepresidentdanquayle.com/speeches_StandingFirm_CCC_3.html.
104. Dow, *Prime-Time Feminism*, 154–55.
105. Janet McCabe and Kim Akass, *Quality TV: Contemporary American Television and Beyond* (New York: I. B. Tauris, 2007), 59.
106. David Blankenhorn, *Fatherless America* (New York: Basic Books, 1995), 69.
107. Charles Murray, "When It Comes to Illegitimacy, We're Living in Separate Worlds: An Update on the White Underclass," Blog.American.com, May 14, 2009, http://blog.american.com/?p=714.
108. Stephen M. Silverman, "Candice Bergen Agrees with Dan Quayle," People.com, July 11, 2002, www.people.com/people/article/0,,624379,00.html.
109. Alan Carter, "The Essential 'Murphy Brown' Interview," *Entertainment Weekly*, May 15, 1992.
110. Larry David, "The Roving Thoughts of a Liberal Insomniac," HuffingtonPost.com, June 28, 2005.
111. Interview with Peter Mehlman, May 12, 2009.
112. Interview with Marta Kauffman, June 23, 2009.
113. Interview with Barbara Fisher, July 6, 2009.
114. Interview with Marta Kauffman, June 23, 2009.
115. Interview with Peter Mehlman, May 12, 2009.
116. Steven Capsuto, *Alternate Channels* (New York: Ballantine, 2000).
117. "Family Outings," *Advocate*, May 30, 1995.
118. Interview with Marta Kauffman, June 23, 2009.
119. Malinda Lo, "Back in the Day: Coming Out with Ellen," AfterEllen.com, Apr. 9, 2005.
120. Richard Natale, "Will Power," *Advocate*, Sept. 15, 1998.
121. James Hillis, "Interview with *Will & Grace*'s Max Mutchnick," AfterElton.com, Mar. 5, 2008.
122. "Q&A: Willie Garson," *Out*, June 2000.

123. Jaime J. Weinman, "The Macleans.ca Interview: Darren Star," Macleans.ca, Apr. 17, 2008.
124. "Interview with Darren Star," *CNN Live Today*, July 17, 2002, http://transcripts.cnn.com/TRANSCRIPTS/0207/17/lt.06.html.
125. "Samantha Jones: Character Bio," HBO.com, www.hbo.com/sex-and-the-city/index.html#/sex-and-the-city/cast-and-crew/samantha-jones/bio/samantha-jones.html.
126. Katey Rich, "Interview: *Sex and the City* Creator and Cast on the Show's Legacy," CinemaBlend.com, May 28, 2010.
127. "Seth MacFarlane," Maxim.com, Sept. 25, 2009.
128. Amy Wallace, "Seth MacFarlane Sounds Off," Details.com, Aug. 2010.
129. Brandon Voss, "BGF: Seth MacFarlane," *Advocate*, Feb.–Mar. 2008.
130. Amy Wallace, "Seth MacFarlane Sounds Off."
131. Brandon Voss, "BGF: Seth MacFarlane."
132. Richard Lawson, "The Most Conservative and Most Liberal Shows on TV," Gawker.com, http://gawker.com/5063314/the-most-conservative-and-most-liberal-shows-on-tv.
133. Lynette Rice, "It Hurts to Laugh," EW.com, Jan. 8, 2007.
134. Nick Juliano, "CBS Sitcom Takes Stealthy Swipe at Fox News," RawStory.com, Oct. 14, 2008.
135. "Tina Fey," Believermag.com, Nov. 2003, www.believermag.com/issues/200311/?read=interview_fey.
136. "Tina Fey on Sarah Palin: 'If She Wins . . . I'm Leaving Earth," HuffingtonPost.com, Oct. 13, 2008.
137. "PBS Weeds Out Tina Fey's Sarah Palin Jokes," Gawker.com, Nov. 16, 2010, http://gawker.com/5691590/pbs-weeds-out-tina-feys-sarah-palin-jokes.

MAKING THE RIGHT CRY

1. Aaron Spelling, *A Prime-Time Life* (New York: St. Martin's, 1996), 3.
2. Ibid., 8.
3. Ibid., 44.
4. Ibid., 36–37.
5. Ibid., 44.
6. Beringia Zen, "Rod Serling," Unitarian Universalist Historical Society, www25.uua.org/uuhs/duub/articles/rodserling.html.
7. Jack Gould, "*Playhouse 90* Gets Under Way with Story About Red Spies, Sneak Attack," *New York Times*, Oct. 5, 1956.
8. Ken Tucker, "Rod Serling: Submitted for Your Approval," *Entertainment Weekly*, Dec. 1, 1995.
9. "Controversy at Moorpark College," RodSerling.com, www.rodserling.com/JMmp-68speech.htm.
10. Karen Anijar, *Teaching Toward the 24th Century: Star Trek as Social Curriculum* (New York: Falmer Press, 2000), 77–79.
11. Brannon Braga, "Every Religion Has a Mythology," International Atheist Conference in Reykjavik, Iceland, June 24 and 25, 2006.
12. James Lileks, "A Conservative Trek," NationalReview.com, Sept. 28, 2007, www.nationalreview.com/articles/222332/conservative-trek/james-lileks#.
13. Nichelle Nichols, *Beyond Uhura: Star Trek and Other Memories* (New York: Putnam, 1994), 196.

14. Daniel Bernardi, *"Star Trek" and History Race-ing Toward a White Future* (New Brunswick, NJ: Rutgers University Press, 1999), 37.
15. Anijar, *Teaching Toward the 24th Century*, 79.
16. Spelling, *Prime-Time Life*, 62–63.
17. Leonard H. Goldenson, *Beating the Odds* (New York: Scribner's, 1991), 324.
18. Spelling, *Prime-Time Life*, 68.
19. Ibid., 65.
20. Ibid., 66–67.
21. Ibid.
22. Kubey, *Creating Television*, 103.
23. Interview with Fred Silverman, May 11, 2009.
24. Interview with Leonard Goldberg, May 20, 2009.
25. Spelling, *Prime-Time Life*, 115.
26. Interview with Leonard Goldberg, May 20, 2009.
27. Spelling, *Prime-Time Life*, 109.
28. Interview with Fred Silverman, May 11, 2009.
29. Interview with Leonard Goldberg, May 20, 2009.
30. Elana Levine, *Wallowing in Sex* (Durham, NC: Duke University Press, 2007), 154.
31. Spelling, *Prime-Time Life*, 110.
32. Ibid., 156.
33. Ibid., 174–75.
34. YouTube.com, "Ed Asner's Message to the 9/11 Truth Movement," International Citizens Inquiry Into 9/11, May 25, 2004, www.youtube.com/watch?v=8dVNDQWhtMc.
35. Interview with Allan Burns, May 26, 2009.
36. Grant Tinker, *Tinker in Television* (New York: Simon & Schuster, 1994), 118.
37. Pete Hamill, "What Does Lou Grant Know About El Salvador?" *New York*, Mar. 15, 1982.
38. Kubey, *Creating Television*, 307.
39. Interview with Fred Silverman, May 11, 2009.
40. Todd Gitlin, *Inside Prime Time* (New York: Pantheon, 1983), 308.
41. Ibid., 306–10.
42. Steven Bochco, "Producer Offers a Prescription for What Ails Network Television," *Los Angeles Times*, Sept. 8, 1992.
43. Interview with Fred Silverman, May 11, 2009.
44. Interview with Joshua Brand, May 11, 2009.
45. Interview with Tom Fontana, Aug. 6, 2009.
46. Goldenson, *Beating the Odds*, 447.
47. Interview with Brandon Stoddard, May 28, 2009.
48. Beth A. Fischer, *The Reagan Reversal: Foreign Policy and the End of the Cold War* (Columbia: University of Missouri Press, 1997), 115–16.
49. Interview with Robert Papazian, June 8, 2010.
50. Interview with Lionel Chetwynd, May 28, 2009.
51. Interview with Nicholas Meyer, June 17, 2010.
52. Fischer, *Reagan Reversal*, 119–20.
53. Jon Niccum, "Fallout from *The Day After*," Lawrence.com, Nov. 19, 2003.
54. Interview with Brandon Stoddard, May 28, 2009.
55. "The Man Behind MacGyver: Swiss Army Knife or Duct Tape?" Lifehacker.com, http://lifehacker.com/5480477/the-man-behind-macgyver-swiss-army-knife-or-duct-tape.

56. Interview with Vin DiBona, June 11, 2009.
57. Ibid.
58. Kubey, *Creating Television*, 155.
59. "Thirtysomething," *Playboy*, June 1990.
60. Lynette Rice, "David E. Kelley Talks Life After 'Boston Legal,'" Hollywoodinsider.ew.com, Oct. 29, 2008.
61. Malinda Lo, "Back in the Day: The Kiss Heard Around the World," AfterEllen.com, Mar. 2005.
62. Interview with Sandy Grushow, Sept. 9, 2009.
63. Interview with Larry Gelbart, Apr. 20, 2009.
64. Interview with Allan Burns, May 26, 2009.
65. Interview with Vin DiBona, June 11, 2009.
66. Rob Owen, "*Boston Legal*'s Kelley Delivers Parting Shots," Post-Gazette.com, Dec. 7, 2008.
67. Jim Halterman, "Interview: Dick Wolf, Sam Waterston on *Law & Order* Turning 19," TheFutonCritic.com, Nov. 5, 2008.
68. Interview with Michael Moriarty, May 6, 2010.
69. Rebecca Dana, "Law and Disorder," *Wall Street Journal*, July 12, 2008.
70. James Hibberd, "O'Reilly Slams 'Law & Order,' Calls Wolf 'Despicable,'" HollywoodReporter.com, Dec. 11, 2009.
71. John Nolte, "dun DUN; Rene Balcer Murdered *Law & Order*," BigHollywood.breitbart.com, Oct. 1, 2010.
72. Adam Serwer, "The Television Justice System," Prospect.org, May 28, 2010.
73. Larry O'Connor, "Teaching the Pig to Dance: Fred Thompson Opens Up About Life, Politics, and *Law and Order*," BigGovernment.com, May 27, 2010.
74. Interview with Michael Moriarty, May 6, 2010.
75. Noel Sheppard, "Laura Ingraham Takes On CSI Creator over Tea Party Bashing Episode," Newsbusters.org, Oct. 14, 2010, www.newsbusters.org/blogs/noel-sheppard/2010/10/14/laura-ingraham-takes-csi-creator-over-tea-party-bashing-episode.
76. Interview with John Langley, May 8, 2009.
77. Interview with Doug Herzog, June 22, 2009.
78. George J. Annas, "Sex, Money, and Bioethics: Watching *ER* and *Chicago Hope*," *Hastings Center Report* 25, no. 5 (1995): 40–43.
79. Ben Feller, "Obama Pleads to Voters: 'Don't Give in to Fear,'" Associated Press, Aug. 16, 2010.
80. Interview with Chris Chulack, May 21, 2009.
81. John Levasque, "Aaron Sorkin Is a Man of Many Words," *Seattle Post-Intelligencer*, Mar. 7, 2000.
82. Peter C. Rollins, John E. O'Connor, *The West Wing: The American Presidency as Television Drama* (Syracuse, NY: Syracuse University Press, 2003), 225.
83. Matthew Miller, "The Real White House," *Brill's Content*, Mar. 2000.
84. "Aaron Sorkin," *NewsHour with Jim Lehrer* transcript, Sept. 27, 2000.
85. Mark Sachleben and Kevan M. Yenerall, *Seeing the Bigger Picture* (New York: Peter Lang, 2008), 26.
86. Interview with Marc Cherry, Aug. 9, 2009.
87. "Laura Bush: First Lady of Comedy?," USAToday.com, May 1, 2005, www.usatoday.com/life/people/2005-05-01-laura-bush-comments_x.htm.
88. Mikey O'Connor, "The Humanist: Shonda Rhimes Hones In on Ethical, Moral Grey Areas," TVGuide.com, Dec. 7, 2009.

89. Aldore Collier, "Shonda Rhimes: The Force Behind *Grey's Anatomy*," *Ebony*, Oct. 2005.
90. Jackie Tithof Steere, "QA with Ian Brennan, Creator of the Hit TV Series *Glee*," Chicagonow.com, May 5, 2010.
91. Charles Winecoff, "Dear Ryan Murphy: Does the 'T' in LGBT Stand for 'Typecast' or 'Totalitarian'?" Bighollywood.breitbart.com, June 18, 2010.
92. "*Glee* Creator Ryan Murphy Q&A," StarPulse.com, Aug. 4, 2010.

"SHUT UP AND CHANGE THE CHANNEL"

1. Interview with George Schlatter, Apr. 21, 2009.
2. Interview with Larry Gelbart, Apr. 20, 2009.
3. Interview with Susan Harris, May 4, 2009.
4. Interview with Gary David Goldberg, May 19, 2009.
5. Interview with Fred Pierce, May 11, 2009.
6. Interview with Brandon Stoddard, May 28, 2009.
7. Interview with Larry Gelbart, Apr. 20, 2009.
8. Interview with Joshua Brand, May 11, 2009.
9. Interview with Larry Gelbart, Apr. 20, 2009.
10. Robert Kubey, *Creating Television* (Mahwah, NJ: Lawrence Erlbaum, 2004), 102.
11. Interview with Marta Kauffman, June 23, 2009.
12. Jim Halterman, "Interview: 'Secret Diary of a Call Girl' Star Billie Piper," TheFuton-Critic.com, Feb. 1, 2010.
13. Norman Lear, "Statement to the Senate Subcommittee on Constitutional Rights," Feb. 8, 1972, www.normanlear.com/backstory_speeches.html.
14. Lisa Robinson, "Mr. MTV," *Spin*, Jan. 1992.
15. Interview with Sandy Grushow, Dec. 9, 2009.
16. Interview with George Schlatter, Apr. 21, 2009.
17. Interview with Larry Gelbart, Apr. 20, 2009.
18. Interview with Gene Reynolds, May 7, 2009.
19. Interview with Susan Harris, May 4, 2009.
20. Interview with Peter Mehlman, May 12, 2009.
21. Interview with Joshua Brand, May 11, 2009.
22. Interview with Gary David Goldberg, May 19, 2009.
23. Interview with Chris Chulack, May 21, 2009.
24. Todd Gitlin, *Inside Prime Time* (New York: Pantheon, 1983), 22–23.
25. Grant Tinker, *Tinker in Television* (New York: Simon & Schuster, 1994), 181.
26. Ibid., 198.
27. Josef Adalian, "Nielsen Failure Foretold by Disco-Era Tactics," TVWeek.com, May 8, 2009.
28. "News FAQs," Nielsen.com, http://en-us.nielsen.com/main/news/news_faqs.
29. Bill Carter, "Who Needs the Sweeps?" *New York Times*, Apr. 24, 2000.
30. Michael Malone, "Media Rating Council Yanks Accreditation for Nielsen Diary Markets," *Broadcasting & Cable*, Nov. 18, 2010, www.broadcastingcable.com/article/460058-Media_Rating_Council_Yanks_Accreditation_for_Nielsen_Diary_Markets.php.
31. Carter, "Who Needs the Sweeps?"
32. "Case Study: Nielsen's People Meter Technology Brings Miami More Accurate Picture of TV Viewers," Nielsen.com, May 29, 2009, http://blog.nielsen.com/

nielsenwire/media_entertainment/people-meter-technology-brings-miami-more-accurate-ratings.

33. Paul Donato, letter to the editor, *Mediaweek*, Jan. 20, 2003.
34. Gitlin, *Inside Prime Time*, 51.
35. Andy Pearch, N. Phillips, and John Terris, "Economy with the Truth—16 Common Agency TV Buying 'Crimes,'" *Admap*, Apr. 1992.
36. James L. Baughman, *Same Time, Same Station* (Baltimore: Johns Hopkins University Press, 2007), 87.
37. Darrell Y. Hamamoto, *Nervous Laughter* (New York: Praeger, 1989), 1.
38. Sally Bedell Smith, *In All His Glory* (New York: Simon & Schuster, 1990).
39. Leonard H. Goldenson, *Beating the Odds* (New York: Scribner's, 1991), 148.
40. Herman P. Miller, "An Appraisal of the 1950 Census Income Data," *Journal of the American Statistical Association* 48, no. 261 (Mar. 1953): 28–43.
41. Robert Halpern, *Rebuilding the Inner City* (New York: Columbia University Press, 1995), 60.
42. "Historical Census of Housing Tables: Ownership Rates," Census.gov, www.census.gov/hhes/www/housing/census/historic/ownrate.html.
43. M. K. Dychtwald, "Marketplace 2000: Riding the Wave of Population Change," *Journal of Consumer Marketing* 14, no. 4–5 (1997): 771–85.
44. Isabelle Szmigin and Marylyn Carrigan, "Learning to Love the Older Consumer," *Journal of Consumer Behavior* 1, no. 1 (Mar. 9, 2001): 22–34.
45. Mary C. Gilly, Valarie A. Zeithaml, "The Elderly Consumer and Adoption of Technologies," *Journal of Consumer Research* 12, no. 3 (Dec. 1985): 353–57.
46. Ibid.
47. Sharon Shavitt, Pamela Lowrey, James Haefner, "Public Attitudes Toward Advertising: More Favorable Than You Might Think," *Journal of Advertising Research* (July–Aug. 1998): 7–22.
48. Michael Pollak, "Paul F. Lazarsfeld: A Sociointellectual Biography," *Knowledge: Creation, Diffusion, Utilization* 2, no. 2 (Dec. 1980): 157–77.
49. Ibid.
50. Paul F. Lazarsfeld, "A Researcher Looks at Television," *Public Opinion Quarterly* 24, Spring, 1960: 24–31.
51. Paul F. Lazarsfeld and Robert K. Merton, "Mass Communication, Popular Taste, and Organized Social Action," (1948) in John Durham Peters and Peter Simonson, eds., *Mass Communication and American Social Thought* (Lanham, MD: Rowman & Littlefield, 2004), 230–31.
52. Sofie Lazarsfeld, *Woman's Experience of the Male* (London: Francis Aldor, 1940).
53. Interview with Leonard Goldberg, May 20, 2009.
54. Szmigin and Carrigan, "Learning to Love the Older Consumer," 22–34.
55. Interview with Mike Dann, May 21, 2009.
56. Ibid.
57. Ibid.
58. Ibid.
59. Interview with Leonard Stern, May 21, 2009.
60. Gitlin, *Inside Prime Time*, 207–8.
61. Interview with Fred Silverman, May 11, 2009.
62. Ibid.
63. Interview with Marty Ransohoff, May 19, 2009.
64. Allan Neuwirth, *They'll Never Put That on the Air* (New York: Allworth Press, 2006), 143.

65. Lawrence Grossman, "Aging Viewers: The Best Is Yet to Be," *Columbia Journalism Review* 36, no 5 (1998): 68–69.
66. Interview with Burt Prelutsky, Jan. 26, 2010.
67. Interview with Leonard Goldberg, May 20, 2009.
68. Steve Sternberg, "Broadcast Networks Are Aging but Time-Shifters Are Younger," BaselineIntel.com, July 12, 2010, www.baselineintel.com/research-wrap?detail/C8/broadcast_networks_are_aging_but_time-shifters_are_younger.
69. Clint Bolick, "Cable Television: An Unnatural Monopoly," Cato.org, Mar. 13, 1984.
70. James Bovard, "Needed: The Separation of Cable and State," Future of Freedom Foundation, May 1998.
71. "Free Press, Consumer Groups Call on Antitrust Authorities and Congress to Investigate 'TV Everywhere,'" FreePress.net, Jan. 4, 2010, www.freepress.net/node/75731.
72. Roger Cheng, "Telcos, Satellite Join Cable's Push to Build Pay Wall on Web," *Wall Street Journal*, Apr. 20, 2009.
73. Grant Tinker, *Tinker in Television* (New York: Simon & Schuster, 1994), 169.
74. Brandon Tartikoff with Charles Leerhsen, *The Last Great Ride* (New York: Turtle Bay Books, 1992), 161.
75. Mark Crispin Miller, *Boxed In: The Culture of TV* (Evanston, IL: Northwestern University Press, 1988), 61.
76. Tartikoff with Leerhsen, *Last Great Ride*, 165.
77. Gitlin, *Inside Prime Time*, 306.
78. Tartikoff with Leerhsen, *Last Great Ride*, 165.
79. Tinker, *Tinker in Television*, 172–73.
80. Interview with Marcy Carsey, July 1, 2009.
81. Louis Chunovic, *One Foot on the Floor* (New York: TV Books, 2000), 112.
82. Interview with Brandon Stoddard, May 28, 2009.
83. Interview with Doug Herzog, June 22, 2009.
84. "*South Park* Takes On Own Network over Ban," Associated Press, Apr. 18, 2006.
85. Interview with Doug Herzog, June 22, 2009.
86. Ben Shapiro, "Exclusive: Comedy Central Head in 2009: We'll Let *South Park* Do Mohammed," BigHollywood.breitbart.com, Apr. 23, 2010.
87. Neuwirth, *They'll Never Put That on the Air*, 195.
88. Interview with Doug Herzog, June 22, 2009.
89. Interview with Fred Silverman, May 11, 2009.
90. Interview with Brandon Stoddard, May 28, 2009.
91. Interview with Marcy Carsey, July 1, 2009.
92. Interview with Barbara Fisher, July 6, 2009.
93. Interview with Mike Dann, May 21, 2009.
94. Larry Gelbart, *Laughing Matters* (New York: Random House, 1998), 109.
95. Interview with Michelle Ganeless, July 6, 2009.
96. James Hibberd, "The Reign of Right-Wing Primetime," *Hollywood Reporter*, Nov. 10, 2010, www.hollywoodreporter.com/blogs/live-feed/right-wing-tv-43558.

THE CELLULOID TRIANGLE

1. James L. Baughman, *Same Time, Same Station* (Baltimore: Johns Hopkins University Press, 2007), 9.
2. Ibid.

3. Ibid., 25.
4. Robert Kubey, *Creating Television* (Mahwah, NJ: Lawrence Erlbaum, 2004), 82–83.
5. Baughman, *Same Time, Same Station*, 26–28.
6. Ibid., 26.
7. Alfred R. Schneider with Kaye Pullen, *The Gatekeeper* (Syracuse, NY: Syracuse University Press, 2001), xiv.
8. "'The Shadow of Incipient Censorship': The Creation of the Television Code of 1952," GMU.edu, http://historymatters.gmu.edu/d/6558.
9. Leonard B. Stern and Diane L. Robison, eds., *A Martian Wouldn't Say That!* (New York: Price Stern Sloan, 1994), 32.
10. Theodor W. Adorno, "How to Look at Television," *Quarterly of Film, Radio and Television* 8, no. 3 (Spring 1954): 213–35; and Paul F. Lazarsfeld, "A Researcher Looks at Television," *Public Opinion Quarterly* 24 (1960): 24–31.
11. Newton N. Minow, "Television and the Public Interest," National Association of Broadcasters, May 9, 1961.
12. Ibid.
13. Tim Brooks, Earle Marsh, *The Complete Directory to Prime Time Network and Cable TV Shows* (New York: Ballantine, 2007), 1256.
14. Leonard H. Goldenson, *Beating the Odds* (New York: Scribner's, 1991), 173–74.
15. Ibid., 174.
16. Allan Neuwirth, *They'll Never Put That on the Air* (New York: Allworth Press, 2006), 210.
17. Schneider with Pullen, *Gatekeeper*, xiv.
18. Ibid., 94–95.
19. Todd Gitlin, *Inside Prime Time* (New York: Pantheon, 1983), 260–61.
20. Kathryn C. Montgomery, *Target: Prime Time* (New York: Oxford University Press, 1989), 111.
21. Gitlin, *Inside Prime Time*, 43–44.
22. James Hibberd, "CBS Adding Three Gay Characters to Shows," HollywoodReporter.com, July 28, 2010.
23. Bill Gorman, "It's Official! CBS Wins the 2009–10 Season in Viewers," TVByTheNumbers.com, May 27, 2010.
24. Henry Mark Holzer, "CAIR KOs *24*," FrontPageMagazine.com, Dec. 4, 2006.
25. Andrew McCarthy, "CAIR's Well-Deserved Expulsion," NationalReview.com, Mar. 24, 2009.
26. Interview with George Schlatter, Apr. 21, 2009.
27. Goldenson, *Beating the Odds*, 322.
28. Schneider with Pullen, *Gatekeeper*, 97–98.
29. "Celebrating 68 Years of Giving," EIFoundation.org, www.eifoundation.org/content/celebrating-68-years-giving.
30. "Showrunner Document: Play Your Part America," Entertainment Industry Foundation, Sept. 25, 2009.
31. Larry O'Connor, "Part II: Obama Controls Your Television Set—Search and Ye Shall Find . . . Left-Wing Advocacy," BigHollywood.breitbart.com, Oct. 15, 2009, http://bighollywood.breitbart.com/sright/2009/10/15/part-ii-search-and-ye-shall-find-left-wing-advocacy.
32. Press Release, "Entertainment Industry Foundation, Mayors From All Over the US Kick Off Two Major Initiatives Encouraging Volunteerism," IParticipate and CitiesOfService.org, September 10, 2009.

33. Deborah Netburn, "NBC's Green Week Gets Overshadowed," *Los Angeles Times*, Nov. 9, 2007.
34. John Davis, "Biodiesel Part of NBC's Green Week," DomesticFuel.com, Apr. 19, 2010.
35. Schneider with Pullen, *Gatekeeper*, 12–14.
36. Ibid., 14–15.
37. Elana Levine, *Wallowing in Sex* (Durham, NC: Duke University Press, 2007), 54.
38. Schneider with Pullen, *Gatekeeper*, 30–33.
39. Ibid., 37, 40, 45.
40. Schneider with Pullen, *Gatekeeper*, 17, 21, 29.
41. Larry Gelbart, *Laughing Matters* (New York: Random House, 1998), 44.
42. Schneider with Pullen, *Gatekeeper*, 101–2.
43. Ibid., 102–3.
44. Ibid., 109–10.
45. Geoffrey Cowan, *See No Evil: The Backstage Battle over Sex and Violence on Television* (New York: Simon & Schuster, 1978), 40–41.
46. Schneider with Pullen, *Gatekeeper*, 113.
47. *Writers Guild of America v. Federal Communications Commission*, 423 F.Supp. 1064 (C.D. Cal. 1976).
48. Barry S. Sapolsky and Joseph O. Taberlet, "Sex in Primetime Television: 1979 Versus 1989," *Journal of Broadcasting & Electronic Media* 35, no. 4 (Fall 1991): 505–16.
49. Levine, *Wallowing in Sex*, 198.
50. Gitlin, *Inside Prime Time*, 252.
51. Interview with Susan Harris, May 4, 2009.
52. Darrell Y. Hamamoto, *Nervous Laughter* (New York: Praeger, 1989), 135.
53. Louis Chunovic, *One Foot on the Floor* (New York: TV Books, 2000), 154.
54. Ibid., 125–26.

THE GOVERNMENT-HOLLYWOOD COMPLEX

1. Jean Edward Smith, *FDR* (New York: Random House, 2007), 757.
2. Robert B. Stinnett, *Day of Deceit: The Truth About FDR and Pearl Harbor* (New York: Simon & Schuster, 2000), 107.
3. Betty Houchin Winfield, *FDR and the News Media* (New York: Columbia University Press, 1994), 109.
4. Monte M. Poen, ed., *Strictly Personal and Confidential* (Columbia: University of Missouri Press, 1999), 165.
5. David Halberstam, *The Powers That Be* (Urbana: University of Illinois Press, 1975), 329.
6. Erik Barnouw, *A History of Broadcasting in the United States* (New York: Oxford University Press, 1977), 144.
7. Dennis Mazzocco, *Networks of Power: Corporate TV's Threat To Democracy* (Boston: South End Press, 1994), 42.
8. Leonard H. Goldenson, *Beating the Odds* (New York: Scribner's, 1991), 274–75.
9. Ibid., 287.
10. Ibid., 189–90.
11. Sally Bedell Smith, *In All His Glory* (New York: Simon & Schuster, 1990).
12. Robert J. Brown, *Manipulating the Ether: The Power of Broadcast Radio in Thirties America* (Jefferson, NC: McFarland, 1998), 15.
13. Smith, *In All His Glory*, 375–76.

14. Joseph D. Straubhaar and Robert LaRose, *Media Now: Understanding Media, Culture, and Technology* (Florence, KY: Thompson Wadsworth, 2006), 214.
15. Tim Brooks and Earle Marsh, *The Complete Directory to Prime Time Network and Cable TV Shows* (New York: Ballantine, 2007), xiii.
16. Michael A. Genovese, *The Watergate Crisis* (Westport, CT: Greenwood Press, 1999), 101.
17. Louis Edward Ingelhart, *Press Freedoms* (Westport, CT: Greenwood Press, 1987), 313.
18. Richard Reeves, "A Media Monster—Who, Me?" *New York*, Nov. 26, 1973.
19. Joel H. Spring, *Images of American Life* (Albany: State University of New York, 1992), 222–23.
20. Nixon Tapes, May 13, 1971.
21. Walter Pincus and George Lardner Jr., "Nixon Hoped Antitrust Threat Would Sway Network Coverage," *Washington Post*, Dec. 1, 1997.
22. Transcript, "Booknotes: Connie Bruck," C-SPAN, July 20, 2003. www.booknotes.org/Transcript/?ProgramID=1737.
23. Connie Bruck, *When Hollywood Had a King* (New York: Random House, 2004), 291–92.
24. Pincus and Lardner, "Nixon Hoped Antitrust Threat Would Sway Network Coverage."
25. Kathleen Sharp, *Mr. and Mrs. Hollywood: Edie and Lew Wasserman and Their Entertainment Empire* (New York: Carroll & Graf, 2003), 322–26.
26. "The Financial Interest and Syndication Rules," Museum.tv, www.museum.tv/eotvsection.php?entrycode=financialint.
27. Interview with Gene Reynolds, May 7, 2009.
28. Interview with Michael Brandman, June 8, 2009.
29. Sharp, *Mr. and Mrs. Hollywood*, 464.
30. Transcript, "Booknotes: Connie Bruck," C-SPAN, July 20, 2003. http://www.booknotes.org/Transcript/?ProgramID=1737
31. Kurt Anderson, "The Clinton-Hollywood Co-Dependency," *Time*, June 7, 1993.
32. Ben Dickenson, *Hollywood's New Radicalism* (New York: I. B. Tauris, 2006), 47.
33. Terry Christensen and Peter J. Haas, *Projecting Politics: Political Messages in American Film* (Armonk, NY: M. E. Sharpe, 2005), 50.
34. Ira Teinowitz, "MTV Inaugural Ball to Celebrate Change, Volunteerism," TVWeek.com, Nov. 2008.
35. Anderson, "Clinton-Hollywood Co-Dependency."
36. Timothy Lynch, "Dereliction of Duty: The Constitutional Record of President Clinton," Cato.org, Mar. 31, 1997.
37. Raymond L. Fischer, "Is It Possible to Regulate Television Violence?" Society for the Advancement of Education, July 1994.
38. Dickenson, *Hollywood's New Radicalism*, 47–48.
39. Bill Carter, *Desperate Networks* (New York: Doubleday, 2006), 145, 150.
40. Brody Mullins, "Studios Take Hit in Tax Bill," *Roll Call*, Oct. 7, 2004.
41. Tamar Brott, "mommy, what does %#!@ mean?" *Los Angeles*, Sept. 2005.
42. Jennifer Hoar, "FCC Firm on Super Bowl Indecency Fine," CBSnews.com, Feb. 23, 2006.
43. Michael Scherer, "The FCC's Cable Crackdown," Salon.com, Aug. 30, 2005.
44. Brott, "mommy, what does %#!@ mean?"
45. Scherer, "FCC's Cable Crackdown."
46. Ibid.
47. Sallie Hofmeister, "Indecency Proposal Getting Static from Cable," *Los Angeles Times*, Apr. 5, 2005.

48. Interview with Gene Reynolds, May 7, 2009.
49. Scherer, "FCC's Cable Crackdown."
50. Hofmeister, "Indecency Proposal Getting Static."
51. Ronald Grover and Todd Shields, "Why Hollywood Loves the White House Again," BusinessWeek.com, July 8, 2010.
52. Ben Shapiro, "NBC's ObamaVision: GE Uses Network to Push Obama's Green Agenda—and Rakes In the Dough," BigHollywood.breitbart.com, Nov. 16, 2009. http://bighollywood.breitbart.com/bshapiro/2009/11/16/propaganda-ge-uses-nbc-to-push-obamas-green-agenda-and-rakes-in-the-dough/print.
53. "President Draws 24.7 Million; *So You Think You Can Dance* Benefits," TVByTheNumbers.com, July 23, 2010, http://tvbythenumbers.com/2009/07/23/wednesday-ratings-the-president-speaks-fox-so-you-think-you-can-dance-win-easily/23356.
54. Howard Kurtz, "The Prez, the Press, the Pressure," *Washington Post*, Aug. 3, 2009.
55. Ibid.
56. David D. Kirkpatrick, "Drug Industry to Run Ads Favoring White House Plan," *New York Times*, Aug. 8, 2009.
57. Ted Johnson, "Show Biz Still Supports the Democrats," Wilshireandwashington.com, July 19, 2010, www.wilshireandwashington.com/2010/07/show-biz-still-supports-the-democrats.html.
58. Marvin Ammori, "TV Competition Nowhere: How the Cable Industry Is Colluding to Kill Online TV," *Free Press*, Jan. 2010.
59. Pub. L. No. 102-385, Sec. 2(a)(2) (1992).
60. "The Failure of Cable Deregulation," U.S. Public Interest Research Group, Aug. 2003. http://cdn.publicinterestnetwork.org/assets/qZPECxJiK5daxX6nCmUS8g/failureofcabledereg.pdf.
61. Ibid.
62. James Bovard, "Needed: The Separation of Cable and State," Future of Freedom Foundation, May 1998.
63. David J. Saylor, "Municipal Ripoff: The Unconstitutionality of Cable Television Franchise Fees and Access Support Payments," *Catholic University Law Review* 35 (Spring 1986): 672.
64. "The Failure of Cable Deregulation," U.S. Public Interest Research Group, Aug. 2003, http://cdn.publicinterestnetwork.org/assets/qZPECxJiK5daxX6nCmUS8g/failureofcabledereg.pdf.
65. Mark Landler, "Gore Urges Cable Industry to Take On the Bells," *New York Times*, Apr. 30, 1996.
66. "A Brief History: The Bell System," AT&T website, www.corp.att.com/history/history3.html.
67. Lawrence Gasman, *Telecompetition: The Free Market Road to the Information Highway* (Washington, DC: Cato Institute, 1994), 52.
68. Bovard, "Separation of Cable and State."
69. *Turner Broadcasting System v. FCC*, 512 U.S. 622 (1994).
70. Ammori, "TV Competition Nowhere."
71. "The Failure of Cable Deregulation," U.S. Public Interest Research Group, Aug. 2003, http://cdn.publicinterestnetwork.org/assets/qZPECxJiK5daxX6nCmUS8g/failure-ofcabledereg.pdf.
72. Brian Stelter and Bill Carter, "Fox Returns to Cablevision," NYTimes.com, Oct. 30, 2010, http://mediadecoder.blogs.nytimes.com/2010/10/30/fox-returns-to-cablevision.
73. Interview with Barbara Fisher, July 6, 2009.

74. Interview with Gary David Goldberg, May 19, 2009.
75. Interview with Michael Brandman, June 8, 2009.
76. "George Clooney Denies Advising Barack Obama," *Daily Mail* (UK), Aug. 14, 2008.
77. "Edward Norton's Obama Documentary Gets a Hollywood Ending," EcoRazzi.com, Nov. 5, 2008.
78. Ira Teinowitz, "Obama Had Hollywood Help on Infomercial," AdAge.com, Oct. 30, 2008.
79. YouTube, www.youtube.com/watch?v=AgHHX9R4Qtk.
80. "Hollywood Woos Obama Volunteers," Associated Press, Oct. 30, 2008.
81. Jeffrey Resner, "Obama's Real Friends in Hollywood," Politico.com, Nov. 19, 2008.
82. Jennifer Parker, "Obama Grants First Family Interview to *Access Hollywood*," ABC-News.com, July 8, 2008.
83. Tina Daunt, "Obama's Filmland Backers Are Asked to Open Wallets," *Los Angeles Times*, Jan. 25, 2007.
84. "Obama's Hollywood Fundraiser Nets $9M," CBSNews.com, Sept. 17, 2008.
85. Ronald Grover and Todd Shields, "Why Hollywood Loves the White House Again," BusinessWeek.com, July 8, 2010.
86. "Barack Obama (D) Inauguration Donors," OpenSecrets.org, www.opensecrets.org/pres08/inaug.php#states.
87. Andrew Malcolm, "A Surprise: Oprah Pays a Real Cost for Supporting Barack Obama," LATimes.com, Apr. 9, 2008.
88. Ibid.
89. Phil Rogers, "Blagojevich Considered Oprah for Senator," NBCChicago.com, June 28, 2010.
90. "Ellen Interviews Barack Obama," WarnerBros.com, Oct. 22, 2008.
91. "McCain Tells Ellen DeGeneres: You Shouldn't Have the Right to Get Married," ThinkProgress.com, May 22, 2008.
92. Marc Malkin, "Ellen DeGeneres on Barack Obama, Prop. 8," EOnline.com., Nov. 5, 2008.
93. Karen Travers and Brian Braiker, "Obama, on *The View*, Discusses the 'Roses' and 'Thorns' of the Presidency," ABCNews.com, July 28, 2010.
94. Saul Alinsky, *Rules for Radicals* (New York: Vintage Books, 1989), 75.
95. Mark Leibovich, "Chevy Chase as the Klutz in Chief, and a President Who Was in on the Joke," *New York Times*, Dec. 29, 2006.
96. Bill Carter, "Comedians Find Obama Jokes a Tough Sell," *New York Times*, July 15, 2008.
97. Ani Esmailian, "Chris Rock: Obama Is Comedian's Worst Nightmare," Hollyscoop.com, Jan. 20, 2009.
98. Joe Garofoli, "For Comedians, Obama Poses a Serious Dilemma," *San Francisco Chronicle*, Nov. 19, 2008.
99. "The Joke's on McCain: Late-Night Comedians Lay Off Obama," LATimes.com, Aug. 21, 2008.
100. Ibid.
101. Interview with Gary David Goldberg, May 19, 2009.
102. "Can *The Daily Show* Survive the Barack Obama Presidency?" *New York*, Nov. 6, 2008.
103. Josh Wolk, "Jon Stewart and Stephen Colbert: Mock the Vote," *Entertainment Weekly*, Sept. 30, 2008.
104. Ibid.

105. Ibid.
106. Carter, "Comedians Find Obama Jokes a Tough Sell."
107. Noel Sheppard, "*Daily Show* Writers Helped Obama with Correspondents' Dinner Jokes," Newsbusters.org, May 3, 2010.
108. Interview with Doug Herzog, June 22, 2009.
109. Interview with Michelle Ganeless, July 6, 2009.
110. Interview with Doug Herzog, June 22, 2009.
111. Kristen Fyfe, "*Boston Legal*: 55 Million McCain/Palin Supporters 'Idiots' and Bloggers 'Entry-Level Life Forms,'" Newsbusters.org, Nov. 18, 2008.
112. Richard Huff, "TV Shows Elect to Take Note of Obama Victory," *New York Daily News*, Nov. 20, 2008.
113. Interview with Michael Nankin, June 3, 2009.
114. Opensecrets.org.

ROBBING THE CRADLE

1. Matea Gold, "No Liberal Bias at PBS, Responds Network President," *Los Angeles Times*, May 25, 2005.
2. David Folkenflik, "CPB Memos Indicate Level of Monitoring," NPR.org, Aug. 19, 2010.
3. Tom Hollis, Greg Ehrbar, *Mouse Tracks: The Story of Walt Disney Records* (Jackson: University Press of Mississippi, 2006), 15–16.
4. L. Wayne Hicks, "Bob Keeshan Interview," TVParty.com, www.tvparty.com/keeshan1.html.
5. Robert W. Morrow, *Sesame Street and the Reform of Children's Television* (Baltimore: Johns Hopkins University Press, 2006), 60.
6. L. Wayne Hicks, "Bob Keeshan Interview," TVParty.com, www.tvparty.com/keeshan1.html.
7. Interview with Mike Dann, May 21, 2009.
8. Norimitsu Onishi, "Evelyn P. Davis, 75, Messenger for *Sesame Street* in Inner City," NYTimes.com, Jan. 13, 1997.
9. Louise Gikow, *Sesame Street: A Celebration of Forty Years of Life on the Street* (New York: Black Dog & Leventhal, 2009), 293.
10. Morrow, *Sesame Street*, 93.
11. "On Sesame Street, 'C' Is for Controversy," NPR.org, Nov. 12, 2009.
12. Peter Hellman, "Street Smart," *New York*, Nov. 23, 1987.
13. Muriel Cohen, "Street Smarts," *Boston Globe*, Oct. 29, 1989.
14. Robin Abcarian, "Divorce Is a Tough Row for *Sesame Street* to Hoe," *Los Angeles Times*, Mar. 27, 1992.
15. Gikow, *Sesame Street: A Celebration*, 161.
16. Larry Elder, "A Christmas Story—in the Mall Parking Lot," *Creators Syndicate*, Jan. 4, 2007, http://townhall.com/columnists/LarryElder/2007/01/04/a_christmas_story_—_in_the_mall_parking_lot.
17. "Learning About Diversity," Sesamestreet.org, www.sesamestreet.org/parents/topics/getalong/getalong06.
18. "Expose Your Child to a World of Diversity," SesameStreet.org, www.sesamestreet.org/parents/topics/getalong/getalong03.
19. Marcella Bombardieri, "Summers' Remarks on Women Draw Fire," *Boston Globe*, Jan. 17, 2005.

20. Michael Jensen, "TCA Weekend Update: Neil Patrick Harris, 'The Starter Wife' and more!" AfterElton.com, July 21, 2008.
21. "Bring the Learning Fun of Sesame Street into Your Classroom," PBS.org, www.pbs.org/teachers/earlychildhood/articles/sesamestreet.html.
22. Morrow, *Sesame Street*, 154–55.
23. Gikow, *Sesame Street: A Celebration*, 252.
24. Ibid., 11.
25. "Top 10 *Sesame Street* controversies," TheWeek.com, Nov. 10, 2009.
26. Randall Herbert Balmer, *Encyclopedia of Evangelism* (Louisville, KY: Westminster John Knox Press, 2002), 495.
27. Daniel Lewis, "Mister Rogers, TV's Friend for Children, Is Dead at 74," NYTimes.com, Feb. 28, 2003.
28. James Gorman, "Of Dinosaurs Why Must This One Thrive?" *New York Times*, Apr. 11, 1993.
29. Lisa de Moraes, "PBS's 'Buster' Gets an Education," *Washington Post*, Jan. 27, 2005.
30. "About the Program," PBS.org, www.pbs.org/parents/arthur/program/prog_summary.html.
31. "Classic Hit 'We Are Family' Remixed to Spread the Message of Diversity and Tolerance to Elementary School Children Nationwide," We Are Family Foundation, Nov. 4, 2004, www.wearefamilyfoundation.org/files/PressRelease_MusicalMessage11.04PR.pdf.
32. "Who We Are," WeAreFamilyFoundation.org, www.wearefamilyfoundation.org/mission.
33. "Children's TV Unites to Launch Pro-Gay Campaign," *American Family Assocation Journal*, Jan. 2005.
34. David D. Kirkpatrick, "Conservatives Pick Soft Target: A Cartoon Sponge," *New York Times*, Jan. 20, 2005.
35. Sally Helgesen, *The Web of Inclusion* (Washington, DC: Beard Books, 1995), 222–23.
36. Allan Neuwirth, *Makin' Toons: Inside the Most Popular Animated TV Shows and Movies* (New York,: Allworth Press, 2003), 58, 62.
37. Kevin Zimmerman, "Not Just for Kids Anymore," *Daily Variety*, Mar. 23, 1995.
38. Brad Stetson and Joseph G. Conti, *The Truth About Tolerance: Pluralism, Diversity, and the Culture Wars* (Downers Grover, IL: InterVarsity Press, 2005), 117.
39. John Stephenson, "Nick News Pushes Leftist Propaganda on Kids," Newsbusters.org, Oct. 31, 2007.
40. "Nick Mulling Post-Spears Pregnancy Show," Associated Press, Dec. 20, 2007.
41. "Respect," Nick.com, www.nick.com/all_nick/everything_nick/kaiser/respect.html.
42. P. J. Gladnick, "Nickelodeon Broadcasts Cartoon Homage to 'Dear Leader' Obama," Newsbusters.org, Mar. 5, 2009, http://newsbusters.org/blogs/p-j-gladnick/2009/03/05/nickelodeon-broadcasts-cartoon-homage-dear-leader-obama.
43. Sharon Kennedy Wynne, "Sex Jokes and Raunch Have Parents Furious with Nickelodeon," TampaBay.com, Nov. 6, 2009, www.tampabay.com/features/parenting/sex-jokes-and-raunch-have-parents-furious-with-nickelodeon/1049771.
44. "Michael Eisner Launches First Animated TV Series Since Leaving Disney," *Guardian* (UK), Mar. 15, 2010.
45. Alana Goodman, "Nickelodeon Game Lets Kids Play at Trying to Look Up Skirt of 'Naughty' Cartoon Teachers," Newsbusters.org, June 14, 2010.
46. Christine Parsons, "Fallout from Breastgate: Is Nickelodeon Marketing MTV to Kids?" *San Francisco Chronicle*, Feb. 11, 2004.

47. Patricia Sellers, "The Women of Viacom," CNN.com, Oct. 11, 2006.
48. Karl Taro Greenfeld, "How Mickey Got His Groove Back," Portfolio.com, Apr. 14, 2008.
49. "Miley Cyrus' New Movie *LOL*: Virginity Loss, Pot Smoking, Lesbian Kisses," HuffingtonPost.com, Aug. 23, 2010.
50. Meg James and Dawn C. Chmielewski, "Teen Sex in *Secret Life* Births Debate over ABC Family Values," *Los Angeles Times*, Feb. 1, 2009.
51. Brian Juergens, "ABC Family's Curious Origins and Bright Future," AfterElton.com, Aug. 26, 2007.
52. " 'Gay Tinky Winky Bad for Children,' " BBC.co.uk, Feb. 15, 1999.
53. "The U.K.'s Answer to Barney: It's 'Teletubbies' Time," CNN.com, Dec. 24, 1997.
54. Joyce Millman, "Tubbythumping," Salon.com, Apr. 3, 1998.
55. Michael Colton, "I'm Sorry, Tinky Winky," Salon.com, Feb. 13, 1999.
56. "Camp Cartoon Star 'Is Not Gay'," BBC.co.uk, Oct. 9, 2002.
57. "SpongeBob Isn't Gay or Straight, Creator Says," Reuters, Jan. 29, 2005.
58. Interview with Andy Heyward, June 12, 2009.

THE END OF TELEVISION?

1. Interview with Carlton Cuse, May 12, 2009.
2. Interview with Susan Harris, May 4, 2009.
3. Interview with Mark Burnett, May 11, 2009.
4. Interview with John Langley, May 8, 2009.
5. Interview with Gene Reynolds, May 7, 2009.
6. Interview with Carlton Cuse, May 12, 2009.
7. Interview with Michael Nankin, June 3, 2009.
8. Interview with Don Bellisario, June 10, 2009.
9. Interview with George Schlatter, Apr. 21, 2009.
10. Interview with Larry Gelbart, Apr. 20, 2009.
11. Interview with Fred Silverman, May 11, 2009.
12. Interview with Allan Burns, May 26, 2009.
13. Interview with Michael Brandman, June 8, 2009.
14. Robin Marantz Henig, "What Is It About 20-Somethings?" *New York Times*, Aug. 18, 2010.
15. "About the Alliance," ANA.net, www.ana.net/content/show/id/afe-about.
16. "Advertisers Earmark $10 Million for Family-Friendly TV," LATimes.com, June 22, 2010.
17. Ibid.
18. Interview with Carlton Cuse, May 12, 2009.
19. Interview with Michael Nankin, June 3, 2009.
20. Interview with Don Bellisario, June 10, 2009.

APPENDIX

1. Alex Leo, "Matt Stone & Trey Parker Are Not Your Political Allies (No Matter What You Believe)," HuffingtonPost.com, Feb. 25, 2010, www.huffingtonpost.com/2010/02/25/matt-stone-trey-parker-ar_n_475744.html.
2. Interview with Don Bellisario, June 10, 2009.

Index

About the Author

BEN SHAPIRO is a graduate of UCLA (which he entered at the age of sixteen) and Harvard Law School. At seventeen, he became the youngest nationally syndicated columnist in the United States. Shapiro is the author of the national bestsellers *Brainwashed*, *Porn Generation*, and *Project President*, and hosts *The Ben Shapiro Show* in Orlando, Florida. He is married and lives in Los Angeles.